TECHTV'S MICROSOFT® WINDOWS® XP FOR HOME USERS

Jim Louderback

CONTENTS AT A GLANCE

A Division of Pearson Technology Group, USA
201 W. 103rd Street
Indianapolis, Indiana 46290

TECHTV'S MICROSOFT® WINDOWS® XP FOR HOME USERS

International Standard Book Number: 0-7897-2651-3

Library of Congress Catalog Card Number: 2001093927

Printed in the United States of America

First Printing: November 2001

04 03 02 4 3

Trademarks

All terms mentioned in this book that are known to be trademarks or service marks have been appropriately capitalized. Que cannot attest to the accuracy of this information. Use of a term in this book should not be regarded as affecting the validity of any trademark or service mark.

Warning and Disclaimer

Every effort has been made to make this book as complete and as accurate as possible, but no warranty or fitness is implied. The information provided is on an "as is" basis. The author and the publisher shall have neither liability nor responsibility to any person or entity with respect to any loss or damages arising from the information contained in this book.

ASSOCIATE PUBLISHER
Dean Miller

ACQUISITIONS EDITOR
Angelina Ward

DEVELOPMENT EDITOR
Mark Cierzniak

MANAGING EDITOR
Thomas F. Hayes

SENIOR EDITOR
Susan Ross Moore

COPY EDITORS
Candice Hightower
Sossity Smith

INDEXER
Kevin Broccoli

PROOFREADER
Harvey Stanbrough

TECHNICAL EDITOR
Kyle Bryant

TEAM COORDINATOR
Sharry Lee Gregory

INTERIOR DESIGNER
Anne Jones

COVER DESIGNER
Planet 10

PAGE LAYOUT
Stacey Richwine-DeRome
Gloria Schurick

TECHTV HEAD OF BUSINESS DEVELOPMENT
Dee Dee Atta

TECHTV VICE PRESIDENT/EDITORIAL DIRECTOR
Jim Louderback

TECHTV MANAGING EDITOR
Andy Guest

TECHTV MANAGING EDITOR—HELP
Phil Allingham

TECHTV LAB DIRECTOR
Andrew Hawn

CONTENTS

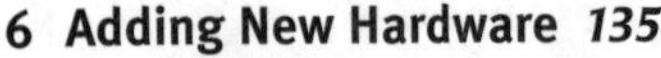

ABOUT THE AUTHORS

Jim Louderback is vice president and editorial director of TechTV. Louderback is responsible for overseeing the network's technical content. Prior to TechTV, Louderback was vice president and editorial director of *PC Week* (now *eWeek*), editor-in-chief of *Windows Sources,* and the director of PC Week Labs.

Louderback grew up in the Northeast. He graduated from the University of Vermont, where he studied mathematics, and holds an MBA in computer applications from New York University.

He is an avid outdoorsman who enjoys living on the Northern California coast where his favorite activities are hiking and sailing.

Michael Miller is a successful and prolific author with a reputation for practical advice and technical accuracy, and an unerring empathy for the needs of his readers.

Mr. Miller has written more than three dozen how-to and reference books since 1989, for Que and other major publishers. His books for Que include *Using Windows 95*, *Using Windows 98 Preview Edition*, *Special Edition Using the Internet and the Web*, and the upcoming *Absolute Beginner's Guide to Computers and the Internet*. He is known for his casual, easy-to-read writing style and his practical, real-world advice—as well as his ability to explain a wide variety of complex topics to an everyday audience.

Mr. Miller is also president of The Molehill Group, a strategic consulting and authoring firm based in Carmel, Indiana. As a consultant, he specializes in providing strategic advice to and writing business plans for Internet- and technology-based businesses.

You can e-mail Mr. Miller directly at `using@molehillgroup.com`. His Web site is located at `www.molehillgroup.com`.

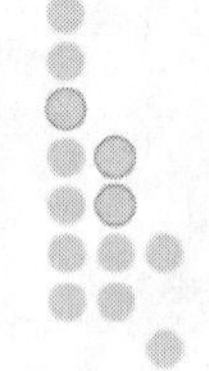

DEDICATION

To Kimberly and Sam

Jim Louderback

ACKNOWLEDGMENTS

I want to thank Paul Allen and Bill Gates for making the operating system, and all the great lab and editorial people I've worked with over the years who have pushed and prodded Microsoft to make better products. And especially to TechTV's labrats, the best product testing organization on earth.

Jim Louderback

Thanks to the usual suspects at Que, including but not limited to Dean Miller, Mark Cierzniak, Kyle Bryant, Susan Moore, Harvey Stanbrough, and Kevin Broccoli.

Michael Miller

TELL US WHAT YOU THINK!

As the reader of this book, *you* are our most important critic and commentator. We value your opinion and want to know what we're doing right, what we could do better, what areas you'd like to see us publish in, and any other words of wisdom you're willing to pass our way.

As an associate publisher for Que, I welcome your comments. You can fax, email, or write me directly to let me know what you did or didn't like about this book—as well as what we can do to make our books stronger.

Please note that I cannot help you with technical problems related to the topic of this book, and that due to the high volume of mail I receive, I might not be able to reply to every message.

When you write, please be sure to include this book's title and author as well as your name and phone or fax number. I will carefully review your comments and share them with the author and editors who worked on the book.

Fax: 317-581-4666

E-mail: `feedback@quepublishing.com`

Mail: Associate Publisher
Que
201 West 103rd Street
Indianapolis, IN 46290 USA

INTRODUCTION

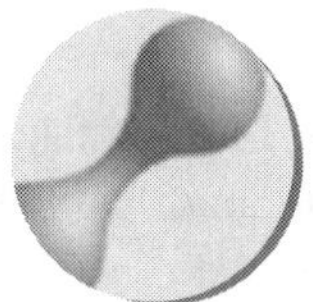

It seems like only yesterday that I was analyzing the innards of Windows 1.0 to complete my Masters degree, but that was in 1985. Since then Windows has gone from academic curiosity to take over the world literally.

Every new release of Windows added, and mostly improved, on what came before. However, every five years or so, Microsoft releases a seminal, essential upgrade to Windows that changes everything. Windows 3.0, released in 1990, finally turned the graphical user interface into a truly useful tool, and from there it became the desktop of choice for most computer users. Then Windows 95 (released in 1995) brought a new, radically easier to use interface, along with a slew of new features and a new 32-bit platform. That spelled the end of almost every other operating system on IBM-compatible machines.

After more than six years, we're overdue for the next groundbreaking version of Windows. And now it's here. Windows XP is clearly the most significant upgrade, and change, to the Windows platform since Windows 95.

It comes wrapped in a brand-new user interface, with a brand-new focus on digital devices and task-based operation. The addition of task panes promises to make it easier to use, and there is a host of new and integrated functions.

Back in 1995, I was editor-in-chief of a popular, but now defunct magazine called *Windows Sources.* That year, we

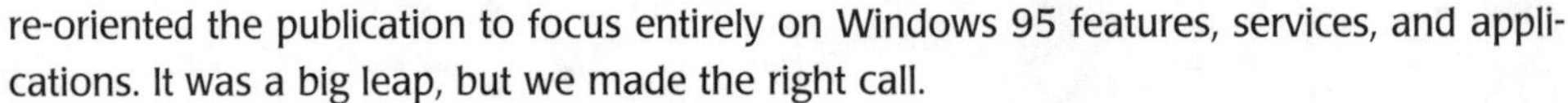

re-oriented the publication to focus entirely on Windows 95 features, services, and applications. It was a big leap, but we made the right call.

But just like the transition to Windows 3.0, and Windows 95, it'll take some time and effort to figure out the new interface, and maximize all the powerful features inside Microsoft's biggest product launch for almost seven years.

And that's where we come in. If you've already adopted Windows XP at home, whether it came pre-installed on a new computer, or you've already done the upgrade, this book will help you uncover all the details, secrets and hidden features of this powerful new tool.

And if you're considering Windows XP, we can help too. This book shows you, in graphical detail, all the new features, capabilities and power inside. We'll help you plan your upgrade, hold your hand during the process, and then help you uncover all the hidden gems inside.

And there's a lot in there from the power of Windows Messaging to drastically cut down long-distance bills, to the capability to create and edit your own audio CDs and movies, to better ways to integrate your digital camera, scanner, and other peripherals.

Let this book be your guide to all the powerful and wonderful features inside Windows XP.

HOW THIS BOOK IS ORGANIZED

To make this book easy for you to use, we've organized its 24 chapters into six major sections, each focusing on a specific group of tasks or operations. This way, you can turn directly to that part of the book that contains the information you want. Or you can read straight through, from front to back, to get the whole Windows XP story.

- **Part I: Getting to Know Windows XP** gets you up and running with this newest version of Microsoft Windows. The first chapter tells you about everything that's new or has been changed since Windows 98 and Windows Me. The second chapter shows you how to customize the Windows XP desktop and operations to look and act the way you want them to.
- **Part II: Working with Files, Programs, and Peripherals** examines all the file-management tools in Windows XP. You'll also learn how to add new software and hardware to your system, and how to control XP's printing function.
- **Part III: Taking Windows Online** is all about Windows XP and the Internet. Here is where you'll learn how to connect to an ISP, how to share an Internet connection, how to use the new features in Internet Explorer 6, and how to chat with other users with the new Windows Messenger instant messaging program.
- **Part IV: Sounds and Pictures** tells you about some of the neatest new features of Windows XP. You'll learn how Windows XP manages the task of importing and viewing pictures from digital cameras and scanners, as well as how you can listen to, rip, and burn digital audio files. (And, yes, you *can* use Windows XP to record MP3 files—although you'll need to buy a $30 add-on utility to do it!)

- **Part V: In the Home and On the Road** is all about using Windows XP on a network or on a portable PC. You'll learn just how easy it is to set up an XP-based home network, how to fast-switch between multiple users, and how to make your notebook PC run faster and look better when you're away from home.
- **Part VI: Maintenance and Troubleshooting** is the place to turn to if you're having trouble with Windows XP. Look here for advice on finding help, performing routine system maintenance, and troubleshooting common problems.

In addition, this book features three appendixes with essential information about upgrading your system to Windows XP, using XP's built-in accessory programs, and implementing XP's accessibility options.

SPECIAL FEATURES IN THIS BOOK

In addition to the main text in this book, you'll find several extra features that give you even *more* information about getting the most out of Windows XP.

Tips

These are pieces of advice—little tricks, actually—that help you use Windows XP more effectively or maneuver around problems or limitations.

To get the most out of Windows XP, I recommend that you configure your system to at least 1024×768 resolution, running at least 16-bit color—and if your video card can handle it, crank the color quality all the way up to the highest setting. Windows XP looks best with 32-bit color. Naturally, you'll need a 17-inch or larger monitor to handle this resolution, which is another one of my recommendations.

Notes

Notes provide information that is generally useful but not specifically needed for what you're doing at the moment. Some are like extended tips—interesting, but not essential.

Prior to Windows 95, filenames were limited to eight main characters plus a three-character extension. Windows no longer has this "8+3" limitation. Filenames can now include up to 255 characters, and can use spaces and special characters.

Cautions

These tell you to beware of a potentially dangerous act or situation. In some cases, ignoring a Caution could cause you significant problem—so pay attention to them!

Installing too many fonts on your system not only consumes a lot of hard disk space, it also eats up system memory and can cause your system to run slower than normal. If your system is running sluggishly, you may want to remove some unused fonts. This enhances the performance of your system performance *and* frees up some disk space.

Shortcut Key Combinations

Shortcut key combinations in this book are shown as the key names joined with plus signs (+). For example, Ctrl+W indicates that you should press the W key while holding down the Ctrl key. (This particular key combination closes the current browser window—useful if you've been plagued with a bunch of advertising pop-ups without the normal Close Window controls.)

Menu Commands

You'll see instructions such as this everywhere in this book:

Choose File, New.

This means that you should pull down the File menu and select New. (This particular example opens the New dialog box in most Windows applications.)

Web Addresses

There are a lot of Web addresses in this book. They're notated like this:

`www.techtv.com`

In all cases, the beginning `http://`, not necessary with Internet Explorer 6, is assumed.

Jim's Top Ten Tips

I end every chapter with a summary of the ten most important points about the topic at hand. If you read nothing else in this book, browse these top ten lists to learn the bare essentials of how to get the most out of Windows XP!

PART I

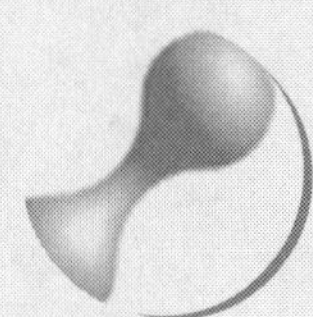

GETTING TO KNOW WINDOWS XP

CHAPTER 1

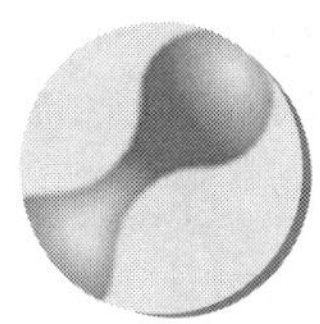

NEW WINDOWS FOR OLD USERS: WHAT'S NEW, WHAT'S CHANGED

- What Windows XP Is—and What It Isn't
- Under the Hood
- Windows XP's New "Look and Feel" Features
- Windows XP's New Internet Features
- Windows XP's New Multiuser and Multiple-PC Features
- Windows XP's New Audio and Video Features
- Windows XP's New System Utilities
- Windows XP's Help and Registration Features
- Feature Comparison
- Old Versus New: How to Do What You Used to Do
- Stuff That Didn't Make the Final Cut
- Jim's Top Ten Tips

I've been using Windows XP (the beta version) for several months now, and I like what I see. Performance- and stability-wise, it's a marked improvement over Windows 98 or Windows Me. It also sports a spiffy new interface, and brings out into the open a lot of common operations that used to be hidden on a pull-down or pop-up menu. Like any new version of Windows, however, it takes a little getting used to—especially if, like me, you've gotten used to the way the old Windows worked.

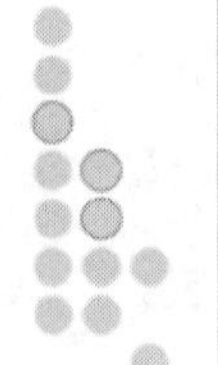

This chapter takes you on a guided tour of Windows XP. I tell you about all the new features of the operating system, and show you how Windows XP changes the way you perform some common tasks. I assume that you're already familiar with some previous versions of Windows, so I won't bore you with basic stuff like how to click your mouse or open a window. Instead, I try to get right to the good stuff–what you need to know to get started using Windows XP *right now*.

WHAT WINDOWS XP IS—AND WHAT IT *ISN'T*

Microsoft has gotten into the habit of bringing out new versions of its Windows operating system every two years or so. The latest big release was Windows 95 (back in 1995), which was a total rewrite of the previous 3.X version of Windows. Windows 98 (which followed in 1998) was a less-significant upgrade, and Windows 98 Second Edition (in 1999) was really no more than a minor bug fix. Windows Me (released in 2000) added a few bells and whistles, but was still basically the same operating system released back in 1995.

Through all those upgrades, the whole Windows 9X/Me product line has been targeted toward individual computer users. Corporations have been encouraged by Microsoft–since the mid-1990s, at least–to use their more robust Windows NT/2000 operating system. This corporate version of Windows was built from the ground up to be a true 32-bit operating system, while the consumer-oriented Windows 9X/Me OS has been saddled with legacy support for 16-bit programs.

In fact, when you open it up and look under the hood, you still find remnants of MS-DOS in the Windows 9X/Me OS. Which means, as most of you know, that the consumer version of windows has not been the most stable of operating systems.

If you wanted better stability, you had to move up to the 32-bit Windows NT/2000 OS. Unfortunately, Windows 2000 (the latest in this line) is not exactly consumer friendly. It doesn't support a lot of the peripherals that are common in home computing, and many popular games and older applications don't run on it.

Which brings us to Windows XP. With XP, Microsoft combines its consumer and corporate operating systems into a single OS. Windows XP is built on the Windows 2000 engine, but includes an interface and driver support built on what was available in 9X/Me. This means that Windows XP should be as stable and robust as Windows 2000, and as easy-to-use as Windows 9X/Me.

All this makes Windows XP the most important operating system release since Windows 95. While you might not have had a good reason to upgrade to Windows 98 or Windows Me, the performance and usability improvements in Windows XP make upgrading a tempting proposition.

Unfortunately, the choice to upgrade isn't clear cut. Mainly, this is because Windows XP has fairly stiff system requirements. (That's a result of using the Windows 2000 engine that has always required more powerful hardware to run.) If you have a relatively new, relatively powerful computer with lot of memory and hard disk space, you're probably okay to upgrade. If you have a computer more than two years old, you should stick with your current operating system.

Microsoft says (and I agree with them) that the best way to experience Windows XP is on a new XP-compatible computer. As you read this book, all new consumer-grade PCs should come equipped with Windows XP as the standard operating system. Buying a new PC with XP installed is certainly a more pleasant experience than going through the whole hassle of upgrading.

If you are upgrading to Windows XP from an older version of Windows, check out Appendix A, "Upgrading to Windows XP." I show you what you need to upgrade, how to prepare, and what to watch out for during the process.

New and Different

When you do move up to Windows XP, you find that all those changes under the hood are just that—under the hood. The main result of the change to the Windows 2000 engine is that the OS doesn't crash nearly as often. That is a good thing, of course, but isn't readily apparent.

What is readily apparent is the new look of the OS. Although, when you get right down to it, Windows XP still looks and acts pretty much like all previous versions of Windows.

There really isn't a lot of new functionality in the core of the OS. A lot of operations that used to be accessible by right-clicking an object are now front-and-center via context-sensitive activity center panes. These panes are activated when you choose to display folders in Web View. They appear in all folder windows and contain lists of the most popular tasks. Just click a task when you want to get something done—much easier than right-clicking items or pulling down menus.

Windows XP has new features, of course. Microsoft's detractors, however, call a lot of these features unnecessary to the operating system's core functionality. They may be right.

Microsoft views these additions as "extensions" to the OS, much as the addition of a Web browser was an extension. The new features of Windows XP include such "extensions" as a more robust media player, a digital video editor, a new instant messaging program that incorporates Internet telephony and video conferencing, and improved support for digital cameras and scanners.

Most of these new features were previously available from third-party providers, and from Microsoft as well. But now that they're built into the operating system, you don't need to obtain them separately. That's good for you (assuming you like Microsoft's versions), and bad for the third-party providers. Whether it's legal or not is up to the courts to decide.

All this functionality is given a high-tech sheen by Windows XP's new "Luna" interface. Luna is the biggest interface change since Windows 95 3-D icons replaced Windows 3.X's flat screen look. This is bright and colorful, with attractive rounded edges and all sorts of visual cues and effects that take full advantage of today's more detailed graphics displays. It may not affect the way XP works, but the new interface makes everything look a little fresher.

Luna is one of the many code words bandied about during the development and testing of Windows XP. XP itself was code-named Whistler.

Different Versions

Microsoft is selling three different versions of Windows XP. Windows XP Home Edition (on which this book is written) is the version of XP for home and small business users. Windows XP Professional is designed for larger businesses and corporate users, and includes the more robust networking and system administration functions required for that environment. Windows XP 64-Bit Edition is designed for workstation-class applications, such as designing bridges and making movies such as *Toy Story* and *Shrek*.

Unless you're running a large network, you don't need XP Professional. And unless you're looking to upgrade a powerful workstation, and are running Intel's new Itanium processor, you don't need the 64-bit version.

Windows XP Home Edition includes all the functionality you need for typical home or small business use, including an improved Network Setup Wizard that makes it easy to set up small home networks or shared Internet connections. XP Home Edition is the version installed on most consumer-grade PCs.

Windows XP Professional is somewhat of a superset of XP Home Edition. Everything you can do with XP Home you can do with XP Pro—and then some.

In case you're curious, these are some of the "and then some" features of XP Professional (not found in XP Home Edition):

- The ability to upgrade from Windows NT 4.0 and Windows 2000 Professional
- Administrative Tools
- Automated System Recovery (ASR)

Automated System Recovery is a new addition to the standard Backup utility, specifically designed for network system administrators.

- Dynamic Disk Support
- Encrypting File System (EFS)
- Fax support
- File-level access control
- Group Policy settings
- IntelliMirror capabilities, including user data management, centrally-managed software installation and updating, user settings management, and Remote Installation Services (RIS)

- Internet Explorer 6 Administration Kit
- Internet Information Services (IIS)/Personal Web Server
- IPSecurity user interface
- Kerberos authentication for enterprise resources
- Multi-language support
- Multi-processor support
- NetWare client service
- Network Monitor
- Remote Desktop
- Roaming user profiles
- SAP Agent
- SNMP support
- System Preparation (Sysprep) utility

As you can see, most of these differences have to do with corporate networking and administration. They aren't necessary for typical home or small business use.

When it comes to Windows XP 64-Bit Edition, you get support for Intel's new Itanium 64-bit processor. The 64-bit version of XP includes pretty much the same feature set as XP Professional, with exceptions of infrared support, DVD support, System Restore, and selected features related to mobile computing—all of which were taken out of the 64-Bit Edition. Suffice to say, you shouldn't be running XP 64-Bit Edition unless you're running some sort of high-end professional workstation.

Changing to a Task-Based Approach

Whichever version of Windows XP you use, you notice one extremely important change in the way this new operating system works. Put simply, Windows XP is much more task-based than its predecessors. Where older versions of Windows forced you to choose an item and then find the desired operation on a pull-down menu (or right-click an item to display a pop-up menu), Windows XP provides a list of likely tasks every time you select an item.

For example, when you select a file in My Computer or the My Documents folder (shown in Figure 1.1), the activity center pane displays a list of possible File Tasks. In this instance, the suggested tasks include Rename this file, Move this file, Copy this file, Publish this file to the Web, E-mail this file, Print this file, or Delete this file. You can still choose an operation from the menu bar (or right-click the file and choose an operation from the pop-up menu), but your most likely actions are listed in the activity center.

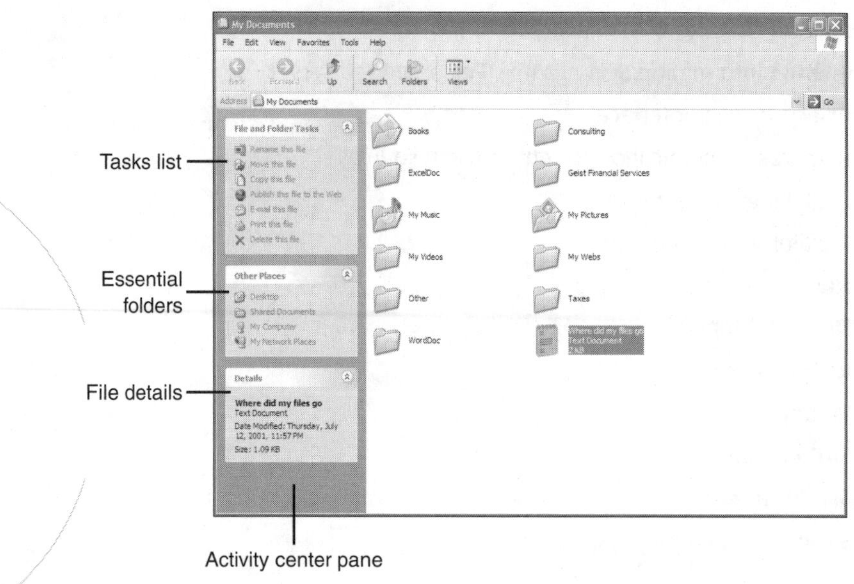

Figure 1.1

The File and Folder Tasks list in the topic bar drives Windows XP's new task-based approach.

Windows XP carries this task-based approach throughout the operating system, using what Microsoft calls an "intelligent user interface." The revamped Start menu, for example, groups your most frequently used files and applications together for quick and easy access. The new Search Companion asks you what you want to search for, in plain English (as opposed to requiring wildcards and file extensions, such as the old Find utility did)—and then offers additional suggestions to help refine your search. The My Pictures folder displays image thumbnails and tasks associated with image management. The My Music folder displays album covers for ripped CDs and tasks associated with digital music playback and recording. And so on.

This whole task-based approach is designed to make Windows work more like you work. This is kind of nice, for a change, to see an operating system adapt to my way of doing things, instead of the other way around!

UNDER THE HOOD

Of all the changes in Windows XP, the biggest one is invisible to the eye. The guts of Windows XP aren't the same guts that were in Windows 9X/Me. Instead, Windows XP uses the underlying engine that is used in the Windows 2000 operating system. If you ignore IBM's old OS/2 Warp (and most people did), this marks the first time a corporate-grade OS has been made available to home users.

A True 32-Bit Operating System

All previous Microsoft home operating systems have evolved from the old 16-bit MS-DOS operating system. The very first version of Windows wasn't much more than a pretty face—a *graphical user interface*, or GUI—grafted onto the underlying DOS command structure. Subsequent versions of Windows improved on the original, but still retained the original MS-DOS underpinnings. This was done to ensure compatibility with older applications—and believe it or not, a fair number of DOS-based apps are in use today.

Windows NT was Microsoft's first operating system *not* based on MS-DOS. NT was designed for corporate use, where system stability was more important than MS-DOS compatibility. By using a 32-bit kernel, Windows NT (and its successor, Windows 2000) was less crash-prone and more reliable.

Windows XP completely abandons the 16-bit engine used in Windows 9X/Me. Instead, it uses the same 32-bit operating system last utilized in Windows 2000. The interface on top of the OS is different, but the guts are pretty much the same.

Improved Stability

The result of this switch to a 32-bit engine is that Windows XP has all the stability of Windows 2000. Which is to say that Windows XP should crash a lot less frequently than Windows 9X/Me did.

If you were used to rebooting your computer at least once a day, or of having frozen programs bring down your whole system, then get used to a better way of doing things. Not that system crashes are completely a thing of the past, but when a program crashes in XP, the rest of your system usually stays up. You find yourself rebooting much less frequently, with far fewer crashes and freezes and the like.

In short, Windows XP features the type of stability and reliability that you've always wished for. Finally, a somewhat-reliable operating system for home use!

System Requirements

This improved performance comes at a price. Like Windows NT and Windows 2000 before it, Windows XP requires some powerful hardware just to get up and running. If you have an older PC, you probably don't have the muscle to run XP. Even if you have a newer PC, you may need to add more memory to handle the overhead of the new OS.

This is what Microsoft recommends for the minimum level of XP compatibility:

- 233MHz or higher processor in the Intel Pentium/Celeron or AMD K6/Athlon/Duron families
- 128MB of random access memory (RAM)
- 1.5GB of available hard disk space
- SuperVGA (800×600) or higher resolution video adapter or monitor
- CD-ROM or DVD drive

That's what *Microsoft* recommends. We've done a lot of testing at TechTV Labs, and based on that testing, I recommend the following:

- Run at least a Pentium III or AMD processor clocked at 500MHz or higher
- Increase your memory to at least 256MB
- Have at least 5GB of free hard disk space
- Set your screen resolution no lower than 1024×768—which means you probably want at least a 17-inch monitor, too

To be fair, Microsoft does offer the following caveat: *"Actual requirements will vary based on your system configuration and the applications and features you choose to install."* And some of the stiffer requirements I suggest can be sidestepped if you don't turn on all of XP's fancy display effects.

Still, memory and hard disk storage are relatively cheap. If you have to do a little hardware upgrading to make XP run well, it won't cost you an arm and a leg.

These basic system requirements are just for running XP with traditional computer software. If you want to perform other types of tasks, you need to have the right peripherals installed on your system. For example:

- For Internet access, you need a 33.6Kbps or higher-speed modem, along with an account with an Internet service provider—or a high-speed DSL or cable connection. (The 33.6Kbps is Microsoft's recommendation. I'd say that 56.6Kbps is the absolute minimum—and if you can get a cable modem or DSL, go for it!)
- For networking, you need a network interface card (NIC) and the proper connections to a network infrastructure.
- For instant voice conferencing and Internet telephony, you need a 33.6Kbps or higher-speed modem or a network connection, along with a microphone, sound card, and either speakers or a headset. (Again, 33.6Kbps is Microsoft's number. My minimum is 56.6Kbps.)
- For video conferencing, you need a 33.6Kbps or higher-speed modem or a network connection, along with a PC camera, microphone, sound card, and either speakers or a headset. (Once again, the 33.6Kbps number comes from Microsoft. From my experience, you won't want to do video conferencing on anything less than a broadband connection.)
- For DVD video playback, you need a DVD drive, DVD decoder card or DVD decoder software, and 8MB of video RAM.
- For digital video editing, you need a video capture card or IE1394 FireWire connection (for a digital video camera), along with a 400MHz or higher processor.

Hardware Support

You'll find that Windows XP is compatible with almost any type of hardware or peripheral you can throw at it. In particular, XP now includes full support for the following technologies:

- DVD-RAMs with FAT32 formatting
- IEEE 1393 Firewire connections
- IEEE 802.11b WiFi wireless networking
- Image Mastering API (IMAPI) for mastering CD-R and CD-RW discs via drag-and-drop
- Infrared Data Association (IrDA) wireless connections
- Intel Itanium 64-bit processor (also supported by the 64-bit version of Windows XP)
- Internet Connection Sharing to share a single Internet connection among multiple computers
- Network bridging, which enables home networks to combine different connection technologies
- Universal Disk Format (UDF) 2.01 for DVD-ROM discs and DVD videos
- Universal Plug and Play (UPnP), to support zero-configuration networking and automatic device discovery
- Universal serial bus (USB), including USB interface keyboards, USB microphones, and array microphones (for video conferencing and telephony)
- Windows Image Acquisition (WIA) for still-image devices

Basically, Windows XP should be compatible with just about any recent piece of hardware you might own—or any new hardware you might be in the market to buy. This is primarily due to the fact that XP is built on the Windows 2000 engine. Windows 2000 has been on the market long enough to have built up an amble and battle-tested library of device drivers. Any hardware driver that works on Windows 2000 *should* work on Windows XP.

However—and this is important—you may need to upgrade older device drivers to the Windows 2000/XP versions of those drivers. I found that when I upgraded from Windows Me to XP, several of my old devices quit working, obviously because I'd installed the Windows 9X/Me drivers. When I installed the Windows 2000 drivers, everything worked fine.

You may be able to use the Windows 2000 drivers that came on your device's installation disk. If not, Windows 2000-compatible drivers should be available for downloading from the manufacturer's Web site.

Windows XP also includes a new AutoPlay feature, which should simplify the use of removable media. AutoPlay lets you connect a new device or media—including flash cards, Zip disks, and CDs—and start using it right away. When you insert the item, AutoPlay determines the content and automatically starts the application. Which means, of course, that you don't have to start the association applications manually any more.

Learn more about adding new peripherals to Windows XP in Chapter 6, "Adding New Hardware."

Software Compatibility

Where hardware support shouldn't be much of a problem with Windows XP, software compatibility could be a different story. Although Microsoft claims that Windows XP is compatible with the top 1000 applications that ran under Windows 9X/Me and virtually all the applications that ran under Windows 2000, the reality might be different.

Many consumer applications that were designed for Windows 9X/Me simply don't run under Windows XP. (They wouldn't run under Windows 2000, either, which is the crux of the problem.) If a Windows 2000 version of a program does not exist, chances are good that you have problems running it under Windows XP. This is especially true with DOS-based programs, and many older PC games.

For example, I couldn't get America Online 6.0 to run under Windows XP. Whenever I tried to start the program, XP displayed a dialog box that told me the program was designed for Windows 95 or Windows 98, and that I needed to install an updated version. After I clicked the Details button, it gave me the option to close the dialog box or start the program.

When I tried to start the program, I got another dialog box. This one told me the program might not function properly with this version of Windows, and gave me another "run or close" option. When I clicked the Run Program button, the program tried to start, but then just as quickly shut down. Thanks to the robustness of the underlying engine, it didn't crash my system—it just didn't start.

A probable reason for this type of problem is that many older applications incorrectly detect which operating system is running. Because Windows XP is based on Windows 2000, these Windows 9X-based programs assume they're installed under Windows 2000—and thus refuse to work.

Microsoft tries to get around this version-sensing problem with Windows XP's Compatibility Mode. The Compatibility Mode uses a new technology called AppFixes, which automatically detects these older applications and tries to fool them into thinking that they're running on an older, more compatible version of Windows.

You can also use the AppFixes technology to manually fool applications that it doesn't catch automatically. Just right-click the application's shortcut, select Properties, select the Shortcut tab, check the Run in Compatibility Mode option, and select which OS you want to emulate. You can also apply compatibility mode through XP's Program Compatibility Wizard. You launch this wizard by clicking the Start button, then selecting All Programs, Accessories, Program Compatibility Wizard.

Microsoft has also specifically addressed potential compatibility problems with DOS-based PC games. Windows XP includes SoundBlaster-compatible sound support and high-resolution VESA video support, which should help to run these older games.

Adding up the pluses and minuses, Windows XP is probably more compatible with legacy applications than was Windows 95, the last big OS upgrade. Even when you have a program crash, it seldom brings down the entire operating system. You should be able to move, resize, minimize, or close a frozen application so that you can continue working in other applications. You can also use the old three-fingered salute (Ctrl+Alt+Del) to open up the Windows Task Manager, which now includes more options than you had in Windows 9X/Me—including the often necessary option of ending the current task.

Oh, and AOL users, never fear. The latest version of AOL, version 7.0, works just fine under XP.

Learn more about using Windows XP with various types of software in Chapter 4, "Running Programs."

WINDOWS XP'S NEW "LOOK AND FEEL" FEATURES

You know that Windows XP is more stable, thanks to its 32-bit Windows 2000 engine. You know that Windows XP employs a more user-friendly task-based approach to things. Now it's time to delve into the details, and examine all the new features of the operating system.

Let's look first at how Windows XP has changed the desktop and user interface. What follows is a list of some of the most important changes to the operating system's look and feel.

Welcome Screen

The first new feature of Windows XP that you see is the new Welcome screen. This screen replaces the old Logon screen, used in previous versions of Windows.

The new Welcome screen is a friendlier, more visual way to handle multiple users. It displays a list of users currently set up on your system, along with an associated image. Click the image to log in as that user—no typing involved—or click the Guest icon to log on as a guest.

You also see the new Welcome screen when you switch users, which you do by clicking the Log Off button on the Start menu.

User Interface

When Windows XP starts, you see the biggest change to the operating system's look and feel. The entire user interface has changed, but in a good way.

Microsoft calls the new interface Luna, and it's much more attractive than any of the previous Windows interfaces. As you can see in Figure 1.2, it features brighter colors, rounder edges, and bigger buttons and icons.

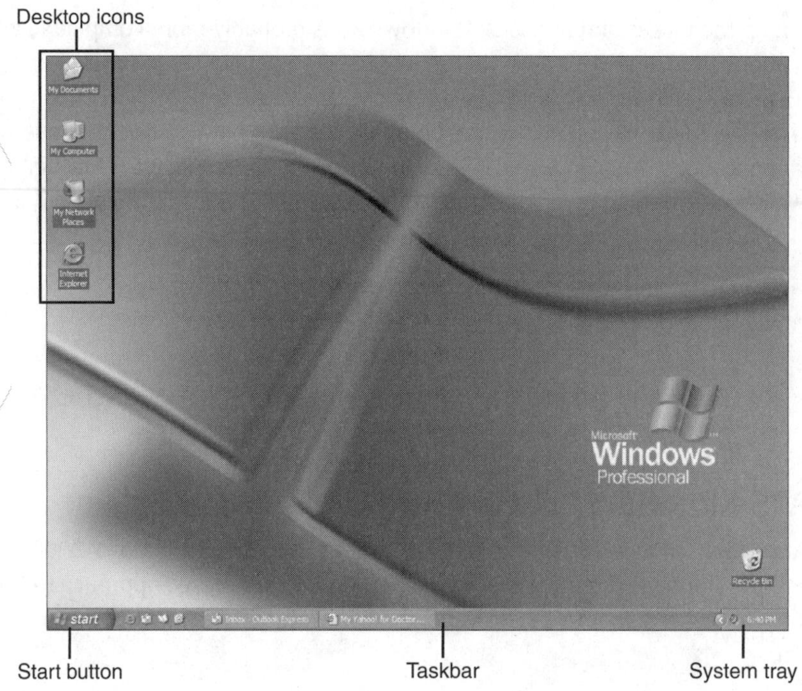

Figure 1.2

Windows XP's new Luna interface—bigger, brighter, and rounder.

You can make Luna look even snazzier by activating a bevy of animation and 3-D effects. These effects include watermarks, fading or scrolling menu transitions, icon text transparency, and drop shadows.

Some of these effects can be activated from the Display Properties dialog box, which you can open from the Windows Control Panel. (Select the Settings tab and click the Effects button.) Other effects have to be activated from the System Properties dialog box, also accessible from the Control Panel. (Select the Advanced tab and click the Settings button in the Performance section.)

Although not much about the new Luna interface changes improves XP's usability, I find that it's a nice change of pace from the traditional hard-edged Windows interface. Notice the nice visual cues, such as the Start button being green (for "go"), and selected buttons being surrounded with an orange glow. If you don't like Luna, you can return to the classic Windows interface from the Display Properties dialog box. Just select the Themes tab and choose the Windows Classic theme, and XP superficially resembles Windows 98.

Learn more about customizing the look and feel of Windows XP (including the Start menu, the Control Panel, folder views, and ClearType) in Chapter 2, "Changing the Way Windows Looks—And Acts."

Desktop

I've seen a lot of desktops on a lot of PCs. Most of them are cluttered to the max, with every type of icon imaginable stuck here and there and everywhere. Windows XP tries to clean up this clutter by removing almost all the icons on initial installation.

You can reclutter your desktop manually, of course. But every few days a Desktop Cleanup Wizard runs and drops any icons you haven't used in awhile back into an Unused Desktop Icons folder. The result is a much cleaner desktop, whether you like it or not. I like it, because I'm a complete desktop slob. This is like having a digital maid!

ClearType

For some reason, this new feature doesn't get a lot of play from Microsoft or the tech press. In fact, it's almost buried in XP's Display Properties dialog box.

That's a shame, because ClearType is one of the most impressive–and most useful–new features of Windows XP.

ClearType is a technology that effectively triples the horizontal display resolution on LCD displays. If you use a portable PC or have one of those expensive flat-panel monitors sitting on your desk, you find that ClearType makes Windows XP a must have operating system.

The difference between ClearType and traditional LCD display technologies is amazing, and is noticeable on every application you use. After you turn ClearType on, you wonder how you ever did without it!

Control Panel

Microsoft has attempted to make the Control Panel easier to use. It now groups applets by type, in what it calls a Category view. In this view, you don't see the applets right off. Instead, you're encouraged to "pick a category" from ten different areas, such as Appearances and Themes, User Accounts, and Performance and Maintenance.

When you click a category, you *then* see the traditional applets–accompanied by a list of tasks under the "pick a task" heading. You can click an applet icon, or click a task, which then opens the appropriate applet.

Although this Category view may be a more task-based approach, it results in more clicking for experienced users. Fortunately, you can turn off the Category view by clicking the Switch to Category View option in the Control Panel's activity center pane.

Folder Views

The folders used to display your computer's files have been completely redesigned in Windows XP.

First, each folder by default displays a context sensitive pane that Microsoft calls an *activity center*. The activity center lists details about the selected file or folder, and displays a list of common tasks you can perform.

You can also customize the look of each folder in a number of ways, including grouping files by type or most-recent use. Choosing custom icons for any folder on your system is also possible—and you can customize folders that contain music or images with a thumbnail of the album art or images they contain.

My Computer

As you can see in Figure 1.3, My Computer looks radically different in Windows XP. In addition to the ever-present activity center pane, My Computer now displays the pieces and parts of your computer system by type. You see a section for hard disk drives, a section for removable storage devices, and a section for other devices (such as digital cameras and scanners).

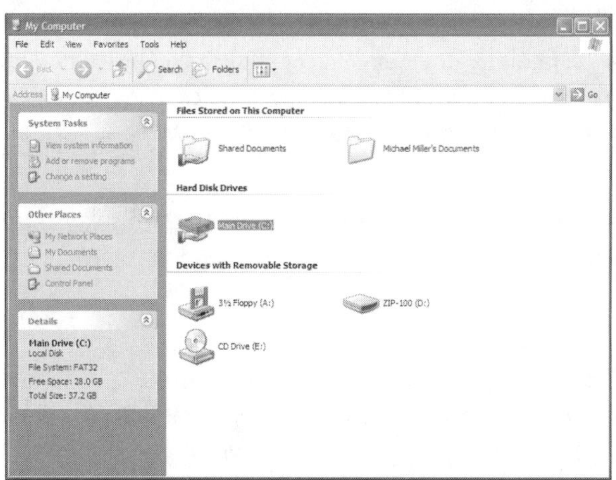

Figure 1.3

Windows XP's new My Computer—more useful than in previous versions.

In addition, the Tasks list contains links that start up the most common system tasks, such as searching for files or folders, or adding or removing programs. These changes work to make My Computer a lot more useful than it was in previous versions of Windows.

Start Menu

Windows XP's Start menu is quite different from the Start menu in previous versions of Windows. It still opens when you click the Start button, but the similarities stop there.

As you can see in Figure 1.4, the new Start menu is greatly simplified. The left side of the menu includes icons for your Web browser and e-mail program, as well as the last six programs used. The right side of the menu contains smaller icons for your essential folders (My Computer, My Documents, My Music, My Pictures, and so on) and key system utilities (Control Panel, Help and Support, and so on).

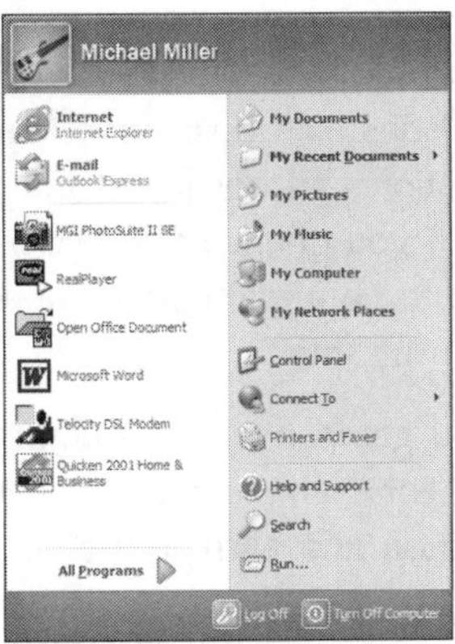

Figure 1.4

The new, simplified Start menu.

All your other programs are accessible from the All Programs link. Just click (or hover over) the green arrow, and the traditional menu of programs pops up.

You can personalize the Start menu by forcing the menu to display programs of your choosing. Whether you use the Start menu as-is or customize it to your liking, I think it's a vast improvement over the cluttered Start menu of old.

System Tray

The big change in Windows XP's System Tray is that it isn't nearly as cluttered as it used to be.

In all previous versions of Windows, just about any utility running in the background showed up in the System Tray. The Tray then expanded to the left to take up valuable display space. In most cases you didn't need to see all those little icons, so the Tray became a big waste of space.

Windows XP takes the System Tray and divides its content into two groups. If it's important for you to see the status of an icon, that icon is placed on the right side of the tray, which is always visible. If an icon doesn't really need to be seen, it's placed on the left side of the tray, which is hidden by default. You can display all the icons by clicking the left arrow button (actually a chevron) to expand the visible area. As you can see in Figure 1.5, though, you'd probably prefer this condensed version of the Tray.

Figure 1.5

The new, more efficient System Tray.

Taskbar

The Taskbar in Windows XP has also been redesigned to reduce clutter. With the old Taskbar, every single application and document that you opened appeared in its own Taskbar button. That meant if you opened five Microsoft Word documents, five buttons would be displayed. This got to be a real pain if you kept a lot of windows open—those Taskbar buttons could get mighty small!

With Windows XP, when you get to a certain number of buttons, the operating system starts to group them by type. For example, those five Word documents are combined into a single button. Click the button and each of the documents are displayed in a pop-up menu. Select a document from the menu to switch to that document.

Windows XP also arranges the Taskbar buttons by similar functions. With previous versions of Windows, Taskbar buttons were arranged in the order they were opened. In Windows XP the buttons are arranged by type—so if you open My Computer, Microsoft Word, and My Documents, the buttons are displayed in this order: My Computer, My Documents, and then Microsoft Word.

This is a small change, but it's a good one.

Interestingly, Windows XP lets you mix and match which interface features you use. For example, if you want to use the old My Computer look and feel with the new Start menu—or vice versa—you can. I tell you how to do this in the next chapter, if you can hold on until then.

WINDOWS XP'S NEW INTERNET FEATURES

Windows XP, like the last few versions of Windows, comes with a Web browser, e-mail client, and instant messaging program. With XP, you get the latest versions of each, complete with a slew of new features and functionality. You also get improved Internet connection sharing features, and a built-in firewall to protect your system from outside dangers.

You don't have to have Windows XP to run Internet Explorer 6. This latest version of IE is available for downloading (for free) from the Web, at `www.microsoft.com/windows/ie/`.

However, XP's Internet integration doesn't stop with browsing, e-mail, and messaging. You have to connect to the Internet to activate Windows XP (you can also activate via a voice call, but that's a real time-waster), and it uses the Internet to automatically update itself through the AutoUpdate and Windows Update features. XP also enables you to e-mail or publish files directly to the Web from any folder, using options on the folder's Tasks list.

Truth be told, you miss a lot if you don't have a regular Internet. You don't have to stay connected all the time, but you definitely need to be connected in some way.

Internet Explorer 6

Windows XP includes Internet Explorer 6, the latest version of Microsoft's market-leading Web browser. As you can see in Figure 1.6, IE6 assumes the look and feel of XP's Luna interface, with new graphics for all its toolbar buttons. It incorporates several new and improved features, including

- A new Media Bar, for streaming audio and video playback (actually a stripped-down version of the Windows Media Player)
- An improved Search Companion for Web searching
- Better handling of Web page images, including a new Image toolbar for saving and printing pictures, and Auto Image Resizing for fitting big images in small browser windows
- The ability to add your own Explorer Bars (those panes that display on the left side of the browser window, such as Favorites and History)

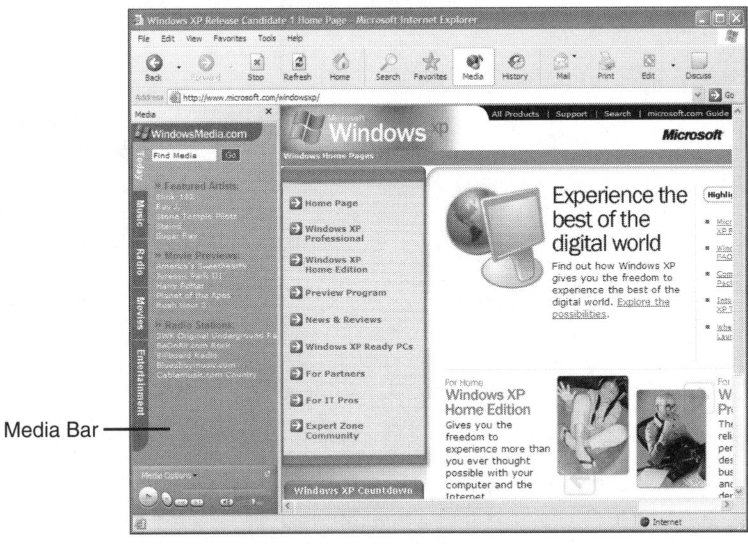

Figure 1.6

XP includes the latest version of Internet Explorer, complete with new Media Bar.

IE6 includes support for all the latest Web development standards, including Document Object Model (DOM) Level 1 and Cascading Style Sheets (CSS). It also incorporates the new Platform for Privacy Preferences (P3P) privacy standard, which gives you more control of how Web sites use your personal data.

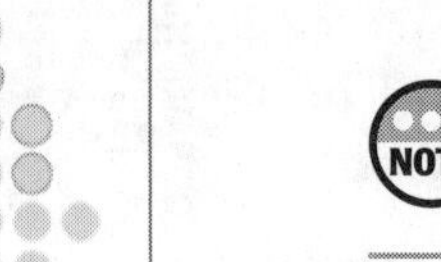

Learn more about Internet Explorer 6 in Chapter 8, "Surfing the Web with Internet Explorer."

Outlook Express 6

Outlook Express 6 is included with Windows XP and is also available for free as part of the Internet Explorer 6 download. The biggest change in this version is improved virus detection, which is accomplished by blocking the downloading of specific types of file attachments. (Not everyone thinks that this is a plus, however, as OE6 blocks downloads of all executable files—and you can't override the block!)

Learn more about Outlook Express 6 in Chapter 9, "Sending and Receiving E-mail with Outlook Express."

Windows Messenger

One of the bigger deals in Windows XP is the new Windows Messenger program, shown in Figure 1.7. Windows Messenger replaces the older MSN Messenger and Netmeeting programs. It functions as an all-in-one program for instant messaging, Internet telephony, and video conferencing.

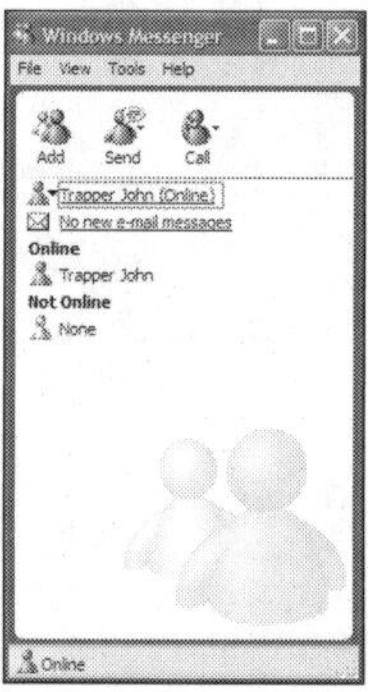

Figure 1.7

Use Windows Messenger for instant messaging, Internet phone calls, and video conferencing.

Windows Messenger enables you to do a lot of communicating from a single program. You can send instant messages to other Messenger users, engage in multiuser online chats, make voice calls to anyone with a telephone or Internet connection, send text messages to cell phones and pagers, and participate in video conferences with anyone connected to the Web.

Windows Messenger is a heck of a program, and one of the key reasons to upgrade to Windows XP.

Learn more about Windows Messenger in Chapter 10, "Chatting Online with Windows Messenger."

Internet Connection Sharing

As more and more users connect to the Internet through high-speed broadband connections, it becomes important to share those fast (and expensive!) connections between multiple computers. Windows XP makes it easy to set up a small network for Internet connection sharing, via the new Network Setup Wizard. This feature lets you share either a dial-up or broadband connection, without a lot of hassle.

Learn more about Internet connection sharing and the Internet Connection Firewall in Chapter 7, "Making the Connection."

Internet Connection Firewall

If you have a broadband connection in your home, you need to install some sort of firewall software to protect your computers from Internet-based attacks. Plenty of third-party firewall programs are available just for this purpose, and now Windows XP includes it's own built-in Internet Connection Firewall. This is not a bad little firewall, and it does the trick for most home users. (Larger business users might want to invest in a more robust firewall, however.)

WINDOWS XP'S NEW MULTIUSER AND MULTIPLE-PC FEATURES

Because Windows XP is built on the Windows 2000 engine, and because Windows 2000 was designed to be a multiuser network-enabled operating system, it makes sense that XP would include a bevy of multiuser and networking features. Chief among these features are XP's new user accounts, the new Home Networking Wizard, and wireless networking support.

XP also includes the ability to set up a single network card with two separate network configurations (great for portable PCs used both at home and at work). You can also use XP's "network bridge" capability to connect two separate network segments—even if those segments use different networking technologies. (For example, you can use XP to "bridge" a wireless network to a wired Ethernet network.)

User Accounts

Windows XP is designed as a multiuser operating system. To that end, XP makes it very easy to set up multiple user accounts, and to switch from one user to another.

You can establish any number of users within Windows XP. Each user can define his own personalizations, documents, and security settings. You choose a user on initial logon, and can switch users at any time by clicking the Log Off button on the Start menu, and choosing a new user from the Welcome screen.

You can also have multiple users logged on at the same time, thanks to the new Fast User Switching feature. Fast User Switching enables you to log on additional users without shutting down the first user's applications. This is a good way to share a single PC among multiple family members—although you need a lot of system memory to make this truly "fast" switching.

Learn more about Windows XP's user accounts in Chapter 16, "Working with Multiple Users."

Network Setup Wizard

Setting up a network is made easy by Windows XP's Network Setup Wizard. Thanks to this feature, you don't have to fiddle with a lot of protocols and configurations. Just answer the questions in the wizard, and you can easily connect two or more computers together in a local area network. You can also use this wizard to set up Internet connection sharing, or even simple printer and peripheral sharing.

Learn more about Windows XP's networking features in Chapter 18, "Setting Up a Home or Small Business Network."

Wireless Networking

If you're contemplating setting up a wireless network, Windows XP supports the 11Mbps IEEE 802.11b standard (also known as WiFi). XP also supports HomePNA phoneline networks. (It doesn't support the new Bluetooth wireless connectivity standard, unfortunately, although Bluetooth hardware vendors make drivers available to support their cards.)

WINDOWS XP'S NEW AUDIO AND VIDEO FEATURES

Today's PCs are used for more than just personal computing. PC use now includes a variety of multimedia activities, from simple picture viewing to advanced CD burning and digital video editing. Windows XP builds the necessary multimedia features into the operating system, so you no longer have to rely on third-party software to perform essential tasks.

Digital Picture Management

Windows XP builds upon Windows Me's enhanced support for digital imaging and fully integrates image management into the operating system. This makes Windows XP an ideal environment for working with digital cameras and scanners.

XP's My Pictures folder is where you store all your digital picture files. This folder includes a number of image-specific functions that simplify the process of transferring, browsing through, printing, and otherwise manipulating images. By default, My Pictures shows all pictures as thumbnails, as shown in Figure 1.8. You can hover over any image and see key details such as resolution, format, and size. You can even display all the pictures in the folder as an onscreen slideshow, or set a picture to be your desktop background.

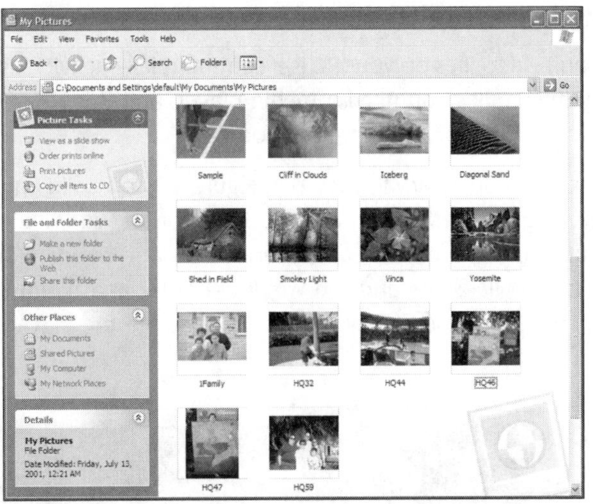

Figure 1.8

The My Pictures folder is where you store, view, and manage all your digital images.

Windows XP incorporates the Windows Imaging Acquisition (WIA) standard. WIA integrates compatible imaging devices, such as digital cameras and scanners, directly into the OS shell. In effect, this lets you see and use any imaging device just like it was a removable drive on your system. So, for example, you could be working in a graphics editing program and open an image file stored on your digital camera, without first saving it to your hard drive.

XP also features the Scanner and Camera Wizard (first included in Windows Me). This wizard lets you easily choose images to download. You can also use the wizard to set up subfolders, delete files directly from your imaging device, and so on.

Finally, XP includes a new Windows Picture and Fax Viewer. When you click a picture in the My Pictures folder, that file is opened from within the Picture and Fax Viewer. From there you can view, rotate, zoom in or out, or print the image file.

Learn more about Windows XP's digital picture management in Chapter 11, "Working with Pictures," and Chapter 12, "Working with Digital Cameras and Scanners."

Online Photo Finishing

The My Pictures folder includes a section on the task pane titled Photo Tasks. One of the tasks in this section is labeled Order Prints From the Internet. When you click this link, XP displays the Online Print Ordering dialog box that lets you send selected image files over the Internet to a professional photo printer.

Microsoft has cut deals with several major firms for online photo finishing services. While some might question whether photo finishing should be part of a computer operating system, it is nice to be able to arrange professional printing with a few clicks of the mouse.

Windows Media Player

Playing audio and video files on your PC is a commonplace activity, especially when you're online. To play media files you need a media player, and Windows XP's Windows Media Player (WMP) for Windows XP is a pretty good one.

The Windows XP version of WMP, shown in Figure 1.9, is a solid improvement over older versions of the program. At first glance the XP version of WMP looks a lot like the previous version, but with the expected Luna interface enhancements. Note, however, that the left taskbar is now collapsible, and the window border and menu are now optional. As with version 7, the XP version of WMP lets you change the player's look and feel with optional "skins."

Figure 1.9

Use Windows Media Player to play back and record a variety of media formats—including MP3 audio and DVD video.

Because WMP for XP can rip at the full speed of your CD drive, copying files from a CD is faster than with version 7. (Version 7 was limited to 2X speed.) The process of creating a playlist is also enhanced. You can now see how much free space you have left while you're in the process.

When you copy music from an audio CD onto your system, the containing folder displays the album art for the CD that was ripped—assuming that you're connected to the Internet to download the cover graphic. If you group CDs in subfolders under a master folder for a particular artist, the artist's folder displays up to four CD album cover images. This is a nice touch that enables you to see at a glance which folder contains which music.

You also find that WMP8 has improved sound and picture quality over previous versions and, as discussed next, now includes support for both DVD video and MP3 audio playback.

Learn more about Windows Media Player in Chapter 13, "Using Windows Media Player."

MP3 Support

Microsoft has introduced rudimentary support for the MP3 format into the XP version of its Windows Media Player. WMP has always supported Microsoft's proprietary WMA format, as well as a variety of streaming audio and video formats. However, this is the first time the player has supported the competing (and vastly more popular) MP3 format.

Don't get too excited about WMP's MP3 support, however. As it ships from the factory, WMP for XP only supports MP3 *playback*, not encoding. You can add MP3 encoding, however, by purchasing an optional add-on software utility called the MP3 Creation Pack. When you install this software, you'll be able to choose from either WMA or MP3 format when you're ripping audio files.

Learn more about MP3s in Chapter 14, "Playing and Recording MP3 and WMA Audio."

DVD Support

WMP8 also includes full-screen playback for DVD videos. It doesn't include its own DVD decoder, however, so you have to use one from a third party. This typically isn't a big deal; if you have a DVD player in your PC, it probably came with decoder software installed. If you don't have DVD decoder software, you can add that capability by purchasing the DVD Decoder Pack add-on software.

CD Burning

You can use Windows Media Player to burn audio files to a CD-R or CD-RW, or you can burn your own CDs directly from any Windows folder. Just open My Computer (or any folder, actually), right-click a file, and select Send To, Recordable CD. (You can also drag files directly to the CD-R/RW drive icon.) When you're done selecting files, use My Computer to open the CD-R/RW drive and select the Burn CD task.

Yes, it's that simple. No confusing utility programs to open, no special configuration to set up. Just click and burn.

Windows Movie Maker

Windows XP supports the IE1394 Firewire standard, which enables the super-fast transfer of files from a digital video camera and your PC. XP also includes Windows Movie Maker, a digital video editing program that first appeared in Windows Me.

Windows Movie Maker, shown in Figure 1.10, enables you to capture both analog and digital video, edit it, add simple transitions and title screens, and then save the final product in Windows Media format. You can then send the saved file back to your VCR, for recording on tape.

Figure 1.10

Perform simple digital video editing with Windows Movie Maker.

While WMM doesn't include a lot of fancy features, it's fine for simple video editing. If you have more sophisticated needs, you need to use a more full-function program.

Learn more about Windows Movie Maker in Chapter 15, "Playing and Editing Digital Movies."

WINDOWS XP'S NEW SYSTEM UTILITIES

Windows XP includes pretty much the same complement of system utilities found in Windows 98 and Windows Me, with a few significant additions and improvements.

System Restore

System Restore was one of the most important additions to Windows Me. Fortunately, this utility continues into Windows XP.

The System Restore utility is a major-league safety net in case you ever experience a catastrophic problem with your computer. Before System Restore, you may have been forced to reinstall your complete operating system. With System Restore, reinstallations are a thing of the past. The utility can automatically restore your system to the state it was in before the problem cropped up.

System Restore works by actively monitoring your system and noting changes made when you install new applications. Each time it notes a change, it automatically creates a snapshot of the key system files on your system. If an installation goes bad, you can run System

Restore and undo any changes made to your system by the installation. This restores your system to the pre-installation state—which should get you up and running again.

Even though it isn't perfect, I thought that System Restore was one of the most important selling points for Windows Me. If you're still using Windows 98 or Windows 95, this utility alone might make it worthwhile to upgrade to Windows XP.

Learn more about System Restore in Chapter 23, "Recovering from System Crashes."

Compressed Folders

File compression, in the form of "zipped" files, has been around since the days of MS-DOS. Until recently, though, you had to do your compressing with a third-party utility, such as the venerable WinZip.

Starting with the Windows 98 Plus! Pack, and continuing into Windows Me, file compression was built into the operating system through what Microsoft calls compressed folders. The compressed folders feature has been enhanced in Windows XP with a new Extraction Wizard. When you right-click a compressed folder and select Extract All from the pop-up menu, the Extraction Wizard starts and walks you through the process of extracting some or all the files from the compressed folder.

This might sound like a small thing, but the Extraction Wizard effectively eliminates the need for any third-party compression software. Because the Extraction Wizard does everything WinZip and other programs do, including the creation and extraction of multiple-disk Zip files, you don't need another utility.

Learn more about compressed folders in Chapter 3, "Managing Files."

Files and Settings Transfer Wizard

This last new utility in Windows XP was designed to help users move between different computers. The Files and Settings Transfer Wizard walks you through the process of transfer important documents, files, and settings to another computer. This is a great way to take all your good stuff with you when you upgrade to a new computer system and you can even run the wizard from the Windows XP CD on a non-XP system.

Learn more about the Files and Settings Transfer Wizard in Chapter 21, "Updating Windows."

WINDOWS XP'S HELP AND REGISTRATION FEATURES

The final changes in Windows XP are to the Help and registration systems. Windows Help has never been something to write home about, and it's still far from great, but at least Microsoft is trying to make it better.

Revamped Help System

The Help system in Windows XP builds on the new Help system that was introduced in Windows Me. Windows XP Help (now called Help and Support) has been enhanced with a better search system, automatic updating with new content from the Internet, and new user-friendly interface.

Microsoft has also integrated a number of system tools into the Help system, including the System Configuration Utility, Advanced System Information, and Windows Update. This puts all the system's troubleshooting tools in one place, which is far superior to the scattershot approach embraced by previous versions of Windows.

Learn more about Windows XP's Help and Support system (including Remote Assistance) in Chapter 20, "Getting Help."

Remote Assistance

Another new component of the Windows XP Help system is called Remote Assistance. This utility lets you turn over control of your computer to another computer—which enables a technician to troubleshoot your system's problems without actually being there. All you have to do is connect your computer to the Internet, and Remote Assistance enables the other person do the driving.

I'm going to use this feature to help support my Dad and his computer—I'm his personal tech support department.

Online Registration and Activation

Finally, if you've already installed Windows XP, you've no doubt noticed that an Internet connection is almost a necessity to complete the installation. For the first time in Windows history, you actually have to get Microsoft's approval to activate Windows on your system. (This is in addition to the normal product registration, which can also be done online.)

Windows XP Product Activation has caught a lot of flack from users afraid that Microsoft is gathering personal information during the activation process. Microsoft claims that isn't so and that it merely encodes information about your system hardware and combines it with the product code on your Windows XP installation CD to create a unique activation code. This machine-specific activation code is meant to prevent you from using a single copy of Windows XP on multiple PCs.

The problem with this Product Activation is that it might also prevent you from reinstalling the operating system on a single PC—especially if you've dramatically changed the configuration of your system. This means that if you have to reinstall Windows, you may need to call Microsoft and sweet-talk a support person into letting you reinstall a program that you already paid good money for.

It remains to be seen if Product Activation really works, or what kind of problems it might cause. It might be a good idea to keep Microsoft's tech support number handy—just in case!

For a more detailed discussion of Windows Product Activation, see Appendix A, "Upgrading to Windows XP."

FEATURE COMPARISON

So, how do all these new and changed features help Windows XP stack up with previous versions of Windows? See for yourself in Table 1.1, which compares the key features of Windows XP with both Windows 98 and Windows Me.

TABLE 1.1—KEY DIFFERENCES BETWEEN WINDOWS XP, 98, AND ME

Feature	Windows XP	Windows Me	Windows 98
32-bit Windows engine	Yes	No	No
Activity center panes	Yes	No	No
ClearType display technology	Yes	No	No
Compressed folders	Yes, improved	Yes	No
Customized folder views	Yes	No	No
Desktop Cleanup Wizard	Yes	No	No
Direct folder-to-CD-R/RW copying	Yes	No	No
DVD video playback	Yes	No	No
Fast user switching	Yes	No	No
Files and Settings Transfer Wizard	Yes	No	No
Hidden icons in System Tray	Yes	No	No
Image Preview utility	Yes	No	No
Internet Connection Firewall	Yes	No	No
Internet Connection Sharing	Yes, improved	Yes	Yes
Internet Explorer 6	Yes	No	No
Luna user interface	Yes	No	No
MP3 encoding	Optional	No	No
Multiple-user Welcome screen	Yes	No	No
My Music folder	Yes, improved	Yes	No
My Pictures folder	Yes, improved	Yes	No
Network Setup Wizard	Yes, improved	Yes	No
Online photo finishing	Yes	No	No
Online support services	Yes, improved	Yes	Yes
Outlook Express 6	Yes	No	No
Personalized Welcome screen	Yes	No	No

TABLE 1.1—CONTINUED

Feature	Windows XP	Windows Me	Windows 98
Product Activation	Yes	No	No
Redesigned Control Panel	Yes	No	No
Redesigned My Computer	Yes	No	No
Redesigned Start menu	Yes	No	No
Remote Assistance	Yes	No	No
Scanner and Camera Wizard	Yes, improved	Yes	No
Search Companion	Yes	No	No
System Restore	Yes	Yes	No
Task-based approach	Yes	No	No
Taskbar button grouping	Yes	No	No
Thumbnail image file display	Yes	Yes	No
User accounts	Yes	No	NO
Web Publishing Wizard	Yes	Yes	No
Windows Image Acquisition for digital pictures	Yes	Yes	No
Windows Media Player	Yes, improved	Yes	No
Windows Messenger	Yes	No	No
Windows Movie Maker	Yes, improved	Yes	No
Windows Update	Yes, improved	Yes	Yes

OLD VERSUS NEW: HOW TO DO WHAT YOU USED TO DO

Everything you used to do with Windows 98 or Windows Me, you can still do with Windows XP. In fact, in most instances you can still perform the same tasks the same way. Windows XP, more often than not, just provides a more efficient way to accomplish your familiar tasks.

This is most apparent when you're working with files and folders. Because all Windows XP folders include an activity center pane, you can use the links on this pane to accomplish your most frequent file management tasks.

Doing It All from a Single Folder

With previous versions of Windows, if you wanted to perform some action on a file, you'd have to pull down the Edit menu or right-click the file to access the pop-up menu. (Most users didn't know about the right-click menus—one of the more productive "hidden" features in Windows 98 and Windows Me.) Now all those right-click options are out in the open, in the activity center's Tasks list.

You might be used to dragging and dropping file icons, or pulling down the Edit menu, or right-clicking. Using the Tasks list is a much faster way to get most things done. You have to get used to some new wording, but when the task is right in front of you like that, it really speeds things up.

In fact, XP really makes a big shift away from the old "drag and drop" paradigm. While XP is still very much mouse-driven, the new paradigm is "select and do." Everything you need to do appears in a single window, so all you have to do is select a file and then choose what you want to do—with no interim menu pulling to get in the way.

The other big change with Windows XP is that you probably, at last, end up abandoning the directory-tree way of doing things, typified by the old Windows Explorer. I've never been a big fan of Windows Explorer, but most power users I know lived inside Explorer, because of its powerful tree view. Well, with Windows XP's new folder views and the creation of the extremely useful activity centers, Windows Explorer has been eliminated. That's right, no more Windows Explorer. Get used to it!

The bottom line is that Windows XP makes a lot of tasks a lot easier than they used to be. You don't *have* to change the way you do things—right-clicking still opens the old pop-up menu—but all the shortcuts and workarounds that Windows power users taught themselves over the years no longer give them any advantage.

In other words, Microsoft finally got it mostly right.

Taking Advantage of the New Utilities

Microsoft also included a handful of new system tools and utilities in Windows XP. These built-in utilities make it easier to do common tasks within Windows, without reverting to third-party programs.

To me, chief among these new utilities is the Extraction Wizard. Over the years I got very used to launching WinZip whenever I needed to compress some files—even after compressed folders were introduced in the Windows 98 Plus! Pack. The Extraction Wizard, however, finally makes compressed folders as easy to use as WinZip, so I don't use the WinZip utility any more. It saves me a little time, and it's more convenient.

Depending on your particular needs, you might say the same thing about XP's integrated folder-to-CD-R/RW file copying, or Windows Media Player's ripping and burning, or the online photo finishing feature, or the Windows Picture and Fax Viewer. More and more common operations are built into the operating system, which reduces the number of application-specific utility programs you need to run. True, some of these XP utilities don't include all the features you might find in a third-party program, but not all users need all those features. You can still use third-party utilities if you like, but you might not need to.

Where Things Are

One last thing about Windows XP. If you go looking for certain files on your hard disk, you find that the location of some important files and folders are different from where they were in previous versions of Windows.

The biggest change is where Windows stores your documents. In Windows 9X/Me, your documents were stored in the My Documents folder, which was one level down from the root directory. In Windows XP, such as Windows 2000, each user has his own My Documents folder, which is stored several levels down. You find the My Documents folder in the following location: c:\Documents and Settings*username*\My Documents\. Within the My Documents folder are the My Music, My Pictures, My Videos, and My Webs subfolders.

Depending on your setup, *username* might be your user name, or it might be "default" or "default user."

Your Favorites folder is also located within the c:\Documents and Settings*username*\ folder. Most templates and configuration files for Microsoft applications (such as Office) have been moved to subfolders within the c:\Documents and Settings*username*\ Application Data\Microsoft\ folder.

In short, look for any user-specific files to be somewhere in the folder with your name on it.

STUFF THAT DIDN'T MAKE THE FINAL CUT

The version of Windows XP you find on store shelves and installed on new PCs isn't quite the version that Microsoft originally intended to release. As with most new product releases, as Windows XP entered the testing phase, some intended features didn't make the cut. Sometimes a feature was cut because Microsoft couldn't get all the bugs out. Other times a feature worked fine, but the company found that users just didn't like it. In any case, Microsoft yanked a handful of features out of the final product—including several that were highly touted beforehand.

Smart Tags

Microsoft generated a lot of noise when they announced that they would build support for Smart Tags into Internet Explorer 6. A Smart Tag is a piece of text that links to a variety of related content—more often than not on Web sites within Microsoft's commercial online service, MSN.

Smart Tags first appeared in Office XP, and their proposed inclusion in IE6 raised a lot of ruckus. That's because the Smart Tags that you would have seen on a Web page were not inserted as part of the page, but were inserted by the browser itself. Microsoft rigged IE6 to tag certain types of words—typically names of companies and other entities—to drive users to Microsoft's own Web sites. As many users pointed out, they're too obvious a for Microsoft-owned content, and interfere with the original design of the underlying Web pages.

Microsoft kept the push on for awhile, even claiming at one point that Smart Tags would rescue users from "under-linked" Web sites. That's the first I've heard of an "under-linking" problem!

After a hearty round of public debate, in which more than one commentator called Smart Tags an attempt to create a Microsoft-sanctioned Internet, Microsoft backed off and pulled Smart Tags from the final release. So IE6 and Windows XP don't include Smart Tags—which is good, because I found them highly annoying!

A better way to find related information is to search for it, or to use the related pages feature already built into both Internet Explorer and Netscape. (In Internet Explorer, you access this feature by selecting Tools, Show Related Links.) Both browsers use this feature to connect to the Alexa service and then display a variety of pages somehow related to the selected page.

Personal and Contact Bars

Two more proposed features for Internet Explorer 6 were dropped before the final release—in this instance, because they simply didn't work very well. Microsoft intended to add a Personal Bar pane to IE6 to display a variety of personalized content, similar to Netscape 6's My Sidebar feature. There was also supposed to be a Contacts Bar that would display names and contact information from the Windows Address Book.

Unfortunately, Microsoft's engineer's couldn't get the bugs out of either of these bars, so they were yanked from the final product.

Professional Interface

When Microsoft's engineers came up with the new Luna interface, they originally felt that it would be too bright and colorful for corporate use. So they came up with an alternative interface, tentatively dubbed the Professional interface, that was more staid and conservative. The thought was to ship XP Home Edition with the Luna interface, and XP Professional with the Professional interface.

During testing, however, Microsoft discovered that even people in corporations really liked the Luna interface, so the Professional interface was dumped. Both the Home and Professional editions of XP now ship with the same interface.

Bluetooth and USB2 Support

As new technical standards are developed, support for those standards eventually find their way into the operating system. Two relatively new standards, however, didn't have the critical mass necessary to warrant inclusion in the first shipping versions of Windows XP.

Bluetooth is a wireless technology primarily designed for cable replacement. With a Bluetooth enabled system, you'd no longer need messy cables between your PC and its component parts or between your PC and your PDA. Even though Microsoft is one of the key members of the Bluetooth Special Interest Group, the powers that be decided it wasn't worth it to include Bluetooth support in Windows XP. (This is a chicken-and-egg situation—not enough critical mass for Bluetooth devices to warrant inclusion in the OS, yet without Windows support there might never be critical mass.)

The situation with the new USB2 standard was slightly different. USB2, which is a faster version of the original Universal Serial Bus, was simply too new to make it into the OS. At some point Microsoft had to freeze the development of the OS, to avoid what the industry calls "feature creep." When the features were frozen, USB2 wasn't ready yet.

That doesn't mean that you aren't able to use Bluetooth and USB2 devices with Windows XP. Expect a number of third parties to supply the appropriate drivers and utilities to make Bluetooth and USB2 devices work with XP. (Or, in the case of USB2, for Microsoft to add this functionality during an automatic update, sometime in the near future.)

JIM'S TOP TEN TIPS

One of Microsoft's big themes for Windows XP is, "it just works." I'd have to agree with that statement. This is the operating system I've been waiting for since the release of Windows 95.

So if you remember nothing else about Windows XP, remember these top ten tips:

1. Windows XP is a 32-bit operating system that melds the stability of Windows NT/2000 with the user friendliness of Windows 9X/Me.
2. You need a relatively new and relatively powerful PC to run Windows XP, with at least 256MB of memory and a 500 MHz Pentium III processor.
3. Three different versions of Windows XP exist. Windows XP Home Edition contains all the features you need for home and small business use and Windows XP Professional contains additional functionality for corporate networks. The third version, Windows XP 64-Bit Edition, isn't a consideration for most users—unless you have Intel's new Itanium 64-bit processor.
4. Most of your old hardware and software should work fine with Windows XP, although some software might have to be run in Compatibility Mode and extremely old scanners and peripherals might be a problem.
5. Windows XP introduces a task-based approach to common operations. Activity center panes in My Documents and other folders list the most common tasks you're likely to perform.
6. If you're viewing Windows XP on a flat-panel monitor or portable LCD display, turn on the ClearType feature. This makes a dramatic difference in the readability of type onscreen.
7. You can configure Windows XP for several different users, each with their own user account—and easily switch between users from the Start menu.
8. Windows XP makes it easy to manage image files from digital cameras and scanners—and includes a useful thumbnail view within the My Pictures folder.
9. All the new functionality built into Windows XP reduces the need for third-party utility programs, such as WinZip.
10. If you're looking for user-specific files (such as document or configuration files), they're likely to be found somewhere in the c:\Documents and Settings*username*\ folder (or related subfolders).

CHAPTER 2

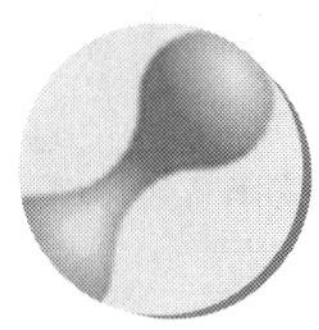

CHANGING THE WAY WINDOWS LOOKS—AND ACTS

- Understanding and Using the Control Panel
- Fine-Tuning the Display
- Configuring the Desktop
- Working With Desktop Shortcuts
- Working with Toolbars, the Taskbar, and the System Tray
- Managing the Start Menu
- Changing Your Cursors
- Changing Your Click
- Using a Screen Saver
- Changing System Sounds
- Adding and Removing Fonts
- Configuring Other System Settings
- Even More Personalization—with Tweak UI
- Making Windows XP Look Like Windows 9X/Me
- Jim's Top Ten Tips

If you're like me, one of the first things you do when you install a new version of your operating system is fiddle around with the desktop and display settings. You want to personalize Windows so that it looks and feels more comfortable to you.

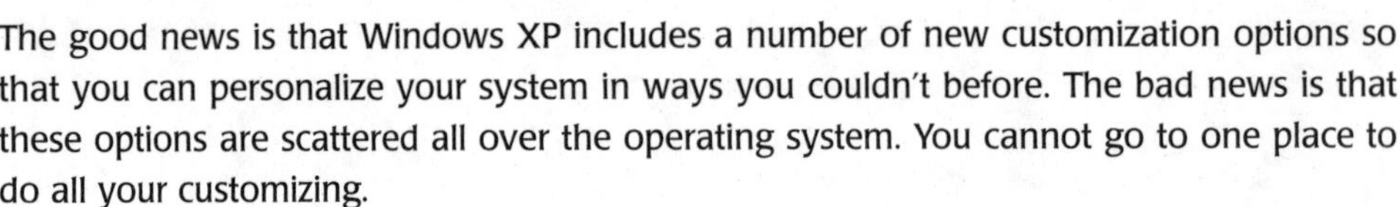

The good news is that Windows XP includes a number of new customization options so that you can personalize your system in ways you couldn't before. The bad news is that these options are scattered all over the operating system. You cannot go to one place to do all your customizing.

Some customization options are accessed from the Display Properties utility. Other options are accessed from the System Properties utility. Still more are found in the Taskbar and Start Menu Properties dialog box and in the Folder Options dialog box.

I'm not sure why Microsoft did such a poor job in drawing attention to all these neat ways to personalize their operating system. They did a *great* job in bringing formerly hidden features to the forefront in other areas of the OS, but took a giant step backward with their configuration options. What were they thinking?

Well, if Microsoft doesn't make it easy for you, I will. In this chapter I show you all the different ways to personalize your Windows XP desktop and interface. The only customization I *don't* cover here is folder customization. For that, you have to turn forward to Chapter 3, "Managing Files."

UNDERSTANDING AND USING THE CONTROL PANEL

Most—but not all—of Windows XP's configuration settings are found somewhere within the Control Panel.

By default, the Control Panel includes a variety of standard Windows XP configuration utilities, such as Add New Hardware and User Accounts. In addition, many applications and utilities install their own Control Panel items. Because of this, the contents of my Control Panel might look slightly different from your Control Panel, although both Control Panels contain the same essential utilities.

When you click an icon in the Control Panel, a dialog box opens that lets you configure settings specific to that item. For example, clicking the Date and Time icon opens the Date and Time Properties utility that enables you to set the date and time of the Windows XP system clock.

Opening the Control Panel

You open the Control Panel by clicking the Start button and then clicking the Control Panel icon. As you can see in Figure 2.1, the Control Panel in Windows XP looks a lot different from the one in previous versions of Windows.

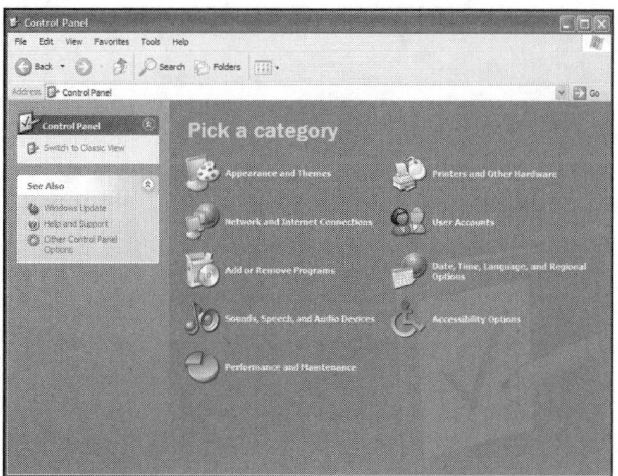

Figure 2.1

The Windows XP Control Panel. The configuration tasks are organized by category.

To launch a particular Control Panel applet, you start by picking a category. When the Pick a task... page appears (shown in Figure 2.2), either click a task or click an icon to open a specific configuration utility. (When you click a task, the appropriate configuration utility is launched.)

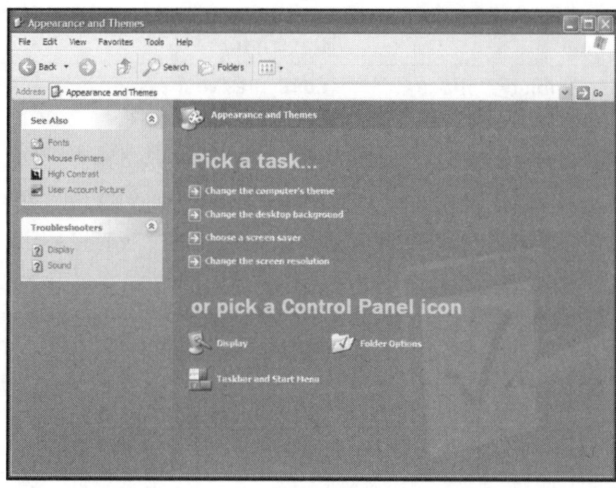

Figure 2.2

After you pick a Control Panel category, you have to pick a task, or click an icon to directly launch a configuration utility.

If you want to bypass all the category and task steps, you can display all the Control Panel utilities at once—just like the way it used to be Windows 9X/Me. To switch to the so-called "classic" view (shown in Figure 2.3), click the Switch to Classic View link in the Control Panel's activity center. (That's the big pane on the left of the Control Panel window.)

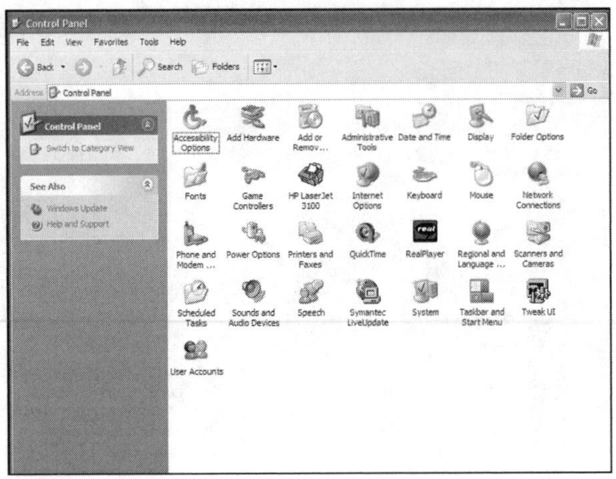

Figure 2.3

Switch to Classic view to display the Control Panel the way it used to be displayed.

Control Panel Items

What can you find in the Control Panel? Table 2.1 details some of the more typical Control Panel icons and their related configuration utilities.

TABLE 2.1—TYPICAL CONTROL PANEL ITEMS

Icon	Name	Description
	Accessibility Options	Configures your system for users with various disabilities. (See Appendix C, "Accessibility Options.")
	Add Hardware	Adds new hardware devices to your system. (See Chapter 6, "Adding New Hardware.")
	Add or Remove Programs	Adds new software to your system, or removes old software programs. (See Chapter 4, "Running Programs.")
	Date and Time	Adjusts Windows XP's time and date settings. (See "Resetting the Time and Date," later in this chapter.)
	Display	Configures settings for your desktop display and monitor. (See "Fine-Tuning the Display," later in this chapter.)
	Folder Options	Configures the look and feel of My Documents and other system folders. (See Chapter 3, "Managing Files.")
	Fonts	Manages your system's fonts. (See "Adding and Removing Fonts," later in this chapter.)
	Gaming Options	Configures any joysticks or game controllers connected to your system. (See Chapter 17, "Playing Games.")

TABLE 2.1—CONTINUED

Icon	Name	Description
	Internet Options	Manages the settings for the Internet Explorer Web browser. (See Chapter 8, "Surfing the Web with Internet Explorer.")
	Keyboard	Configures your PC's keyboard. (See Chapter 6.)
	Mouse	Configures the operation of your mouse and other pointing devices. (See Chapter 6.)
	Network Connections	Configures your PC's connection to a local area network. (See Chapter 18, "Setting Up a Home or Small Business Network.")
	Phone and Modem Options	Configures your PC's modem and telephony settings. (See Chapter 7.)
	Power Options	Determines how and when your computer powers down when not in use. (See Chapter 19, "Using Windows XP on Portable PCs.")
	Printers and Faxes	Configures Windows XP to work with your printer. (See Chapter 5, "Controlling Printers."
	Regional and Language Options	Adjusts currency and number formats for where you live. (See "Changing Your Locality," later in this chapter.)
	Scanners and Cameras	Configures Windows XP for digital camera and scanner use. (See Chapter 12, "Working with Digital Cameras and Scanners.")
	Scheduled Tasks	Schedules selected system maintenance activities. (See Chapter 22, "Keeping Windows Healthy and Happy.")
	Sounds and Audio Devices	Changes the sounds you hear when you initiate certain operations, and configures your system's audio settings. (See "Changing System Sounds," later in this chapter.)
	Speech	Configures your system for text-to-speech translation. (See Appendix C, "Accessibility Options.")
	System	Lets you view and configure technical aspects of your computer system. (See Chapter 22.)
	Taskbar and Start Menu	Configures the Windows Taskbar and Start menu. (See "Working with Toolbars and the Taskbar" and "Managing the Start Menu," later in this chapter.)
	User Accounts	Sets up your computer to be used by multiple users. (See Chapter 16, "Working with Multiple Users.")

Most of these configuration utilities should work fine without additional configuring. In fact, you may never have to open some of these utilities. On the other hand, when you want to reconfigure any part of your system, chances are you find what you need right here in the Control Panel.

FINE-TUNING THE DISPLAY

Windows has always enabled you to change the resolution and number of colors displayed on your computer screen. Windows XP works like previous versions in this regard, and adds the ability to improve the look of LCD displays via the new ClearType technology.

Changing the Display Resolution

Assuming you have a powerful enough video card, you can configure your computer's display to run at a variety of screen resolutions. Make sure you've selected the proper display setup for your video card, however if you set up your display to run at a higher resolution than your card is capable of, you could end up with a lot of gibberish on your screen, and could even damage your monitor.

To get the most out of Windows XP, I recommend that you configure your system to at least 1024×768 resolution, running at least 16-bit color—and if your video card can handle it, crank the color quality all the way up to the highest setting. Windows XP looks best with 32-bit color. Naturally, you'll need a 17-inch or larger monitor to handle this resolution, which is another one of my recommendations.

To change the resolution of your desktop display, follow theses steps:

1. From the Control Panel, click the Display icon. (You can also right-click anywhere on the desktop and select Properties from the pop-up menu.)
2. When the Display Properties utility appears, select the Settings tab (see Figure 2.4).

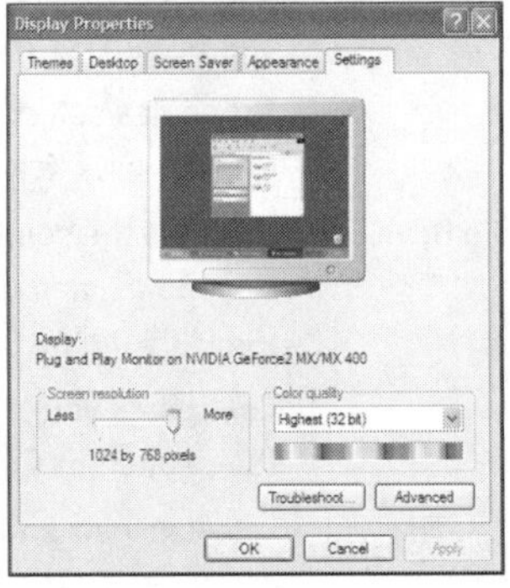

Figure 2.4

Access the Display Properties utility from the Control Panel, or by right-clicking the desktop and choosing Properties.

3. To change the resolution of your display, adjust the Screen Resolution slider. (The sample display changes to reflect your new settings.)
4. To change the number of colors displayed (more is better), choose the desired setting from the Color Quality drop-down list.
5. Click OK to activate your new display settings.

Some video drivers add new tabs to the Display Properties dialog box. If so, you need to click this driver-specific tab to make changes to certain video and display properties.

To confirm your video card configuration, click the Advanced button to display the Advanced Display Properties dialog box, and then click the Adapter tab.

Enabling ClearType

ClearType is a new display technology that effectively triples the horizontal resolution on LCD displays. (In other words, it makes things look sharper—and smoother.) If you have a flat-panel monitor or a portable PC, you definitely want to turn on ClearType.

To turn on ClearType, follow these steps:

1. From the Display Properties utility, select the Appearance tab.
2. Click the Effects button.
3. When the Effects dialog box appears, check the Use the Following Method to Smooth Edges of Screen Fonts option, and select ClearType from the pull-down list.
4. Click OK, and then click OK again.

If you have a normal tube-based monitor, you might want to give ClearType a try. At TechTV Labs, our opinions are divided on whether ClearType is a plus or a minus for normal monitors. Personally, I think it makes the display look fuzzier. Be your own judge.

Setting Up Windows for Two Monitors

Some computer-related activities are easier if you can see two things at once. For example, programmers might like to see their code on one monitor, and the results of that code on a second screen. If you're running a PowerPoint presentation, you could use one monitor to display your presentation, and a second monitor to display your private notes.

If you have two monitors—and two video cards—installed in your system, you can configure Windows XP to run two separate displays. Just follow these steps:

1. Make sure that when you install Windows XP, you have only one video card installed in your system. After Windows XP installation is complete, shut down your computer and add the second display card to your system, following the installation instructions from the card's manufacturer.
2. From the Control Panel, click the Display icon.
3. After you've installed your second video card, the Display Settings dialog box has a new tab, labeled Monitors, that replaces the standard Settings tab. Select the Monitors tab.
4. Your primary monitor should already be configured properly. Select the secondary display/monitor combination, and choose to Use This Device as Part of the

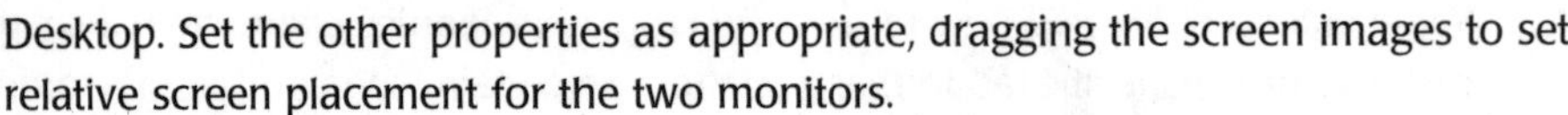

Desktop. Set the other properties as appropriate, dragging the screen images to set relative screen placement for the two monitors.

5. To change the resolution of the second monitor, click the Settings button and make the appropriate changes.
6. Click OK to register your changes.

You need to know that the dual-monitor feature has not always worked perfectly in older versions of windows. If you really want multi-monitor support as easily as possible, with great performance, consider a "dual-head" graphics card. Dual head cards put both graphics cards on one board, so you don't have to add another card into a slower PCI slot. Matrox (`www.matrox.com`) makes my favorite dual-head card these days.

CONFIGURING THE DESKTOP

Windows XP presents a lot of different ways to personalize the look and feel of your desktop. In fact, one of the great things about Windows XP is how quickly you can make the desktop look like *your* desktop, different from anybody else's.

Assuming you know where to make the changes, of course.

Changing Your Desktop Theme

Desktop themes are specific combinations of background wallpaper, colors, fonts, cursors, sounds, and screen savers—all arranged around a specific look or topic. When you choose a new theme, the look and feel of your entire desktop changes.

To change desktop themes, follow these steps:

1. From the Control Panel, click the Display icon.
2. When the Display Properties utility appears, select the Themes tab (shown in Figure 2.5).

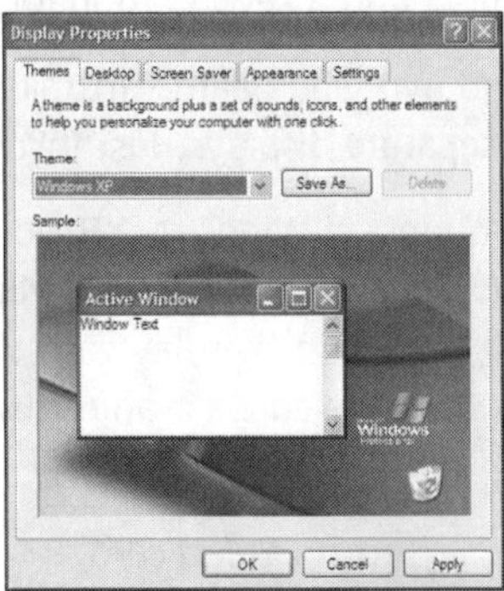

Figure 2.5

Choose from one of several desktop themes available with Windows XP.

3. Select a new theme from the Theme pull-down list; the new theme is displayed in the Sample window.
4. Click OK to accept the new theme and close the dialog box.

Although changing themes is the fastest way to change the look of all your desktop elements, you can also change each element separately.

Personalizing the Desktop Background

To keep your desktop interesting, you can easily change your desktop's background pattern or wallpaper. You can choose from the many patterns and wallpapers provided by Windows XP, or select a graphic of your own choosing.

To select a new pattern or wallpaper, follow these steps:

1. From the Control Panel, click the Display icon.
2. When the Display Properties utility appears, select the Desktop tab (shown in Figure 2.6).

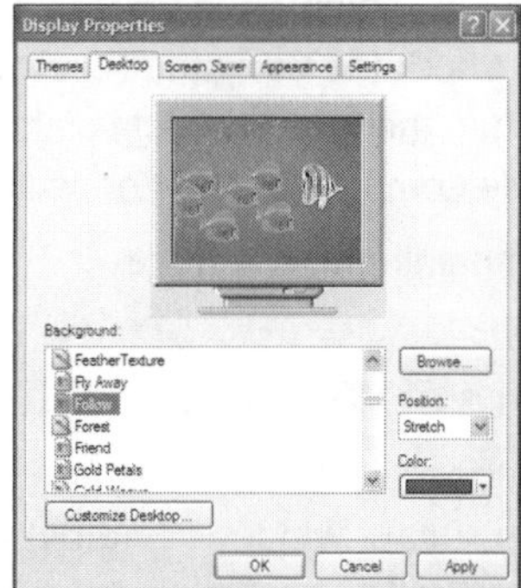

Figure 2.6

Change the background of your Windows XP desktop.

3. To choose one of XP's built-in backgrounds, make a selection from the Background list. Your new background is shown on the example screen.
4. To select your own graphics file, click the Browse button and navigate to the file you want to use. Click the Open button to add this file to the Background list.
5. To determine how the image file is displayed on your desktop, choose one of the options from the Position pull-down list: Center, Tile, or Stretch.
6. If you'd rather display a solid background color with no graphic, select None from the Background list and select a color from the Color list.
7. Click OK to register your changes.

Using a Web Page as a Background

You can also choose to display a Web page as your desktop background. When you do this, your desktop background functions like a live Web page whenever you're connected to the Internet. (This is a great way to put your favorite Web page or list of links at your fingertips.)

Follow these steps:

1. From the Control Panel, click the Display icon.
2. When the Display Properties utility appears, select the Desktop tab and click the Customize Desktop button.
3. When the Desktop Items dialog box appears, select the Web tab.
4. To use your home page as the desktop background, select it from the Web pages list.
5. To use another page as the desktop background, click the New button to display the New Active Desktop Item dialog box. Enter the URL of the page into the Location box, and then click OK.
6. To automatically update the content of this Web page, click the Properties button and select the Schedule tab. Check the Using the Following Schedules option, and then click the Add button. When the New Schedule dialog box appears, set a time for updating, check the If My Computer Is Not Connected… option, and then click OK.
7. Click OK to close the remaining dialog boxes.

Changing the Appearance of Windows and Buttons

By default, Windows XP uses the rounded windows and buttons of the new Luna interface. If you'd rather go back to the square windows and buttons of Windows 9X/Me, you can make that change from within the Display Properties dialog box.

To change the appearance of XP's windows and buttons, follow these steps:

1. From the Control Panel, click the Display icon.
2. When the Display Properties utility appears, select the appearance tab.
3. Pull down the Windows and Buttons list and select a different style.
4. Choose OK to use the new windows and button style.

Changing the Color Scheme

The default Windows XP desktop uses a predefined combination of colors and fonts. If you don't like this combination, you can choose from several other predefined schemes.

To change to a new color scheme, follow these steps:

1. From the Control Panel, click the Display icon.
2. When the Display Properties utility appears, select the Appearance tab (shown in Figure 2.7).

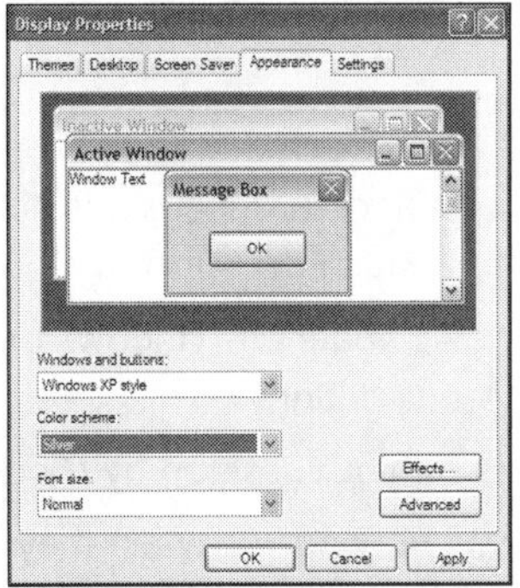

Figure 2.7

Change the way Windows XP looks by selecting a new color scheme.

3. Pull down the Color Scheme list and select a new theme. (The new color scheme is shown in the example window.)
4. Choose OK to use the displayed color scheme.

In previous versions of Windows you could change the color of each screen element individually. You can't do this in Windows XP. You have to use one of the preselected schemes.

However, if you click the Advanced button on the Appearance tab, you open an Advanced Appearance dialog box that makes it seem like you can change the colors of individual screen elements. This is not the case. This dialog box will change the individual colors if you've switched to Classic-style windows and buttons, but *not* if you're using XP-style elements. (This dialog box *will* let you change the *size* of some elements, however.)

This is a little confusing, but just get used to using the standard XP color schemes as-is—and ignore the Advanced button.

Adding Special Effects

All sorts of special effects are included with Windows XP. These effects are applied to the way certain elements look, or the way they pull down or pop up onscreen.

Some of these special effects can be changed from the Display Properties utility. Others are changed from the System Properties utility.

Let's look first at the special effects available with the Display Properties utility. To change these special effects, follow these steps:

1. From the Control Panel, click the Display icon.
2. When the Display Properties utility opens, select the Appearance tab and click the Effects button.

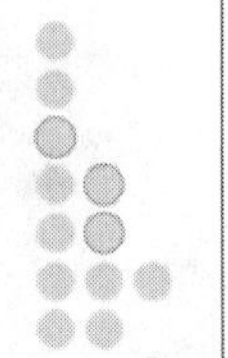

3. When the Effects dialog box appears, as shown in Figure 2.8, make the following choices:
    - Make menus and tooltips scroll or fade in and out by checking the Use the Following Transition Effect for Menus and Tooltips option, and selecting either Scroll Effect or Fade Effect from the pull-down list.
    - Display drop shadows under all Windows menus by checking the Show Shadows Under Menus option.
    - Display large icons on your desktop by checking the Use Large icons option.
    - Display the contents of windows when they're being dragged by checking the Show Window Contents While Dragging option.
    - Hide those underlined letters on menu items by checking the Hide Underlined Letters for Keyboard Navigation… option.
4. Click the OK button to register your changes.

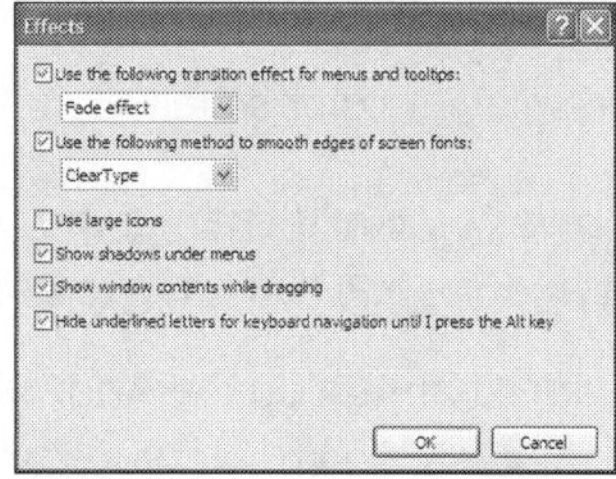

Figure 2.8

Add menu transition and shadow effect in the Effects dialog box.

Now let's look at the much longer list of effects available from the System Properties utility.

1. From the Control Panel, click the System icon.
2. When the System Properties utility opens, select the Advanced tab and click the Settings button (in the Performance section).
3. When the Performance Options dialog box appears, click the Visual Effect tab (shown in Figure 2.9) and choose from the following effects. Most of these effects are self-explanatory, although some are extremely subtle. All degrade the performance of your system to some degree.
    - Animate windows when minimizing and maximizing.
    - Draw gradient in window captions.
    - Enable per-folder type watermarks.
    - Fade in taskbar.
    - Fade out menu items after invocation.
    - Fade/slide menus into view.

- Fade/slide tooltips into view.
- Hot-track menu items and other elements.
- Show alpha blended selection rectangle.
- Show shadows under menus.
- Show shadows under mouse pointer.
- Show window contents while dragging.
- Slide icons over background images in folders.
- Slide open combo boxes.
- Slide taskbar buttons.
- Smooth edges of screen fonts.
- Smooth-scroll list boxes.
- Use drop shadows for icon labels on the Desktop.
- Use visual styles on windows and buttons.
- Use Web view in folders.

4. Click OK to register your changes.

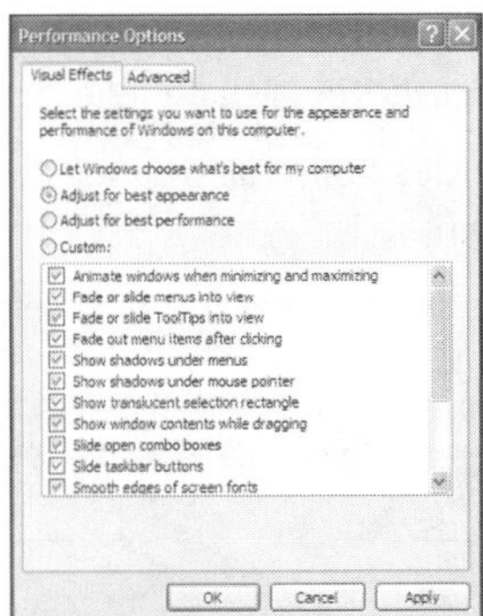

Figure 2.9

Turn on and off a variety of visual effects from the Performance Options dialog box.

Not all these effects are turned on by default. If you want to get the full effect of the new Windows XP interface, you have to manually turn on those settings that are turned off by default.

As you can see, some of these settings duplicate the settings in the Effects dialog box. Turning them off or on in one place turns them off in the other, as well.

XP offers an even easier way to select visual effects in the Performance Options dialog box. When you select the Adjust for Best Appearance option, all the effects are turned on. When you select the Adjust for Best Performance option, all the effects are turned off. (You

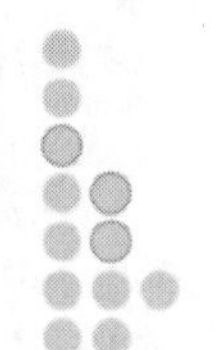

also have the option of having Windows figure it out for you, by selecting the Let Windows Choose What's Best for My Computer option.)

If your system has the horsepower—especially in RAM, and on your graphics card—you should try turning on all these special effects. It really makes Windows XP a lot more enjoyable to use!

If your system is running sluggishly, click the Best Performance button to turn off all the resource-draining visual effects.

WORKING WITH DESKTOP SHORTCUTS

Desktop icons, called *shortcuts*, are just that—shortcuts for starting applications and opening documents. Placing a shortcut on your desktop is an alternative to launching items from the Start menu or a Windows folder.

Changing Desktop Icons

Tired of the default icons for My Computer, the Recycle Bin, and other basic desktop items? Then change them!

Just follow these steps:

1. From the Control Panel, click the Display icon.
2. When the Display Properties utility opens, select the Desktop tab and click the Customize Desktop button.
3. When the Desktop Items dialog box appears, select the General tab (shown in Figure 2.10).

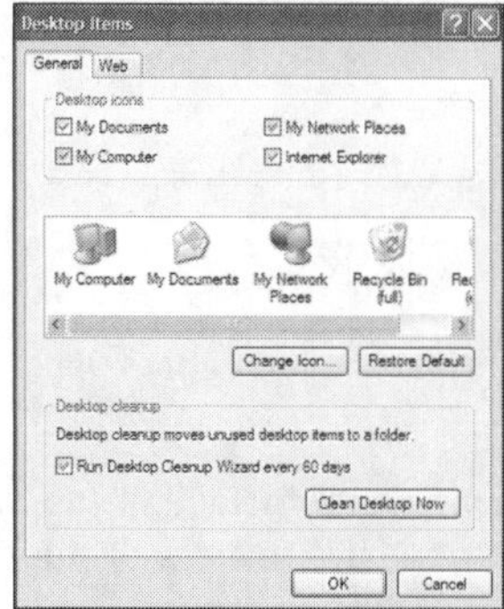

Figure 2.10

Change your desktop icons—or run the Desktop Cleanup Wizard.

4. Check those icons you want to display on your desktop; uncheck those items you don't want to display.
5. To change an icon, select the icon and click the Change Icon button.
6. When the Change Icon dialog box appears, select a new icon from those listed, or click the Browse button to select another file full of icons.
7. Click OK when done.

You can return to the original icons by clicking the Restore Default button.

Creating New Shortcuts on the Desktop

To put a new shortcut on your desktop, follow these steps:

1. From within My Computer or any Windows folder, navigate to the application or document for which you want to create a shortcut.
2. Right-click the file icon, and then select Send To, Desktop (Create Shortcut).

You can also create a shortcut by right-dragging a file icon directly to the desktop, or by right-clicking on the desktop and selecting New, Shortcut from the pop-up menu.

To remove a shortcut icon from the desktop, just drag it into the Recycle Bin.

Changing the Name of a Shortcut

When you create a new shortcut icon, its name is automatically prefixed with the words "Shortcut to…." To change the name of a shortcut, follow these steps:

1. Right-click the shortcut on your desktop.
2. When the pop-up menu appears, select Rename.
3. The shortcut's name is now highlighted on your desktop. Use the Delete or Backspace keys to erase parts of the existing name, and then type a new name. Press Enter when you've finished entering the new name.

Changing Shortcut Properties

You can change certain things about the way a shortcut behaves. To change the properties of a shortcut, follow these steps:

1. Right-click the shortcut icon and select Properties from the pop-up menu.
2. When the Shortcut Properties dialog box appears, click the Shortcut tab (see Figure 2.11).

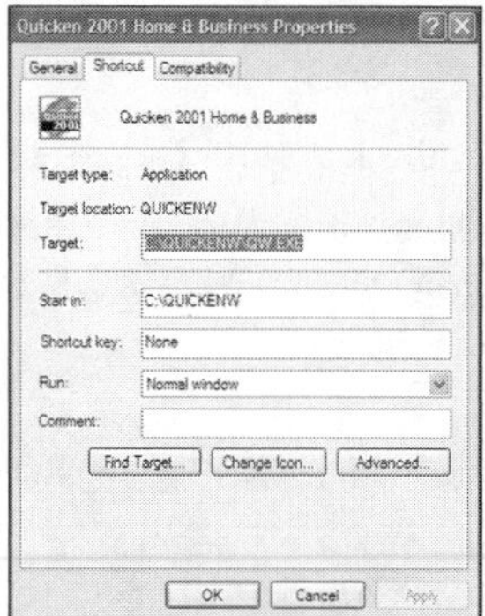

Figure 2.11

Right-click a shortcut icon to change its properties.

3. Choose the property you want to change, as detailed in Table 2.2.
4. Click OK to accept the changes and close the dialog box, or click Apply to make the changes while keeping the dialog box open.

TABLE 2.2—SHORTCUT PROPERTIES

Property	Description
Target	Identifies the file that the shortcut opens.
Run in Compatibility Mode	Determines whether an older program should run in XP's Compatibility Mode.
Start In	Identifies the specific folder from which the program starts.
Shortcut Key	Identifies the shortcut keys that activate the shortcut.
Run	Determines whether the program is launched in a normal, maximized, or minimized window.
Comment	Information about the file.
Find Target	Click this button to find the specific program file for this shortcut, if not correctly listed in the Target box.
Change Icon	Click this button to change the icon used for the shortcut.
Advanced	Click this button to run this shortcut as another user, or to run in separate memory space.

Not all properties are available for all shortcuts.

Arranging Icons on the Desktop

Desktop shortcut icons give you easy access to your programs, especially when you arrange them in a way that works best for you. To arrange your icons, right-click a blank area of the desktop and choose from the options presented in Table 2.3:

TABLE 2.3—OPTIONS FOR ARRANGING ICONS ON YOUR DESKTOP

Command	Action
Name	Sort items alphabetically by file name.
Size	Sort items by file size, from smallest to largest.
Type	Sort items by file type. Files with the same extension are grouped together.
Modified	Sort items by date, from oldest to the most recent.
Auto Arrange	When checked, this choice automatically arranges icons at the left side of the desktop.
Align to Grid	When checked, your icons automatically snap to an invisible grid. (This is a good option if you have lots of icons scattered around your desktop.)
Show Desktop Items	Displays the icons for My Computer, My Documents, the Recycle Bin, and other essential desktop items.
Lock Web Items on Desktop	Locks the items on your desktop, so you can't change them accidentally.

The Align to Grid command does nothing if the Auto Arrange option is toggled on because auto arranging keeps the icons aligned automatically. Turn Auto Arrange off if you want to spread your icons across the desktop, not crowded to the left side. Then use the Align to Grid command to line them up on the invisible grid in their same general vicinity.

Cleaning Up Your Desktop Shortcuts

By default, Windows XP runs the Desktop Cleanup Wizard every 60 days. This wizard sweeps all your unused desktop icons into an Unused Desktop Icons folder, thus cleaning up a cluttered desktop. If you don't like this automated housecleaning, you can turn off the wizard, or choose to clean up your desktop manually.

To clean up your desktop manually, follow these steps:

1. From the Control Panel, click the Display icon.
2. When the Display Properties utility opens, select the Desktop tab and click the Customize Desktop button.
3. When the Desktop Items dialog box appears, select the General tab.
4. To turn off the Desktop Cleanup Wizard, uncheck the Run Desktop Cleanup Wizard Every 60 Days option. Although you can't change how often it runs, you can only turn it on and off.
5. Click the Clean Desktop Now button to run the Wizard now.

WORKING WITH TOOLBARS, THE TASKBAR, AND THE SYSTEM TRAY

By now you're probably familiar with the Windows Taskbar; the solid bar that typically sits at the bottom of your screen and holds buttons for any applications that are open at the time. You're probably less familiar with Windows toolbars, which look kind of like the Taskbar, but hold specific groups of icons.

Read on to learn how to customize the Taskbar, the toolbars, and the System Tray that sits to the right of the Taskbar at the bottom of the screen.

Moving the Taskbar

The default position for the Taskbar is horizontally across the bottom of the screen. If you don't like it there, you can move it to the top or to either side of the screen.

Just follow these steps:

1. Point to a part of the Taskbar where no buttons appear.
2. Click with the left mouse button and drag the Taskbar to another edge of the screen. You see a shaded line that indicates the new position of the Taskbar.
3. Release the mouse button.

Windows XP introduces the concept of locking the Taskbar. When the Taskbar is locked, you can't move it. To lock or unlock the Taskbar, right-click an open area of the Taskbar, and either check or uncheck the Lock the Taskbar option.

Hide the Taskbar

If you're running Windows XP on a small display (640×480 resolution, for example), you might not want the Taskbar taking up screen space all the time. For these situations, Windows XP lets you hide the Taskbar and recall it only when you need it.

1. Right-click an open area of the Taskbar and select Properties from the pop-up menu.
2. When the Taskbar and Start Menu Properties dialog box appears, select the Taskbar tab, shown in Figure 2.12.
3. Check the Auto-Hide the Taskbar option.
4. Click OK to close the dialog box.

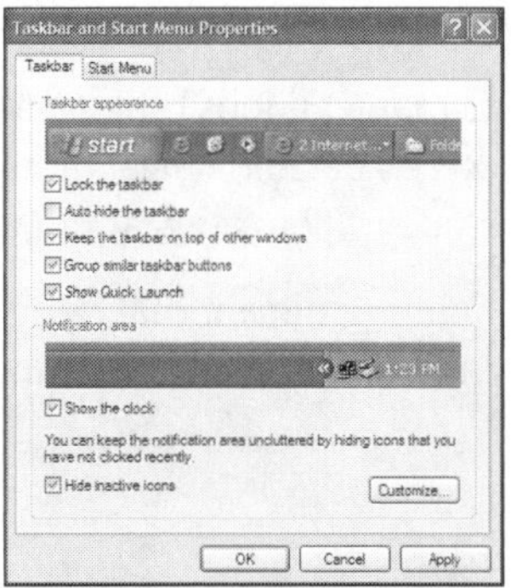

Figure 2.12

Change the appearance of the Taskbar from the Taskbar and Start Menu Properties dialog box.

This configuration automatically hides the Taskbar so that your applications can use the entire screen. To display the Taskbar again, all you have to do is move your cursor to the very bottom of the screen. The Taskbar then pops up for your use.

If you'd rather have the Taskbar constantly visible, check the Keep the Taskbar On Top Of Other Windows option.

Resizing the Taskbar

You may have noticed that when the Taskbar is positioned horizontally, the Taskbar buttons become smaller the more applications you open. If you open too many applications, the Taskbar buttons become so small that you can't read the whole name of each application.

By adjusting the size of the Taskbar, you can create a taller Taskbar so that multiple buttons can stack on top of each other. In addition, if you choose to position the Taskbar along one of the sides of the desktop, you may want to adjust the Taskbar width to display wider or narrower buttons.

However your Taskbar is positioned, you can resize it by following the same steps:

1. Position your cursor at the edge of the Taskbar, where the pointer becomes a double arrow. (If the Taskbar is at the bottom of the screen, just point to the upper edge of the Taskbar.)
2. Click the left mouse button and drag the edge to the size you want.
3. Release the mouse button.

If you make a vertical Taskbar narrow enough, only the application icons show, without words. (If you point to the icons, a ToolTip pops up to show you its name.)

Grouping Taskbar Buttons

The old problem of having too many buttons on too small a Taskbar has been addressed by a new feature in Windows XP. By default, similar buttons are grouped together and multiple documents (for the same application) are stacked together on a single button.

If you'd rather not use this button-grouping feature, open the Taskbar and Start Menu Properties dialog box, select the Taskbar tab, and uncheck the Group Similar Taskbar Buttons option.

Adding Toolbars to the Taskbar

Windows XP also lets you dock additional toolbars to the Taskbar. Each toolbar contains a group of icons that enables you to perform selected tasks—such as launching programs or connecting to Web sites.

Windows XP has several predesigned toolbars, including the following (all shown in Figure 2.13):

- **Address**—This toolbar is an URL box. Type the address for any Web page into this box, press Enter, and Windows connect to the Internet, launch Internet Explorer, and display the Web page you entered.
- **Links**—This toolbar displays five selected links (by default, five links on Microsoft's Web site).
- **Desktop**—This toolbar displays all the shortcut icons currently on your desktop. It's a good way to have ready access to your shortcuts if your desktop is perpetually cluttered.
- **Quick Launch**—This toolbar displays three icons for basic Internet use: Internet Explorer, Outlook Express, and my personal favorite, Show Desktop (which minimizes all open windows on your computer, so you can actually see your desktop).

Figure 2.13

The four toolbars built into Windows XP.

To dock a toolbar to the Taskbar, follow these steps:

1. Right-click anywhere on the Taskbar.
2. When the pop-up menu appears, select Toolbars, and then select the toolbar you want to display.

To remove a toolbar from the Taskbar, follow these steps:

1. Right-click anywhere on the toolbar to display the pop-up menu.
2. Select Toolbars, and then deselect that particular toolbar.

You can resize any toolbar you've added to the Taskbar. Just move your cursor to the far left of the toolbar until the cursor changes to a double-arrow, click the left mouse button, and drag the toolbar to the desired size. You can also stack toolbars on top of one another, as shown in Figure 2.13.

Adding Icons to the Quick Launch Toolbar

Microsoft lets you add your own icons to the Quick Launch toolbar. I use this to add those programs I use most often to that toolbar, so they are always a single-click away. (In my case, I've added icons for Lotus Notes and my virtual private network to the toolbar.)

The easy way to add an icon to the Quick Launch toolbar is to grab a program icon from the Programs menu or My Computer and drag it onto the toolbar. You can also add icons by using My Computer to open the \Documents and Settings*username*\Application Data\Microsoft\Internet Explorer\Quick Launch\ folder, and then selecting File, Create Shortcut. Note that this is a hidden folder—you have to tell Windows to show hidden folders to use this method.

Creating a New Toolbar

In addition to the four preselected toolbars I just told you about, you can also create your own personal toolbars.

Just follow these steps:

1. Right-click anywhere on the Taskbar.
2. When the pop-up menu appears, select Toolbars, and then select New Toolbar.
3. When the New Toolbar dialog box appears, choose a disk or folder or enter a Web address and click OK.
4. The new toolbar now appears, docked to the Taskbar. If you selected a disk or folder, the contents of that disk or folder appear in the toolbar. If you entered a Web address, that address appears in the toolbar.

You can also create a toolbar by dragging a disk or folder from My Computer onto the Taskbar. If you drag a disk or folder from My Computer to another side of the screen, a new toolbar is created there instead of on the Taskbar.

Configuring Toolbars

Windows XP provides several ways for you to customize how your toolbars are displayed. You can adjust the size of the icons and how the icons appear.

1. Right-click in an open area of the toolbar you want to configure. This displays a pop-up menu.
2. To display the title of the toolbar, check Show Title. Uncheck this option to hide the name of the toolbar.

3. To display large icons on the toolbar, select View and check Large. To display small icons, select View and check Small.
4. To display a label for each icon, check Show Text. Uncheck this option to hide labels.

To move a toolbar to another side of the screen, simply drag the toolbar to the desired spot and then release the mouse button. If you drop the toolbar into the middle of your screen, it becomes an open window on your desktop.

Manage the System Tray

The System Tray is that part of the screen that displays icons for utilities that Windows runs in the background. Sometimes other applications put their own icons in the System Tray, too. These third-party icons sometimes indicate that a program is running, and sometimes make it easier to launch that program (by clicking on the icon in the Tray).

The problem with the System Tray is that it gets abused. If you have a lot of little utilities running and a lot of programs that have installed their own icons in the Tray, the Tray gets awfully crowded and starts to expand. The more icons in the Tray, the wider the Tray is. If the Tray gets too wide, it starts borrowing space from the Taskbar, which is also prone to overcrowding. You only have so much space along the bottom of the screen, after all.

Windows XP introduces a solution to this overcrowding problem by hiding those System Tray icons that you really don't need to see. The important icons, such as the system clock remain visible in what Microsoft now calls the Notification Area. The other icons are now hidden until you click the left-arrow button at the edge of the Tray (shown in Figure 2.14).

Figure 2.14

Click the arrow to expand the System Tray.

If you don't like hiding your icons, you can turn off this feature by following these steps:

1. Right-click an open area of the Taskbar and select Properties from the pop-up menu.
2. When the Taskbar and Start Menu Properties dialog box appears, select the Taskbar tab.
3. Uncheck the Hide Inactive Icons option.
4. Click OK.

By default, the system clock is always displayed in the Notification Area. If you'd rather not display the clock, uncheck the Show the Clock option.

If you're really into the details, you can configure the "hide when inactive" status for each icon in your system tray. Just go to the Taskbar tab in the Taskbar and Start Menu Properties dialog box and click the Customize button. When the Customize Notifications dialog box appears (as shown in Figure 2.15), select a particular icon and set it's Hide When Inactive behavior. Check the item to hide it, uncheck it to make sure that it's always visible.

Figure 2.15

Choose to hide or display every icon in the System Tray on an item-by-item basis.

MANAGING THE START MENU

The Start menu in Windows XP is a lot different from the Start menu you got used to in previous versions of Windows. It does a good job of hiding things you don't use that often, while keeping your most frequently used programs front and center.

Changing the Way the Start Menu Works

Windows XP applies a handful of special effects to the Start menu. You can animate the Start menu when it opens, force submenus to open when you hover over them, and highlight new applications.

To change these special effects, follow these steps:

1. Right-click the Start button and select Properties from the pop-up menu.
2. When the Taskbar and Start Menu Properties dialog box appears, select the Start Menu tab and click the Customize button.
3. When the Customize Start Menu dialog box appears, select the Advanced tab (shown in Figure 2.16).
4. To animate the Start menu, check the Animate Start Menu As It Opens option.
5. To make submenus open when you point at them, check the Open Submenus on Hover option.

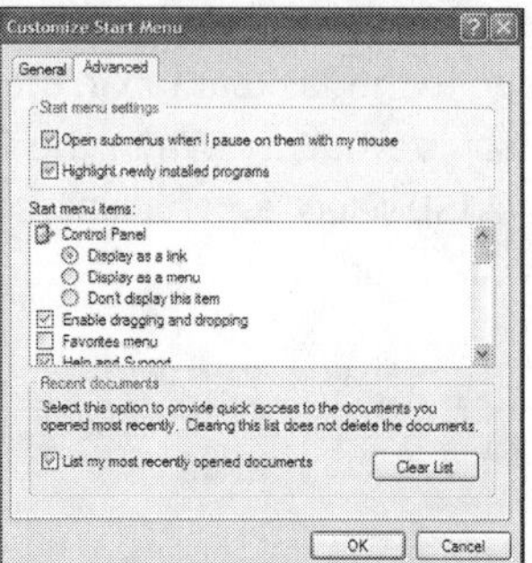

Figure 2.16

Change the way Start menu behaves—and what it displays.

6. To highlight the newest applications, check the Highlight Newly Installed Applications option.
7. Click OK when done.

Changing the Size of Start Menu Icons

You can also choose from two sizes of icons in the Start menu. Follow these steps:

1. Right-click the Start button and select Properties from the pop-up menu.
2. When the Taskbar and Start Menu Properties dialog box appears, select the Start Menu tab and click the Customize button.
3. When the Customize Start Menu dialog box appears, select the General tab (shown in Figure 2.17).

Figure 2.17

Change the size of the Start menu icons, as well as how many programs it displays.

4. Check Small Icons to display smaller icons than normal. Check Large Icons to display the normal large icons.
5. Click OK.

Displaying More—or Fewer—Programs

By default, the Start menu displays the five most-recent applications you've run. You can reconfigure the Start menu to display more (up to nine) or fewer (as few as zero!) applications at a time.

To display more or fewer programs, follow these steps:

1. Right-click the Start button and select Properties from the pop-up menu.
2. When the Taskbar and Start Menu Properties dialog box appears, select the Start Menu tab and click the Customize button.
3. When the Customize Start Menu dialog box appears, select the General tab.
4. Select a new number from the Number of Programs on Start Menu list.
5. Click OK.

If you want to start the Start menu with a clean slate, click the Clear List button. This opens the Start menu with no programs displayed.

Hiding (or Changing) the Browser and E-mail Icons

Also by default, the Start menu displays icons for your Web browser and e-mail client. For most users, that's probably Internet Explorer and Outlook Express. (If you have Office installed on your PC, Microsoft Outlook may be displayed as the e-mail client.)

You don't have to display these icons and you don't have to link them to Microsoft programs.

Follow these steps to delete or reconfigure these two items:

1. Right-click the Start button and select Properties from the pop-up menu.
2. When the Taskbar and Start Menu Properties dialog box appears, select the Start Menu tab and click the Customize button.
3. When the Customize Start Menu dialog box appears, select the General tab.
4. To display the icons for other browser or e-mail clients, go to the Show on Start Menu section and select new programs from the Internet and E-mail lists.
5. To not display one or both of these icons, uncheck the Internet and/or E-mail options.
6. Click OK when done.

Selecting Which Icons to Display—and How

The default Start menu also displays icons for the Control Panel, My Computer, My Documents, My Pictures, My Music, Network Connections, Help and Support, and the Run command. You can configure Windows XP to not display any of these icons or to display some of the icons as menus.

Follow these steps:

1. Right-click the Start button and select Properties from the pop-up menu.
2. When the Taskbar and Start Menu Properties dialog box appears, select the Start Menu tab and click the Customize button.
3. When the Customize Start Menu dialog box appears, select the General tab.
4. In the Show These Items on the Start Menu box, click As Link to display an icon as a link to the main item; As Menu to display a pop-up menu when an icon is clicked; or Never to not display an item.
5. Click OK when done.

When you choose the As Link option, clicking an icon displays the related item. For example, when you click the My Documents icon, the My Documents folder opens in a separate window.

When you choose the As Menu option, clicking an icon displays a pop-up menu that contains all the options in the selected item. For example, when you click the My Documents icon, a pop-up menu appears that lists all the folders and files in the My Documents folder.

Which option you choose depends on how you work. If you like to work from folders, choose the As Link option. If you like to work from menus, choose the As Menu option.

Adding a Program to the Start Menu Permanently

If you're not totally comfortable with the way programs come and go from the Start menu, rest assured the tried-and-true Programs menu still exists. Just click the All Programs link on the Start menu, and the Programs menu appears, just like you remember it.

If you'd rather display a program on the Start menu than the Programs menu, but don't want the icon going away if you don't use it, you're in luck. You can add any program to the Start menu—*permanently*. Just follow these steps:

1. From the Start menu, click the All Programs link to display the Programs menu.
2. Navigate to the program you want to add to the Start menu, and right-click that program.
3. From the pop-up menu, select Pin to Start Menu.

The program you selected now appears on the Start menu, just below the browser and e-mail icons.

To remove a program you've added to the Start menu, right-click its icon and select Unpin From Start Menu.

You can use this same method to add *any* program file to the Start menu even if it doesn't appear on the Programs menu. Just use My Computer to navigate to an application file, and then right-click the file and select Pin to Start Menu from the pop-up menu.

Changing Back to the Old Style Start

If you don't like Windows XP's new Start menu, you can easily switch back to the "classic" Windows 9X/Me version.

Follow these steps:

1. Right-click an open area of the Taskbar and select Properties from the pop-up menu.
2. When the Taskbar and Start Menu Properties dialog box appears, select the Start Menu tab (shown in Figure 2.18).

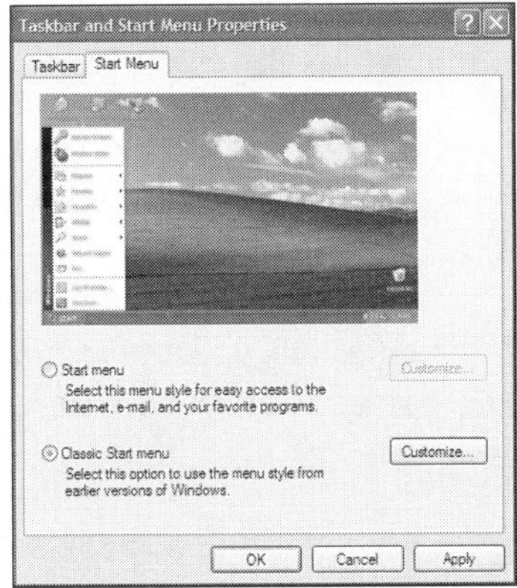

Figure 2.18

Switch between new and classic Start menus.

3. Check the Classic Start Menu option.
4. Click OK.

CHANGING YOUR CURSORS

Another item you can personalize with Windows XP is the *cursor scheme* that appears onscreen. Different schemes use different kinds of cursors. You can choose from normal cursors, 3D cursors, extra-large cursors, animated cursors, and so on.

To change your cursor scheme, follow these steps:

1. From the Control Panel, click the Mouse icon.
2. When the Mouse Properties utility opens, select the Pointers tab (shown in Figure 2.19).

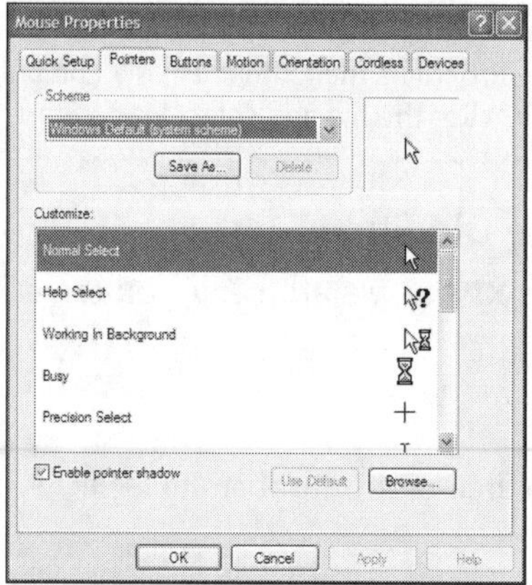

Figure 2.19

Choose a new cursor scheme with the Mouse Properties utility.

3. Select a new cursor scheme from the Scheme pull-down list. Alternatively, you can change a specific cursor by highlighting the cursor in the Customize list and clicking the Browse button to select a new cursor from the Cursor folder.
5. Click OK when you've finished.

While you're in the Mouse Properties utility, you might want to check the Enable Pointer Shadow option. This puts a drop shadow under your cursor, similar to the one you can display under all your Windows menus.

CHANGING YOUR CLICK

How do you click? Do you like to double-click the icons on your desktop? Would you prefer to single-click your icons, the same way you click hyperlinks on a Web page? Should the names of your icons be plain text, or underlined like a hyperlink?

However you like to click, Windows XP can accommodate you. You just have to know *where* the configuration options are for desktop clicking because they're not in an obvious place.

Believe it or not, the XP's click options for the entire operating system are buried in the Folder Options dialog box. I certainly wouldn't have thought to look for them there. If you're like me, you would have thought that a Folder Options dialog box controlled the way My Documents and other folders look and feel. You would have only been partially right.

So how exactly do you change the way Windows clicks? Just follow these steps:

1. Open My Documents, My Computer, or any other system folder.
2. Select Tools, Folder Options to open the Folder Options dialog box, shown in Figure 2.20.

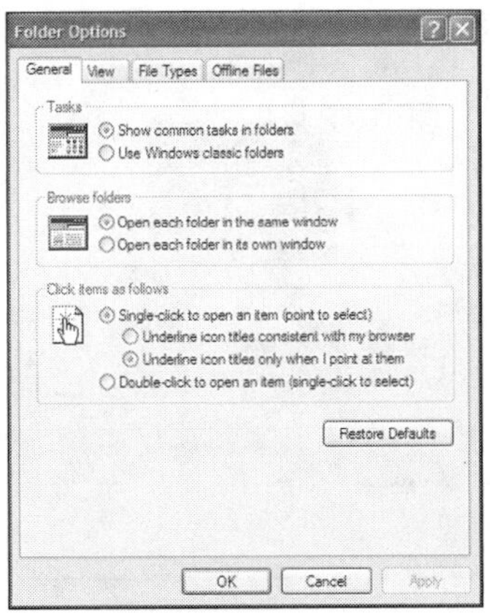

Figure 2.20

You have to open a folder to change your click.

3. If you want to use traditional double-clicking, check the Double-Click to Open an Item option.
4. If you want to use Web-like single-clicking, check the Single-Click to Open an Item option.
5. If you select single clicking, you can choose to underline the titles of all desktop icons (Underline Icon Titles Consistent With My Browser) or only underline titles when an item is hovered over (Underling Icon Titles Only When I Point At Them).
6. Click OK to register your settings.

This is probably one of the most important Windows settings, and it's buried in a place (and described in a way) that most users never find . Why would anyone want to hide this important setting? I have no idea, but now that you know where it is—use it!

USING A SCREEN SAVER

Screen savers display moving designs on your computer screen when you haven't typed or moved the mouse for a while. This prevents static images from burning into your screen.

Although screen burn-in is rarely a problem with newer monitors, screen savers can still be entertaining and hide any work you have on your screen when you leave your desk. You can even assign a password to the screen saver so that only *you* can reactivate the screen.

To activate one of the screen savers included with Windows XP, follow these steps:

1. From the Control Panel, select the Display option.
2. When the Display Settings utility opens, select the Screen Saver tab, shown in Figure 2.21.

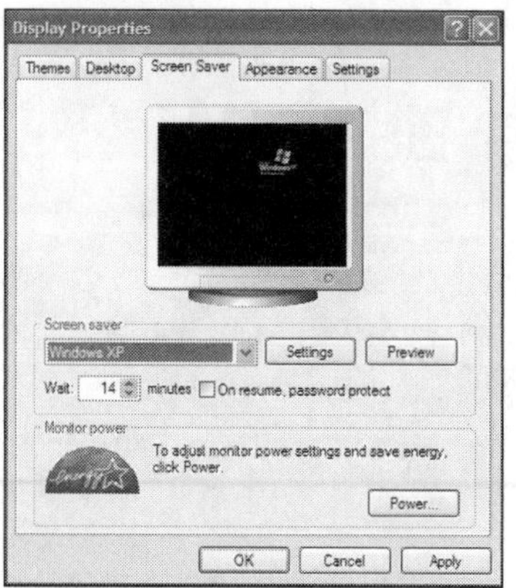

Figure 2.21

Put on a fancy show with a Windows XP screen saver.

3. Select a screen saver from the Screen Saver drop-down list. A sample of the screen saver appears on the sample display. For a full-screen view, click the Preview button and click the screen to return from the preview.
4. Change the properties of the selected screen saver by clicking the Settings button. The options available differ for each screen saver you choose, but usually include things such as speed and colors. Make your selections and then choose OK.
5. In the Wait section, select the number of minutes you want the screen to be idle before the screen saver activates.
6. If you want your system to display the Welcome screen when the screen saver stops, check the Return to Welcome Screen option. (Select this option if you want to require a password for reactivating your system after a nap.)
7. Click OK when done.

CHANGING SYSTEM SOUNDS

Just as you can change the way Windows XP looks, you can also change the way it sounds.

Every operation in Windows can or does have a sound associated with it. When you first turn on your computer and launch Windows, you hear a sound. When you get dinged with an error message, you hear another sound. When you open and close applications, you hear even more sounds.

When you take all the sounds together, you have a sound scheme—which is similar to a color scheme, but with sounds. (Naturally.)

Windows XP lets you change the entire sound scheme, or individual sounds within the scheme. Just follow these steps:

1. From the Control Panel, select the Sounds and Audio Devices icon.
2. When the Sounds and Audio Devices Properties utility opens, select the Sounds tab (shown in Figure 2.22).

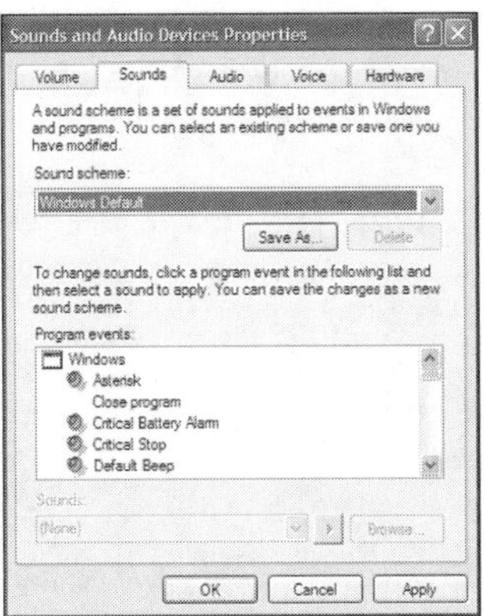

Figure 2.22

Personalize the sounds you hear when something happens onscreen.

3. To change sound schemes, pull down the Sound Scheme list and select a new scheme.
4. To change an individual sound, select an item in the Program Events list and then select a new sound from the Sounds list. (You can choose from a wider variety of sounds by clicking the Browse button and navigating to any sound file stored on your hard disk.)
5. Click OK when done.

ADDING AND REMOVING FONTS

Windows XP comes with a large number of common fonts pre-installed for use in your favorite software programs. You use these fonts to both display text onscreen and to print out text from your printer.

Previewing Fonts

To see what fonts are installed on your system, follow these steps:

1. From the Control Panel, click the Fonts icon.
2. When the Fonts window is displayed, as shown in Figure 2.23, double-click any font icon to view a sample of that font at various type sizes.
3. Click the Print button to print a sample of the font.
4. Click the Done button to close the display window.

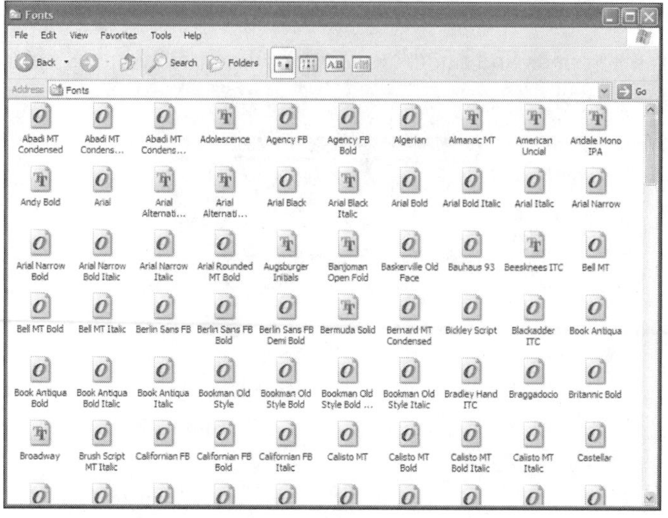

Figure 2.23

Manage all your system fonts from the Fonts window.

Installing New Fonts

Although Windows XP installs many font files during setup, you may want to add additional fonts from third-party vendors or Web sites. To install a new font, follow these steps:

1. From the Control Panel, click the Fonts icon.
2. When the Fonts window appears, select File, Install New Font.
3. When the Add Fonts dialog box appears, select the drive and folder that holds the fonts you want to install.
4. Fonts available at the location you specified are listed now. Select the font(s) you want to add.

To select multiple fonts, hold down the Ctrl key while clicking additional listings.

5. Select the Copy Fonts to Fonts Folder check box.
6. Click OK to add the fonts you selected.

You can also install fonts directly from My Computer. Simply copy the new font files from an installation disk and paste them into the \Windows\Fonts folder.

Installing too many fonts on your system not only consumes a lot of hard disk space, it also eats up system memory and can cause your system to run slower than normal. If your system is running sluggishly, you may want to remove some unused fonts. This enhances the performance of your system performance *and* free up some disk space.

Removing Unwanted Fonts

If you find you have too many fonts installed on your system or fonts that you seldom use, if ever, you can use the Control Panel to delete these font files from your system.

1. From the Control Panel, click the Fonts icon.
2. When the Fonts window appears, right-click the icon for the font you want to delete and select Delete from the pop-up menu.
3. Windows asks if you're sure you want to delete this font. Choose Yes to delete, and the font file is uninstalled from your system and sent to the Recycle Bin.

You can also delete fonts directly from My Computer. Just select a font file from the \Windows\Fonts folder and select Delete This File.

CONFIGURING OTHER SYSTEM SETTINGS

While that takes care of the major system settings, there are a handful of other settings you probably need to know about, just in case. Chances are they're fine as-is—but you never know!

Resetting the Time and Date

The time and date for your system should be automatically set when Windows XP is first installed. If you find that you need to change or reset the time or date settings, follow these steps:

1. From the Control Panel, click the Date and Time icon.
2. When the Date and Time Properties utility opens, select the Date & Time tab (shown in Figure 2.24).

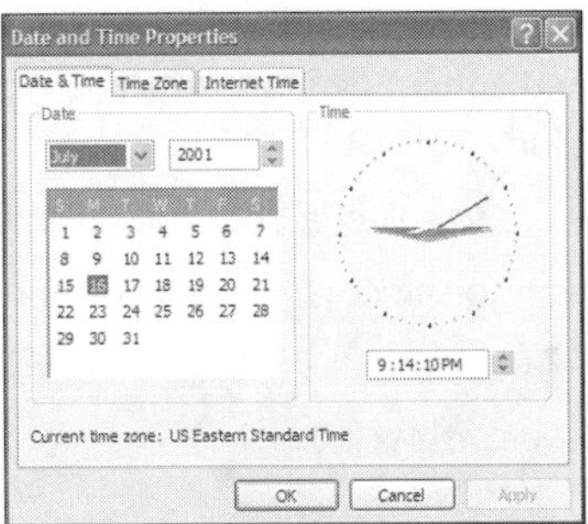

Figure 2.24

Click the Date and Time icon to set your system's date and time.

3. Choose the correct month and year from the pull-down lists, click the correct day of the month on the calendar, and set the correct time on the clock.

4. Now select the Time Zone tab. Select the correct time zone from the pull-down list. For most states, you should also select Automatically Adjust Clock for Daylight Saving Changes.
5. If you want to automatically set your PC's clock from a time server on the Internet, select the Internet Time tab and check the Automatically Synchronize With an Internet Time Server option. You can choose from several different servers listed in the Server pull-down list. This is one of my favorite new features, because it always seems like one of my systems has a dying battery, and the clock is never right.
6. Click OK when done.

You can also access the Date/Time Properties utility by double-clicking on the time in the System Tray.

Changing Your Locality

Copies of Windows XP sold in English-speaking countries, by default, are configured for American-style currency and number formats. By changing XP's regional settings properties, you can switch between different international character sets, number formats, currency formats, and date and time displays. This essentially sets up Windows XP for use in other countries.

Changing the language and country formats does not change the language used in Windows menus and dialog boxes. (For that you need a local-language version of Windows.) It, however, affects the data in applications that take advantage of these regional features.

To change the regional settings of Windows XP, follow these steps:

1. From the Control Panel, click the Regional and Language Options icon.
2. When the Regional and Language Options utility opens, select the Region Options tab to select your region.
3. Select the Languages tab to select a different input language.
4. Select the Advanced tab to select languages for non-Unicode programs and code page conversion tables.
5. Click OK when done.

EVEN MORE PERSONALIZATION—WITH TWEAK UI

Now it's time for me to let you in on one of my favorite Windows utilities. Tweak UI is a "power toy" from Microsoft that lets you further customize your desktop beyond what

Windows XP normally lets you do. Microsoft says that Tweak UI is for so-called power users, but I think anyone reading this book finds it indispensable.

Even though it's developed by Microsoft engineers, Tweak UI isn't included with Windows XP. Instead, you have to download it from Microsoft's Web site and install it separately.

When Tweak UI is installed, a Tweak UI icon is automatically added to the Control Panel. This makes it easy to start the utility when you want to reconfigure some parameter of your system.

You should know that as of this writing, an official version of Tweak UI just for Windows XP does not exist. Instead, you have to use the Windows 2000 version of the utility, version 1.33. This version works just fine, and adds a lot of new personalization features to the OS.

Microsoft is working on a Windows XP version of Tweak UI, which will probably be available by the time you read this. It will be part of the Windows XP PowerToys, a collection of utilities that all power users will find extremely useful. Check with Microsoft's official Windows XP site (`www.microsoft.com/windowsxp/`) for details about downloading Tweak UI and the Windows XP PowerToys.

Follow these steps to install and run the program:

1. Direct your Web browser to `www.microsoft.com/ntworkstation/downloads/PowerToys/Networking/NTTweakUI.asp` and click the Download Now link.
2. After the file is downloaded, use My Computer to navigate to the downloaded file. (It was probably saved in the \windows\temp\ folder.) Right-click the file to extract the program files.
3. Right-click the tweakui.inf file and select Install from the pop-up menu.
4. If the Tweak UI installation opens a Help window, close it. Then open the Control Panel and click the Tweak UI icon to launch the Tweak UI utility.
5. Click the tabs described in Table 2.4 and make the selections you want.
6. Click OK to register your changes and close the utility.

TABLE 2.4—TWEAK UI SETTINGS

Tab	Description
Desktop	Determines which standard system icons are displayed on your desktop. This is the way to get rid of pre-installed icons—such as the icon for the Microsoft Network—that you can't delete normally.
My Computer	Determines which drives are displayed in the My Computer window, and the location of special Windows folders.
Control Panel	Determines which icons are displayed in the Windows Control Panel—a great way to hide little-used utilities.

TABLE 2.4—CONTINUED

Tab	Description
Logon	Enables you to log on to your network automatically at system startup and eliminates the need to type your username and password every time you start your computer.
New	Adds or removes items from the New submenu displayed when you right-click the desktop. The New submenu lets you create new documents of the selected types.
Mouse	Calibrates your mouse's speed and double-clicking and dragging sensitivity. You can also choose to have whichever window the mouse is over be your active window (the Activation Follows Mouse option), and select how you use your mouse wheel for scrolling.
General	Turns on or off various Windows effects (such as window animation and smooth scrolling). Also prevents applications from stealing focus.
Explorer	Changes the way shortcuts are displayed on the desktop (with small arrows, large arrows, no arrows, or a custom icon) and turn on or off the "Shortcut to" prefix on new shortcuts. This tab alone makes Tweak UI worthwhile!
IE	Turns on or off various Internet Explorer settings, including the detection of accidental double-clicks.
Add/Remove	Removes listings from the installed programs listing in the Add/Remove Programs utility. This is quite useful if the manual deletion of a program left its listing in the Add/Remove Programs list.
Boot	Turns on or off various options for Windows behavior at start-up. You can make function keys available for a preset number of seconds, start the Windows GUI automatically, display the Windows splash screen while loading, enable the F4 key to boot another operating system, and to always show the boot menu. You can also select how to run ScanDisk on startup if you have a system failure, but never after prompting, or without prompting
Repair	Rebuilds any damaged icons on your desktop, as well as repairs any corrupted or overwritten system files, resets Registry Editor to its default parameters, and restores the default file type icons and associations. This is a great tool in case things go wrong with your system that you can't fix.
Paranoia	Clears various system tracking mechanisms (Run history, Document history, Find Files history, Find Computer history, Internet Explorer history, and Last User settings). Also turns on or off the ability to play audio or data CDs automatically, and the ability to log errors to the FAULTLOG.TXT files.

I could have devoted a chapter of this book to Tweak UI. I use this utility myself, and I find it quite useful.

Admittedly, Windows XP now incorporates some of the functions that previously were available only with Tweak UI. That's okay. Even with a little duplication, Tweak UI still provides a lot of options that aren't available in the OS.

If you're an experienced and interested user, I recommend you install Tweak UI and play with it awhile. Then you can discover for yourself all the power it adds to your system!

MAKING WINDOWS XP LOOK LIKE WINDOWS 9X/ME

My final tip in this chapter is for all you older Windows users who don't like the new look and feel of Windows XP. If you're dead set against embracing change, you don't have to. You can make the Windows XP interface look like the "classic" interface you're used to using.

This is how you do it:

1. Open the Display Properties utility, select the Themes tab, select Windows Classic from the pull-down list, and click Apply.
2. Select the Desktop tab, select the Windows 2000 Background, and then click Apply.
3. Select the Appearance tab, select Windows Classic Windows and Buttons and the Windows Classic Color Scheme, and then click Apply.
4. Click the Effects button and uncheck the following options: Use the Following Fade Effect for Menus and Tooltips, Use the Following Method to Smooth Screen Fonts, Show Shadows Under Menus, and Hide Underlined Letters.... Click OK when done.
5. If you want to change the colors of individual desktop items, click the Advanced button to display the Advanced Appearance dialog box, shown in Figure 2.25. Make changes to individual items, and then click OK.

Figure 2.25

When you select the Windows Classic theme and color scheme, you can change the color for each desktop element separately.

6. Click OK to close the Display Properties utility, and then open the System Properties utility.
7. Select the Advanced tab, and then click the Settings button (in the Performance section). When the Performance Options dialog box appears, select the Visual Effects tab and click the Best Performance button. Click OK to close this dialog box, and then click OK again to close the System Properties utility.
8. Open the Control Panel and click the Switch to Classic View option.

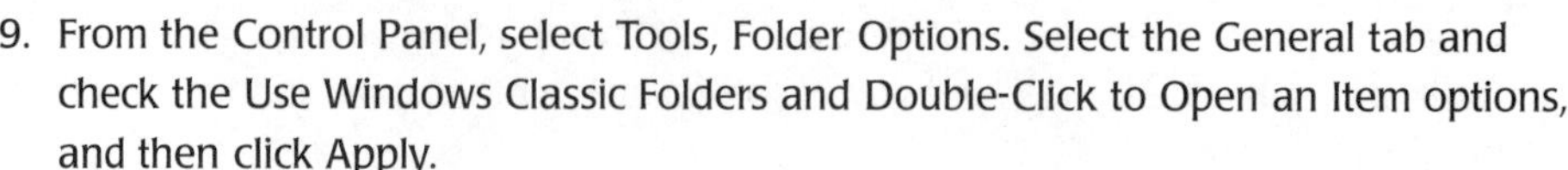

9. From the Control Panel, select Tools, Folder Options. Select the General tab and check the Use Windows Classic Folders and Double-Click to Open an Item options, and then click Apply.
10. Select the View tab and uncheck the following options: Show Pop-Up Animation for Folder and Desktop Items, and Use Search Companion for Searching. Click the Like Current Folder button, and then click OK.
11. Right-click the Start button and select Properties. When the Taskbar and Start Menu Properties dialog box appears, select the Start tab, check the Classic Start Menu option, and then click Apply.
12. Select the Taskbar tab and uncheck the following options: Group Similar Taskbar Buttons, and Hide Inactive Icons. Click OK when done.
13. Open My Documents, right-click anywhere in the files area, select Arrange Items By from the pop-up menu, and uncheck Show In Groups.

If you perform all these steps, Windows XP looks and behaves pretty much the same way Windows 98 or Windows Me did. (See Figure 2.26 for a peek.) The fact that you have to reconfigure *so many* settings tells you how much Microsoft changed in Windows XP. (A lot!)

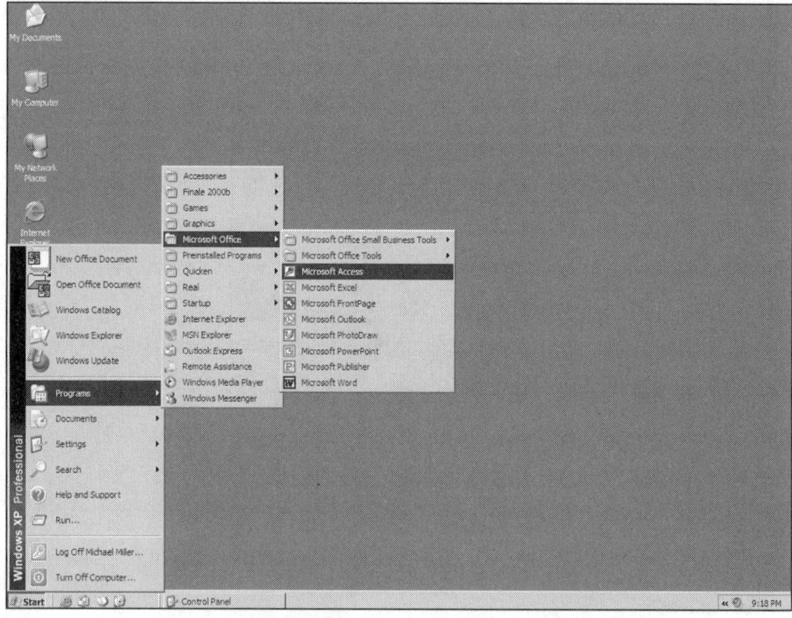

Figure 2.26

Is this Windows 98 or Windows XP reconfigured to look like Windows 98?

If you don't want to go to *all* this work, just complete steps 1, 2, and 3. That will change the major parts of interface back to "classic" Windows style, which is good enough for most users.

JIM'S TOP TEN TIPS

These are the ten most important things to remember about configuring your copy of Windows XP:

1. Most configuration settings for Windows XP are found somewhere in the Control Panel. (The Display Settings utility is a good place to look.)
2. Windows XP's Control Panel has been redesigned to have a task-based approach, although you can return it to its traditional look by clicking the Switch to Classic View link.
3. With Windows XP you can change the overall desktop theme, the desktop background, and the color scheme. You can't change the colors of individual desktop elements.
4. A variety of special effects in XP make the interface look more sophisticated. Some of these effects are accessed via the Display Properties utility, and others via the System Properties utility.
5. By default, Windows XP groups like items on the Taskbar—and hides inactive icons in the System Tray.
6. By default, the Start menu displays the last five active programs. You can customize the Start menu to display more or fewer programs, and to permanently add your favorite programs to the Start menu. (Right-click the Start button and select Properties to display the Taskbar and Start Menu Properties dialog box.)
7. Windows XP adds the ability to synchronize your PC's system clock with a time server on the Internet. Just open the Date and Time utility, select the Internet Time tab, and check the Automatically Synchronize With an Internet Time Server option.
8. You can configure Windows XP for either single-clicking or double-clicking of icons and files. (Open My Computer and select Tools, Folder Options.)
9. To gain even more control over the way Windows XP looks and acts, install the Tweak UI utility (available from Microsoft's Web site).
10. To make Windows XP look like the previous versions of Windows, select the Windows Classic theme and color scheme, and then move through all the configuration options and make minor changes as necessary.

PART II

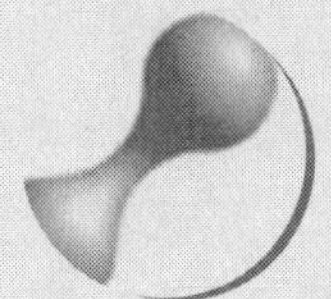

WORKING WITH FILES, PROGRAMS, AND PERIPHERALS

CHAPTER 3

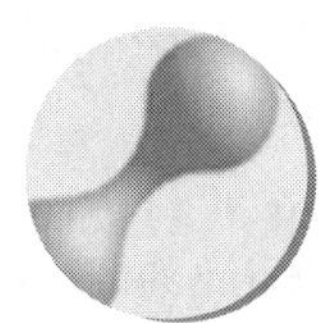

MANAGING FILES

- Understanding Files and Folders
- Windows XP's File Management Tools
- Configuring File and Folder Views
- Basic Navigation and Operations
- Essential File Management
- Compressing and Decompressing Files
- Working with File Types and Associations
- Jim's Top Ten Tips

Every computer user has to work with files. Whether you're downloading MP3 files from the Internet or sharing Word documents with a friend or colleague, you need to know several essential file-related tasks. You have to know how to copy files, delete files, move files, and rename files. And you have to know which file management tools to use to perform these tasks.

Windows XP really doesn't add anything new in terms of what you can do with your files. What it does add is a much easier way to perform essential file management tasks. Everything you need to do is out in the open, instead of being hidden behind pull-down menus or obscure right-click commands.

In addition, Windows XP tries to anticipate what you want to do when you select a file. If you select an image file, for example, you are presented with a list of image-related operations. If you select an MP3 file, you are

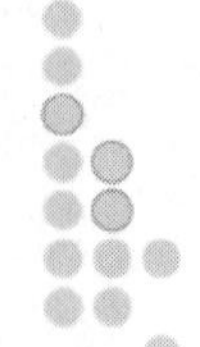

presented with a different list of audio-related operations. This context sensitivity isn't perfect, but it does a pretty good job of helping you do what needs to be done.

I think that these improvements to file management offer a compelling reason to upgrade to Windows XP. The simple addition of an activity center panel in My Computer doesn't sound like that big a deal, but its impact is tremendous. That one little panel makes so many things so much easier to accomplish. It's amazing.

My only wish is that Microsoft had incorporated this type of file management years ago. This is the kind of thing that should have been in Windows from the beginning. Fortunately for us, it's here now. A few years late, perhaps, but welcome nonetheless.

UNDERSTANDING FILES AND FOLDERS

Before I get into Windows XP's new method of file management, let's spend a little space on a files-and-folder refresher course. (Just in case you forgot, of course.)

The files and folders on your computer are like the files and folders in a typical filing cabinet. Your computer is the filing cabinet, and it contains folders that contain individual files.

On your computer, every file and folder has a unique name and occupies a distinct location. A filename consists of a main name and a three character "extension," separated by a period. A typical filename looks something like this: main name of this file.ext.

Extensions are typically identified with specific types of files. For example, Microsoft Word documents have a .doc extension. Whenever you see a file ending in .doc, you know it's a Word document.

Prior to Windows 95, filenames were limited to eight main characters plus a three-character extension. Windows no longer has this "8+3" limitation. Filenames can now include up to 255 characters, and can use spaces and special characters.

Files are stored on your disk in folders. A folder can contain both files and additional folders. (A folder within a folder is called a *subfolder*.)

The exact location of a file is called its *path* and contains all the folders leading to the file. For example, a file named filename.doc that exists in the system folder that is contained in the windows folder on your c:\ drive has a path that looks like this: c:\windows\system\filename.doc

What current versions of Windows call "folders," Windows 3.x and MS-DOS called "directories." Some older computer users—like me—occasionally slip and refer to folders as directories. Don't get confused. A folder and a directory are the same thing.

Learning how to use files and folders is a necessary skill for all computer users. You may need to copy files from one folder to another, or from your hard disk to a floppy disk. You certainly need to delete files every now and then.

Any time you have to work directly with files or folders, you use one of Windows XP's file-management tools or upper-level Windows folders. I show you how to use each of these tools in the next section.

WINDOWS XP'S FILE MANAGEMENT TOOLS

All the key file management tools in Windows XP look and work very similarly. Whether you're using My Computer or My Documents (or any other system folder), everything looks and works pretty much the same. It's like you have a single tool with multiple interfaces—and each interface is customized for its own particular task!

My Computer

The main file-management tool in Windows XP is My Computer. You can open My Computer from its desktop icon or from the Start menu.

My Computer lets you manage your hard drive(s), mapped network drives, peripheral drives, folders, and files. As you can see in Figure 3.1, Windows XP's version of My Computer looks quite a bit different from the My Computer in previous versions of Windows.

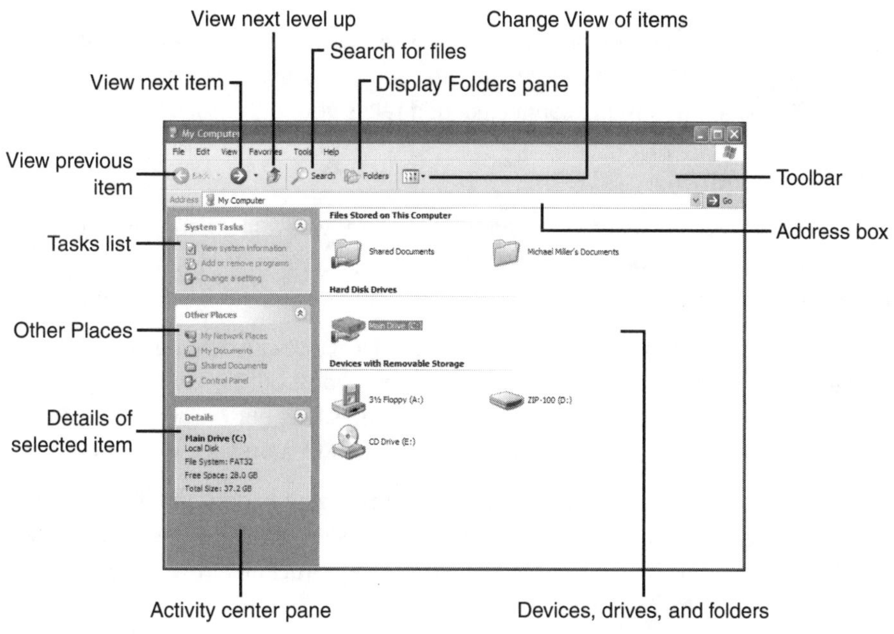

Figure 3.1

Use My Computer to access all the devices attached to your system.

By default, all the devices on your computer are displayed, and arranged by type in the right pane. The left pane is the activity center that displays core Tasks, a list of Other Places (other file management tools), and Details about a selected item.

You can adjust the width of the activity center pane by grabbing the right edge of the pane with your mouse and dragging it to resize.

You can open any device, drive, or folder by clicking its icon. When you open an item, its contents are displayed in the right pane.

When you hover your cursor over an icon, My Computer displays details about that item in the Details section of the activity center. The Tasks list also changes to reflect tasks specific to the selected item.

The toolbar at the top of My Computer is the same one displayed in all Windows XP's file management tools. From this toolbar you can perform the following operations:

- Go Back to the last item you were looking at
- Go Forward to the next item
- Go Up one level in the folder hierarchy
- Search for files or folders (displays the Search Companion)
- Display a list of Folders in a hierarchical "file tree"
- Change the View of the items in the right pane

You can also use My Computer as a Web browser by entering the URL for a Web page into the Address box. When you enter an URL and press Enter, Windows connects to the Internet (if you're not already connected) and takes you to the specified page.

Windows Explorer

In previous versions of Windows, Windows Explorer was a file-management tool that displayed files in a hierarchical "tree." In Windows XP, however, Windows Explorer no longer exists. That is, there's no icon for it anywhere, and no place for it on the Start menu.

That's because the old Windows Explorer hierarchical tree can now be displayed within My Computer. All you have to do is click the Folders button on the My Computer toolbar. As you can see in Figure 3.2, the activity center pane slides out of the way and is replaced with a "file tree" that lists all the devices, folders, and files on your system.

Many users prefer this hierarchical approach to managing folders and files because it gives you two panes worth of folders and files to work with. The left Folders pane contains all the devices and folders on your system, in a tree-like structure. The right pane displays the contents of any item selected in the Folders pane.

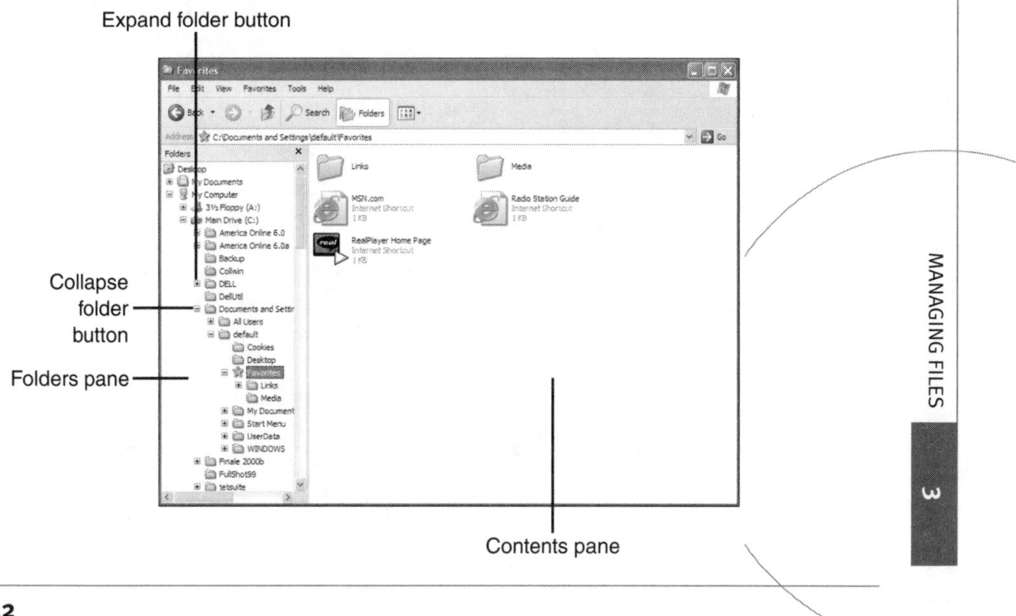

Figure 3.2

Change My Computer to look like Windows Explorer by displaying the Folders pane.

In the Folders pane, drives or folders that contain other folders have a "+" beside them. Click the "+" to expand the folders. When the drive or folder is fully expanded, the "+" changes to a "–"; click the "–" to collapse the contents again.

My Documents and Other Windows Folders

Windows XP tries to group related types of user files into master folders. Basic documents (for Word, Excel, and other applications) are grouped into the My Documents folder. Image files are grouped into the My Pictures folder. MP3 and other audio files are grouped into the My Music folder. Digital video files are grouped in the My Videos folder. And user-created Web pages are grouped into the My Webs folder.

These upper-level Windows folders have several interesting things about them. First, they all look and act just like My Computer—including the new activity center panes. Second, in addition to the standard Tasks list, some of these folders (My Music and My Pictures, in particular) include an additional list of tasks specific to their type of files. Third, like My Computer, you can choose to display a Folders pane instead of the normal activity center pane.

Let's look at My Documents first. Figure 3.3 shows a typical My Documents folder. In this screen shot, the subfolders contained in My Documents are grouped by name. (I show you how to do this in the "Grouping Files and Folders" section later in the chapter.) Select a folder and key details are displayed in the Details section of the activity center.

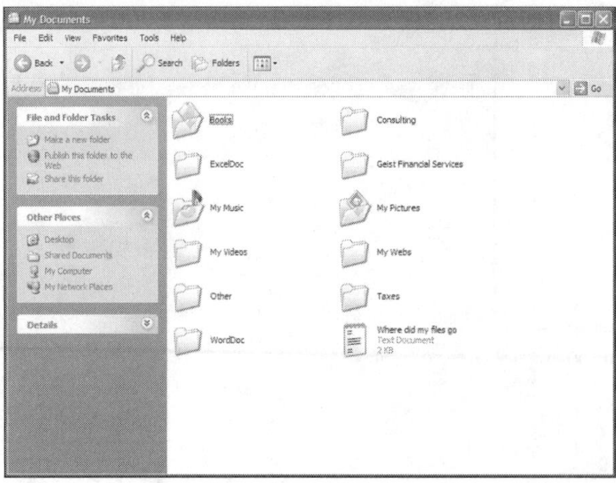

Figure 3.3

My Documents looks and acts just like My Computer, except that it displays key user-created files and folders.

Figure 3.4 shows another folder displayed from within My Documents. Here you can see how different files look, and how the Tasks and Details sections of the activity center have adapted. In this view, My Documents is identical to My Computer. (They really are the same tool!)

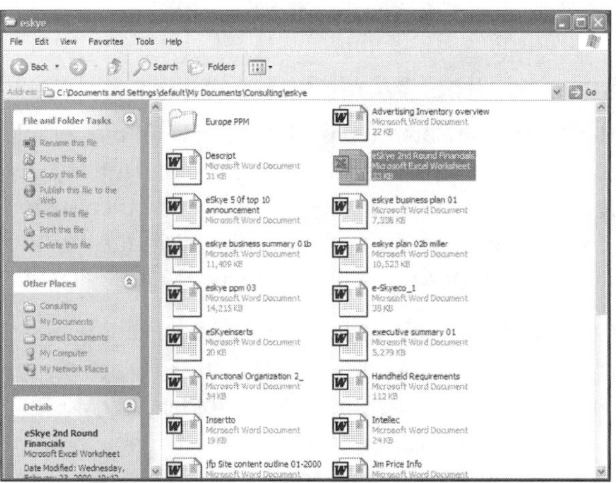

Figure 3.4

Individual files in the My Documents folder.

My Pictures, shown in Figure 3.5, is a subfolder of the My Documents folder. As you can see, image files are displayed as thumbnails (instead of the typical boring file icons). A new Pictures Tasks section is in the activity center pane, and the Details section also displays the selected thumbnail—along with key image information.

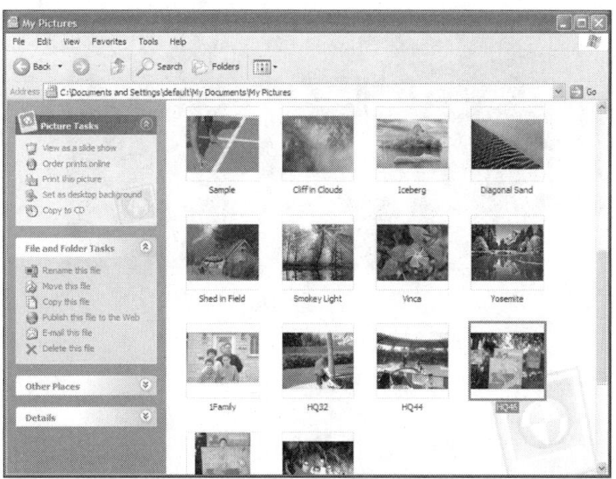

Figure 3.5

My Pictures is a variation of My Documents, specific to image files.

For more information about My Pictures, see Chapter 11, "Working with Pictures."

The other upper-level folders (My Music, My Videos, and My Webs) are similar to My Pictures in that they're customized for their specific types of files.

The Command Prompt

There's one more file-management tool in Windows XP that bears mentioning—even though it really isn't related to My Computer and the other tools. This tool is the Command Prompt that you can use to execute old DOS commands.

Even though Windows XP isn't built on the MS-DOS engine (like Windows 9X/Me was), you still might have some old DOS applications installed on your system. Or you may have learned how to use computer in those ancient pre-Windows days, and can't quite give up that old command-line orientation. Whatever the case, XP still includes a DOS-emulation utility for you to use.

You access the Command Prompt by selecting Start, All Programs, Accessories, Command Prompt. As you can see in Figure 3.6, the Command Prompt window looks pretty much like the old MS-DOS window in Windows 9X/Me, and works pretty much the same way, too. You enter a DOS command at the prompt, and then press Enter. (To close the window, just enter EXIT.)

You old-timers out there will be pleased to know that a good number of MS-DOS commands are still available in Windows XP. Which means you can COPY and DEL and DIR to your heart's content.

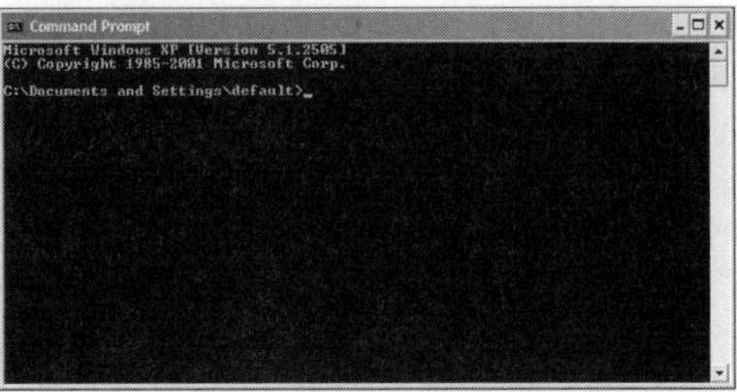

Figure 3.6

It's still there—the Windows XP Command Prompt window.

CONFIGURING FILE AND FOLDER VIEWS

Leaving DOS behind (hopefully forever!), let's return to Windows XP's other file management tools. All these tools are basically the same, and all can be customized in the same ways. You can change a lot about My Computer, My Documents, and the other system folders, to create a truly personalized file management environment.

Activating Web View

If you can see the activity center pane in My Computer or My Documents, your version of Windows XP has Web View turned on. Web View enables each folder to be displayed with custom HTML content, like you might see on the World Wide Web. (The activity center pane is generated by HTML code, actually.) To take full advantage of Windows XP, you definitely want to have Web View activated.

To turn Web View on or off, follow these steps:

1. From within any folder, select Tools, Options.
2. When the Folder Options dialog box appears, select the General tab (shown in Figure 3.7).

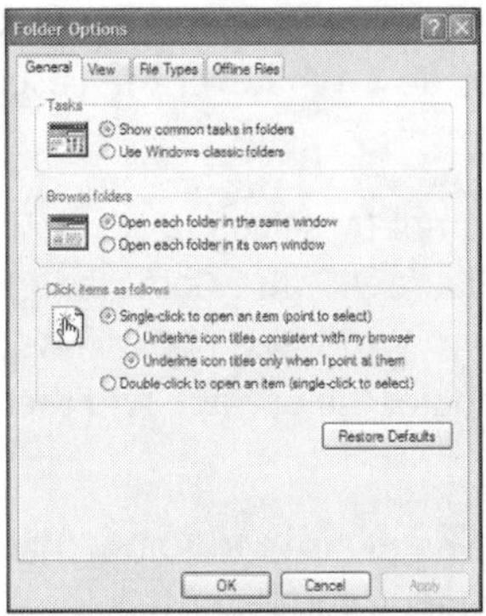

Figure 3.7

To use XP's activity centers, turn on Web View.

3. In the Web View section, check the Enable Web Content in Folders option.
4. Click OK.

In addition, activating Web View enables you to treat all file and folder icons as you would objects on a Web page. Instead of double-clicking to launch an object, you can now single-click. Just select the Single-Click to Open an Object option.

Changing the Way Files Are Displayed

You can choose to view the contents of a folder in a variety of ways. Just click the Views button and choose from the following options:

- **Thumbnails**—Best for image files, as shown in Figure 3.8
- **Tiles**—Big icons with selected file details, shown in Figure 3.9
- **Icons**—Small icons with no file details, shown in Figure 3.10
- **List**—Filenames only with no details, shown in Figure 3.11
- **Details**—Filenames only with selected details, shown in Figure 3.12

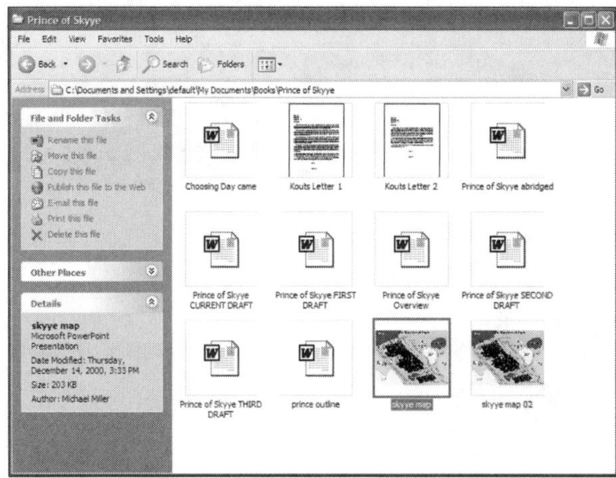

Figure 3.8

Displaying files as thumbnails.

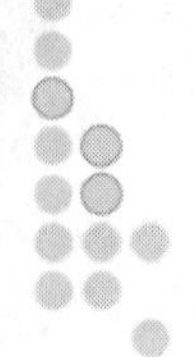

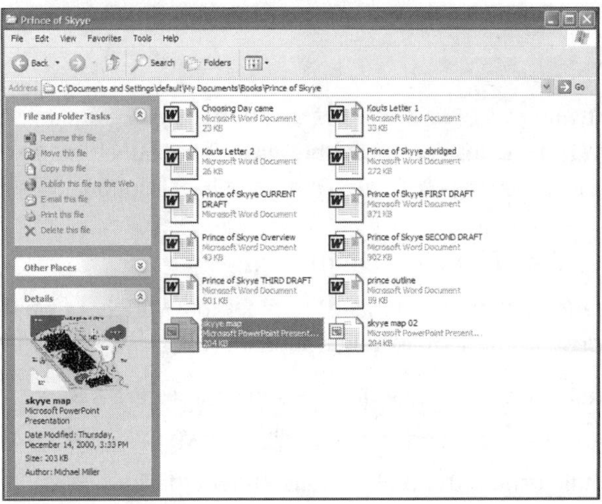

Figure 3.9

Displaying files as tiles.

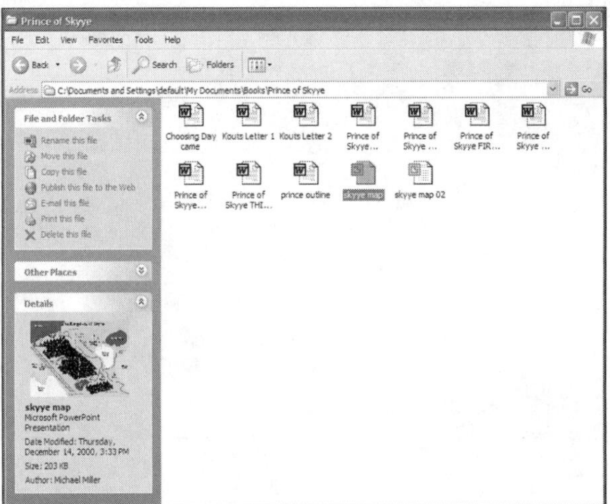

Figure 3.10

Displaying files as icons.

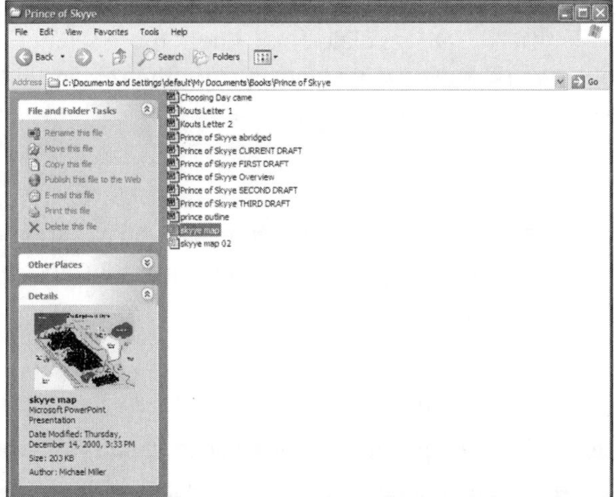

Figure 3.11

Displaying files in a list.

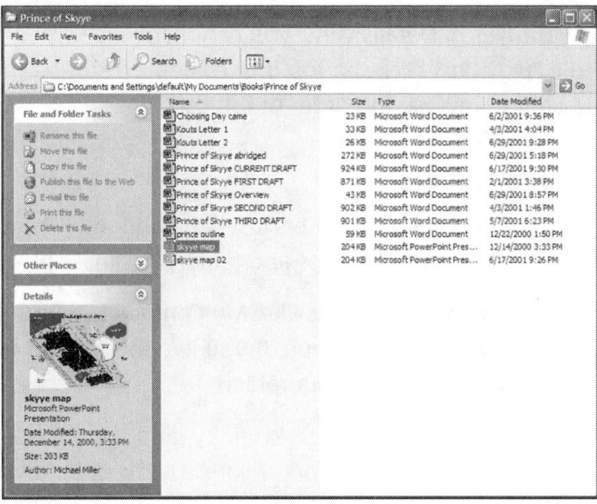

Figure 3.12

Displaying files in a list with details.

If you have moved, copied, or deleted some files and folders but don't see the changes, you need to update your display. Select View, Refresh, or press the F5 key.

If you choose Details view, you can select which details are displayed. Select View, Choose Details to display the Detail Settings dialog box. Check those settings you want to display, and use the Move Up and Move Down keys to place the settings in the order you want. Click OK to lock in your new configuration.

Sorting Files and Folders

When viewing files in My Computer or My Documents, you can sort your files and folders in a number of ways. To do this, select View, Arrange Icons By, and then choose from the following options:

- **Name**—Sorts files by filename, alphabetically
- **Size**—Sorts files by size, smallest to largest
- **Type**—Sorts files by file type: applications, configuration files, and so on
- **Modified**—Sorts files by date and time last modified

You can also sort your icons by right-clicking in an open area of the folder and selecting Arrange Icons By.

If you're viewing your files in Details view, you can manually sort your files by any setting you've chosen to display. Just click the top of a column to sort by that column. (Click the column a second time to reverse the order of the sort.)

Grouping Files and Folders

I'm not done with displaying files and folders just yet. Windows XP includes another option that I really like—the ability to display files and folders in similar groups.

You've already seen what grouping looks like. My Computer groups items by device type, with a title and thin line above each group. If you like this type of organization, you can apply similar grouping to any and all your folders.

To turn on grouping, select View, Arrange Icons By, and then check the Show In Groups option. Windows now groups your files and folders by the criteria you used to sort those items. For example, if you sorted your files by date, they'll now be grouped by date, as shown in Figure 3.13. (Actually, by Today, Last Week, Last Month, and so on.) If you sorted your files by type, they'll be grouped by file type. And so on, for all the different ways of sorting your files.

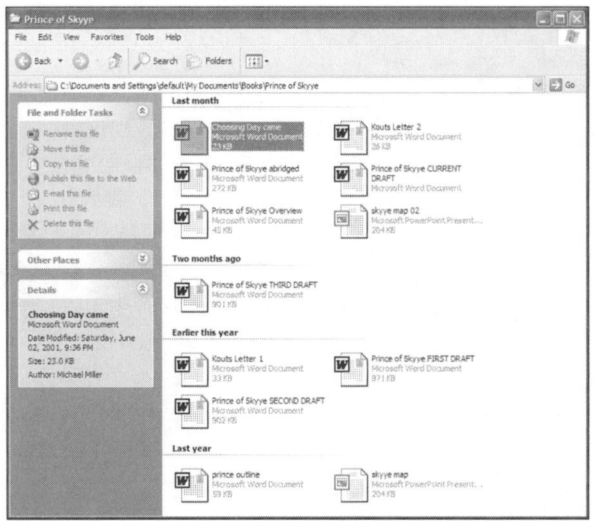

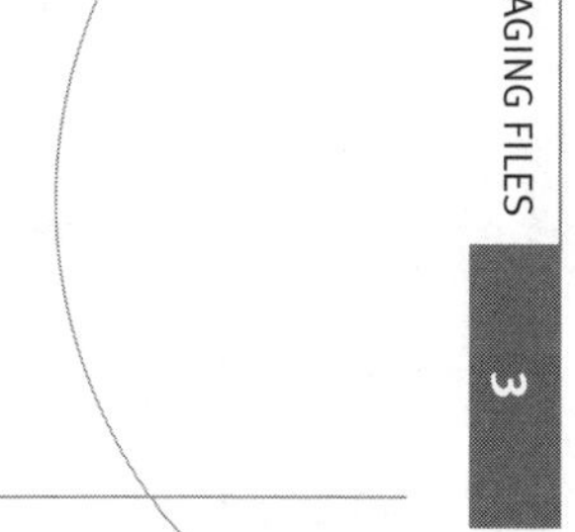

Figure 3.13

Configure Windows XP to group your files by date, type, name, or size.

Individual or Universal Views

The neat thing about selecting various views, sorts, and groups is that you can combine all these options in a lot of different ways. For example you can display details sorted and grouped by date, or tiles sorted and grouped by file type. However you want to view your files, you can.

You need to know one more thing about all these different folder views. You can select different views for different folders, or you can choose to apply a custom view to all your folders.

By default, when you customize a folder, that view is specific to that folder. To apply a folder view to all the folders on your system, follow these steps:

1. Open the folder that looks the way you want it to look, and then select Tools, Options.
2. When the Folder Options dialog box appears, select the View tab (shown in Figure 3.14).

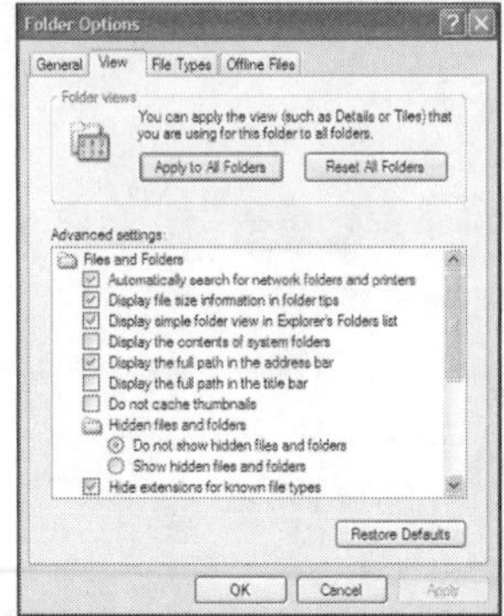

Figure 3.14

Make all your folders look like the current folder.

3. Click the Like Current Folder button.
4. Click OK.

To return your folders to their default state, click the Reset All Folders button.

While you're in the Folder Options dialog box, take a look at the Advanced Settings list on the View tab. As you can see, this list contains a number of more obscure configuration settings, like hiding file extensions and displaying the full path in the title bar. Remember this list if you need to change one of these settings.

Changing Folder Icons

You're not through customizing folders just yet. Windows XP also lets you change the icon used to represent a folder. Just follow these steps:

1. From within the folder, select View, Customize This Folder.
2. When the Properties dialog box appears, select the Customize tab, shown in Figure 3.15.
3. To select a new icon for the folder, click the Change Icon button and select a new icon from the New Icon dialog box.
4. To select a picture to use when this folder is displayed in thumbnail view, click the Choose Picture button and browse to the desired image file. (If you don't choose a picture, up to four thumbnails from this folder's documents are displayed.)
5. Click OK.

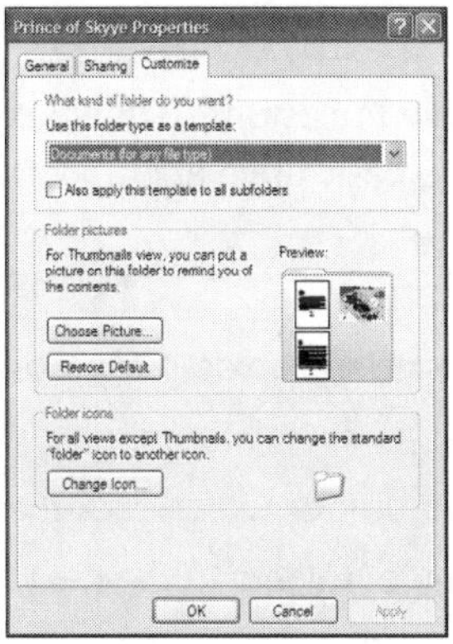

Figure 3.15

Change the properties of the current folder, including the folder's icon.

Personalizing the Send To Menu

With the advent of Windows XP's activity center pane, you'll probably find that you're doing less right-clicking. (In older versions of Windows, you had to right-click to access many of the common tasks. These same tasks are now on the activity center Tasks list.

That doesn't mean that you should give up right-clicking entirely. The pop-up menu that appears when you right-click a file or folder still contains the Send To menu, which is one of the fastest ways to send a file from one place to another. You can use the Send To menu to send a file to another disk, to another folder, to another user via e-mail, or to a printer for printing.

Because using the Send To menu is a quick way to work with files, you might want to add other actions to the menu. For example, you might want to create a Send To item for a Zip drive or commonly used folder. This way you can right-click a file and use the Send To command to copy the file automatically.

This is how you add options to the Send To menu:

1. Use My Computer to navigate to the \Documents and Settings*username*\SendTo folder.
2. Select File, New, Shortcut.
3. When the Create New Shortcut wizard appears, enter the name of the file, folder, or drive you want to add to the Send To menu. (Click the Browse button to search your system for the item.) Click Next to proceed.
4. Enter the name you want to appear on the Send To menu, and then click Finish.

The next time you right-click a file and select Send To, your new item appears in the list of Send To options.

Because I use the Send To menu a lot, this is one of my favorite tips. I hope you can use it!

BASIC NAVIGATION AND OPERATIONS

Now that you've looked at how to customize the look and feel of Windows XP's folders, let's turn our attention to some basic drive and folder navigation and operations.

Navigate Disks and Folders

You can navigate through disks and folders My Computer, My Documents, and other folders in several ways:

- To view the contents of a disk or folder, click the selected item.
- To move up the hierarchy of folders to the next highest folder or disk, click the Up button on the toolbar.
- To move back to the disk or folder previously selected, click the Back button on the toolbar.
- To choose from the history of disks and folders previously viewed, click the down arrow on the Back button and select a disk or folder. View the complete history by selecting the History icon on this pull-down menu.
- If you've moved back through multiple disks or folders, you can move forward to the next folder by clicking the Forward button.
- Go directly to any disk or folder by entering the path in the Address Bar (in the format *x:\folder\subfolder*) and pressing Enter or clicking the Go button.

You can also go directly to any folder by clicking the Folders button to display the Folders pane, and then selecting the folder in the Folders list.

Selecting Files and Folders

Sometimes you want to perform an action on a single file. To select a single file, just hover your cursor over the file until it is highlighted; the filename and icon changes color, and information about the selected file appears in the Details section of the activity center pane. (If you're using double-click mode, you have to single-click a file to display the Details.)

At other times, however, you want to perform a single action on multiple files. To select multiple files, hover your cursor over the first file you want to select, and then hold down the Ctrl key on your keyboard. Select additional files by hovering your cursor over them until they are highlighted. Keep holding down the Ctrl key until you've selected all desired files.

Creating Folders

Folders act kind of like drawers on your hard drive to hold other folders or files. They enable you organize your hard drive by putting common files or subfolders together.

This is how you create new folders:

1. Navigate to the current drive or folder that contains the new folder.

2. Select File, New Folder—or click the Make a New Folder task in the File and Folder Tasks panel of the activity center pane.
3. A new, empty folder appears, with the filename "New Folder" highlighted. Type a name for your folder (which overwrites the "New Folder" name) and press Enter.

One of Microsoft's most important "little" changes is the addition of the "make new folder" command in so many places within each folder window. Used to be you could only access this command from the File menu. Now you can create a new file directly from the activity center pane, or by right-clicking anywhere in the folder window.

Thanks, Microsoft!

Finding Files

Locating a file on your system can be difficult, especially with today's extra-large hard disk drives. Windows XP includes a new Search Companion utility that makes it relatively easy to find specific files on your system.

The Search Companion replaces the old Find utility, found in previous versions of Windows. Not only do you get the companionship of an animated dog (named Rover), you also get some decent help and advice on how to fine-tune your search.

To search for a particular file, follow these steps:

1. Open the Start menu and click the Search icon. (Alternately, you can click the Search button found on the toolbar in any Windows folder.) This displays the Search Companion pane, as shown in Figure 3.16.

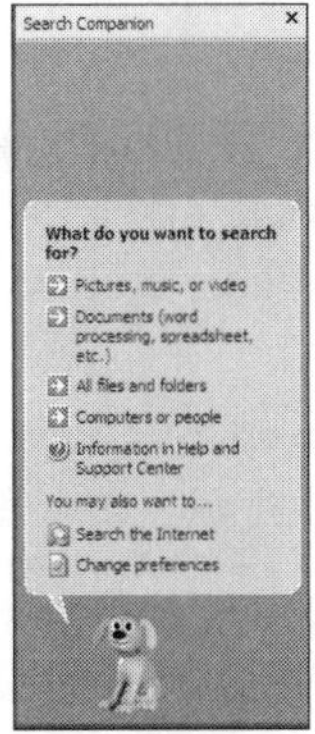

Figure 3.16

Use the new Search Companion to find files on your hard disk.

2. Select what type of file you want to search for. If you're not sure what file type to select, select All Files and Folders.
3. The pane that appears next depends on which type of file you wanted to search for. In most cases, you can choose to search by all or part of the filename, as well as choose where (what drive or folder) you want to look for the file.

PART 2 WORKING WITH FILES, PROGRAMS, AND PERIPHERALS

4. If available (and if relevant to your search), select one or more of the advanced search options, such as when the file was last modified, or the file size.
5. Click the Search button to start the search.
6. The Search Companion now displays a list of files that meet your search criteria—along with advice on how to refine the search. To narrow down your results, click one of the suggestions, and follow the onscreen advice.

Just as you could with the old Find utility, you can use "wildcard" characters when searching with the Search Companion. For example, if you use an asterisk(*) in place of multiple characters, searching for file* finds filename, filetype, and files. If you use a question mark (?) in place of a single character, searching for file? finds only files.

By the way, you can change the animated character that appears in the Search Companion pane—or get rid of it completely. To change the animated character, click the Change Preferences link and then click With a Different Character. Windows XP comes with four characters built in.

To kill the Search Companion character, click the Change Preferences link and then click Without An Animated Screen Character. Bye bye Rover!

ESSENTIAL FILE MANAGEMENT

Now it's time to address the most common things you do with files—renaming, deleting, copying, and moving them. Virtually all these activities can now be accessed directly from the activity center pane in any Windows folder.

Renaming Files and Folders

Naming your files and folders in a way that somehow describes their contents is a good idea. Sometimes, however, you may need to change the name of a file or folder. Fortunately, it's relatively easy to rename an item.

Folder and filenames can include up to 255 characters—including many special characters. Some special characters, however, are "illegal," meaning that you can't use them in folder or filenames. Illegal characters include the following: \ / : * ? " ⇠ ⇢ |.

To rename a file or folder, just follow these steps:

1. Select the file or folder you want to rename.
2. Click Rename This File from the File Tasks list (or Rename This Folder from the Folder Tasks list).
3. The filename is now highlighted. Type a new name for your folder (which overwrites the current name) and press Enter.

A faster way to rename a file is to select the file and press F2 to automatically highlight the filename. (This is one of my favorite tips!)

Deleting Files and Folders

Because disk space is a resource you don't want to waste, you should delete files and folders you no longer need.

1. Select the file or folder you want to delete.
2. Click Delete This File from the File Tasks list (or Delete This Folder from the Folder Tasks list).

You can also delete a file by dragging it from the folder window onto the Recycle Bin icon on the desktop, or by highlighting it and pressing the Del key.

Restoring Deleted Files

If you delete a file and later decide you made a mistake, you're in luck. For a short period of time, Windows XP stores deleted files in a special file called the Recycle Bin. If you've recently deleted a file, it should still be in the Recycle Bin.

This is how you can restore a deleted file:

1. Open the Recycle Bin by clicking its icon on the desktop.
2. When the Recycle Bin opens (see Figure 3.17), select the file or folder you want to restore.
3. Click Restore This Item from the Recycle Bin Tasks list.

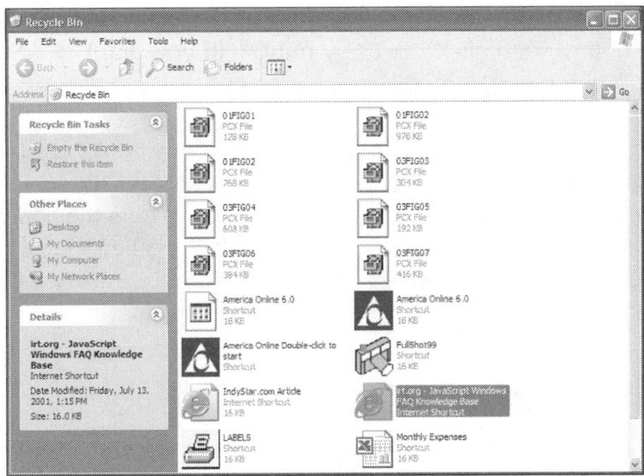

Figure 3.17

Bring a deleted file back to life from the Recycle Bin.

Managing the Recycle Bin

The Recycle Bin is where deleted files are stored after you delete them. Files do not stay in the Recycle Bin indefinitely, however.

By default, the deleted files in the Recycle Bin can occupy 10 percent of your hard disk space. When you've deleted enough files to exceed this 10 percent, the oldest files in the Recycle Bin are automatically and permanently deleted from your hard disk.

If you want to manually remove files from the Recycle Bin, follow these steps:

1. Click the Recycle Bin icon on your desktop.
2. When the Recycle Bin opens, select Empty the Recycle Bin from the Recycle Bin Tasks list.
3. When the Confirm File Delete dialog box appears, click Yes to completely erase the files, or click No to continue storing the files in the Recycle Bin.

Copying Files and Folders

Copying a file or folder is how you place a copy of it at another location while still keeping the original where it is.

Copying is different from moving. When you copy an item, the original remains. When you move an item, the original is no longer present in the original location.

This is how you copy a file or folder with Windows XP:

1. Select the file or folder you want to copy.
2. Click Copy This File from the File Tasks list (or Copy This Folder from the Folder Tasks list).
3. When the Copy Items dialog box appears , navigate to and select the new location for the item, and then click the Copy button. (If you want to copy the item to a new folder, click the New Folder button first.)

You can copy a file in several other ways. You can select the file and then select File, Copy to Folder. You can right-click it and select Send To from the pop-up menu. You can hold down the Ctrl key and drag it from one location to other. You can even drag the file with the *right* mouse button—when you drop the file into a new location, you see a pop-up menu that asks whether you want to move it or copy it.

Moving Files and Folders

Moving a file or folder is different from copying it. Moving cuts the item from its previous location and places it in a new location. Copying leaves the original item where it was *and* creates a copy of the item elsewhere.

In other words, when you copy something you end up with two of it. When you move something, you only have the one thing.

To move a file or folder, follow these steps:

1. Select the file or folder you want to move.
2. Click Move This File from the File Tasks list (or Move This Folder from the Folder Tasks list).
3. When the Move Items dialog box appears, navigate to and select the new location for the item, and then click the Copy button. (If you want to move the item to a new folder, click the New Folder button first.)

You can move a file several other ways. You can select the file and then select File, Move to Folder. You can drag the file from one location to another. You can even do the right-drag trick discussed earlier. When you drop the file into a new location, you see a pop-up menu that asks whether you want to move it or copy it.

Unprotecting Read-Only Files

If you have a file that you want to edit or delete but you can't, chances are the file is designated as *read-only*.

Read-only files can't be changed or deleted. You can read these files, but you can't touch them.

If you need to edit or delete a read-only file, you need to change that file's *attributes*—such as whether it's hidden, or read-only. Follow these steps:

1. Select the file or folder you want to change and select File, Properties.
2. When the Properties dialog box appears (see Figure 3.18), select the General tab and then check or uncheck the desired attributes. For example, to make a read-only file editable, uncheck the Read-only check box.
4. After you've made the desired changes, click the OK.

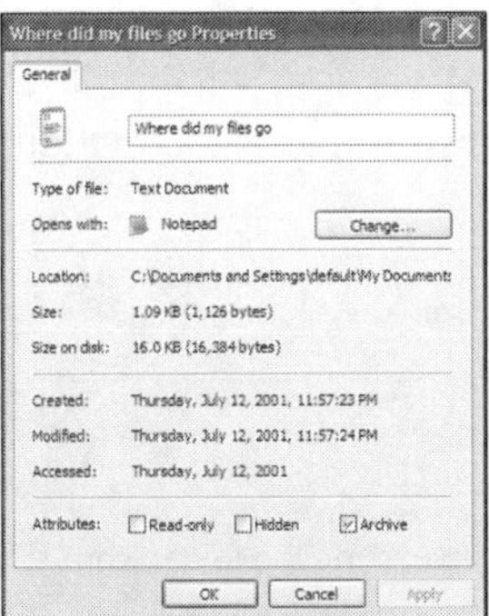

Figure 3.18

You can change the attributes of a file from the Properties dialog box.

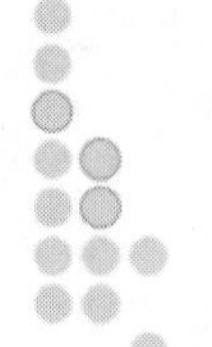

You can change the following file attributes in the Properties dialog box:

- *Read-only* files are files you can read but not edit or delete.
- *Hidden* files are files—typically sensitive system files—that you normally can't view from My Computer.
- *Archive* files are files that have changed since last backed up.

COMPRESSING AND DECOMPRESSING FILES

Files are getting bigger.

If you want to transfer a really big file to another computer, you can run into all sorts of problems. If you're copying the file to floppy disk, the file might be too big to fit on a single floppy disk. If you're sending the file via e-mail, the file might be so big it exceeds your ISP's limits on attachment size.

No matter how you look at it, big files are a bother.

Fortunately, Windows XP includes a way to make big files smaller. Compressed folders take big files and compress them down in size, which makes them easier to copy or move. After the file has been transferred, you uncompress the file back to its original state.

Compressing a File

Compressing a file is a relatively easy task from within any Windows folder. You can even compress multiple files into a single compressed folder.

Just follow these simple steps:

1. Select the file(s) you want to compress.
2. Right-click the selected file(s) and select Send To, Compressed Folder.

That's it—that's all you have to do! Windows creates a new folder, such as the one in Figure 3.19, that contains compressed versions of the file(s) you selected. You can now copy, move, or e-mail this folder, which is a lot smaller than the original file(s).

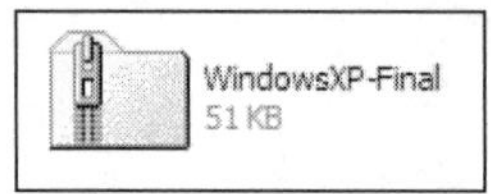

Figure 3.19

A compressed folder—notice the little "zipper" on the folder icon.

The compressed folder is actually a file with a .ZIP extension, so it can be used with other compression/decompression programs, such as WinZip. You can add files to a compressed folder by dragging and dropping them onto the compressed folder icon.

If you install a third-party Zip program on your system, Windows removes Compressed Folders from the Send To menu and replaces it with a link to the new compression program.

One thing to keep in mind about XP's compressed folders. While the Extraction Wizard can extract multiple-disk .ZIP files, Windows XP cannot *create* multiple-disk files. If you need to create a compressed folder that's too big to fit on a single floppy disk, you have to use a third-party utility, such as WinZip. (By the way, you can download WinZip from `www.winzip.com`.)

To better identify compressed folders, you can configure Windows XP to display them in blue. Just open the Folder Options dialog box, select the View tab, and check the "Display compressed files and folders with alternate color options.

Extracting Files

The process of decompressing a file is actually an *extraction* process. That's because you *extract* the original file(s) from the compressed folder.

In Windows XP, this process is eased by the use of the Extraction Wizard. This is how it works:

1. Right-click the compressed folder and select Extract All.
2. When the Extraction Wizard launches, click the Next button.
3. When the Select a Destination page appears, select which folder you want to extract the files to, and then click the Next button.
4. The wizard now extracts the files, and displays the Extraction Complete page. Click the Finish button.

If the compressed folder comprised a multiple-disk set, the Extraction Wizard prompts you to insert each disk in the set, as needed.

WORKING WITH FILE TYPES AND ASSOCIATIONS

As you browse the files and folders on your system, you notice that some files have specific icons. These icons enable you know what type the file is. The file type determines more than just the icon, however. It also determines the application that is used to open the file.

Displaying or Hiding File Types

Windows XP can (and does) hide certain types of files—specifically sensitive system files. Because you don't want to accidentally delete or change a system file, hiding these files is probably a good idea.

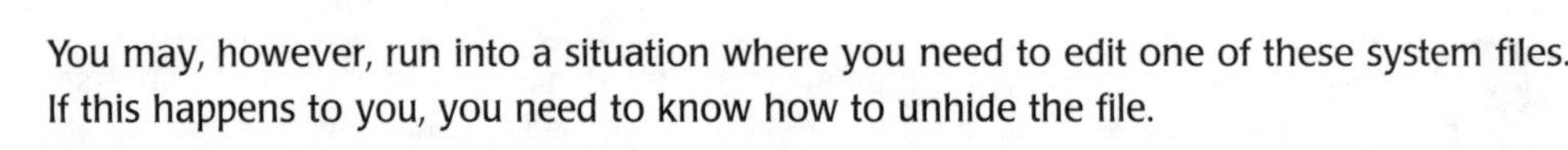

You may, however, run into a situation where you need to edit one of these system files. If this happens to you, you need to know how to unhide the file.

To unhide all the hidden files on your system, follow these steps:

1. From the Control Panel, click the Folder Options icon.
2. When the Folder Options dialog box appears, select the View tab.
3. Open the Hidden Files and Folders item and check the Show Hidden Files and Folders option.
4. Click OK to register your changes.

Associating a File Type with an Application

When you install a new application, it usually registers its file types automatically. That is, Windows associates that file type with a specific application. You may also need to reassociate a file type, however, if you install a new program that hijacks the original file associations for itself—and you'd rather go back to the default associations.

To associate a file type with a particular application, follow these steps:

1. From the Control Panel, click the Folder Options icon.
2. When the Folder Options dialog box appears, select the File Types tab and click the Change button.
3. When the Open With dialog box appears, select the application you want to associate with the file type. (If the program you want isn't listed, click the Click Here link to search for and select another program.)
4. Click OK.

Changing Icons for File Types

Each file type is represented by a specific icon. If you don't like a particular icon, you can easily choose another icon for any file type.

Follow these steps:

1. From the Control Panel, click the Folder Options icon.
2. When the Folder Options dialog box appears, select the File Types tab.
3. Choose the file type you want to change from the Registered File Types list, and then click the Advanced button.
4. When the Edit File Type dialog box appears, click the Change Icon button.
5. When the Change Icon dialog box appears (see Figure 3.20), select a new icon or click the Browse button to choose an icon from another file.
6. Click OK to register your change.

Figure 3.20

Change the icon associated with a particular file type.

Removing File Types

Sometimes you find file types registered that don't even exist on your system. This can happen after you uninstall a program and its associated files.

To clean up your system by removing unused file types, follow these steps:

1. From the Control Panel, click the Folder Options icon.
2. When the Folder Options dialog box appears, select the File Types tab.
3. Choose the file type you want to remove from the Registered File Types list, and then click the Remove button.
4. Click OK.

JIM'S TOP TEN TIPS

When you're working with files and folders, these are the ten most important things to remember:

1. Use My Computer to manage all the drives and devices attached to your system. Use My Documents to manage your documents.
2. When Web View is activated, My Computer and other folders display an activity center pane. This pane contains a context-sensitive Tasks list that makes it easy to perform most common file operations.
3. In Windows XP, My Computer, My Documents, and other system folders are all essentially the same tool.
4. Since Windows Explorer has been removed from Windows XP, you can display a "file tree" view by clicking the Folders button in My Computer or My Documents.
5. The My Pictures and My Music folders are customized with views and commands useful for their specific types of files.
6. Windows XP lets you display different icon views, and group icons by type, date, size, or name.
7. The fastest way to copy a file is to right-click the file and select Send To from the pop-up menu.
8. If you right-drag a file to a new location, Windows displays a pop-up menu that lets you choose to either copy or move the file.
9. All files you delete are sent to the Recycle Bin folder. Until the Recycle Bin is filled up, you can restore any file you've recently deleted.
10. To reduce the size of files you want to copy or e-mail, used Windows XP's compressed folders feature—which creates compressed .ZIP files.

CHAPTER 4

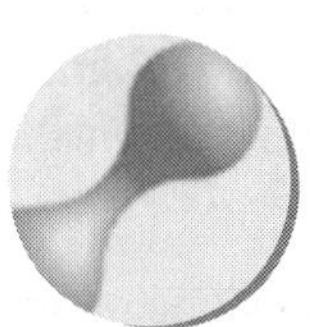

RUNNING PROGRAMS

- Adding and Removing Software
- Installing Programs from the Internet
- Launching Programs
- Launching Programs When Windows Starts
- Switching Between Programs
- Arranging Windows on Your Desktop
- Closing Stuck Programs
- Jim's Top Ten Tips

What use is an operating system if you don't have any software to run on it?

In many ways, the operating system exists as the infrastructure that enables you run various software programs on your PC. If the operating system is doing its job, you almost forget that it's there. You use the OS to launch your programs, but after they're launched, it stays out of your way.

In this chapter I show you how to use Windows XP to launch your programs. I also show you how to use Windows XP to install and remove programs from your computer system. I even give you a few tips on what to do if a program freezes on you.

When you get your programs up and running, however, you're on your own!

ADDING AND REMOVING SOFTWARE

Even though most new computers come with a decent selection of software installed, at some point in time you're going to want to add something new. When you need to add a new program—or remove an old one—you find that Windows XP works pretty much the same way Windows 9x/Me did. Which means, of course, that if you already know how to add and remove software, you don't have much to learn.

Installing New Programs

Almost all software programs have their own built-in installation program. Installing the software is as easy as running this built-in program.

If the program you're installing comes on a CD-ROM, all you have to do is insert the program's main or installation CD in your computer's CD-ROM drive. The program's installation program should then start automatically, and all you have to do is follow the onscreen instructions.

If the installation program *doesn't* start automatically, you have to launch it manually. To do this, click the Start button, click the Run icon, and then enter *x*:\setup into the Run dialog box. (Replace *x* with the letter of your CD-ROM drive.) Click OK to run the installation program. (If this doesn't work, know that some older programs name their installation programs install instead of setup, so change the filename if necessary.)

If you're installing from floppy disks, you launch a program's setup program by inserting the first floppy disk into your PC's disk drive, selecting Start, Run, entering a:\setup into the Run dialog box, and then clicking OK.

If the program you're installing doesn't have an automated setup program, or if you prefer to install a new program manually, you can run Windows XP's Add or Remove Programs utility.

Follow these steps:

1. From the Control Panel, click the Add or Remove Programs icon.
2. When the Add or Remove Programs utility opens, click the Add New Programs button (shown in Figure 4.1), and then click the CD or Floppy button.
3. When the Install Program from Floppy Disk or CD-ROM dialog box appears, insert the program's installation disk or CD in the appropriate drive and click the Next button.
4. Windows now searches for the installation program and displays the command line in the Run Installation Program dialog box. If the Wizard did not find the installation program, click the Browse button to locate it manually.
5. Click the Finish button to run the program's installation program and make sure you follow all the onscreen instructions to complete the installation.

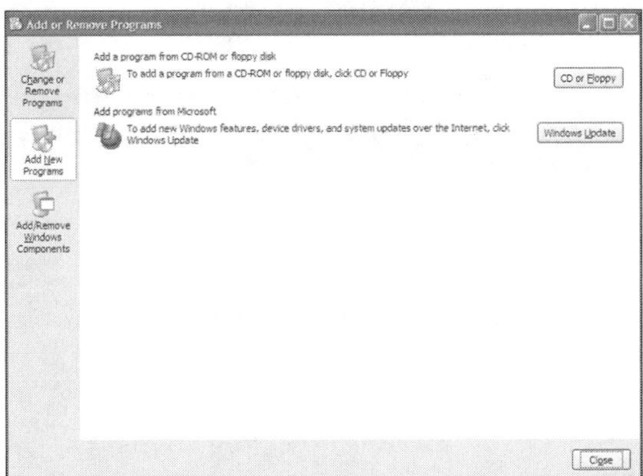

Figure 4.1

Manually installing a new program.

Removing Old Programs

Removing a software program from your system can be easy—or it can be complicated.

Most newer Windows programs include their own utilities to uninstall the program automatically. If you want to uninstall a program, you should use this publisher-supplied utility when it exists. You can generally find the program's uninstall utility in the folder where the program's other files reside.

If you want to remove a Windows application that doesn't include its own uninstall utility, you should use Windows' Add or Remove Programs utility. This utility identifies every component of the application you want to remove, and automatically deletes them from your hard disk.

A well-behaved uninstall program should *not* remove your personal files, even if they are stored in the application's folders. Just to be safe, however, you should move any personal files you want to keep to a new folder before removing the application.

To remove a software program from your PC, follow these steps:

1. From the Control Panel, click the Add or Remove Programs icon.
2. When the Add or Remove Programs utility opens, click the Change or Remove Programs button (shown in Figure 4.2). This part of the dialog box looks a bit different from the one in Windows 9X, in that it provides more detail about the programs listed. It works the same way as the old Windows 9X version, however.

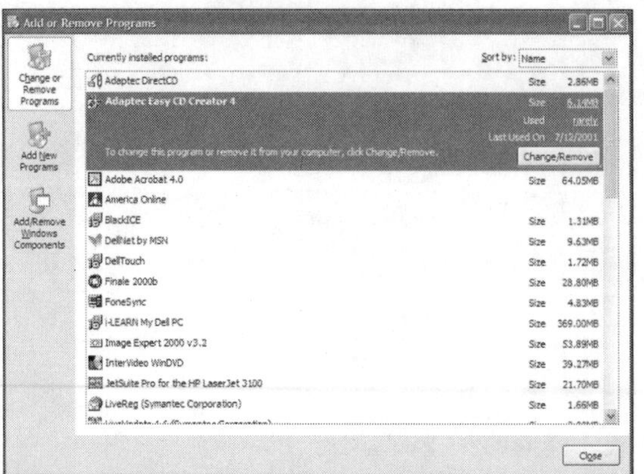

Figure 4.2

Choose a program to remove from your system.

3. Select the program's name from the Currently Installed Programs list, and then click the Change/Remove button. (For some applications, this is a single Remove button.) If prompted, confirm that you want to continue to uninstall the application.
4. Answer any other prompts the uninstall utility presents for removing the program. Some programs, such as Microsoft Word, may require you to insert the original installation disks or CD to perform the uninstall.
5. After the uninstall routine is completed, click the Close button to close the Add or Remove Programs utility.

If you've manually created any Start menu or desktop shortcut icons for the deleted program, the uninstall program might not know they exist—and thus might not delete them. If this is the case, you have to delete these icons manually.

If the program you want to remove does not have an automatic uninstall utility, you have to delete the program's files manually, using My Computer. The problem with trying to delete a program in this way is that miscellaneous files associated with the program are often scattered throughout various folders on your hard disk. You may want to purchase a third-party uninstall program (such as Norton CleanSweep, available at `www.symantec.com/sabu/qdeck/ncs/`) to find and remove all program remnants from your system.

INSTALLING PROGRAMS FROM THE INTERNET

Nowadays many software publishers make their products available via download from the Internet. Many users like this because it provides immediate gratification via instant download. However, it only works if the download is a relatively small file, or if you have a fast broadband connection to the Internet. If you try to download a big file over a slow connection, you're going to get really tired of waiting for the download to complete.

Downloading Commercial Programs

When you download a program from a major software publisher, the process is generally fairly easy to follow. You probably have to read a page of do's and don'ts, agree to the publisher's licensing agreements, and then click a button to start the download. After you specify which folder on your hard disk you want to save the downloaded file, the download begins.

A dialog box should alert you when the download is complete. From this point, installing the program is almost identical to installing from CD or floppy disk. Use My Computer to navigate to where you saved the downloaded file, and then launch the file. The software's installation program should then take over, and lead you through the rest of the process step-by-step.

If you expect to do a lot of downloading, you might want to create a dedicated My Downloads folder in your My Documents folder, and use this folder to hold all your downloaded files.

Downloading Shareware and Freeware

You can also find a wealth of shareware and freeware programs that you can download free-of-charge. (If it's a shareware program, you typically receive some sort of free evaluation period, after which you need to pay to continue using the program.) These programs are typically found in large Web-based archives, and can be easily downloaded with your Web browser.

Web-Based Archives

The biggest of these download archives includes thousands of applications and utilities of all different types. You'll want to search for programs that are Windows XP-compatible, of course—although any program that works on Windows 2000 should also work on Windows XP, with few if any problems.

If you're searching for freeware and shareware, these are some of the best software archives to check out:

- CNET's Download.com (`download.cnet.com`)
- FileMine (`www.filemine.com`)
- Jumbo (`www.jumbo.com`)
- Shareware Place (`www.shareware.place.com`)
- Shareware.com (`www.shareware.com`)
- Tucows (`www.tucows.com`)
- ZDNet Downloads (`www.zdnet.com/downloads/`)

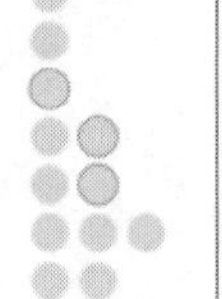

If you download a lot of files, check out the Go!Zilla download manager (`www.gozilla.com`). Go!Zilla lets you schedule your downloads for low traffic periods, organize and categorize your downloaded files, and even resume broken downloads without having to start over.

All these archives offer typical Web-based downloading. Some other file sites use a different protocol, called FTP (File Transfer Protocol) for file downloading.

FTP Servers

FTP servers can be accessed via special FTP client software, or with your Internet Explorer browser. You access an FTP site with IE by entering the address of the FTP site into the Address box, but with *FTP* (instead of *HTTP*) in front of the address. For example, the full address of the Microsoft FTP server looks like this: `ftp://ftp.microsoft.com`.

If you prefer to download with a dedicated FTP client, check out CuteFTP (`www.cuteftp.com/products/cuteftp/`), LaplinkFTP (`www.laplinkftp.com`), or WS_FTP (`www.ipswitch.com/Products/WS_FTP/`).

When you access an FTP site with IE, the directories and subdirectories on the server are displayed as folders and files in the browser's main window, as shown in Figure 4.3. (This makes Internet Explorer look—and work—just like My Computer or My Documents.) Downloading is as simple as clicking on the icon for a specific file.

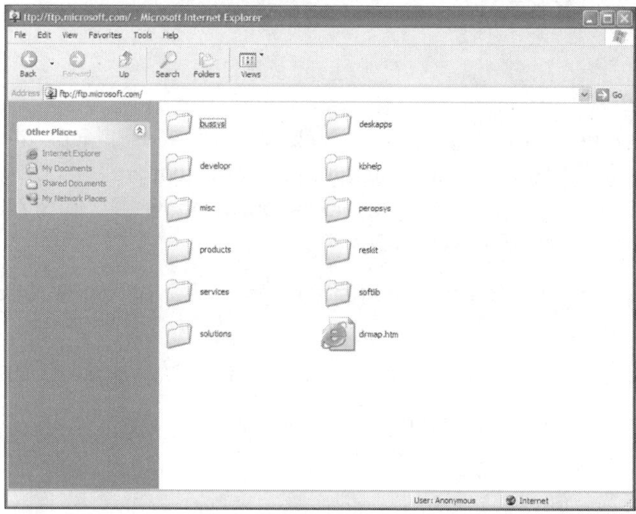

Figure 4.3

Viewing the folders and files on Microsoft's FTP site with Internet Explorer.

If an FTP site asks for your ID and password, it doesn't support anonymous login. And any site that doesn't support anonymous login is likely to be off-limits to the general public and reserved for some private use.

Hunting for an FTP server is a bit of a task because there are not as many FTP Servers as Web servers. You can find lists of FTP servers at the following Web sites:

- FtpFind (`www.ftpfind.com`)
- LaplinkFTP (`www.laplinkftp.com`)
- Lycos FAST FTP Search (`ftpsearch.lycos.com`)
- TILE.NET/FTP (`tile.net/ftp-list/`)

Checking for Viruses

A computer virus is a malicious program that can infect other files, and do untold damage to your computer system. One of the most common ways of contracting a computer virus is through program files downloaded from the Internet.

If you're downloading from a commercial software publisher or major software archive, you probably don't have to worry about accidentally downloading a computer virus. Almost all publishers and archives virus-check their files before they're posted for download.

If you download from a smaller or independent site, however, the possibility exists that you could be downloading infected files. Sites that offer games, pirated software for download, or quite openly cater to hackers, are high-risk for viruses.

Sites that specialize in providing bootleg software and hacked code are sometimes called *warez* sites. (That's pronounced "wares," as in "softwares.")

Windows XP provides no built-in defense against computer viruses. Which means you need to install a third-party antivirus program. I recommend any of the following programs:

- Dr. Solomon's AntiVirus (`www.drsolomon.com`)
- McAfee VirusScan (`www.mcafee.com`)
- Norton AntiVirus (`www.symantec.com/securitycheck/`)
- PC-cillan (`www.antivirus.com/pc-cillin/`)
- Sophos Anti-Virus (`www.sophos.com`)

Whichever antivirus program you choose, you need to go online periodically to update the program's virus definition database. New viruses are being created every week—and they need to be tracked!

LAUNCHING PROGRAMS

After you have all your software installed, you can use Windows XP in several ways to launch your programs. You should use the method that's most convenient to you.

Launching from the Start Menu

Using the Start menu is probably the simplest way to launch an application. If you've used the program recently, it appears on the left side of the Start menu. If not, you need to open the Programs menu and launch the program from there. Just follow these steps:

1. Click the Start menu and select All Programs. The Programs menu now appears next to the Start menu, as shown in Figure 4.4.

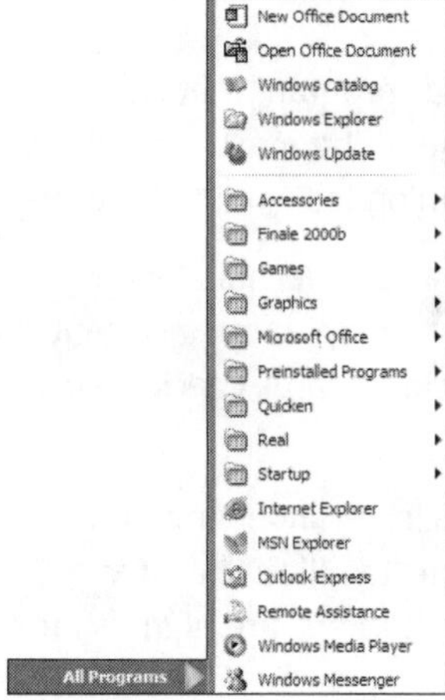

Figure 4.4

Launching an application from the Programs menu.

2. Point to the application's folder or name on the menu. When you point to a menu item with an arrow, a submenu opens. If the item you want is on that submenu, point to it. The item you point to is highlighted.
3. Click the highlighted item to launch the application.

To learn how to place a permanent shortcut icon on the Start menu, see the "Managing the Start Menu" section in Chapter 2.

Launching from My Computer

Another way to launch applications is to click the application file from My Computer.

Follow these steps:

1. From within My Computer, navigate to the folder that contains the program you want to start.

2. Click the folder icon to display the files stored within that folder.
3. Click the icon for the application file that you want to open. The application starts automatically.

You can also launch an application by right-clicking an application file and selecting Open from the pop-up menu.

Launching from a Desktop Shortcut Icon

Although Windows XP tries to force you into an uncluttered desktop, you can still create desktop shortcuts to launch your favorite programs. Many users feel that using a desktop shortcut is the fastest way to launch those programs they use all the time. Clicking an icon is certainly a lot quicker than wading through layers and layers of menus and folders.

To launch a program from a desktop shortcut, all you have to do is click the program's icon.

To learn how to create a desktop shortcut, see the "Working with Desktop Shortcuts" section in Chapter 2.

Launching from the Run Command

If you know the name and location of the program you want to run, you can use Windows XP's Run command to launch the program. The Run command is the Windows equivalent of the old DOS command line, when it comes to launching programs.

To use the Run command, follow these steps:

1. Click the Start button and then click the Run icon.
2. When the Run dialog box appears, as shown in Figure 4.5, enter the path and name of the application file into the Open box. If you don't know the location of the file, click the Browse button to find it.
3. Click the OK button to launch the program.

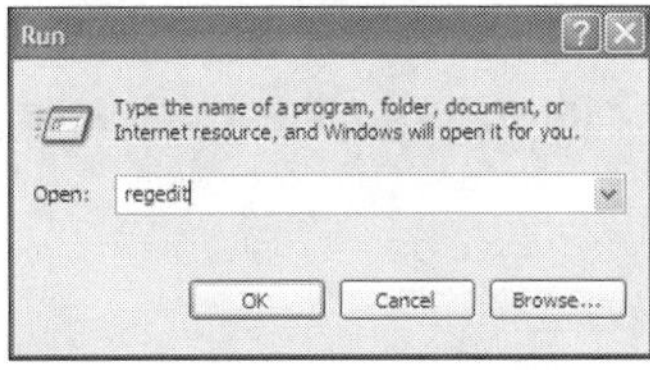

Figure 4.5

Use the Run command to launch a program directly.

LAUNCHING PROGRAMS WHEN WINDOWS STARTS

If you want a particular program to always launch whenever you turn on your computer, you can add that program to Windows' Startup menu. Any file in the Startup menu launches whenever Windows starts.

This is how you do it:

1. From My Computer, navigate to the \Documents and Settings\All Users\Start Menu\Startup\ folder.
2. Select File, New, Shortcut.
3. When the Create Shortcut wizard opens, enter the location of the program you want to launch, or use the Browse button to navigate to and select that file. Click Next.
4. Enter a name for the shortcut, and then click the Finish button.

You can also add a program to the Startup menu by dragging the icon for that program onto the Startup folder.

SWITCHING BETWEEN PROGRAMS

After you've launched a program, it's easy to switch between that program and other open programs. You can

- Click the application's Taskbar button.
- Click the application's title bar.
- Click any visible part of the application's window.
- Hold down the Alt key and then press the Tab key repeatedly until the application window you want is selected. (This cycles through all open windows.) When you're at the window you want, release the Alt key.

If you have multiple windows open at the same time, you can determine which is currently the active window by its title bar. The title bar for the active program is brighter, and the title bar text is bright white. An inactive title bar is more dull, with off-white text. If you have overlapping windows on your desktop, the window on top is always the active one. The active application's Taskbar button looks like it's pressed in.

ARRANGING WINDOWS ON YOUR DESKTOP

Some users like to run all their programs full-screen. Others like to look at all their open programs at once, in overlapping windows. Still other users like to arrange their windows neatly on their desktop.

If you're a neatnik, it's easy to have Windows arrange your windows for you. All you have to do is right-click an open area of the Taskbar and then select one of the following options from the pop-up menu:

- *Cascade Windows* Creates a stack of windows starting at the top-left corner of your screen and continuing diagonally down and to the right, as shown in Figure 4.6.
- *Tile Windows Horizontally* Creates horizontal rows of windows on your desktop, as shown in Figure 4.7.
- *Tile Windows Vertically* Creates vertical columns of windows, as shown in Figure 4.8.

Figure 4.6

Arrange your windows in a cascade effect.

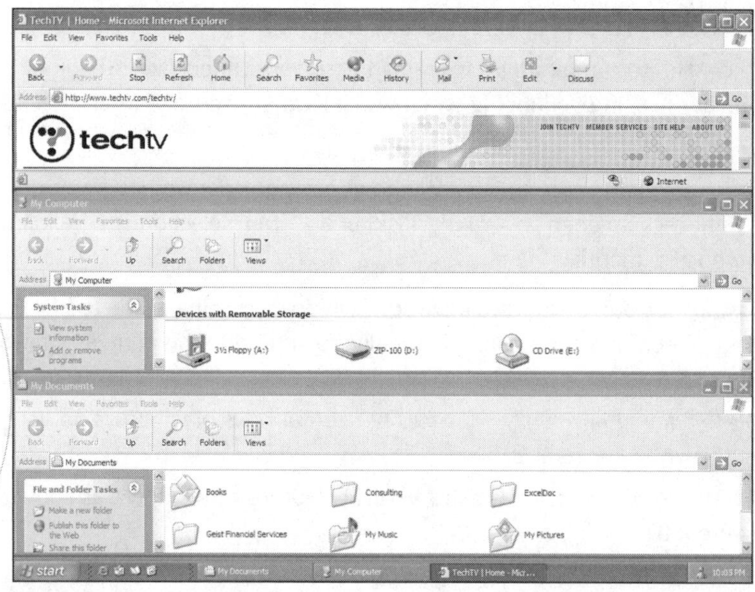

Figure 4.7

Arrange your windows in horizontal rows.

Figure 4.8

Arrange your windows in vertical columns.

CLOSING STUCK PROGRAMS

As robust as Windows XP is, there still are occasions where a program freezes on you. This is typically a less serious situation than with older versions of Windows, when a stuck program could bring down your entire system. Now when a program freezes, it seldom affects anything else. All you have to worry about is closing the stuck program.

The first thing to look at is whether the program is really stalled, or whether it's just slow. If your computer is low on memory, some programs might take *forever* to do some complex operations. You can run into this situation if you have a lot of programs open at the same time, or if you're printing a large file while you're trying to do something else.

You should probably wait a minute or so to see if the program eventually responds. If it doesn't, you should try switching to another open program, either from the Windows Taskbar or by pressing `Alt+Tab` to shuttle through all open programs.

If the program is definitely frozen, press `Ctrl+Alt+Del` (what old-timers call the "three-fingered salute") to display the Windows Task Manager. This is a souped-up version of the old Close Program dialog box found in previous versions of Windows, and it offers a lot more functionality. I discuss this utility in more depth in Chapter 22, "Keeping Windows Healthy and Happy," but for now let's just focus on using it to close frozen programs.

You can also open the Windows Task Manager by right-clicking the Taskbar and selecting Task Manager from the pop-up menu.

When the Windows Task Manager opens, select the Applications tab (shown in Figure 4.9). This tab displays a list of all programs currently running on your system.

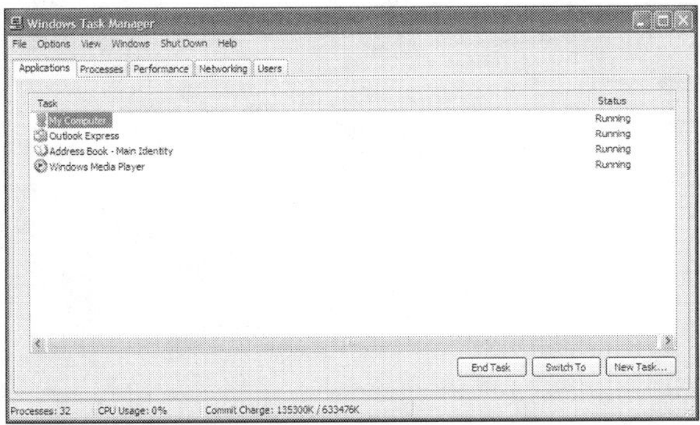

Figure 4.9

Use the Windows Task Manager to unstick stuck software.

If a program is frozen, this might be indicated in the Status column. Or it might not. In any case, you want to select the frozen program, and then click the End Task button. Nine times out of ten, this should take care of your problem.

If this doesn't make the program close, go back to the Windows Task Manager and click the Processes tab. Find the file that's frozen, select it, and then click the End Process button.

If you're forced to use the "end processes" method to shut down a program, you probably should restart Windows to clear up any loose ends still floating around system memory.

The worst-case scenario is that you can't close the frozen program no matter what you try, and it then starts to affect the rest of your system. If this happens to you, you need to restart Windows. If things get so bad you can't restart the operating system, you have to reboot your computer by pressing `Ctrl+Alt+Del` twice.

Very occasionally, that doesn't work either.

Then it's time to turn to sterner stuff. Try pressing your computer's on/off button. If that doesn't work, unplug your computer, or if you have a notebook, unplug it and remove the battery. That should work.

JIM'S TOP TEN TIPS

Installing, removing, and launching programs with Windows XP are all fairly commonsense activities. Just remember these top ten tips:

1. Whenever possible, use the built-in installation program that comes with a new software program.
2. If you have to install a program manually, use Windows XP's Add or Remove Programs utility.
3. You also use the Add or Remove Programs utility to uninstall programs from your hard disk.
4. Downloading and installing a commercial software program from the Internet is similar to installing the program from CD—after you sit through the program download, of course.
5. If you're looking for freeware or software programs to download, make sure they're Windows XP/2000-compatible. If you're not downloading from a major software archive, make sure you check the files for viruses.
6. With Windows XP, you can launch programs from the Start menu, from My Computer, from a desktop shortcut icon, or from the Run command.
7. To switch between open programs, click the appropriate Taskbar button—or press Alt+Tab to cycle through all open programs.
8. If you want a program to always launch when you start Windows, add the program to the Startup menu.
9. To neatly arrange all the open windows on your desktop, right-click the Taskbar and select one of the cascade or tile options.
10. To manually close a frozen program, press Ctrl+Alt+Del to open the Windows Task Manager, and then select the program and click the End Task button.

CHAPTER 5

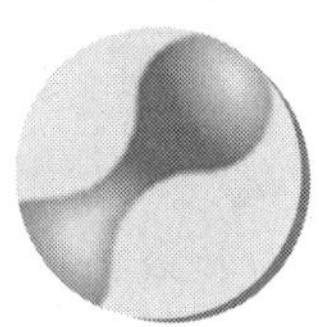

CONTROLLING PRINTERS

- Adding and Removing Printers
- Configuring Printers
- Managing the Printing Process
- Jim's Top Ten Tips

Windows has been pretty good at printer management for several versions now. You install the proper printer drivers, tell Windows which is your main (default) printer, and then you're ready to print. Unless you run into problems during a particular print job, printing is as simple as clicking the Print button from inside your favorite application.

Yes, you can still pause and cancel print jobs in progress. Yes, you can still install multiple printers on your system, and choose between then when it's time to print. (I show you how to do all these things, of course.) But, more often than not, I just click and print.

One relatively new feature in Windows XP is the ease in which you can set up a small network, and then share a printer between several different computers. If you're interested in this type of printer sharing, go directly to Chapter 18, "Setting Up a Home or Small Business Network." In that chapter I show you how to use Windows XP's Network Setup Wizard. You use this to set up all your networked peripherals.

ADDING AND REMOVING PRINTERS

Windows XP lets you hook up as many printers to your system as you have ports for. You can even install virtual printers (such as fax software) that enable you "print" to a file or program instead of to a physical printer.

In most cases, adding a new printer to your computer is as simple as plugging it in. Read on and I tell you all about it.

Adding a New Local Printer

If you have a Plug and Play-compatible printer, Windows XP, in most cases, recognizes your new printer the next time you start Windows. If your printer is not Plug and Play-compatible, Windows XP uses the Add Printer Wizard to assist you with installation.

To run the Add Printer Wizard, follow these steps:

1. From the Control Panel, click the Printers and Faxes icon.
2. When the Printers and Faxes utility opens, click the Add Printer icon to start the Add Printer wizard. When the first screen of the wizard appears, click the Next button.
3. If you're adding the printer to this PC, check the Local Printer option. If it's a PnP printer (and it probably is), you should also check the Automatically Detect and Install My Plug and Play Printer. Click the Next button.
4. When the next screen of the Wizard appears, select the printer's manufacturer in the Manufacturers list box (see Figure 5.1). Select the specific model of the printer in the Printers list box, and then click Next.

If your printer is not on the list, either choose the Generic Manufacturer and Generic/Text Only printer or click the Have Disk button and follow instructions to install a vendor-supplied driver.

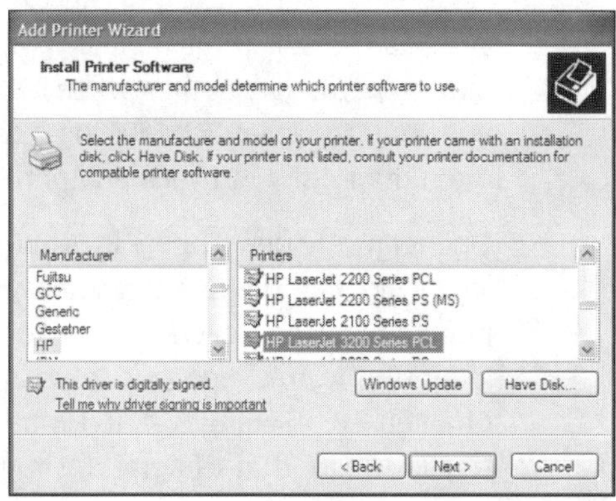

Figure 5.1

To install a new local printer, just pick the right make and model from the list.

5. When the next screen of the Wizard appears, select the port to which the printer is connected, and then click Next.
6. In the Printer Name text box, type a name for the printer or keep the name that is displayed. Select the Yes option button if you want this to be your default printer. (If a different printer is the default printer, choose No.) Click the Next button.
7. The Printer Sharing page now appears. If you want to share this printer with other computers on the network, check the Share Name option and enter a "share name" for the computer. (This is the name other users see when they print to this printer.) If you don't want to share, check the Do Not Share This Printer option. Click Next.
8. When the next page appears, select Yes if you want to print a test page, and then click Next.
9. The test page prints (if you selected Yes). Click the Finish button, and the proper drivers are installed to your system, and your installation is complete.

If the test page does not print correctly, you can work through any potential problems with Windows XP's Print Troubleshooter. Just click the Start button and select Help and Support. When the Help and Support Services window appears, click the Printing and Faxing link, click Printing, and then click Fix a Printing Problem. Follow the onscreen steps to track down and fix your specific problem.

Adding a Connection to a Network Printer

If your computer is part of a network (even a small home network), you need to add a connection to the network printer.

If the printer has been configured, on its host computer, as a "shared" printer, your work may have already been done for you. In many cases, shared printers automatically show up in the printers list of all computers connected to the network.

This section assumes that the printer is connected to another computer on your network. If the printer is connected to the current computer, you don't have to do anything beyond the normal printer installation.

If the shared printer *doesn't* appears in your printers list, this is what you need to do:

1. From the Control Panel, click the Printers and Faxes icon.
2. When the Printers and Faxes utility opens, click the Add Printer icon to start the Add Printer wizard. When the first screen of the wizard appears, click the Next button.
3. To setup a connection to a network computer, check the Printer Connection option and then click Next.
4. When the Specify a Printer screen appears (shown in Figure 5.2), click the Browse For a Printer option, and then click Next.

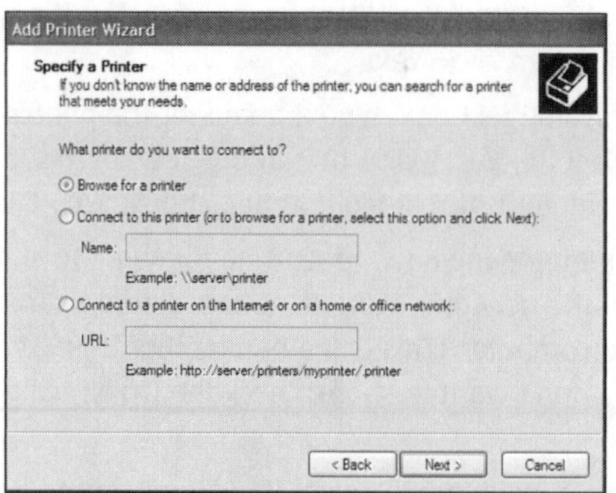

Figure 5.2

Choose a printer on your network that you want to share.

5. When the Browse for Printer screen appears, select the printer you want to connect to, and then click the Next button.

Only those printers that have been designated for printer sharing are available in the Add Printer Wizard. As described in Chapter 18, you set printer sharing from the computer that the printer is physically attached to.

6. Follow the onscreen instructions to finish connecting to the network printer.

Deleting an Existing Printer

If you no longer need to have a particular printer installed, you can delete it from your system by following these steps:

1. From the Control Panel, click the Printers and Faxes icon.
2. When the Printers and Faxes utility opens, select the printer you want to delete.
3. Click Delete This Printer in the activity center Tasks list.
4. Windows asks if you are sure that you want to delete the printer. Choose Yes. The printer icon is deleted.
5. Windows then asks if it can remove files that were used only for this printer. Choose Yes. (However, if you plan to reattach this printer in the future, choose No.)

That's that. Just make sure that you physically disconnect the printer, or else Windows "rediscovers" the printer and try to reinstall it.

CONFIGURING PRINTERS

Normally you don't have to do any configuration to your printers beyond what takes place during installation. However, it is possible to configure your printers for specific types of printing and it's relatively easy to do.

Setting Printer Properties

After you install a printer in Windows XP, you can make changes to the configuration to customize it for different printing requirements. You make these changes in the printer's Properties dialog box.

1. From the Control Panel, click the Printers and Faxes icon.
2. When the Printers and Faxes utility opens, select the printer you want to reconfigure, and then click Set Printer Properties in the activity center Tasks list.
3. The Properties dialog box opens, as shown in Figure 5.3). This dialog box contains several tabs. Select each tab to view the various settings, as explained in Table 5.1. Properties vary according to each printer's capabilities.

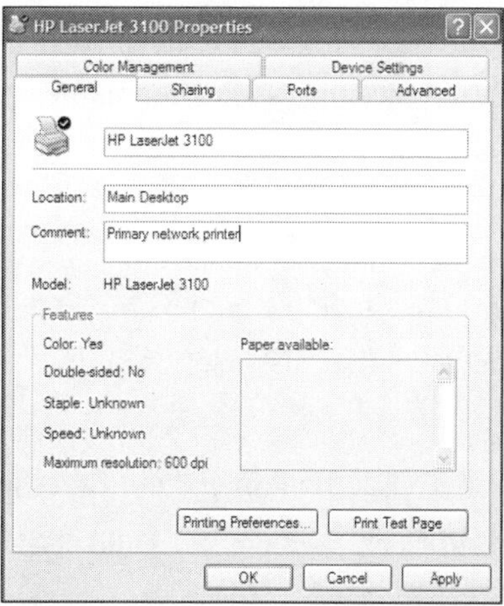

Figure 5.3

Use the Properties dialog box to configure your printer.

4. Change settings as desired, and then choose OK to save the new settings. Choose Cancel if you prefer to abandon all changes.

TABLE 5.1—PRINTER PROPERTIES

Tab	Properties
General	Enters comments about this printer. Click the Print Test Page button to test your printer's output. Click the Printing Preferences button to set orientation, page order, and default tray for the printer.
Sharing	Determines whether your printer is shared by other users on your network.
Ports	Selects and configures which port your printer uses.
Advanced	Sets printer availability, print spooling, and other advanced settings.
Device Settings	Determines settings specific to your model printer, such as print density, print quality, and printer memory.

The tabs in the Properties dialog box may vary depending on the type of printer you have. For example, many color printers have a Color Management tab you can use to set the printer's color options. Please adjust my instructions dependent on the tabs present in your specific configuration.

Renaming an Existing Printer

The Add Printer Wizard gives you an option to name the printer when you install it. You can rename the printer later without reinstalling it. The name is changed throughout Windows after you rename the printer.

1. From the Control Panel, click the Printers and Faxes icon.
2. When the Printers and Faxes utility opens, select the printer you want to rename, and then click Rename This Printer in the activity center Tasks list.
3. Type a new name to replace the highlighted name and press Enter.

Selecting the Default Printer

The *default* printer is the printer that your applications automatically use when you choose to print a document. If you have multiple printers hooked up to your computer—including printers shared over a network—you need to select one of them as your default printer.

Follow these steps:

1. From the Control Panel, click the Printers and Faxes icon.
2. When the Printers and Faxes utility opens, right-click the printer you want as your default printer.
3. When the pop-up menu appears, select Set as Default Printer.

The default printer appears with a check mark next to its icon in the Printers and Faxes window.

Choosing Between Multiple Printers

When you go to print a document from any Windows application, the document is automatically printed to the default printer. (This happens when you click the Print button, or select File, Print.)

If you want to print to another printer, you have to do a little extra work. Just follow these steps:

1. From within your application, select File, Print.
2. When the Print dialog box appears, pull down the Printer list and select the printer you want to use.
3. Make any other selections from this dialog box, and then click the OK button to begin printing.

MANAGING THE PRINTING PROCESS

After you've started printing, the print job is first sent to a buffer on your computer, and then to a buffer in your printer. If it's a particularly long print job, this arrangement enables you to pause or cancel the job in mid-stream.

Managing Print Jobs from Print Manager

Print Manager is used to control print jobs sent to a printer. A separate manager for each printer is installed on your system. If the jobs you have sent to a printer aren't so small that they go directly to the printer, you should have time to double-click the printer icon that appears in the Windows System Tray. After the printer icon disappears from the System Tray, you can only control the print job at the printer itself.

You can open the Print Manager by clicking a particular printer icon in the Printers and Faxes utility, or by double-clicking the printer icon in the System Tray.

Checking the Status of a Print Job

After you open the Print Manager, you can quickly check the status of any print jobs in process.

First, you can look at the jobs in the queue and view their status (printing, paused, or spooling) in the Status column, as shown in Figure 5.4. You can also view the status bar to see the number of jobs remaining to be printed. Select View, Status Bar to turn the status bar on and off.

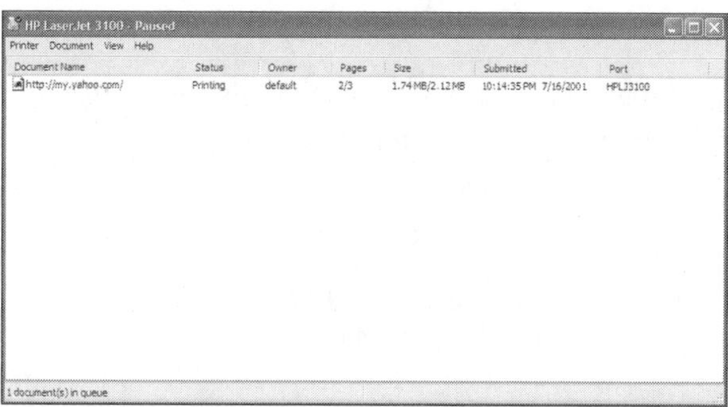

Figure 5.4

Use Print Manager to view the status of all current print jobs.

Pausing a Print Job

If you have multiple print jobs on a single printer, you can choose to pause specific print jobs and continue printing all jobs that are not paused.

To pause a print job, follow these steps:

1. Double-click the printer icon in the System Tray to open the Print Manager.

2. Select one or more documents from the print queue list.
3. Select Document, Pause Printing.

To pause a document quickly, right-click its entry in the print queue and then choose Pause Printing from the pop-up menu.

Pausing a specific print job is not the same as pausing all printing. To pause all current print jobs from Print Manager, select Printer, Pause Printing.

Resuming a Paused Print Job

Usually you pause a print job so that you can restart it later. Maybe you want to change to a different paper stock or change the toner. The job remains paused in Print Manager until you restart it or cancel it.

To continue printing a paused print job, follow these steps:

1. Double-click the printer icon in the System Tray to open the Print Manager.
2. Select the paused document.
3. Select Document, Pause Printing. The selected document no longer displays a Paused status and begins printing in its place in queue.

Canceling a Print Job

You can cancel a print job in the print queue even if it has started to print.

Follow these steps:

1. Open the Print Manager by double-clicking the printer icon on the System Tray.
2. Select one or more documents from the print queue list.
3. Select Document, Cancel Printing.

To cancel printing a document quickly, right-click its entry in the print queue and then choose Cancel Printing from the pop-up menu.

When you cancel a print job, it disappears immediately from the print queue. You may want to try pausing the job first to be sure you are canceling the right job.

Purging All Print Jobs

Purging removes all the queued print jobs. You can purge all the jobs that have not started to print.

Follow these steps:

1. Double-click the printer icon in the System Tray to open the Print Manager.
2. Select Printer, Purge Print Jobs.

JIM'S TOP TEN TIPS

I told you that printing was easy with Windows XP! These are the ten most important points to remember:

1. You can install multiple printers on a single PC, although you have to select one of these printers as your default printer.
2. Use the Add Printer Wizard to add new printers—both local printers and printers installed on other computers on a network.
3. You can use the Add Printer Wizard to enable sharing of a printer with other computers on a network.
4. Settings for each printer are set via individual Properties dialog boxes.
5. When you have more than one computer connected to your system, use your application's Print dialog box to select which printer to print to.
6. The Windows Print Manager enables you to manage all print jobs in progress. You open the Print Manager by clicking a printer's icon in the Printers and Faxes dialog box, or by double-clicking the printer icon in the Windows System Tray.
7. To temporarily pause a print job, double-click the printer icon in the System Tray, select the print job, and then select Document, Pause Printing.
8. To resume a paused print job, double-click the printer icon in the System Tray, select the print job, and then select Document, Pause Printing.
9. To cancel a specific print job, double-click the printer icon in the System Tray, select the print job, and then select Document, Cancel Printing.
10. To purge all pending print jobs, double-click the printer icon in the System Tray, and then select Printer, Purge Print Jobs.

CHAPTER 6

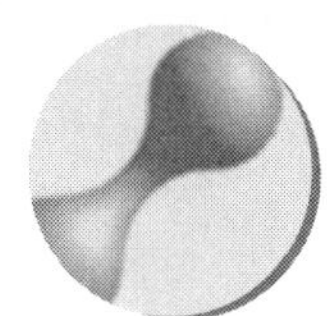

ADDING NEW HARDWARE

- Understanding Ports
- Installing New Peripherals
- Updating Device Drivers
- Solving Device Conflicts
- Most Popular Peripherals
- Working with Hardware Profiles
- Jim's Top Ten Tips

In the early days of personal computing (not that long ago, really), adding new hardware to a computer system was a pain in the rear. You had to work with jumpers and manually install device drivers and get your hands dirty with all sorts of system configuration files. And then, after all that hassle, half the time the new hardware still wouldn't work.

I don't miss those days. At all.

Fortunately, technology has improved. And the operating system has improved. So now it's relatively easy to plug in something new, and have it work like it should—first time out.

A lot of this improvement is due to better device recognition and compatibility in Windows. Microsoft introduced Plug and Play (PnP) technology several years ago, with the express purpose of easing installation headaches. And, while early versions were more like "plug and *pray*," PnP works pretty good in Windows XP.

Which is a good thing, given all the peripherals we plug into our PCs these days. It's not unusual to soup up a factory-standard machine with a printer or two, a scanner, a PC camera, a digital still camera, a joystick, a CD burner, and a network connection. That's a lot of stuff to hook up to a single PC, but Windows XP will handle it.

Read on and I'll tell you how.

UNDERSTANDING PORTS

Everything that's hooked up to your PC is connected via some kind of *port*. A port is simply an interface between your PC and another device—whether that connection is internal (inside your PC's system unit) or external (via a connector on the back of the system unit).

There are many different kinds of ports, each optimized for a different type of data communication. Different types of hardware connect via different types of ports.

You can take a look at all the ports on your PC, and the devices connected to them, with Windows XP's Device Manager utility. As you can see in Figure 6.1, the Device Manager displays all your devices by type. When you double-click a device type, you see the specific devices of that type that are installed on your system. Double-click a specific device to display the Properties dialog box for that device.

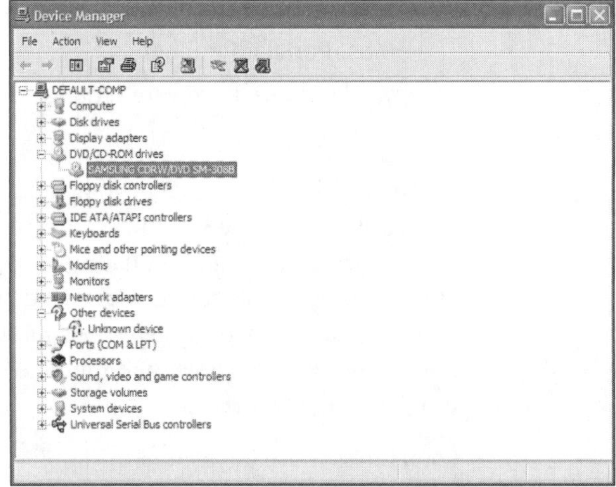

Figure 6.1

Use the Device Manager to examine all the ports and devices on your system.

You open the Device Manager like this:

1. From the Control Panel, click the System icon to open the System Properties utility.
2. Select the Hardware tab, then click the Device Manager button.
3. When the Device Manager opens, select View, Devices by Type.

You can also open Device Manager by right-clicking on My Computer and selecting Properties from the pop-up menu.

Serial Ports

A serial port is an interface that allows communication one bit at a time. That means that a device can't send multiple streams of data, and it also means that data can only flow in one direction at a time. Serial ports are used to connect modems, printers, mice, and similar peripherals.

Parallel Ports

A parallel port is an interface that can handle communications going in two directions at once. Parallel ports are typically used to connect printers, and are often referred to as printer ports.

USB Ports

A Universal Serial Bus (USB) port is a newer, faster, more intelligent type of serial port. USB devices can be added while the computer is still running, and be automatically recognized by the operating system. You can use USB ports to connect just about type of device, including printers, scanners, modems, CD-ROM/DVD drives, hard drives, Zip drives, PC cameras, digital still cameras, keyboards, mice, and joysticks.

Windows XP supports the original USB standard, but does not yet support the newer USB2 standard—which ups the transmission speed beyond FireWire and SCSI levels. Expect USB2 support to be added via an update at some later date.

FireWire Ports

FireWire (also called IEEE 1394) is an interface that enables hot-pluggable high-speed data transmission. It's typically used to connect digital video cameras and recorders—although some external hard drives and CD burners are coming out with FireWire connections, as well. I eventually expect FireWire devices to become even more popular as XP takes off—eventually supplanting USB as the most common external device interconnection port.

SCSI Ports

The Small Computer System Interface (SCSI, pronounced "skuzzy") port is a high-speed parallel interface. You use SCSI ports to connect hard disks, CD-ROM and DVD drives, Zip drives, tape backups, and other mass storage media—as well as some scanners and printers. You should know, though, that SCSI is quickly losing ground to the faster FireWire.

PCMCIA Ports

The Personal Computer Memory Card International Association (PCMCIA) established the standard for the PC Card interface used on most of today's portable PCs. On a portable PC, the PC Card slot can be used to connect everything from modems, miniature hard disks, and additional system memory.

INSTALLING NEW PERIPHERALS

In most cases, connecting a new device to your computer is a simple operation that goes something like this:

1. Close Windows and turn off your PC.
2. Connect the new device.
3. Restart your computer.
4. As Windows starts, it should recognize the new device, and either install the proper drivers automatically or ask you to supply the device drivers (via CD-ROM or diskette).
5. Windows installs the drivers and finishes the startup procedure. Your new device should now be operational.

A device driver is a small software program that enables your PC to communicate with and control a specific device. Windows XP includes built-in device drivers for many popular peripherals. If Windows doesn't include a particular driver, you can typically find the driver on the peripheral's installation disk, or on the peripheral manufacturer's Web site.

This procedure should work with both external devices and boards that you insert into your PC's internal slots.

Installing a new device is this easy because of the almost-universal support of Plug and Play. It's because of PnP that Windows recognizes the new devices you connect.

In fact, if you're connecting a FireWire or USB device, you don't even have to turn off your PC. The USB connection is more intelligent than other types of connections, and a USB can be plugged in and operational without rebooting your machine.

There are still occasions, however, where Windows doesn't recognize a new peripheral. There are many causes for this. The device might be an older one that isn't PnP-compatible. Windows might not have a record of that particular device in its internal database. Or it could just be that the moon and the stars aren't aligned quite right.

Whatever the cause, if Windows doesn't recognize your new device, you have to install the device manually. With Windows XP, even manual installation is automated, thanks to the Add Hardware Wizard.

This wizard walks you step-by-step through the installation process. It starts by trying to recognize the new device itself. If it still doesn't recognize the device, it asks you to identify the device, and to supply the proper device driver. Once the driver is supplied, it completes the installation for you.

To use the Add Hardware Wizard, follow these steps:

1. From the Control Panel, click the Add Hardware icon.
2. When the Add Hardware Wizard opens, click the Next button.
3. Windows now evaluates your system and displays a list of installed devices, as shown in Figure 6.2. To add a new device, select Add a New Hardware Device from the list, and click the Next button.

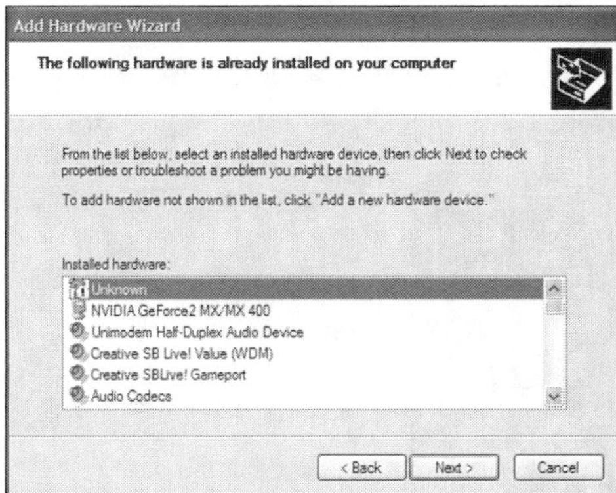

Figure 6.2

The Add Hardware Wizard starts by identifying all the hardware installed on your PC.

4. When the next screen appears, select Search For and Install the Hardware Automatically, then click Next.
5. Windows now looks for new PnP hardware. If it can identify the new hardware, the wizard will continue with the installation. If it can't find a new device, it will tell you so. If this is your situation, click Next to begin a manual installation.
6. Select the type of device you want to install, then click Next.
7. On the next screen, select the manufacturer and specific device. If you want to install the drivers that came with the device, click the Have Disk button. To use a built-in Windows driver, click the Next button.
8. When the necessary files have been loaded, follow the onscreen instructions to complete the installation.

UPDATING DEVICE DRIVERS

The most appropriate drivers for your hardware are installed when Windows XP is first installed, or when you install a new peripheral. You can upgrade your drivers at any time,

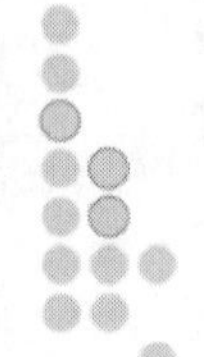

however—if new drivers are available. (Manufacturers constantly update their drivers, typically to fix bugs or incompatibilities.)

To upgrade a specific device driver:

1. From the Control Panel, click the System icon.
2. When the System Properties utility opens, select the Hardware tab and then click the Device Manager button.
3. When the Device Manager utility opens, select View, Devices by Type, and then navigate to the device you want to update.
4. Double-click the device's icon to open the Properties dialog box.
5. When the Properties dialog box appears, click the Driver tab, and then click the Upgrade Driver button.
6. When the Hardware Update Wizard appears (as shown in Figure 6.3), check the Install the Software Automatically button and click the Next button.

Figure 6.3

Use the Hardware Update Wizard to find and install updated device drivers.

7. Follow the onscreen instructions to find and install the updated driver. If you have the latest version of the driver already installed, the wizard will tell you this.

If you think you need an updated device driver (of any type), go to DriverGuide.com (`www.driverguide.com`), Drivers.com (`www.drivers.com`), or WinDrivers.com (`www.windrivers.com`). All these sites contain massive databases of drivers and related resources, all available for easy download.

SOLVING DEVICE CONFLICTS

The Device Manager can also be used to review hardware settings and to determine where devices may have conflicts. A conflict happens when two devices try to use the same port, and get in each other's way. You can generally resolve these conflicts by assigning one of the devices to another port.

When you open the Device Manager, look for items that have an exclamation point displayed next to their names. These are the devices that are currently acting up.

Double-click the problematic device to display the Properties dialog box, and then click on the General tab. You'll see a message indicating the basic problem, and advising what steps to take to fix it. (If the dialog box displays a Troubleshooting button, click this button to initiate a more comprehensive troubleshooting procedure.)

Following the instructions provided in this dialog box will generally solve your problem. If not, make sure you write down any problem code or number displayed in the Properties dialog box. They might come in useful if you have to deal with technical support.

If you've just installed a new device and run into immediate problems, chances are that the new driver is the cause. Windows XP provides a way to back your way out of new installation problems, by "rolling back" the driver to a previous version. Just select the Driver tab in the driver Properties dialog box, and then click the Roll Back Driver button. Windows will now uninstall the new driver and reinstall the old one—which should put your system back in the same working shape it was before.

If you still have problems, click the Uninstall button to completely delete the problematic driver, and then start the installation process again from scratch. Sometimes you have to do things twice to get them to work.

For more detailed information on finding and fixing system problems, see Chapter 24, "Troubleshooting Common Problems."

MOST POPULAR PERIPHERALS

When it comes to adding stuff to your PC, what are the most popular peripherals? Here's a top ten list of hardware you can add to or upgrade on your system, along with some tips on how Windows XP might handle the new devices.

Video Cards

If you want to display a higher-resolution picture on your computer screen, you have to start with a higher-performance video card. This procedure is as simple as swapping out the old card for a new one. Windows should recognize your new video card on restart, and make the necessary configuration changes automatically.

Even if Windows automatically identifies your new video card, it might not always uninstall your old card. You may need to do this manually, from the old video card's Properties dialog box (accessible from the Device Manager).

You can also install additional video cards to use with multiple monitors. To learn more about Windows XP's multiple-display capabilities, turn to the "Setting Up Windows for Two Monitors" section in Chapter 2, "Changing the Way Windows Looks—and Acts."

Sound Cards

If you play high-end games, listen to high bit-rate MP3s, watch surround-sound DVD movies, or mix and record digital audio, you may want to upgrade your PC's sound card. While the replacement is a simple procedure, you may need to tweak your system's audio configuration to take advantage of all the functionality of the new card.

You can configure all sorts of audio properties by clicking the Sounds and Audio Devices icon in the Control Panel. This displays the Sound and Audio Devices Properties utility.

Select the Audio tab (shown in Figure 6.4) to select and configure specific devices for sound playback, sound recording, and MIDI music playback. Select the Voice tab to select and configure devices for voice playback and recording. Select the Hardware tab to configure the properties for specific multimedia drivers.

Figure 6.4

Use the Sound and Audio Devices Properties utility to configure your new sound card.

Keyboards

Installing a new keyboard is as simple as unplugging the old one and plugging in the new one. You may want to replace your PC's standard keyboard with a more ergonomic model, or with a wireless keyboard. (Or both—I particularly like Logitech's ergonomic wireless keyboard, which lets me type while I'm leaning back with my feet up on my desk!) You can even have two keyboards at once—by adding a USB keyboard to your system.

Once you install a new keyboard, you can set various properties that affect the way it works. In particular, you can set the character repeat rate, cursor blink rate, the language, and the keyboard type. You can also select multiple languages for your keyboard and switch between them.

You change keyboard properties by opening the Control Panel and clicking the Keyboard icon. This opens the Keyboard Properties utility, as shown in Figure 6.5. Most of what you want to adjust can be found on the Speed tab.

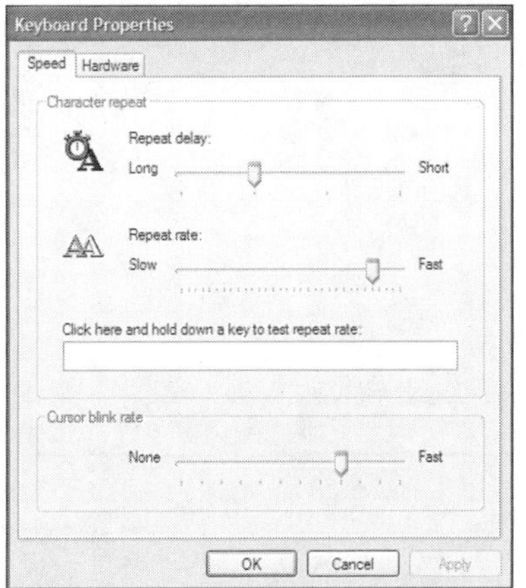

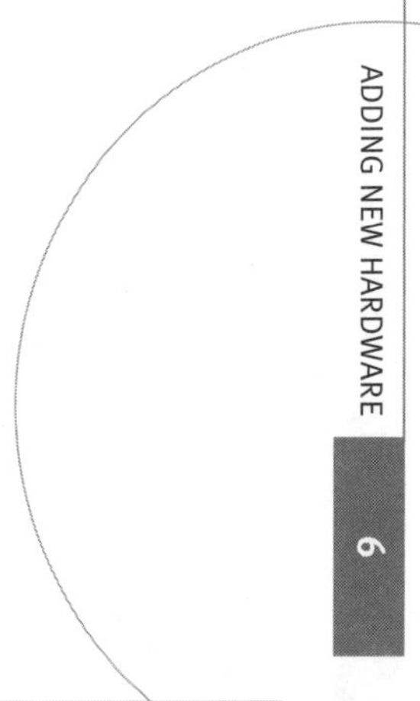

Figure 6.5

Use the Keyboard Properties utility to change various keyboard options, such as repeat rate and delay.

Mice

Replacing your mouse is as easy as replacing your keyboard. If you're still using the generic mouse that came with your PC, you should definitely take a look at the newer models available today. You'll find optical mice, wireless mice, and alternative mice (trackballs, and so on). I guarantee that you'll find some kind of input device that you like better than the one you're currently using!

Since some mice have extra buttons or wheels, it's likely that the mouse will come with it's own installation program. When you run this program, the proper device drivers will be installed—and additional features added to Windows' Mouse Properties utility.

You open the Mouse Properties utility by clicking the Mouse icon in the Control Panel. As you can see in Figure 6.6, all mice share the same basic tabs (Buttons, Pointers, Pointer Options, and Hardware). Some mouse models add their own proprietary tabs for their own specific features. It might be worthwhile to click through the tabs to see what kinds of functionality your specific mouse offers—and select the desired settings, as appropriate.

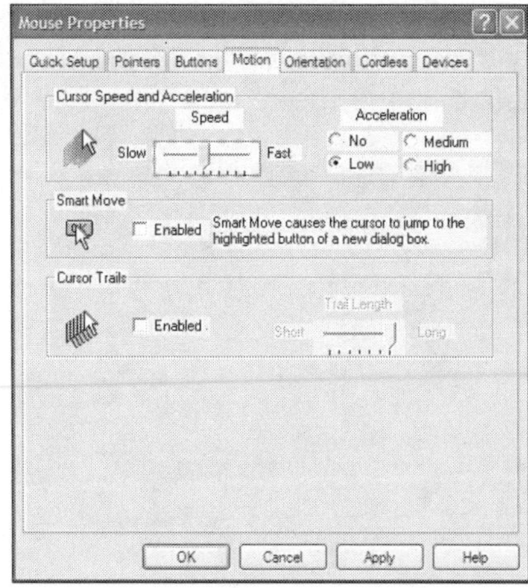

Figure 6.6

Configure your mouse with the Mouse Properties utility.

Joysticks

There are many brands and types of joysticks and game controllers available for use with PC games. Connecting a new device is as simple as plugging it in (and running the installation program, if there is one). Go with a USB joystick and you get the immediate gratification of using it as soon as you plug it in.

You can configure a new game controller by clicking the Game Controllers icon in the Control Panel. This opens the Game Controllers dialog box. Select the Settings tab to calibrate your joystick and configure additional settings.

Learn more about using Windows XP with games and gaming devices in Chapter 17, "Playing Games."

Modems

Most new PCs come with an internal 56.6Kbps modem installed. This is the fastest dial-up modem available today, so you probably won't have any need to install a new one.

If you do need to install a new modem, you can choose from an internal or an external model. Internal modems are less hassle, even though you have to open up your system unit to plug them in. External modems take up valuable desk space, need to be plugged in to a power supply, and are sometimes more difficult to configure. If you have a choice, go with an internal one.

When you need to change the settings for your modem, click the Phone and Modem Options icon in the Control. This opens the Phone and Modem Options utility, where you can set a number of configuration options.

To set driver, performance, and other settings specific to your modem, select the Modems tab, select the modem, and click the Properties button. To configure *how* your modem dials, select the Dialing Rules tab, select your location, and click the Edit button. This opens the Edit Location dialog box (shown in Figure 6.7), which lets you specify which number the modem dials to get an outside line, whether or not to disable call waiting, and so on.

If you intend to use your modem from another location, or from a hotel room, click the New button on the Dialing Rules tab to create a new location with different dialing rules.

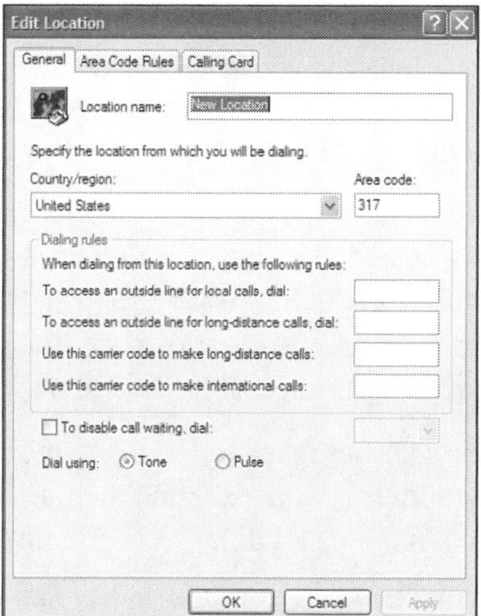

Figure 6.7

Don't forget to set the dialing rules for your modem—or create new rules for a new location.

If you're setting up your system for use with a broadband Internet connection–via DSL or a cable modem–the setup is completely different. Yes, you'll still use a modem (typically supplied by your Internet service provider), but the modem will either connect to a network card in your PC, or through your PC's USB port. See Chapter 7, "Making the Connection," for more information on this type of hookup.

DVD and CD-ROM Drives

Most PCs come with either a CD-ROM or a DVD drive as standard. (A DVD drive will also read CD-ROM discs.) If you have a CD-ROM drive, you may want to upgrade to or add a DVD drive. You may also want to add a recordable/rewritable CD drive to burn your own CDs.

Recordable CDs are designated CD-R, and rewritable CDs are designated CD-RW. Most drives can burn both recordable and rewritable CDs, and are designated as CD-R/RW drives.

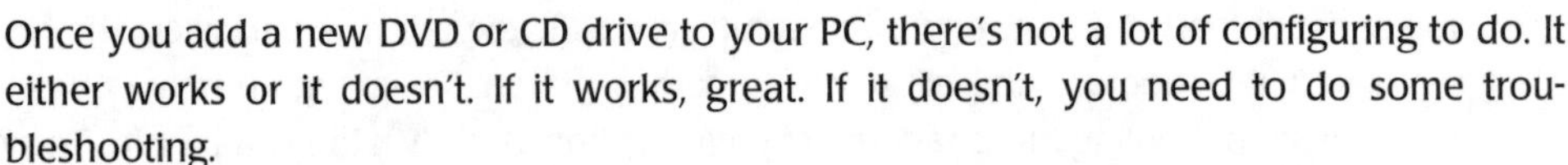

Once you add a new DVD or CD drive to your PC, there's not a lot of configuring to do. It either works or it doesn't. If it works, great. If it doesn't, you need to do some troubleshooting.

When a DVD or CD drive is properly installed, it should appear in My Computer as a new Device with Removable Storage, alongside your floppy diskette and Zip drives. You can access the contents of the drive from My Computer as you would any other drive. If you have a CD-R/RW drive, you can copy files and folders to a blank disc by using Windows' normal copy command—or by dragging and dropping files onto the CD-R/RW drive icon.

Hard Drives

Managing new hard drives is easier in Windows XP than in Windows 9X/Me, because there are fewer options. In most instances you don't have to do a lot of formatting or partitioning, because XP recognizes and works with today's very large hard disks.

Windows XP recognizes three different hard disk file systems: NTFS, FAT, and FAT32. NTFS is Microsoft's preferred file system, because it works best with ultra-large hard disks. It's also compatible with Microsoft's Active Directory service, which is used by network administrators to manage network security. Know, however, that most current disk utilities don't work with NTFS yet, although this is bound to change over time.

If you want to convert an older hard disk to NTFS, the process is surprisingly easy. If your hard disk is blank (or if you don't mind losing all the data on it), you can *format* the disk as NTFS. If you want to retain the disk's data, you can *convert* the drive from FAT or FAT32 to NTFS.

After you convert from FAT32 to NTFS, you can't go back. Also, if you're using NTFS, you can't boot your computer from DOS. In addition, you can't convert to NTFS is you're using a dual-OS box, like if you're running both Linux and Windows from the same hard disk—or running an older version of Windows along with XP.

To convert an existing drive, you have to open the Command Prompt utility and then run the following command:

convert *x*: /fs:ntfs

Naturally, you replace *x* with the letter of the drive you want to convert.

Formatting a drive is a more destructive process—although it's amazingly simple to do. Just follow these steps:

1. From within My Computer, select File, Format.
2. When the Format Disk dialog box appears (as shown in Figure 6.8), confirm the drive's capacity, select NTFS as the File System, and select Default Allocation Size as the Allocation Unit Size.
3. Click Start to begin the formatting process.

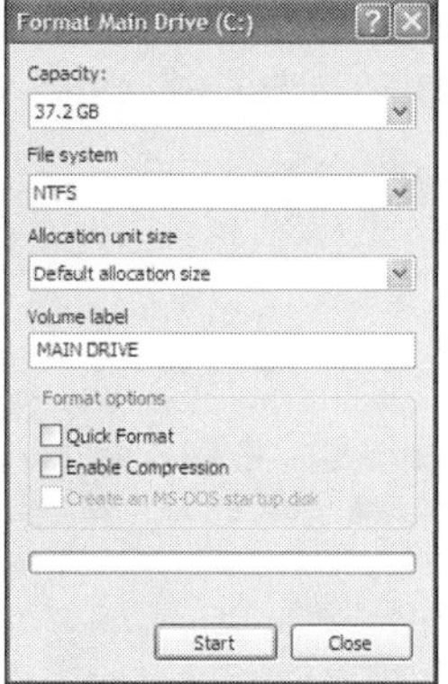

Figure 6.8

Formatting a hard disk is easy—*too* easy, if you're not careful!

Formatting a drive permanently erases all data stored on the drive. You cannot format the hard disk that contains your PC's system information (typically drive c:).

Scanners

A desktop scanner is an essential part of many users' PC systems. Scanners have come down in price to where they're quite affordable, and they're relatively easy to install and use.

If you have the option, go with a scanner that connects via your computer's USB or FireWire port. USB and FireWire scanners require very little setup. When you connect the scanner, Windows XP will recognize it and begin the driver installation process. If you're lucky Windows will have a device driver for your scanner. If not, you'll have to insert the scanner's installation disc to download the proper driver.

If Windows does not recognize your scanner, you can add the scanner to you system via the new Scanners and Cameras utility. Just click the Scanners and Cameras icon in the Control panel, and when the utility opens, click the Add Device icon. This starts the Scanner and Camera Installation Wizard, which walks you step-by-step through the installation.

When your scanner is installed, you can link the scanner to a particular program. For example, you can configure Windows to automatically open a specific image editing program when you click a scanned image anywhere on your system.

Follow these steps:

1. From the Control Panel, click the Scanners and Cameras icon to open the Scanners and Cameras utility.
2. Select the scanner you want to configure, then click View Device Properties from the activity center Tasks list.

3. When the Properties dialog box appears, select the Events tab.
4. In the Scanner Events section, select the event you want to link to a program.
5. In the Send to This Application section, select the program you want to link to the selected event.
6. Click OK.

To learn more about using Windows XP with scanners and cameras, see Chapter 12, "Working with Digital Cameras and Scanners."

Digital Cameras

One way to get digital images into your PC is by scanning existing photographs with a desktop scanner. A better method is to take your photographs digitally to begin with, and then transfer those digital files directly to your hard disk.

You take digital photographs with a digital camera. Digital cameras connect to a PC pretty much the same way scanners do—ideally, via your system's USB port. In fact, the way Windows XP handles digital cameras is identical to the way it handles scanners. Use the Scanners and Cameras utility to both install your camera and configure it, then work with it from My Computer as you would any other device.

PC Cameras

A PC camera is a small camera that sits on top of or beside your computer monitor, and transmits live video images directly to your computer. You can use PC cameras to take digital photographs or videos of yourself, which you can then send via e-mail or post on your Web site. You can also use a PC camera to create a Webcam, which is a live stream of photographs, updated every few minutes, which are transmitted over the Web for all to see.

Webcams are very popular these days, partly because PC cameras are so cheap and easy to use. If you buy a USB model, installing it is as easy as plugging it in. Windows handles the PC camera as it would any other type of input device, such as a digital still camera. Your chief chore will be interfacing the camera with your Webcam software, configuring your Webcam software to work with your Web site, and coding your Web site to display your Webcam pictures.

There are many Web sites that offer Webcam hosting services. Most of these sites also provide the information and software necessary to set up your own Webcam. If you're really interested in Webcasting your activities all across the Internet, check out the information and services at AllCam (`www.allcam.com`), Camarades (`www.camarades.com`), WebCam World (`www.webcamworld.com`), or WebCam Resource (`stage.webcamresource.com`). Then get ready to put your life on display, 24/7!

There's an eleventh peripheral that should be added to this top ten list—the network interface card. Instead, I devote an entire chapter to installing network cards and setting up a home network. Flip forward to Chapter 18, "Setting Up a Home or Small Business Network," to learn more.

WORKING WITH HARDWARE PROFILES

After you get all the hardware and peripherals on your system set up and ready to go, you should be set—right? That might be true if your PC is a desktop model, but if you have a laptop that you use both at work and at home, you're faced with a new problem. You can configure your laptop for all the peripherals you use at work, but what do you do when you bring the computer home? Now you have to hook it up to a completely different set of peripherals, which can be a royal pain to reconfigure.

Fortunately for laptop users, Windows XP lets you create multiple hardware profiles for your PC, each with a different configuration, for the changing equipment you use. A laptop used with and without a docking bay is a prime system for creating additional profiles—one profile for docked operation, and a second for undocked mode.

I'll level with you. Hardware profiles are notoriously difficult to use. So difficult that few people use them. (I know I don't!) The reality is that Windows XP does a pretty good job recognizing what's hooked up and what's not, so that you really don't need to create separate profiles for different locations.

Still, if you want to play around with profiles, be my guest. Read on and I'll tell you how.

Creating New Hardware Profiles

You create a new profile by copying and renaming an existing profile. When a hardware profile is highlighted and copied, its exact configuration is assumed by the new copy. All you have to do is assign a new name to reflect the new configuration.

Here's how you create a new hardware profile:

1. From the Control Panel, click the System icon to open the System Properties utility.
2. Select the Hardware tab and then click the Hardware Profiles button.
3. When the Hardware Properties dialog box appears (see Figure 6.9), select a hardware profile (such as Original Configuration) and click the Copy button.

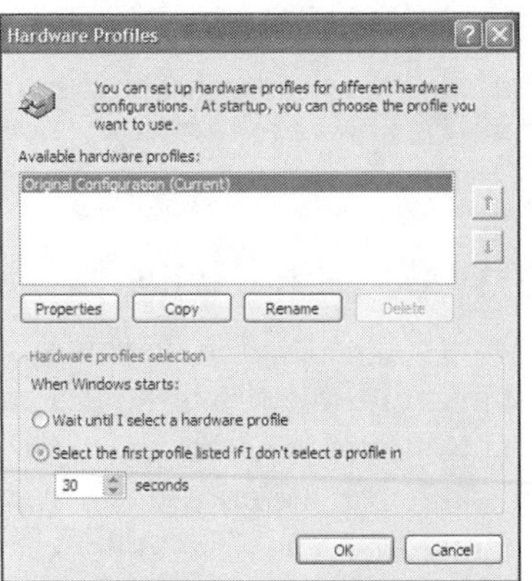

Figure 6.9

Create a new hardware profile for a laptop computer.

4. When the Copy Profile dialog box appears, type a new name for the profile over the original name in the To field, then click OK.

Configuring Hardware Profiles

Once you've created a new profile, you can configure it by selecting which devices are used by that profile. Here's how to do it:

1. Open the Device Manager and double-click a device.
2. When the device Properties dialog box appears, select the General tab and pull down the Device Usage list. If you want to use this device in the current profile, select Use This Device; if you don't want to use this device, select Do Not Use This Device In the Current Hardware Profile.
3. Repeat Step 2 for any devices you want to activate or deactivate for the current hardware profile.

You can also configure some general settings for each of your hardware profiles.

1. In the Hardware Profiles dialog box, select the profile you want to configure, then click the Properties button.
2. When the Properties dialog box appears, check if you're configuring a portable computer, then select the docking state for this profile. You should also check the Always Include This Profile As an Option When Windows Starts option, then click OK.
3. Back in the Hardware Profiles dialog box, select whether Windows should wait until you select a hardware profile, or select the first profile listed if you don't make a choice.
4. Click OK when done.

JIM'S TOP TEN TIPS

Adding new hardware doesn't have to be a hassle. Just remember these ten important tips:

1. You can add all sorts of peripherals to your computer, including video cards, sound cards, keyboards, mice, joysticks, modems, DVD and CD-ROM drives, hard drives, scanners, digital cameras, and PC cameras.
2. Choose the right port for the peripheral you're adding.
3. When you have a choice, go with a FireWire or USB connection—both are fast and intelligent, and you don't have to restart your PC when you add a new device.
4. In most cases, Windows XP's Plug and Play function will recognize a new peripheral as soon as you restart your computer.
5. If Windows *doesn't* recognize a new device, use the Add Hardware Wizard to install the device manually.
6. Windows XP includes built-in drivers for many peripherals. You can also choose to install the drivers included on your peripheral's installation disk.
7. Older drivers can sometimes cause operational problems. You can use the Windows Device Manager to search for and install new versions of problematic drivers.
8. The Device Manager is also a good place to start if you think you have a conflict between two drivers.
9. Windows XP lets you "roll back" a new driver to its previous version—very useful if you upgrade a driver and start experiencing problems.
10. If you have a laptop computer, you may want to create separate hardware profiles for home and office (or docked and undocked) use. Or not. Profiles are difficult to use, and not always necessary.

PART III

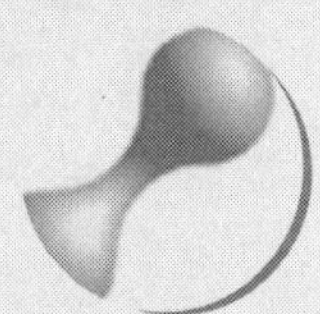

TAKING WINDOWS ONLINE

CHAPTER 7

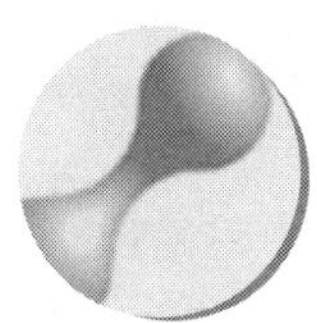

MAKING THE CONNECTION

- Connecting via MSN
- Understanding Broadband Internet
- Sharing an Internet Connection
- Activating the Firewall
- Jim's Top Ten Tips

The Internet has been around long enough to be an important part of most people's lives. Can you imagine trying to get by without e-mail, or without your favorite Web sites? I certainly can't.

You might not remember this, but Microsoft was slow to embrace the Internet. It wasn't until Bill Gates personally got turned on to the Net—and then forced everyone who worked for him to open their eyes to the online world—that Microsoft started taking the Internet seriously.

That was then, this is now.

Today, if Microsoft had their way, they'd own the entire Internet. (You can never accuse Bill Gates and crew of thinking small!) The entire company is in the midst of their .NET initiative, which aims to turn all their traditional software programs into Web-based applications. To date, they've tried to integrate the Internet into as many of their products as possible—in whatever ways they can come up with.

This Web integration is everywhere in Windows XP. From the initial installation, where Windows uses the Internet to both activate and register the operating system, to the Help and Support section (covered in Chapter 20, "Getting Help"), which kicks you out to the Web when you need advanced help, Windows depends on the Internet.

In fact, it's hard to imagine using Windows XP without being hooked up to the Internet. If you're not connected, there's so much you can't do. You can't get automatic updates to the OS. You can't search for missing or outdated drivers. You can't contact Microsoft if you need help. (Okay, you could try calling them—but good luck getting through on those overloaded technical support lines!)

Most important, if you're not connected to the Internet, you can't do everything else you've grown accustomed to doing online, which is as good a reason as any for Microsoft to make it as easy as possible for you to get connected—directly from the operating system.

CONFIGURING A NEW ACCOUNT

If you upgraded an existing system to Windows XP, your old Internet connection should still be there, waiting for you to make a connection. There is nothing in the upgrade process that should screw up any existing connection information.

If you just purchased a new PC, you need to set up a new Internet connection from within Windows XP. You do this with the New Connection Wizard, a special utility that automates the creation and configuration of new Internet connections.

You can use the New Connection Wizard to set up a completely new Internet account, or to configure your system for an existing account with your ISP. All you need to do is input the appropriate information, and the wizard does the rest of the job–including setting up your e-mail and USENET newsgroup accounts.

Creating a Completely New Account

If you don't yet have an account with an Internet Service Provider (ISP), you can use the New Connection Wizard to find and subscribe to an ISP. All you have to do is follow these steps:

1. Click the Start button, then select Connect To, Show All Connections. When the Network Connections window opens, select Create a New Connection from the Network Tasks panel. When the New Connection Wizard dialog box appears, click the Next button.
2. When the Network Connection Type screen appears, check the Connect to the Internet option and then click the Next button.
3. When the Getting Ready screen appears (see Figure 7.1), check the Choose From a List of Internet Providers option.
4. When the next screen appears, check the Select From a List of Other ISPs option, then click the Finish button.

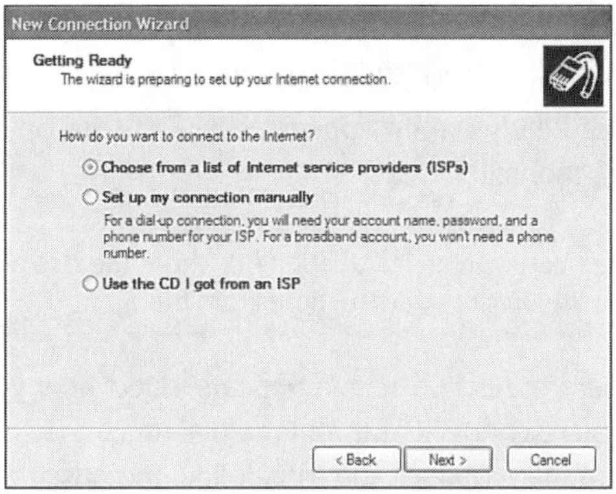

Figure 7.1

Use the New Connection Wizard to set up your Internet connection.

5. Windows now opens the Online Services window. You can choose from one of the providers listed here, or click the Refer Me to More Internet Services Providers Icon.
6. If you choose to look for more ISPs, the wizard now dials into the Microsoft Internet Referral Service and downloads a list of available ISPs. Select an ISP from this list and follow the onscreen instructions to sign up for a new account.

The Microsoft Internet Referral Service isn't always accurate or complete, and may not always find all the ISPs available in your area. If it can't find *any* ISPs, you'll need to obtain your own ISP subscription and then enter the information manually via the second option in the Internet Connection Wizard.

When you've selected an ISP, the wizard does everything else for you—including setting up a new connection within Windows.

You can view details of each connection on your PC by clicking the Internet Options icon from within the Control Panel, and then selecting the Connections tab. Select a connection from the Dial-Up Settings list, then click the Settings button.

Setting Up a Manual Dial-Up, LAN, or Broadband Connection

If you already have an account set up with an ISP, you can create a new connection for that ISP by entering its settings manually. You use this same technique to set up a cable or DSL connection, or a connection made through your company's local area network.

Just follow these steps:

1. Click the Start button, then select Connect To, Show All Connections. When the Network Connections window opens, select Create a New Connection from the Network Tasks panel. When the New Connection Wizard dialog box appears, click the Next button.

2. When the Network Connection Type screen appears, check the Connect to the Internet option and then click the Next button.
3. When the Getting Ready screen appears, check the Set Up My Connection Manually option, then click Next.

If your ISP provided you with an installation CD, check the Use the CD I Got From an ISP option, and follow the onscreen instructions from there.

4. When the Internet Connection screen appears, select how you want to connect to the Internet. If you're connecting through a dial-up connection, check the Connect Using a Dial-Up Modem option, and then follow the onscreen instructions to complete your connection. If you're connecting via a DSL or cable modem connection that requires manual log in, check the Connect Using a Broadband Connection That Requires a User Name and Password option. If you're connecting through an "always on" LAN, cable modem, or DSL connection, check the Connect Using a Broadband Connection That Is Always On option. Click Next when you've made your selection.
5. Follow the onscreen instructions for your specific type of installation. You'll probably need to enter your user name, password, and specific information about your ISP. The wizard now completes your connection. (Not much to it, really.)

Transferring an Existing Account to This PC

If you already have an account with an ISP (but on another PC), you'll need to transfer those settings to your new Windows XP PC. With previous versions of Windows, you'd have to do this manually—by writing down all your settings from your old PC, and then reentering them by hand into your new machine.

With Windows XP this entire process is automated as part of the File and Settings Transfer Wizard. When you use this wizard to transfer key settings from one PC to another.

To learn how to use the File and Settings Transfer Wizard, see the "Transferring Files and Settings" section of Chapter 21, "Updating Windows."

CONNECTING VIA MSN

If you haven't yet subscribed to an Internet Service Provider, Microsoft would very much like it if you signed up for their own proprietary online service. This service, called MSN (it used to be called the Microsoft Network, hence the initials) functions both as a traditional ISP and as a commercial online service that competes directly with America Online. Although there's nothing within Windows that forces you to sign up for MSN, Microsoft certainly goes out of its way to make MSN easy to subscribe to.

MSN is listed as one of the available ISPs when you run the New Connection Wizard. When you select the MSN option, the MSN sign-up program launches. From here, signing up to MSN is as easy as following the onscreen instructions (and providing the appropriate personal information—including your credit card number).

MSN is a decent ISP, although its proprietary content isn't near as wide or as deep as that found on AOL. You use the MSN Explorer program, shown in Figure 7.2, to access all of MSN's features. MSN Explorer is a customized version of the Internet Explorer browser, but with more content features built-in—similar to the way the AOL interface works.

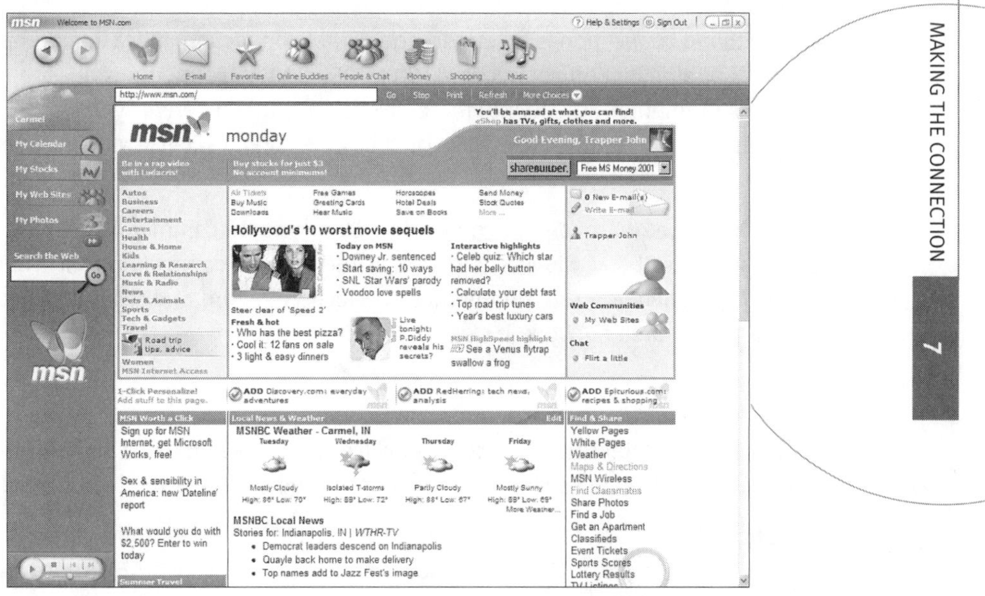

Figure 7.2

You access MSN with MSN Explorer, which looks and acts suspiciously like Internet Explorer.

Most of the content on MSN is also available free-of-charge to any user with a Web browser. So what you're really paying for is the Internet access—the content is just a bonus. (Not that there's anything wrong with MSN's content. Some of the MSN sites, such as Expedia and Carpoint, are definitely best-of-category.)

So if you want a good solid Internet connection, MSN fits the bill. You can connect to MSN and then use Internet Explorer and Outlook Express to surf the Web and access your e-mail. You don't have to use MSN Explorer if you don't want to.

MSN's monthly rates are competitive with AOL's, and with those from other national and local ISPs. While there's no reason that you have to sign up with MSN just because you have Windows XP, there's also no reason *not* to—if you need a new ISP, that is.

UNDERSTANDING BROADBAND INTERNET

Even the best dial-up connection to the Internet can be maddeningly slow. This gets to be a real problem as more and more Web sites add more and larger graphics and multimedia files. Because every single item on a Web page must be downloaded to your computer before you can view it, the typical 56.6Kbps dial-up pipeline just isn't big enough to download everything instantaneously.

This is why it takes such a long time to access some Web pages. And even longer to download large files, or receive e-mails with large attachments.

Fortunately, there's a way you can speed up your connection to the Internet. All you have to do is dump your dial-up connection and subscribe to a broadband Internet service.

A broadband connection is an end-to-end digital connection, at least ten times faster than a typical analog dial-up connection. While DSL and cable modems are the most popular methods of Internet broadband, there are actually five different types of broadband connections available today: ISDN, DSL, digital cable, digital satellite, and broadband wireless access.

Whichever type of broadband you choose, Windows XP can handle it. In the case of DSL, cable, and broadband wireless, XP handles the Internet connection as it would a network connection. Then you run the Internet Connection Wizard and tell it that you're connecting via a local area network. It's easy, and it's fast.

ISDN

ISDN stands for Integrated Services Digital Network. It was the first digital connection technology, and it's still in use in many locations in the United States and around the world.

Although ISDN is faster than analog modems, it's much slower than other forms of broadband. ISDN connects at 128Kbps, which is only twice as fast as a 56.6Kbps connection. The big drawback to ISDN is that it's generally more expensive than faster types of broadband, and it's a hassle to hook up. Choose ISDN only if you have no other options available.

To obtain this modest increase in speed, you have to deal with an unwieldy, unreliable, and costly technology—which is why, in most areas of the country, ISDN is being supplanted by the lower-cost (and much faster) DSL technology.

DSL

DSL (Digital Subscriber Line) is the fastest-growing broadband technology today. It piggybacks on your existing telephone lines, and is relatively easy to install and configure.

DSL provides speeds of at least 384Kbps—and more typically in the 500Kbps–1Mbps range. For just $40–$50 per month (which includes the cost of an ISP), it's easy to see why DSL is so popular today.

If you choose DSL, make sure you go with a provider that's on firm financial footing. Several third-party DSL providers have gone belly-up in recent months, leaving subscribers high and dry—and without an Internet connection. If you're looking for stability, go with the DSL service provided by your local phone company.

Digital Cable

Cable modems are also very popular, as they connect to the same digital cable lines that are working their way into homes across the country. That makes for a very easy—and a very fast—connection.

Digital cable delivers an even faster connection than what you typically get with home DSL. Even the slowest connections will hit somewhere around 500Kbps, and it's not unusual to clock downstream rates between 1Mbps–2Mbps. Cable internet service is priced competitively with DSL, and is typically much easier to install and set up.

Digital Satellite

The same company that offers DIRECTV digital satellite service also offers DirectPC satellite-based Internet access. With DirecPC you can choose from one-way service (fast satellite down to your PC, slower phone lines back out to the Internet) or the latest two-way service (fast signals down from the satellite, and fast signals back from your dish into outer space).

As a plus, you can use the same dish for both your digital Internet and your digital television services. Downstream connection speeds average around 400Kbps. However, two-way satellite service is typically priced at about $80 a month—almost twice the price of one-way service.

Broadband Wireless Access

Wireless broadband systems use microwave technology to transmit and receive Internet data at broadband speeds—without any wires or cables, whatsoever. All you have to do is install a special antenna on your roof (and a modem in your PC), and then your connection is up and ready to go.

Broadband wireless access is faster than DSL, and almost as fast as the best cable modem connections. Most users average about 1Mbps with their wireless connections.

SHARING AN INTERNET CONNECTION

Do you have more than one PC in your home? If so, you probably want them both to be connected to the Internet.

This is particularly true if you have a broadband connection coming into your home. With a broadband connection you have enough bandwidth to connect multiple computers to the Internet at the same time—by sharing a single Internet connection.

Windows XP includes special Internet Connection Sharing (ICS) technology, which enables a single "gateway" computer to manage a shared Internet connection for other computers on your home network. You activate ICS via the Network Setup Wizard, which I discuss in more detail in Chapter 18, "Setting Up a Home or Small Business Network." For now, I'll focus on using the wizard to set up a shared Internet connection.

Naturally, you'll need to have network cards installed in each of your computers. You can go with either 10Mbps cards or 100Mbps cards. Either type will be faster than the speed of your broadband connection. (For other networking tasks—such as transferring files between machines—you're better off with the faster cards.)

With ICS, the gateway computer is called the *host*, and all the other computers on the network are called *clients*. The host computer and the clients have to be set up separately, as described in the following sections.

Setting Up the Host Computer

Before you can configure ICS on your lead computer, you first have to install *two* network cards. (That's for the host PC only; the other PCs only need one card each.) In the host PC one card is used to connect to your DSL, cable, satellite, or wireless broadband modem, and the second card is used to connect to your network hub.

Once you have the cards installed and configured, there are two ways you can activate Internet Connection Sharing.

If you already have your home network up and running, you don't need to run the Network Setup Wizard to set up ICS. All you have to do is follow these steps:

1. Open the Control Panel and click the Network Connections icon.
2. When the Network Connections utility launches, right-click the icon for the Internet connection that you want to share, and select Properties from the pop-up menu.
3. When the Properties dialog box appears (as shown in Figure 7.3), select the Advanced tab and check the Allow Other Network Users to Connect Through This Computer's Internet Connection option.
4. Click OK to activate ICS.

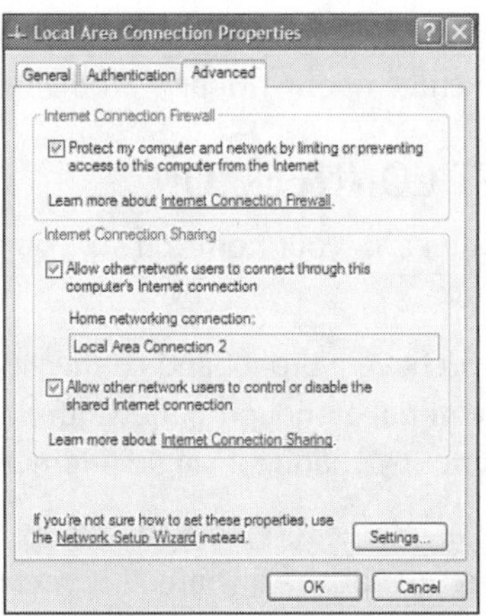

Figure 7.3

If your network is already up and running, activating Internet Connection Sharing is as easy as checking a checkbox.

If you're just now setting up your home network, you can activate ICS via the Network Setup Wizard. You start the wizard by clicking the Start button and then selecting All Programs, Accessories, Communications, Network Setup Wizard.

When you run the Home Networking Wizard, you want to choose the This Computer Connects Directly to the Internet option, as shown in Figure 7.4. You'll also have to select which Internet connection you want to share, as well as which of your two network cards are connected to what. (One card connects to your broadband modem, the other card connects to your home network—probably through a hub.)

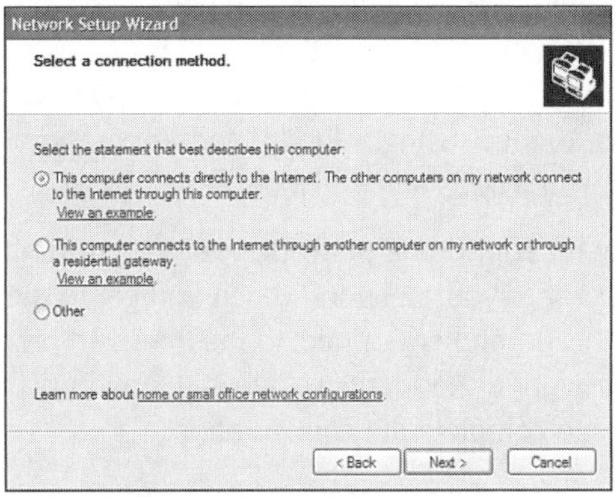

Figure 7.4

Use the Network Setup Wizard to set up Internet Connection Sharing.

After you click through the balance of the wizard, you're done—with the host computer. Now it's time to configure the other computers on your network.

Setting Up the Client Computers

You have to figure each client computer on your network to share your Internet connection. If the computers are all running Windows XP, the process is fairly straight ahead. If any of the computers are running older versions of Windows, you'll need to run the Network Setup Wizard directly from your Windows XP installation CD.

Windows XP's Internet Connection Sharing only works with computers running Windows XP, Windows 2000, Windows Me, or Windows 98. If you have a PC that's running Windows 95, you'll either need to upgrade that PC to a newer version of Windows, or use a third-party connection sharing utility instead. (The same goes with Macs—you'll need a third-party utility to share your connection with a Macintosh computer.)

To run the Network Setup Wizard on a pre-XP machine, follow these steps:

1. Insert the Windows XP installation CD in the PC's CD-ROM drive.
2. When the setup program launches, click the Perform Additional Tasks option.

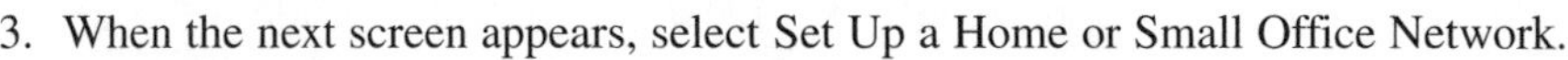

3. When the next screen appears, select Set Up a Home or Small Office Network.
4. Follow the onscreen instructions to activate Internet Connection Sharing.

To be honest, setting up Internet Connection Sharing is easier if all your computers are running Windows XP. Not only do you have fewer compatibility issues when all your machines are running the same operating system, but Windows XP makes the whole process a lot easier than it used to be.

If a Windows XP client computer is already connected to the Internet, it's extremely easy to activate Internet Connection Sharing. All you have to do is follow the steps outlined in the "Sharing a Broadband or LAN Connection" section, earlier in this chapter. The key thing is to run the New Connection Wizard, choose the Set Up My Connection Manually option, and then choose the Connect Using a Broadband Connection That Is Always On option. Follow the onscreen instructions and you'll be all set.

If you haven't yet set up your home network, you need to run the Network Setup Wizard to connect the computer to your network. When you get to the Select a Connection Type screen, choose the This Computer Connect to the Internet Through Another Computer on My Network or Through a Residential Gateway option. Then follow the remaining onscreen instructions to complete the configuration.

Repeat these steps for each client computer (but *not* your gateway computer!) on your network.

Establishing the Connection

After you've restarted the last computer on your network, Internet Connection Sharing should be fully operational across all your PCs. As long as your gateway computer is connected to your broadband connection and turned on, all the other PCs should also have a live, always-on connection.

If your host PC isn't turned on, none of your other PCs will be able to connect to the Internet.

ACTIVATING THE FIREWALL

When you connect to the Internet via a broadband connection, your connection is always on. Unlike a dial-up connection, where you have to dial up every time you want to go online, a broadband connection keeps you constantly connected to the Internet. No dialing, no waiting, just an always-on connection.

The downside to an always-on connection is that it's much easier for hackers and crackers to break into your system from the Internet. In fact, if you have multiple computers sharing a connection, a dedicated cracker can attack your entire network and access data on all your computers.

You can protect against this type of Internet-based attack by installing a *firewall* between your gateway computer and the Internet. Firewall software acts as a kind of gatekeeper that keeps undesirable users out.

A firewall works by checking all communications that travel between your computer/network and the Internet. It's selective about what information is passed through, and it also works to keep the addressed of your network's client computers hidden from other users on the Internet. In effect, your computers are protected because they can't be seen from the other side of the firewall.

There are lots of third-party firewall programs available, including BlackICE Defender (`www.networkice.com/products/blackice_defender.html`), McAfee Firewall (`www.mcafee.com`), and Norton Personal Firewall (`www.symantec.com/securitycheck/`). With Windows XP, however, you don't have to invest in one of these additional programs; XP includes its own built-in firewall.

Windows XP's Internet Connection Firewall (ICF) is a basic firewall best-suited for small network use. If you have fewer than a half-dozen computers connected in a home or small-business network, ICF should do an adequate job of protecting your computers from outside attack.

The Internet Connection Firewall is automatically activated when you set up a shared Internet connection via the Home Networking Wizard. You can also activate (or deactivate) the firewall manually, by following these steps:

1. From your host (gateway) computer, open the Control Panel and click the Network Connections icon.
2. When the Network Connections utility opens, right-click the Internet connection you want to connect, and then select Properties from the pop-up menu.
3. When the Properties dialog box appears, select the Advanced tab and check the Internet Connection Firewall option. (Uncheck this box to disable the firewall.)
4. Click OK to activate the firewall.

Once you have ICF activated, there are a number of advanced settings you can configure. Most users shouldn't have to bother with these settings. But if you're running your own Web site or just like to fiddle with power user settings, you might want to take a look at these settings.

You access the firewall settings from the Advanced tab of the Properties dialog box for your protected Internet connection. Click the Settings button to display the Advanced Settings dialog box (shown in Figure 7.5) and you'll see three tabs worth of very technical settings. Don't mess with these settings if you're not familiar with them. If you *are* familiar with them, you don't need me to go through all the details. Consult your Windows XP manual or the Microsoft Knowledge Base if you need more information.

Figure 7.5

Advanced firewall settings—don't mess with them unless you have to!

JIM'S TOP TEN TIPS

Configuring Windows XP for any type of Internet connection is much, much easier than it used to be. Gone forever are the days where you have to manually install and configure the TCP/IP protocol stack—and, boy, am I glad! Hooking up to the Internet shouldn't be a major production. In my opinion, Windows XP does it right. Just remember these ten key points:

1. If you already have an account with an ISP, you can use the New Connection Wizard to create a new connection with your existing settings.
2. If you don't yet have an ISP account, use the New Connection Wizard to find an ISP in your area—and then sign up, online.
3. Windows XP also lets you connect to the Internet via a LAN, or through a broadband connection. Just run the New Connection Wizard and choose the Set Up My Connection Manually option.
4. As you might expect, Microsoft tries very hard to entice you to use MSN for your ISP. If you need a new ISP, MSN isn't a bad choice—and you don't even have to use the MSN Explorer interface, if you don't want to.
5. If you want a faster Internet connection, you should dump your dial-up and go with a broadband connection. (Windows XP handles all sorts of broadband, from ISDN to broadband wireless.)
6. DSL is a broadband connection that comes through your phone lines. Typical connection speeds are in the 384Kbps to 1Mbps range.
7. Many digital cable systems offer broadband connections via cable modem. Typical connection speeds run from 500Kbps to 2Mbps.
8. Another popular type of broadband connection is via a digital satellite system. You can get DirecPC service in either one-way or two-way versions, with connection speeds in the 400Kbps range.
9. If you have a high-speed Internet connection, you can share it with all the computers in your home via Internet Connection Sharing. You set up ICS via Windows XP's Network Setup Wizard. (If your network is already up and running, you don't even need to run the wizard. Just open the Properties dialog box for the connection you want to share, select the Advanced tab, and check the appropriate option to turn on Internet Connection Sharing.)
10. To protect any computers connected via an always-on broadband connection, activate Windows XP's Internet Connection Firewall. This software acts as a gatekeeper between your computers and the Internet, and keeps your home network safe from outside attack.

CHAPTER 8

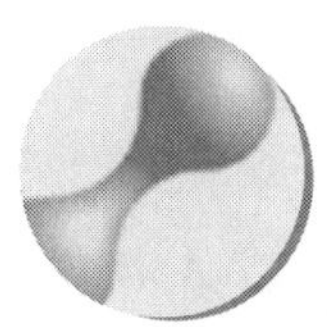

SURFING THE WEB WITH INTERNET EXPLORER

- Introducing Internet Explorer 6
- Personalizing the Browser Interface
- Configuring the Browser
- Surfing Safely
- Speeding Up Your Browser
- Working with Web Sites
- Alternative Browsers
- Jim's Top Ten Tips

If you followed the government's anti-trust case against Microsoft, you know that one of the key issues was Microsoft's "bundling" of a Web browser with their operating system. Like it or not, the Internet Explorer browser is now an essential part of Windows. And Windows XP includes the latest and greatest version of Internet Explorer—Internet Explorer 6 (IE6).

IE6 is a sleek and versatile program, updated to reflect XP's Luna interface, and crammed full of new and useful features. If you're like most users, IE6 will be the browser you use to surf the Web. It's not the only browser available (see the end of this chapter for some other options), but it's the most popular one.

Of course, that begs the question, Is Internet Explorer popular because it's the best browser, or because it's included with every copy of Windows? In the case of IE6, the answer is probably "both." Yes, it's easy to default to IE6 because it's right there. But IE6 is also a darned good browser, better, in my opinion, than the latest version of Netscape.

I think you'll like the latest changes in IE6. The apparent changes are relatively minor (which is a good thing), so the basic browser operation is similar to what it was with previous versions. The new and changed features actually make the browser easier to use, which is a good thing.

Read on to learn more about the latest version of this popular Web browser.

INTRODUCING INTERNET EXPLORER 6

Before we get into all the fancy features of IE6, let's take a few pages for a brief refresher course on Internet Explorer basics.

The Internet Explorer Interface

Internet Explorer 6 looks like most previous versions of the program, but with a slicker look and feel and some new icons and graphics. By default, the toolbar buttons are displayed with minimal text, so the new look might take a little getting used to. (I'll show you how to change the button display later in this chapter.)

Figure 8.1 details the various parts of the IE6 interface.

As you will see, other than the look of the buttons, there's not much new here.

Basic Web Surfing

If you're at all familiar with the Internet, you already know how to use IE6 to surf the Web. If you need a quick refresher course, follow these steps:

1. When you first launch Internet Explorer, it loads your predefined home page.

To change Internet Explorer's home page, select Tools, Internet Options, select the General tab, and enter a new URL into the Address box in the Home Page section. Even easier, you can simply drag a page's icon from the Address box onto the Home button on the toolbar.

2. Enter a new Web address in the Address box and press Enter (or click the Go button). Internet Explorer loads the new page.
3. Click any link on the current Web page. Internet Explorer loads the new page.
4. To return to the previous page, click the Back button. If you've backed up several pages and want to return to the page you were on last, click the Forward button.
5. To return to your start page, click the Home button.

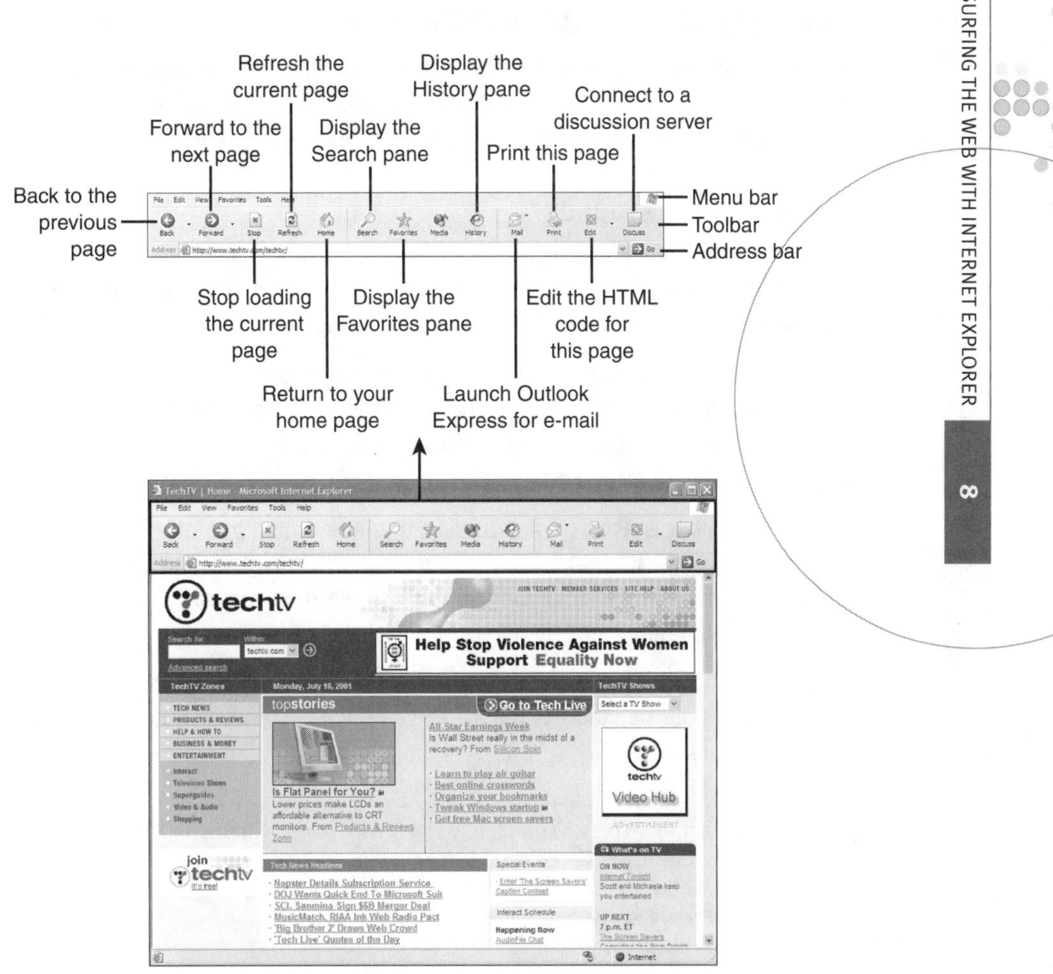

Figure 8.1

Internet Explorer 6, with the new-look buttons and menus.

Printing

To print the currently displayed Web page (as-is), click the Print button. To see a preview of the page before it prints, select File, Print Preview.

To print only a selected frame or selected text within a page, select File, Print to display the Print dialog box. Make the appropriate selections there, then click the OK button to initiate printing.

PERSONALIZING THE BROWSER INTERFACE

There are several ways you can change look of the IE6 interface. You can add or delete buttons from the Toolbar, add your own personal links to the Links bar, or decide which of the many sidebar panels—what IE6 calls *Explorer Bars*—to display.

Move the Bars Around

The easiest change you can make to the interface concerns all the different "bars" displayed on screen. By default, you have a Toolbar, an Address bar, and a Taskbar. You can choose *not* to display any of these bars—or to display them in a different order.

Before you can fiddle with any of the toolbars, you first have to *unlock* them. (This is a new feature of IE6.) You unlock all the toolbars at once by selecting View, Toolbars, and then unchecking the Lock the Toolbars option. When this option is checked, you can't move or edit any of IE6's onscreen elements.

Moving a toolbar is as easy as grabbing the little dotted line at the far left of the toolbar, and then dragging the bar to a new position. You can stack the toolbars on top of each other, or move them so that they share a single row. You can also resize them within a row, also by dragging the left side of the toolbar.

To choose which toolbars are displayed, select View, Toolbars and then check or uncheck the Standard Buttons, Address Bar, or Links options. (Standard Buttons is how IE6 refers to the main Toolbar.)

If you want to display a completely clean Web page, with the minimal amount of browser interface, use IE6's full-screen mode. Just press F11 (or select View, Full Screen), and your Web page will be displayed full screen, with only a minimal toolbar visible. Press F11 again to return to normal mode.

Customizing the Toolbar

Don't like the standard Internet Explorer Toolbar buttons? Then change them!

The first thing you can change is how the buttons are displayed. With IE6, you have the option of displaying large icons (shown in Figure 8.2), small icons (see Figure 8.3), text labels, or selected text on right (see Figure 8.4). You access these options by selecting View, Toolbars, Customize, and then making the appropriate changes in the Customize Toolbar dialog box (shown in Figure 8.5).

You can also use the Customize Toolbar dialog box to add, remove, or rearrange Toolbar buttons. To add a button, select the button from the left-hand list and click the Add button. To remove a button, select it from the right-hand list and click the Remove button. To rearrange buttons, select the button to move in the right-hand list and click either the Move Up or Move Down buttons. Click the Close button when you're done messing with things.

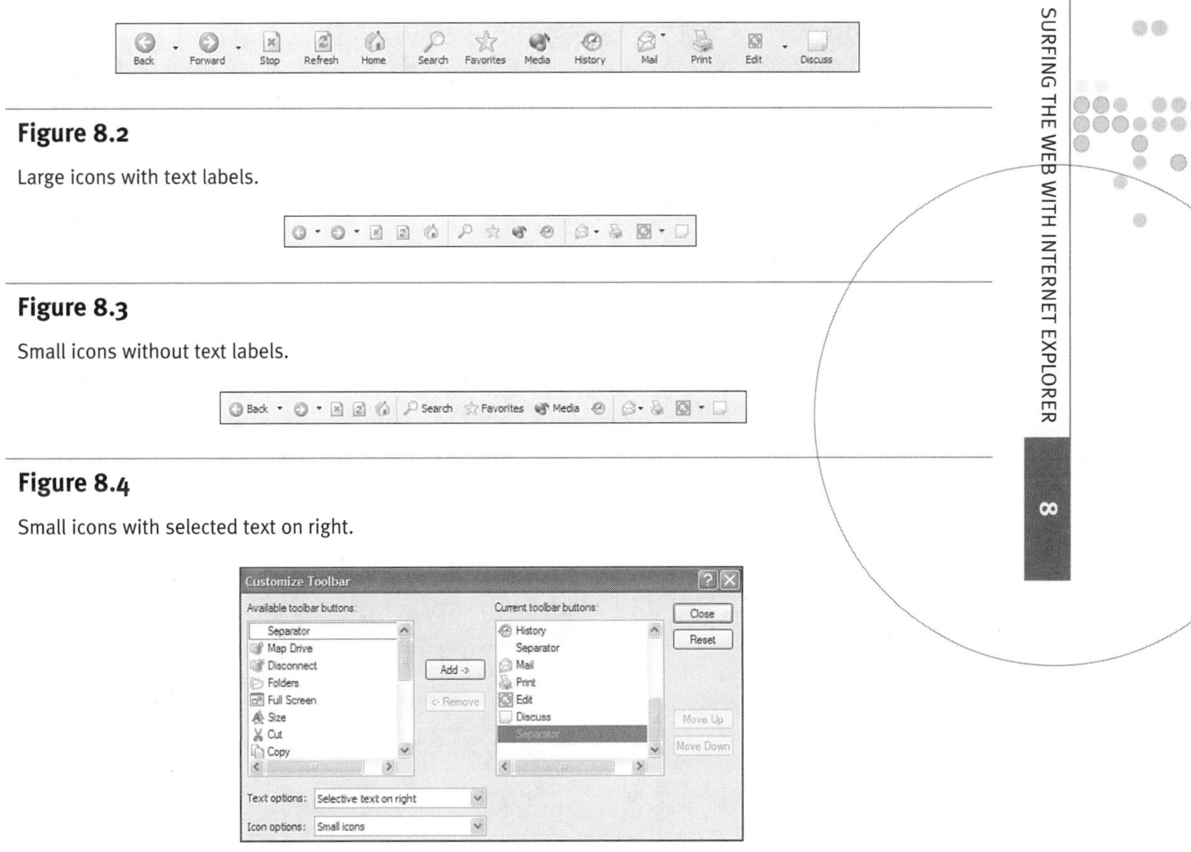

Figure 8.2

Large icons with text labels.

Figure 8.3

Small icons without text labels.

Figure 8.4

Small icons with selected text on right.

Figure 8.5

The Customize Toolbar dialog box—where you make desired changes to the IE6 Toolbar.

Adding Links

The Links bar is your opportunity to put your favorite links right in front of your face. When you add a Web site to the Links bar, you can jump to that site with the click of a button.

To add a site to the Links bar, all you have to do is drag the site's icon from the Address bar onto the Links bar. You can rearrange buttons on the Links bar by dragging them from one position to another.

CONFIGURING THE BROWSER

You can change many options in Internet Explorer to make it better suit your personal needs. For example, you may want to change the color of links you have visited—or, if you're concerned about security, you may want to turn on warnings when entering an unsecured site

To change Internet Explorer's default configuration:

1. From within Internet Explorer, select Tools, Internet Options. (You can also open the Control Panel and click the Internet Options icon.)
2. When the Internet Options dialog box appears, configure the appropriate options.
3. After you have Internet Explorer configured as you like, click the OK button.

I'll explain some of these options in the following sections.

General Options

The General tab in the Internet Options dialog box (as shown in Figure 8.6) will be the tab you use most often. Here is where you can:

Figure 8.6

Manage your home page, temporary files, and browser history from the Internet Options General tab.

- Set the default start page (what IE6 calls your Home page) for your browser
- Delete all the cookie files from your computer
- Delete all temporary Internet files, and select how much disk space is kept for these temporary files
- Select how many days to store the history of Web sites you've visited—or clear your history completely
- Change your browser's default background, text, and link colors
- Change the default fonts displayed in your browser
- Change the default language for your browser display
- Configure selected accessibility options

Security Options

The Security tab (shown in Figure 8.7) is where you assign so-called "content zones" for your browser. You use content zones to ensure your system's security while you're browsing individual Web pages. (See the "Security Zones" section later in this chapter for more information.)

Figure 8.7

Configure your system's security zones from the Internet Options Security tab.

Privacy Options

The Privacy tab (shown in Figure 8.8) is where you set the privacy level for the sites you visit. (See the "Privacy Preferences" section later in this chapter for more information.)

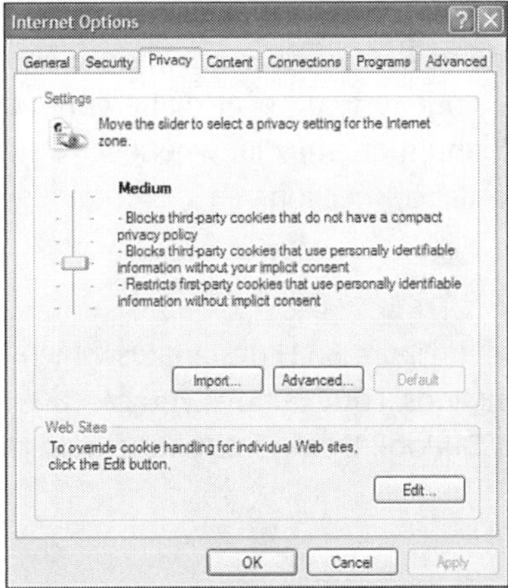

Figure 8.8

Manage your browser's privacy protection from the Internet Options Privacy tab.

Content Options

The Content tab (shown in Figure 8.9) lets you manage the Web content that can be viewed with your browser. You can enable the Content Advisor to make certain types of Web sites inaccessible, which is a good way to protect younger users from inappropriate content. (See the "Content Advisor" section later in this chapter for more information.)

Figure 8.9

Configure IE6 to block inappropriate content from the Internet Options Content tab.

Connections Options

The Connections tab (shown in Figure 8.10) is where you manage all the Internet connections installed on your PC. You can change the settings for any existing connection, or click the Setup button to create new connections using the New Connection Wizard. You can also use this tab to have your system never dial a connection (if you're connected via a LAN or always-on broadband modem), dial whenever a networking connection isn't present, or always dial a specific connection.

Programs Options

The Programs tab (shown in Figure 8.11) designates which "helper" programs are used for which Internet-related functions. For example, you can use this tab to designate FrontPage as your HTML editor and Outlook Express as your e-mail client.

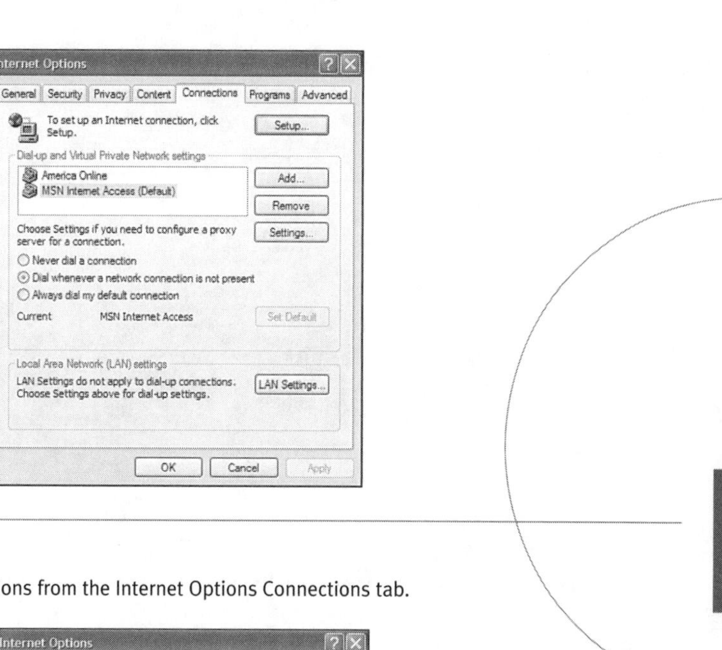

Figure 8.10

Manage all your Internet connections from the Internet Options Connections tab.

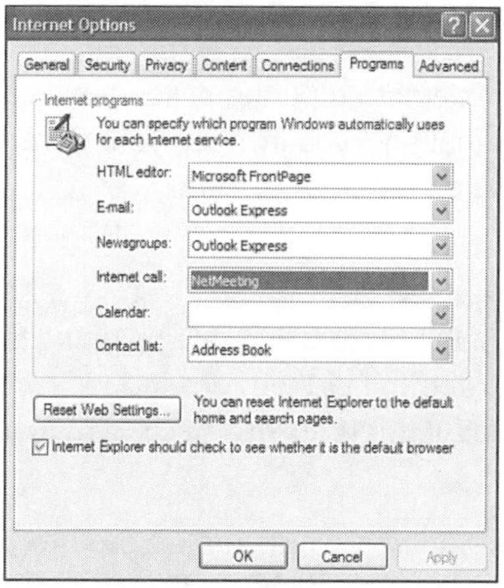

Figure 8.11

Designate default helper programs from the Internet Options Programs tab.

Advanced Options

The Advanced tab (shown in Figure 8.12) might be one you naturally shy away from—even though it contains some of the most useful configuration settings.

Basically, this tab lists, using a tree structure, all manner of configuration settings. The options are too numerous to mention them all here, but include everything from automatically checking for browser updates to turning on or off IE6's Java console. If you can't find a particular option anyplace else, chances are it's somewhere on this tab!

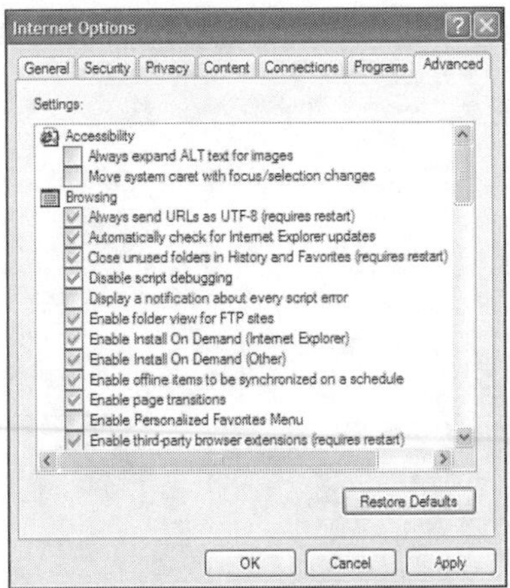

Figure 8.12

Configure all sorts of useful settings from the Internet Options Advanced tab.

SURFING SAFELY

Three of the tabs in the Internet Properties dialog box deal with safer surfing. In particular, IE6 includes features that help you increase your privacy and security, and shield your children from inappropriate Web-page content.

Content Advisor

Let's start with that last point, because kid-safe browsing is a major issue for anyone with children on the Web. Far too many Web sites include content that just isn't appropriate, especially for younger kids. If this is an area of concern to you, you need to look into IE6's content-filtering features.

IE6 includes the Content Advisor, which can be used to block access to sites that meet specified criteria. For example, you might configure Content Advisor to block all sites that include nudity, or that contain bad language. Content Advisor enables you to set your own tolerance levels for various types of potentially offensive content, and then blocks access to sites that don't pass muster.

Here's how to activate and configure the Content Advisor:

1. From the Internet Options dialog box, select the Content tab.
2. From within the Content Advisor section, click the Enable button. (If you're prompted for a password, enter it now.)
3. When the Content Advisor dialog box appears, as shown in Figure 8.13, select the Ratings tab and select a category (Language, Nudity, Sex, or Violence).

Figure 8.13

Use the Content Advisor to filter out inappropriate language, nudity, sex, and violence.

4. Adjust the ratings slider to the right to increase the tolerance for this type of content. (Leaving the slider all the way to the left is the least tolerant level.) Click OK when done.
5. To create a list of Web sites that are either always viewable or never viewable, select the Approved Sites tab. Enter the URL in the Allow This Web Site box, and then click the Always button (to always view the site, regardless of its rating) or the Never button (to completely block access to the site.)
6. Click OK, and you'll be prompted to create a supervisor password. After you enter a password and click OK, the Content Advisor will be activated.
7. To disable Content Advisor, return to the Content tab in Internet Options dialog box and click the Disable button. (You'll again be prompted for your Supervisor Password; enter your Windows password and click OK.)

You should know that while Content Advisor is a great way to protect your kids, you might find it annoying when you surf the Web. That's because Content Advisor (especially when set to the least tolerant levels) is likely to block access to a lot of sites you're used to visiting on a normal basis. News sites, in particular, include stories about sex and violence and hatred that can activate the Content Advisor filter.

If you find that Content Advisor is blocking too many sites, try turning down the tolerance level. You can also add your favorite sites to the list on the Approved Sites tab.

IE6's Content Advisor settings are specific to the user currently logged in. If you switch users (via Windows XP's Fast User Switching, discussed in Chapter 16, "Working with Multiple Users") the Content Advisor settings change to reflect that user's preferences. Which means you'll need to set separate Content Advisor settings for each of your kids, if they log on as different users.

Security Zones

Internet Explorer incorporates a technology called ActiveX. ActiveX, developed by Microsoft, enables Web designers to add a variety of active and multimedia content to their pages. Unfortunately, ActiveX also provides a potential "hole" into your computer system.

ActiveX controls can be automatically downloaded from a Web page to your PC, in the background and without your knowledge. Most of the time ActiveX controls are good things, adding functionality to your Web pages. On occasion, however, ActiveX controls can be configured to use your system's resources and even write to your hard disk. The result is that crafty developers can use ActiveX to breach your system, upload personal information, and download viruses and other harmful programs.

Microsoft's workaround for these ActiveX security issues is to enable you to set different *security zones* for different Web sites. Each security zone is assigned either Low, Medium, or High security levels.

Low security provides no warning if you're about to run potentially damaging ActiveX content. Medium security prompts you before running questionable items. High security simply won't let you run anything potentially dangerous.

These security levels are applied to different Web page by assigning each page to a specific security zone. IE6 lets you assign four different zones:

- **Internet Zone**—This is IE6's default zone. Any site not previously visited falls into this zone. The default security level is Medium.
- **Local Intranet Zone**—This zone is dedicated to pages on your company's local Intranet. You can't manually add sites to this zone. The default security level is Medium.
- **Trusted Sites Zone**—This zone contains sites that you know are completely safe. The default security level is Low.
- **Restricted Sites Zone**—This zone contains sites you don't trust. The default security level is High.

By default, all Web sites are assigned to the Internet Zone. To assign a Web site to either the Trusted Sites or Restricted Sites zone, follow these steps:

1. From the Internet Options dialog box, select the Security tab.
2. Select either the Trusted Sites or Restricted Sites icon and then click the Sites button.
3. When the zone dialog box appears, enter the URL for the new site in the Add This Web Site To the Zone box, then click the Add button.
4. Click OK when done, then click OK again to close the Internet Options dialog box.

If you select Local Intranet Zone, you will see a dialog box pertaining to various Intranet/proxy server/firewall options. Click the Advanced button to add the current page to this zone.

The security zone for the current Web page is always shown on the right side of the Internet Explorer status bar.

Privacy Preferences

Internet privacy relates to what personal information of yours is shared by a particular Web site. This personal information can be stored in a cookie, or on a Web's database.

A cookie is a small file, stored on your computer's hard disk, that contains information about your visits to a particular Web site. An e-tailing site, for example, might store your user name and password in a cookie. The next time you visit that site, your cookie information is read and processed.

If you're concerned about how your personal information is used, go to the Privacy tab of the Internet Options dialog box. Here you can set your allowable Privacy Preferences. There are three settings to choose from:

- **Low**—At this setting, your browser allows cookies from all sites, and doesn't check for any other privacy policies or reporting. In other words, every site will be accessible, no matter what.
- **Medium**—This is the default privacy setting for IE6. At this setting, your browser allows cookies from all sites, but does not allow any unsatisfactory third parties to save cookies on your system. The browser will also check for a site's privacy policy, and compare that policy to your preferences.
- **High**—This setting offers the highest level of protection, but will also block access to a large number of sites. At this setting, your browser prohibits any cookies from being saved to your system. (Because many sites depend on cookies to function properly, you may not be able to enter these sites at this setting.)

As much as some users rail against the use of cookies, not accepting cookies will severely limit your use of the Web. It's kind of like the issue some people have with credit cards. Yes, obtaining a credit card creates a credit file that follows you everywhere, for the rest of your life. But trying to exist *without* a credit card is simply impractical. So most people trade off some degree of privacy for the convenience of using a credit card.

It's the same thing with cookies. You make the trade off between complete privacy and the convenience of accessing and using a broad variety of Web sites.

In other words, cookies aren't as bad as some people make them out to be—and really aren't worth worrying about.

SPEEDING UP YOUR BROWSER

While we're on the topic of configuring IE6, there are a handful of settings you can adjust to speed up your Web browsing. If you connect through a particularly slow connection, you should consider reconfiguring these settings.

Set a Larger Cache

IE6 uses a section of your hard disk to hole previously viewed Web pages and graphics. This disk space is called a *cache,* and the bigger it is, the faster you browser will be in reloading older pages. The most significant speed enhancement you can make comes from resizing this cache. The bigger the cache, the faster your browser—when visiting pages you've already been to.

Of course, if you select too large a cache, you'll eat up valuable hard disk space. So you have to choose some sort of compromise between size and performance. If you're continually waiting for your favorite pages to load, your cache may be too small. Choose a larger setting and see how that affects performance.

If you have a very large (10Gb+) hard disk with lots of free space, consider assigning between 500Mb and 1Gb to the cache.

To change the IE6's cache size, follow these steps:

1. From the Internet Options dialog box, select the General tab.
2. In the Temporary Internet Files section, click the Settings button.
3. When the Settings dialog box appears (as shown in Figure 8.14), go to the Temporary Internet Files section and adjust the slider to the desired size, in MB.
4. Click OK to accept this new cache size.

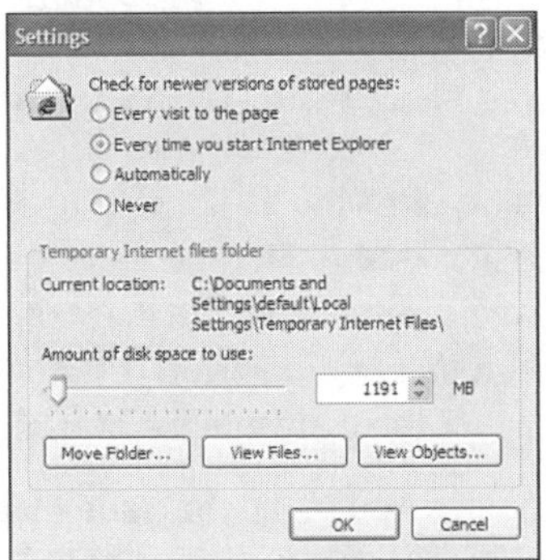

Figure 8.14

Use the Settings dialog box to adjust IE6's disk cache.

If your hard disk is getting too full (or if your browser keeps loading old versions of certain pages), you should clear your browser cache. You do this by clicking the Delete Files button on the General tab of the Internet Options dialog box.

Don't Check for Updates

Of course, a cache is no good if your browser downloads every single element every time you visit a page. Faster performance can be had by forcing your browser to use the cache. This way IE6 will only check for new content periodically.

If you turn off page verification entirely, you run the risk of not always loading the latest Web page content.

To configure this Web page verification, follow these steps:

1. From the Internet Options dialog box, select the General tab, and then click the Settings button.
2. When the Settings dialog box appears, go to the Check For Newer Versions of Stored Pages section, and make your desired selection. You can choose from Every Visit to the Page, Every Time You Start Internet Explorer (this is the default setting), Automatically, or Never.
3. Click OK to activate your new settings.

Turn Off the Graphics

Another, more drastic, thing you can do to speed up your browser is to not load graphics. While this approach definitely reduces the appeal of most Web pages, it can help you cope with an extremely slow Internet connection.

Here's how you prevent IE6 from loading Web-page graphics:

1. From within the Internet Options dialog box, select the Advanced tab.
2. Scroll down to the Multimedia section, and uncheck the Show Pictures option.
3. Click OK.

WORKING WITH WEB SITES

Once you have IE6 configured to your liking, it's time to start browsing the Web. There are some specific features of IE6 that help you keep track of the sites you visit—or to find those sites in the first place—and I'll talk about those features next.

Managing Your Favorite Sites

When you find a Web page you like, you can add it to IE6's Favorites list. With this feature, you can access any of your favorite sites just by choosing it from the list.

To add a page to your Favorites list:

1. Go to the page you want to add.
2. Select Favorites, Add to Favorites to display the Add Favorite dialog box.
3. Confirm the page's Name, and then click the Create In button to extend the dialog box.
4. Select the folder where you want to place this link, and then click OK.

To view a page in your Favorites list:

1. Click the Favorites button. The browser window automatically splits into two panes. Your favorites are displayed in the left pane, as shown in Figure 8.15.

Figure 8.15

Click the Favorites button to display the Favorites pane; click on any link to display that page in the right pane.

2. Click any folder in the Favorites pane to display the contents of that folder.
3. Click a favorite page and that page will be displayed in the right pane.
4. Click the Favorites button again to hide the Favorites pane.

If you add a lot of pages to your Favorites list, it can become unwieldy. To reorganize the Favorites list, use your mouse to drag a favorite page into a new folder or position. To delete a favorite, just highlight it and press Delete.

Revisiting History

Internet Explorer has two ways of keeping track of Web pages you've visited, so that you can easily revisit them without having to reenter the URL.

To revisit one of the last half-dozen or so pages you've visited, click the down-arrow on the Back button. This drops down a menu containing the last nine pages you've visited. Highlight any page on this menu to jump directly to that page.

To revisit pages you've viewed in the past several days, you use IE6's History pane. Just follow these steps:

1. Click the History button. The browser window will automatically split into two panes, with your history for the past several days displayed in the left pane (see Figure 8.16).

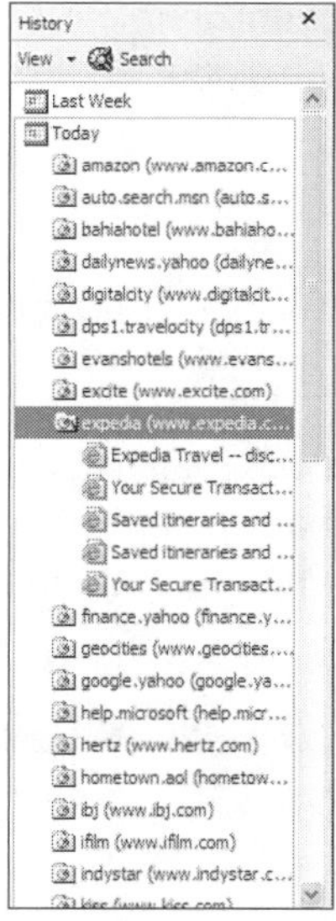

Figure 8.16

Click the History button to revisit pages you've recently viewed, organized by day and by site.

2. Your history is organized into folders for each of the past several days. Click any folder in the History pane to display the sites you visited that day.
3. Each site you visited on a particular day has its own subfolder. Click a subfolder to display the pages you visited within that particular site.
4. Click a specific page to display that page in the right pane.
5. Click the History button again to hide the History pane.

To sort the sites in the History pane by site, by most visited, or by most visited today, pull down the View menu within the pane and make a new selection. To increase or decrease the number of days' history displayed, select Tools, Internet Options and then go to the History section of the General tab and enter a new value for Days to Keep Pages in History. (The default value is 20—which may be too much history for you!)

Searching for Sites

Internet Explorer has two features that make Web searching easier. In both cases, you can initiate your searches from within the browser, without having to go directly to Yahoo! or Google or any other search site.

The first feature to take note of is called Autosearch, which enables you to enter a search query directly into the Address bar. Just enter a question mark followed by one or more search words (like this: **? red balloon**), then press Enter. IE6 will now initiate a search and display the results in the browser window.

To select which search service is used when you search from the Address bar, click the Search button to open the Search Companion, and then click the Customize button to display the Customize Search Settings window. Now click the Autosearch button, and select which search service you want to use.

The second IE6 search feature is the Search Companion. When you click the Search button, IE6 displays the Search Companion pane, shown in Figure 8.17. Enter your query in the text box, then click the Search button to begin the search.

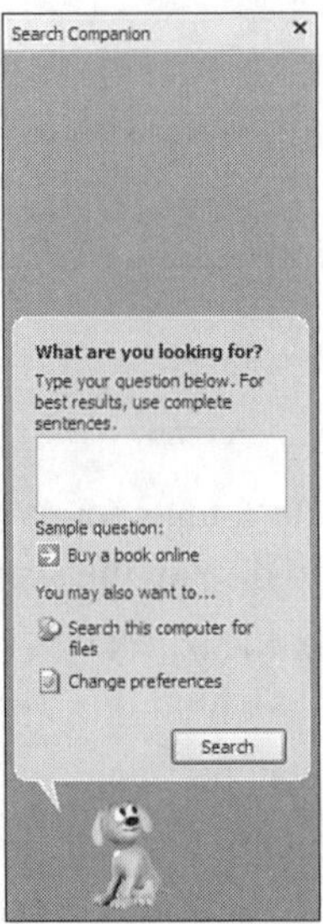

Figure 8.17

Click the Search button to initiate in-browser Web searching.

The Search Companion will now return results from your favorite search engine—along with some other suggested activities, all listed in the Search Companion pane. Probably the most useful activity, if the first set of results isn't to your liking, is to automatically send your results to other search engines. Click this option and the Search Companion displays a list of other search engines, and displays results from the first engine on the list. Click any other search engine to use it for a further search.

To customize the search services used by the Search Companion, click the Change Preferences option in the Search Companion pane, then select Change Internet Search Behavior. When the Internet Search Behavior pane appears, you can select which search service you want to use by default, or you can choose to turn off the Search Companion and go back to the old-style Classic Internet search.

After you've accessed a specific Web site, select Tools, Show Related Links. This displays a Related List pane that contains a list of Web sites that are somehow related to the displayed page. This feature is powered by technology supplied by Alexa. (Go to `www.alexa.com` to learn more about Alexa's full menu of navigation services.)

ALTERNATIVE BROWSERS

That pretty much does it for the new and cool features of Internet Explorer 6. You should know, however, that Internet Explorer is not the only Web browser available. Even though IE6 comes included with Windows XP, you can choose not to use it—and use another Web browser, instead.

Internet Explorer is the most popular Web browser available, but there are two other browsers you can choose to use, if you want—Netscape and Opera.

Netscape

Netscape was one of the first Web browsers, and for a while was the most popular one. After Netscape's purchase by America Online, however, Microsoft started winning the browser wars. Netscape is still out there, still available for free, but now a distant second to Internet Explorer, in terms of number of users.

In terms of how Netscape works, the answer is "pretty much like Internet Explorer." Both browsers perform the same functions, in pretty much the same manner. I've found that the most-recent version of Netscape (version 6.1) is a tad slower and buggier than IE6, but that might change with future updates.

If you're curious, you should download Netscape for yourself and give it a spin. (It's okay to install more than one browser on your system. It won't hurt anything.) If you do a lot of surfing, it's a good idea to have both browsers anyway. Occasionally a site that doesn't work with IE will work, or look better, with Netscape.

You can download the latest version of Netscape (for free) at `home.netscape.com/download/`.

Opera

While Internet Explorer and Netscape are far and away the two most-used Web browsers, there is a third browser that is gaining a lot of attention among the techie crowd. Opera, developed by Opera Software, is known for its speed and small file size, and is available for all versions of Windows, Linux, BeOS, OS/2, and the Macintosh.

Unlike Internet Explorer and Netscape, Opera is not necessarily free. Opera Software does offer a no-charge version of the software, but it's advertising supported, so you have to deal with ads in the interface. If you want an ad-free version of the browser, you'll have to pay $39. Go to `www.opera.com` for more information and to download the software.

JIM'S TOP TEN TIPS

If you're like most users, you browse the Web for at least an hour every day. Which means that you'll get a lot of use out of the new Internet Explorer 6 included with Windows XP.

Just make sure you remember these ten important points:

1. Windows XP includes a new version of Internet Explorer, version 6, which features the new Luna interface and some improved functionality.
2. Before you can customize IE6's toolbars, you first have to unlock them. (Select View, Toolbars, then uncheck Lock the Toolbars.)
3. You can move IE6's toolbars around, hide or display individual toolbars, or add/delete/rearrange buttons on the main Toolbar.
4. Most of IE6's configuration options are found in the Internet Options dialog box. (Select Tools, Internet Options—or click the Internet Options icon in the Windows Control Panel.)
5. The most-used settings are found on the General tab. From here you can set the browser's Home page, delete temporary files, set the size of the disk cache, delete cookies, and manage history files.
6. To manage your Internet connections, go to the Connections tab. (You can also start the New Connection Wizard from here.)
7. To filter out sites that contain inappropriate content, go to the Content tab and activate the Content Advisor.
8. You can save your favorite Web sites to the Favorites list. Click the Favorites button to select a site from your Favorites list.
9. You can search directly from the browser by entering a query (preceded by a ?) into the Address bar.
10. To query multiple search engines, click the Search button to display the Search Companion.

CHAPTER 9

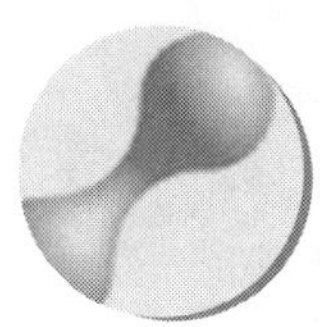

SENDING AND RECEIVING E-MAIL WITH OUTLOOK EXPRESS

- Introducing Outlook Express 6
- Configuring Outlook Express
- Protecting Against E-mail Viruses
- Sending and Receiving E-mail
- Sending Fancy Messages
- Connecting to Web Mail
- Working with Folders and Message Rules
- Using the Address Book
- Using Outlook Express with Newsgroups
- Alternative E-mail/Newsreader Clients
- Jim's Top Ten Tips

As popular as the Web is, the true "killer app" for the Internet is e-mail. More people use the Internet to communicate than they do for any other purpose. And for most users, communication means e-mail.

When it comes to communicating, Windows XP includes a good all-purpose program in the form of Outlook Express. Outlook Express is used both for e-mail and for accessing Usenet newsgroups. It's similar to the version of Microsoft Outlook included with Microsoft Office, except without all the contact management and scheduling functions. That makes it an easier program to learn, and an easier program to use.

The latest version of Outlook Express, version 6, isn't a lot different from the previous version 5. The big differences are the adoption of XP's Luna interface and slightly more effective protection against e-mail viruses.

INTRODUCING OUTLOOK EXPRESS 6

The basic Outlook Express window is divided into three panes, as shown in Figure 9.1. The pane on the top left is called the Folder list, and it's where you access your Inbox and other message folders. The pane on the bottom left is your Contacts list, and it contains all the names in your Address Book. The top-right pane is the Message pane, and it lists all the messages stored in the selected folder. The bottom right pane is the Preview pane, and it displays the contents of the selected message.

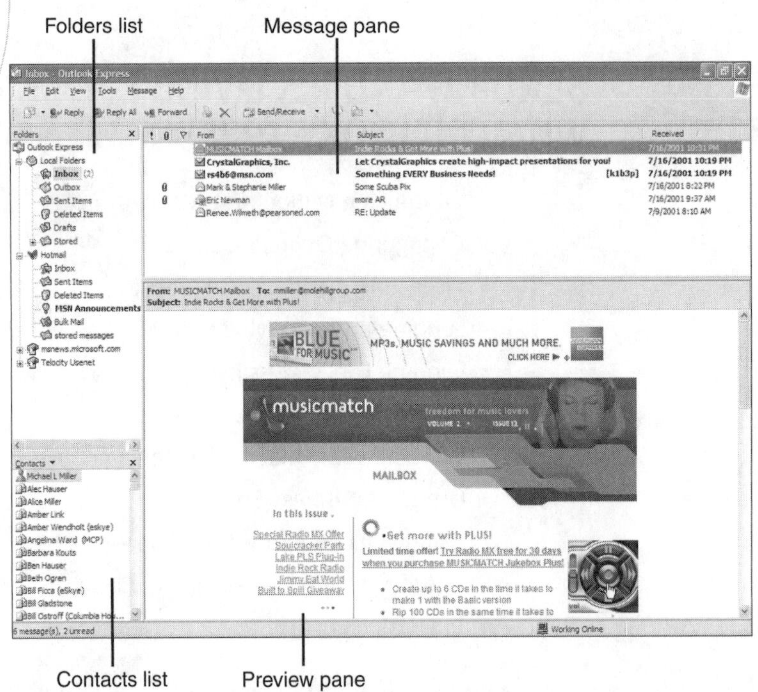

Figure 9.1

The main Outlook Express window, divided into four panes.

You access incoming e-mail message by clicking the Inbox icon in the Folder List. Message headers for your Inbox are displayed in the Message pane. Select a message header and the contents of that message are displayed in the Preview pane.

CONFIGURING OUTLOOK EXPRESS

Before you can use Outlook Express, you have to configure it for your current e-mail and newsgroup accounts. You can also reconfigure the interface to look a little more sophisticated—like the interface for the Microsoft Outlook program.

Setting Up E-mail Accounts

Outlook Express has to be set up for each and every e-mail account you might have. If you used the Internet Connection Wizard to create your Internet connection, Outlook Express was automatically configured at that time. If you didn't use the Internet Connection Wizard, you'll need to configure Outlook Express manually. You'll also have to manually configure Outlook Express if you add a new e-mail account to your portfolio.

To add a new e-mail account to Outlook Express, you'll need to have the following information handy:

- Your e-mail address (in the form of *xxx@xxx.xx*) for the new account
- The names of the new account's incoming and outgoing e-mail servers (may be the same)
- The new e-mail POP account name and password

Once you have the proper information in hand, follow these steps to set up a new account:

1. From within Outlook Express, select Tools, Accounts.
2. When the Internet Accounts dialog box appears, select the Mail tab, and then click the Add button and select Mail.
3. Outlook Express now launches a subset of the Internet Connection Wizard. Follow the onscreen instructions to complete your new account's configuration.

If you have more than one e-mail account, or accounts with multiple ISPs, repeat these steps to add your additional accounts.

The first time you use Outlook Express, a wizard will launch automatically to walk you through the new account setup.

Setting Up Usenet Accounts

While you're setting up Outlook Express, you also need to configure to access Usenet newsgroups from your ISP's newsgroup server. As with the e-mail setup, if you used the Internet Connection Wizard to create your Internet connection, Outlook Express was automatically configured at that time. If you didn't, you'll need to configure Outlook Express manually for your newsgroup server.

Follow these steps:

1. From within Outlook Express, select Tools, Accounts to display the Internet Accounts dialog box.
2. Select the News tab, click the Add button, and then select News.
3. Outlook Express now launches a subset of the Internet Connection Wizard. Follow the onscreen instructions to complete your account configuration.

Outlook Express will let you access multiple news servers. For example, you may want to access the newsgroup server at your ISP for standard newsgroups, but access Microsoft's news server (`msnews.microsoft.com`) for discussions specific to Microsoft software. This is a good strategy when you find newsgroups that aren't available on a specific server.

Personalizing the Interface

The Outlook Express window can be configured for a number of different views. For example, you may want to change the traditional "tree" view of the Folders list into an icon-driven sidebar more like the one used in Microsoft Outlook.

Figure 9.1 showed the Outlook Express window in standard configuration. Figure 9.2 shows a different configuration, with the Outlook bar to the left, folder bar to the top, and preview pane underneath the message pane.

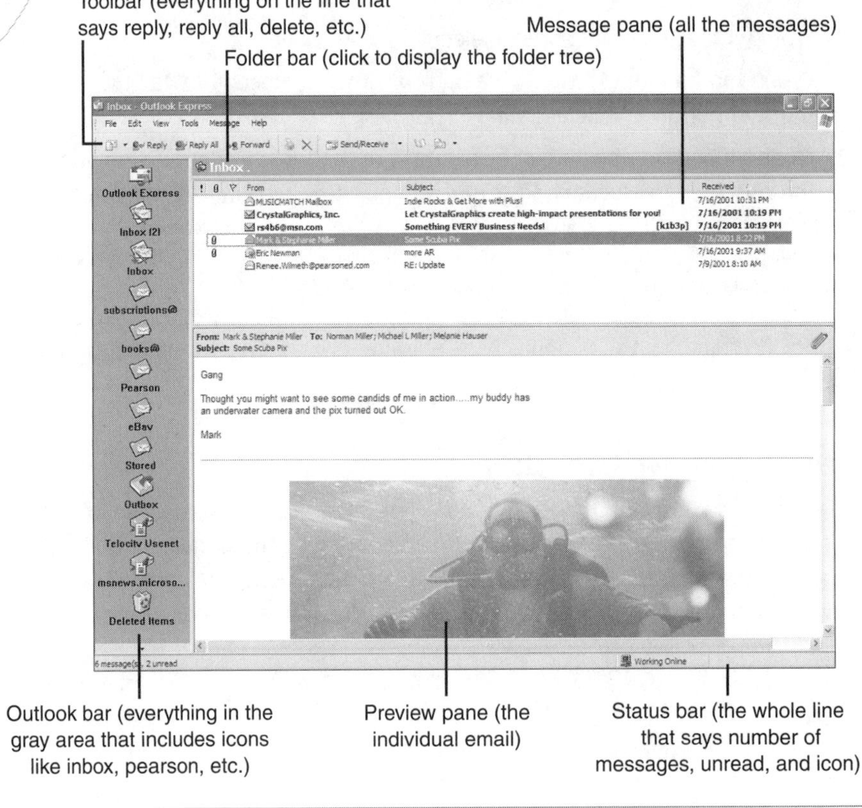

Figure 9.2

A alternate configuration for Outlook Express, mimicking Microsoft Outlook's look and feel.

To configure the Outlook Express window:

1. Select View, Layout to display the Window Layout Properties dialog box, shown in Figure 9.3.

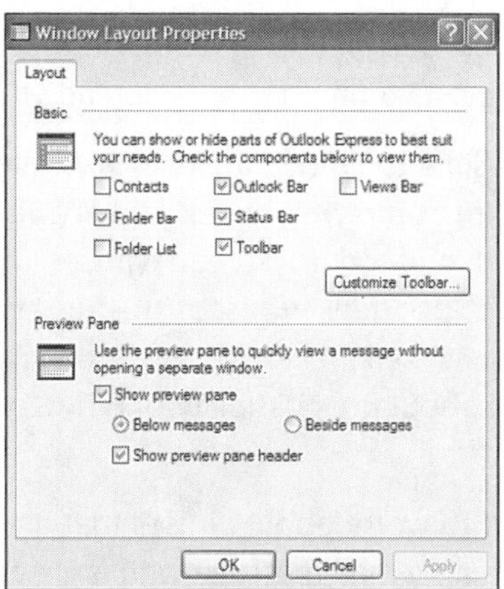
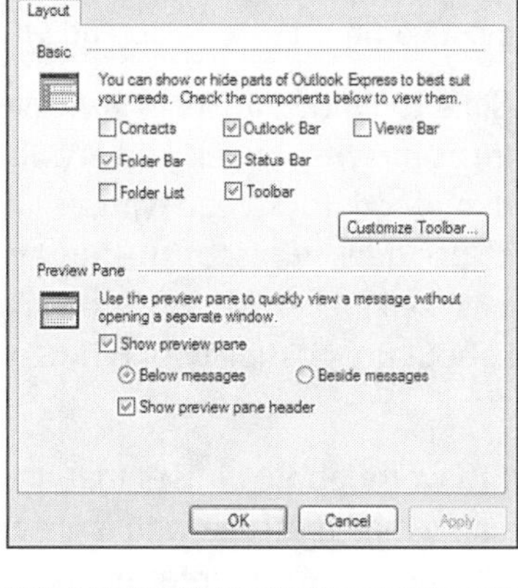

Figure 9.3

Use the Windows Layout Properties dialog box to customize the program's look and feel.

2. To display or hide various other parts of the interface, check or uncheck the options in the Basic section of the dialog box.
3. To display a preview pane, check the Show Preview Pane option. You can also choose to display the preview pane below or beside your messages, and to display a header for the preview pane.
4. To add, delete, or rearrange the buttons on the toolbar, click the Customize Toolbar button. When the Customize Toolbar dialog box opens, make your selections. (You can also configure how the buttons are displayed—with large or small icons, no labels, normal labels, or selected text to the right.)
5. Click OK when done.

You can also select which columns are displayed in the Message pane. Select View, Columns to display the Columns dialog box. Check those columns you want to show, and uncheck those you want to hide. Use the Move Up and Move Down buttons to rearrange the columns to your liking, then click OK.

PROTECTING AGAINST E-MAIL VIRUSES

One of the big problems with the Internet is that all the near-instant communication makes it easy for computer viruses to spread quite rapidly. Every way you can communicate online is also a way for viruses to spread.

E-mail is not exempt from this. One of the more popular ways of spreading viruses is through attachments to e-mail messages. I'll discuss attachments in more detail later in this chapter, but for this discussion all you need to know is that an attachment is a file, of any type, that hitches a ride on an e-mail message. Because a virus is just a computer file, it's quite easy for viruses to tag along on e-mail messages.

It used to be that you couldn't catch a virus just by receiving or reading an e-mail. You actually had to run or open a file attached to an e-mail in order to infect your machine with a virus. (And this is still the most common way to spread viruses via e-mail.)

However, because it's possible to embed a virus via ActiveX or Java into HTML code, it's also possible to catch a virus simply by reading an HTML-format e-mail message. This is still a relatively little-used method to spread viruses, however, and Microsoft issues patches to its software as new viruses of this type are discovered. (Go to `www.microsoft.com/technet/security/` for Microsoft's latest list of security bulletins.) I wouldn't get too paranoid about the possibility of HTML e-mail viruses, but it is one more thing to worry about.

I think it's more important to worry about viruses that are spread by e-mail attachments. It's just too easy to receive an e-mail message with a file attached, click the file to open it, and then launch the virus file. Boom! You're infected.

Viruses can be found in many different types of files. The most common file types for viruses are .EXE, .VBS, .BAT, .COM, and .PIF. Viruses can also be embedded in Word or Excel files, using VisualBasic macro code. You *can't* catch a virus from a picture file, so viewing .JPG, .GIF, .TIF, and .BMP files is completely safe.

If you think about it, it should be fairly easy to avoid catching a virus. Just don't open any .EXE, .VBS, .BAT, .COM, or .PIF files you receive via e-mail—especially if they come from people you don't know.

Worried that a file—even a Word .DOC file—might contain a virus? Then open the file in Notepad or Wordpad. Both these programs open any program as plain text, so you can read what's there—without activating any potential virus code.

The problem is that people are curious. When you see an e-mail with the subject line "Nude pictures of your neighbor's wife" or "I love you," you might be tempted to take a look. That temptation is what gets you.

It gets worse when the virus developers try to "hide" the file's extension. What would you think if you saw a filename that looked like this: nude pictures.jpg.vbs? You *might* think it's a .JPG file—especially if the file name was so long that the ".VBS" part was hidden off to the side. And, since .JPG files are safe, you might open it. Even though it's not really a .JPG. (It's a .VBS—VisualBasic Script—file with a ".JPG" in the middle of the filename.)

You can see how tricky the virus developers are. They've even developed viruses that implant themselves in your machine and then use Outlook Express to e-mail copies of themselves to all the contacts in your Address Book. Then your friends see an e-mail from you, with some sort of file attached, and naively open the file. (If it's from you, it must be safe—right?) Boom! Another system infected. And another. And another.

The only way to completely protect yourself against e-mail viruses is to never open any e-mail attachments. That's probably too drastic for most users, so Outlook Express 6 has added some virus-protection features that you should find useful.

You access Outlook Express' virus-protection by selecting Tools, Options to display the Options dialog box, then selecting the Security tab. As you can see in Figure 9.4, the top half of this tab is devoted to virus protection.

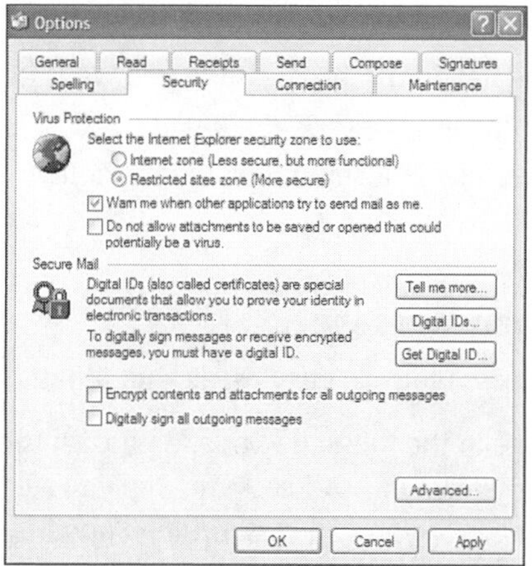

Figure 9.4

Configure Outlook Express to protect you from e-mail viruses.

The key features here are the two checkboxes. The first one, Warn Me When Other Applications Try to Send E-Mail As me, protects you from viruses hijacking Outlook Express to e-mail themselves to your contacts. The second option, Do Not Allow Attachments To Be Saved or Opened That Could Potentially Be a Virus, blocks the receipt of any .EXE, .VBS, or .PIF file.

For the best protection, you should check both these options. The only problem you might have with that is if you even need to receive a legitimate application file (.EXE extension) from another user. With the second option enabled, you couldn't receive the program.

The solution, of course, is to leave the option checked until you know you're going to receive an .EXE file. Then you can uncheck the option, receive the file, and then go back and turn the option back on.

SENDING AND RECEIVING E-MAIL

In case you're new to e-mail, it's time to present a quick Outlook Express e-mail how-to. Read on to learn how to use Outlook Express' most common operations.

Reading an E-mail Message

If you've received new e-mail messages, they will be stored in Outlook Express' Inbox. To read a new message

1. Click the Inbox icon in the Folder list. All waiting messages will now appear in the Message pane.
2. Click the message header of the message you want to read. This displays the contents of the message in the Preview pane.
3. To display the message in a separate window, double-click the message in the Message pane.

Replying to an E-mail Message

Replying to an e-mail message is as easy as clicking a button. Just follow these steps:

1. Select the message in the Message pane, then click the Reply to Author button on the toolbar. (Alternately, you can click the Reply to All button to reply to all recipients of the message—or you can click on the Forward button to send the message to a completely different recipient.)
2. A Re: window appears, as shown in Figure 9.5. The original message sender is now listed in the To: box, with the original message's subject referenced in the Subject: box. The original message is "quoted" in the text area of the window, with > preceding the original text.

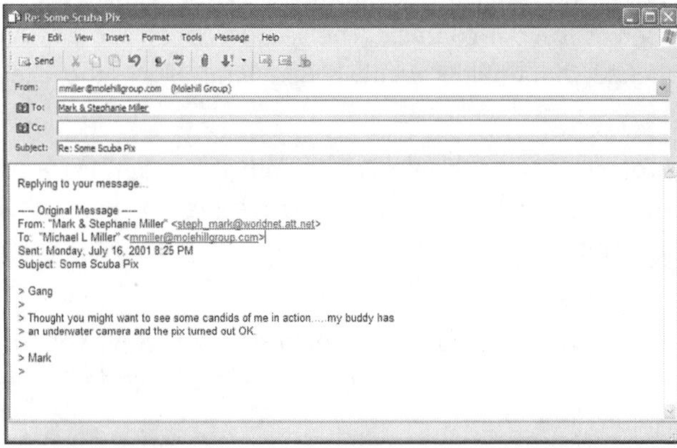

Figure 9.5

Replying to a message is similar to creating a new one—but with the original message's text automatically quoted.

3. Type your reply in the text area above the quoted text.
4. Click the Send button to send this reply to your Outbox.

Unless reconfigured otherwise, Outlook Express does not automatically send your new messages out over the Internet when you click the Send button. The Send button only "sends" the message to your Outbox. To send all waiting messages from your Outbox out over the Internet, click the Send and Receive button on the main Outlook Express toolbar.

Creating a New E-mail Message

Creating a new e-mail message is similar to replying to a received message. Follow these steps:

1. Click the New Mail button.
2. When the New Message dialog box appears, enter the e-mail address of the recipient(s) in the To: field and the address of anyone you want to receive a carbon copy into the Cc: box.

Separate multiple addresses in the To: or Cc: fields with a semicolon (;) but no spaces, like this: fflintstone@bedrock.com;gjetson@sprockets.com.

3. You can also select names from your Address Book by clicking the Address Book icon next to the To: or Cc: fields. When the Select Recipients dialog box appears (as shown in Figure 9.6), select the name(s) of whomever you want to send the message to and click the To: button. Select the name(s) of whomever you want to send a carbon copy of the message to and click the cc: button. Click OK when done.

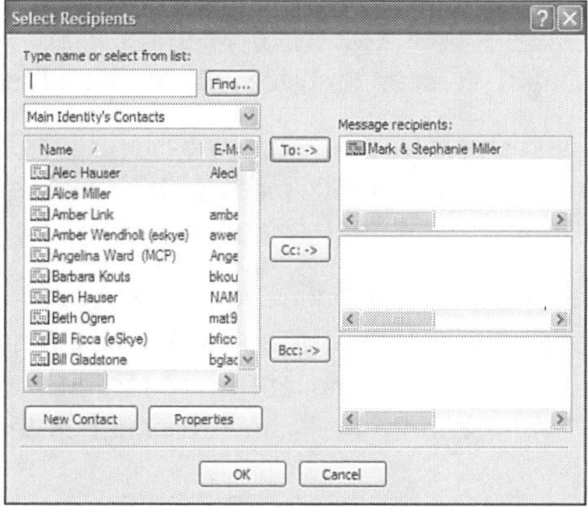

Figure 9.6

Use the Address Book to automatically add recipients to your new message.

4. Enter the subject of the message in the Subject: field.
5. Move your cursor to the main message area and type your message.
6. You can choose to send your message in either plain text or HTML format. (HTML messages are discussed in the next section.) If you choose to send it in HTML format, you can use the formatting buttons on the toolbar to add boldface, italic, underlined, or aligned text. To select HTML formatting, select Format, Rich Text (HTML).

If you type a standard Web URL into an HTML e-mail message, Outlook Express will automatically create a hyperlink for you—you don't have to do it manually.

7. If you're sending the message in HTML format, you can add background colors and graphics. If you simply want to use a background color, select Format, Background, Color, and then pick a color from the color list. If you want to use a background picture, select Format, Background, Picture, and then enter the name of the graphics file you want to use. You can also add a background sound to your message by selecting Format, Background, Sound.
8. When your message is complete, send it to the Outbox by clicking the Send button.

SENDING FANCY MESSAGES

You're probably used to e-mail messages containing nothing but boring plain text. It doesn't have to be that way. Outlook Express lets you send e-mail with fancy HTML formatting, personalized signatures, and attached files.

Creating HTML Mail

Most e-mail messages are just plain text—because that's all you're sending, in most cases. But Outlook Express can also send and receive fully formatted text, with backgrounds and colors and embedded HTML hyperlinks.

You turn on HTML formatting for a specific message by selecting Format, Rich Text (HTML) from the message window. You turn *off* HTML formatting by selecting Format, Plain Text.

You can configure Outlook Express so that all your messages are sent in HTML, by default. Just select Tools, Options to display the Options dialog box, then select the Send tab and choose the HTML option in the Mail Sending Format section. If you'd rather send all your messages in text-only format, choose the Plain Text option instead.

Some older or corporate-oriented e-mail programs will not be able to display fancy HTML formatting—and might reject HTML e-mail outright. So if you're sending message to a user and you don't know whether they can receive HTML e-mail, you'll want to send that message as a text-only (*not* HTML!) message.

Using Stationary

Outlook Express lets you create custom backgrounds and text for your messages. When your create this *stationery*, it is used as the default background for all your new HTML-formatted messages.

To create a default stationery for your new messages:

1. Select Tools, Options to display the Options dialog box.
2. Select the Compose tab.
3. Check the Mail option in the Stationery section, then click the Select button.
4. When the Select Stationery dialog box appears, choose a format and click OK.

Adding a Signature

An important part of any e-mail message is your "signature," a two- or three-line message that is added to the bottom of all your messages. To create a signature in Outlook Express, follow these steps:

1. Select Tools, Options to display the Options dialog box.
2. Select the Signatures tab.
3. Click the New button and add the text for your signature in the Edit Signature box.
4. Check the Add Signatures to All Outgoing Messages option. (If you don't want to add your signature to replies and forwards, check the Don't Add Signatures to Replies and Forwards option.)
5. Click OK.

Signatures are not HTML-dependent. They can be added to any e-mail message, plain text or HTML.

Working with Attachments

Some e-mail messages have additional files "attached" to the mail message. Attaching files to an e-mail message is a way to send files from user to user over the Internet.

What kind of files can you attach to e-mail messages? Here's a short list:

- Graphics, such as pictures of your kids and family
- Audio, such as MP3 song files or audio clips from your favorite television programs
- Video clips, such as files captured from your videotaped home movies
- Documents, such as word processing files from Microsoft Word or spreadsheets from Microsoft Excel

As you read earlier, you can also attach virus files to e-mail messages—but the less said about that the better.

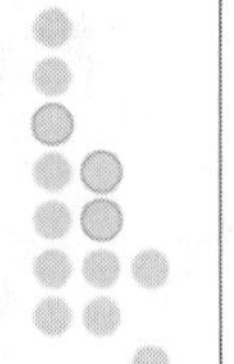

If a message contains an attachment, you'll see a paperclip icon in the message header and a paperclip button in the preview pane header. When you receive a message with an attachment, you can open it or save it to your hard disk.

To view or open an attachment, click the paperclip button in the Preview pane header, then click the attachment's filename. This will open the attachment in its associated application. (If you're asked whether you want to save or view the attachment, select view.)

To save an attachment to your hard disk, click the paperclip button in the preview pane header, then select Save Attachments. When the Save Attachments dialog box appears, select a location for the file and click the Save button.

If you want to attach a file to an outgoing e-mail message, start with a new message and then click the Attach button in the message's toolbar. When the Insert Attachment dialog box appears, locate the file you want to send and then click Attach. The attached file is now listed in a new Attach: field below the Subject: field. When you click the Send button, the e-mail message and its attached file are sent together to the Outbox.

CONNECTING TO WEB MAIL

If you're like me, you have a standard POP e-mail account with your ISP, and an auxiliary e-mail account with a Web-based e-mail provider, such as Hotmail or Yahoo! Mail. The advantage of a Web mail account is that you can check that account from any computer, using any Web browser. It's also a great way to establish a second identity on the Internet, for those times you want to be someone other than yourself.

Outlook Express lets you add your Web-based e-mail accounts to its basic configuration. This way you can use Outlook Express to send and receive e-mail to and from Hotmail and other Web mail services.

Here's how you set it up:

1. From within Outlook Express, select Tools, Accounts to display the Internet Accounts dialog box.
2. Select the Mail tab and click Add, Mail.
3. When the Your Name screen of the Internet Connection Wizard appears, enter your Display Name and click Next.
4. On the Internet E-Mail Address screen, select I Already Have an E-Mail Address That I'd Like to Use, enter that address, and click Next.
5. On the E-Mail Server Names screen, pull down the My Incoming Mail Server list and select HTTP.
6. If you're setting up Outlook Express for Hotmail, pull down the My HTTP Mail Server Provider list and select Hotmail. If you're setting up another service, select Other.
7. Enter the URL of your service's e-mail server into the Incoming Mail Server box, then click Next.

In almost all cases the URL of your service's e-mail server is *not* the URL you use to access the service. You'll need to obtain the server address from your Web mail service before you configure Outlook Express—and be sure to enter the full address, including the `http://`.

8. When the Internet Mail Logon screen appears, enter your account name and password into the appropriate blanks, select the Remember Password option, then click Next.
9. When the Congratulations screen appears, click Finish.

When you return to Outlook Express, you'll find a new listing for your Web mail provider in the Folder List. You can now access this Web mail account just as you do your POP e-mail account

WORKING WITH FOLDERS AND MESSAGE RULES

Receiving e-mail is a simple task–until you start getting a lot of it. Every time I log on to my ISP I have to slog through dozens and dozens of e-mail messages. And most of them are nothing but junk!

Fortunately, e-mail has a way to organize and manage that avalanche of messages. All you have to do is separate the messages into folders, just like the ones in your physical file cabinets.

Managing Folders

Outlook Express lets you store messages in folders. The Inbox, for example, is a folder. You can create as many folders as you like, and use them to organize your messages however you want.

To create a new folder, go to the Folders list and select Local Folders. Select File, New, Folder to display the Create Folder dialog box, then enter a name for the new folder and click OK.

You can next folders in subfolders by selecting a different folder and then going through the above procedure. You can also choose which folders you display on the Outlook bar (if you have the Outlook bar displayed) by right-clicking the folder and selecting Add To Outlook Bar.

Using Message Rules

Okay, now you have a bunch of folders. Maybe you've assigned them labels by letter of the alphabet, or by sender ("Messages From Uncle Bob"). In any case, the folders are there, and waiting to be used.

Outlook Express includes a set of *message rules* that let you determine what to do when you receive messages from certain senders. You could set up a rule, for example, that automatically sends any message from Uncle Bob to the "Messages From Uncle Bob" folder, completely bypassing your normal inbox. If you manage your message rules right, you'll really clear up a lot of that inbox clutter.

To create a new message rule, follow these steps:

1. From within Outlook Express, select Tools, Message Rules, Mail. This opens the New Mail Rule dialog box, as shown in Figure 9.7.

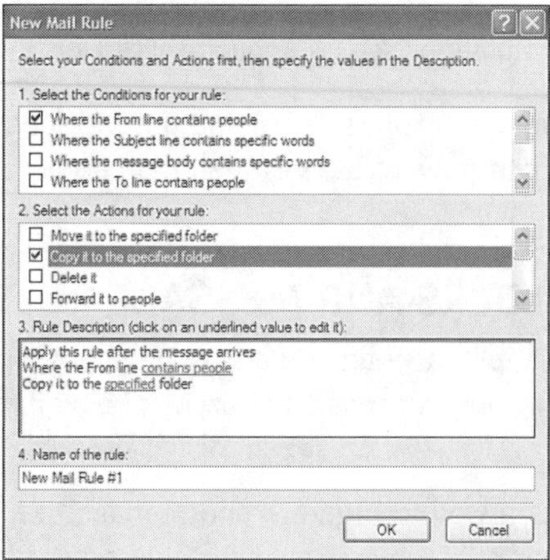

Figure 9.7

Create message rules to manage the messages you receive.

2. Select a condition from the top list. For example, to manage mail from particular senders, you would select Where the From Line Contains People.
3. Select an action from the second list. For example, to send messages to a particular folder, you would select Move It To the Specified Folder.
4. The rule you've created now appears in the Rule Description box—but you're not done yet. You still have to specify the senders or folders that you want the rule to apply to. Click any blue underlined text to make specific selections.
5. Enter a name for the rule in the Name of the Rule box, then click OK.

Blocking Unwanted Messages

When it comes to unwanted e-mail, spam ranks just below viruses. In fact, you'll get a lot more spam than you'll ever get viruses. If you're like me, not a day goes by that you don't get a half-dozen junk e-mails in your inbox. It's a huge bother, at the least.

While it's impossible to completely eliminate spam, it is possible to configure Outlook Express to block messages from identified offenders. You can also use this feature to block messages from real people that you don't want to hear from anymore.

At your request, Outlook Express can add specific users (or entire Internet domains) to its Blocked Senders list, through a kind of built-in message rule. When e-mail is received from any address on this list, it's sent immediately to the Deleted Items folder. You never see it.

When you receive a message from someone that you want to block, all you have to do is highlight the message in the Message pane, then select Message, Block Sender. That sends the sender to the Block Senders list, and you won't have to worry about them again.

You can also manually add addresses to the Block Sender list. Select Tools, Message Rules, Blocked Senders list to display the Message Rules dialog box with the Blocked Senders tab displayed. Click the Add button to display the Add Sender dialog box, enter the user's address or an entire domain name (such as microsoft.com), then click OK. That sender or domain will now be blocked from your inbox.

If you want to start receiving e-mail from someone you've previously blocked, return to the Blocked Senders tab, select the sender, and click the Remove button.

USING THE ADDRESS BOOK

The Windows Address Book is a handy way of keeping track of everyone's addresses. It also lets you assign simple names in place of complicated e-mail addresses. You can use the Address Book to store names and e-mail address information for those people you send e-mail to most often.

To add a new contact to the address book, follow these steps.

1. From within Outlook Express, click the Addresses button on the toolbar. (You can also select Tools, Address Book.)
2. When the Address Book window appears, as shown in Figure 9.8, click the New button and then select New Contact.

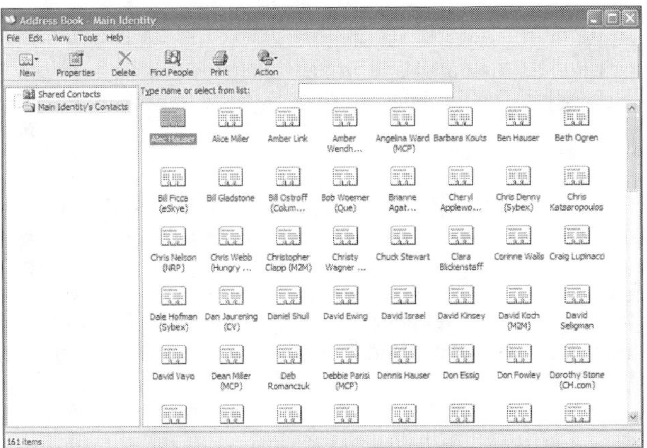

Figure 9.8

Use the Windows Address Book to manage all your e-mail recipients.

3. When the Properties dialog box appears, select the Name tab (shown in Figure 9.9). Enter the first and last name of the new contact, as well as the name you want to show in the Address Book's Display. Now enter the person's e-mail address (or addresses). Click the Add button to register each new e-mail address.

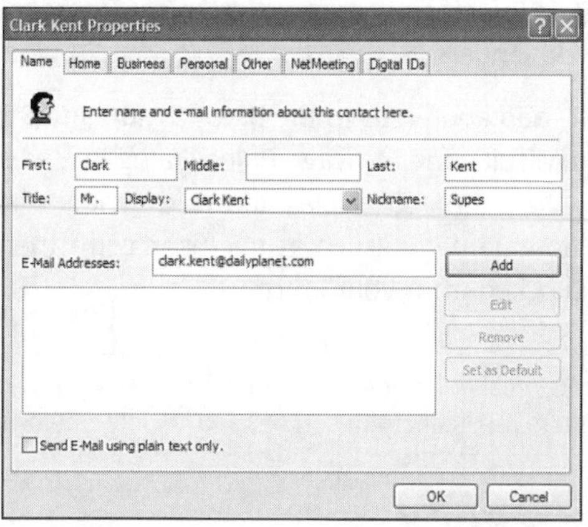

Figure 9.9

Add new contact names to your Address Book.

If this person can't receive HTML mail, check the Send E-Mail Using Plain Text Only option.

4. If you want to enter other information about the contact (street address, phone number, business info, and so on), select the appropriate tabs and enter the information.
5. Click the OK button when done.

You can quickly add the name of anyone who sends you an e-mail to your Address Book by right-clicking his or her name and selecting Add Sender to Address book from the pop-up menu.

The contents of your Address Book will appear in the Outlook Express Contacts list. Your contacts will also be available when you compose new e-mail messages.

If you type the first few letters of a contact's name in the To: or Cc: fields of a new message, Outlook Express will automatically fill in the rest of the contact's name and e-mail address from the Address Book.

USING OUTLOOK EXPRESS WITH NEWSGROUPS

In addition to being an e-mail program, Outlook Express also functions as a newsreader for Usenet newsgroups. Newsgroups are online discussion boards where you can read and post messages (called *articles*) about specific topics. There are more than 40,000 different newsgroups, each focused on a specific topic.

Earlier in this chapter I showed you how to configure Outlook Express for a specific newsgroup server. Most ISPs host their own newsgroup servers, and provide access for all their subscribers. When you want to access a specific newsgroup, you'll probably be connecting to your ISP's newsgroup server.

Selecting and Subscribing to Newsgroups

After you're connected to a newsgroup server, you can then access specific newsgroups. You can simply go to a newsgroup manually, or you can "subscribe" to selected groups. When you subscribe to a newsgroup, there is no formal registration process. All this means is that you've added this newsgroup to a list of your favorites. It's easier to jump to one of a small list of subscribed groups than it is to search for one group out of the 40,000 or so total groups offered by Usenet.

To find and access a newsgroup, follow these steps:

1. From within Outlook Express, click the icon in the Folder for your particular newsgroup server.
2. If you are not currently subscribed to any newsgroups, you'll be prompted to view a list of all newsgroups. Click Yes and proceed to Step 4.
3. If you have already subscribed to one or more newsgroups, you'll now see a list of your subscribed newsgroups. Double-click on a newsgroup to view its contents, or click the Newsgroups button on the toolbar to view a list of all available newsgroups.
4. When the Newsgroup Subscriptions dialog box appears (see Figure 9.10), click the All tab (at the bottom of the dialog box) and select a newsgroup from the main list. You can scroll through the list or search for a specific group by entering key words in the Display Newsgroups Which Contain box.
5. If you want to add this newsgroup to your subscribed list, click the Subscribe button, or double-click the newsgroup item.
6. To choose a newsgroup from your subscribed list, click the Subscribed tab and select the newsgroup you want to read.
7. To go directly to the selected newsgroup, click the Go To button.

Once you've entered a newsgroup, you can then view articles, respond to articles, and create and post your own articles.

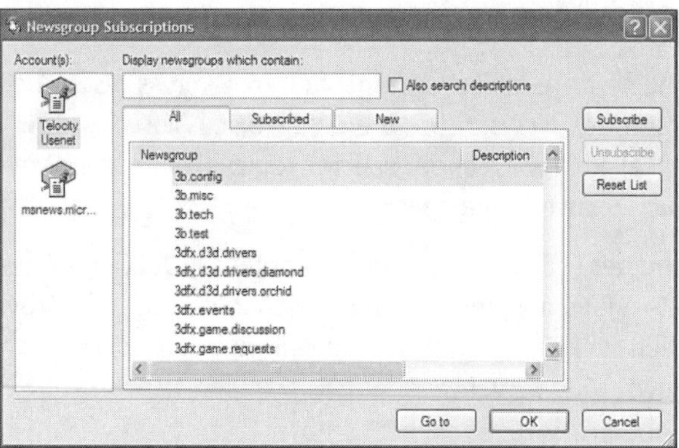

Figure 9.10

Searching for specific newsgroups with Outlook Express.

Reading Newsgroup Articles

Within Outlook Express, articles from the selected newsgroup are displayed in much the same fashion as are e-mail messages. As you can see in Figure 9.11, all the articles from a newsgroup are displayed in the Message pane; the selected message is displayed in the Preview pane. You can read a message in the Preview pane, or double-click on the message header to view the article in its own window.

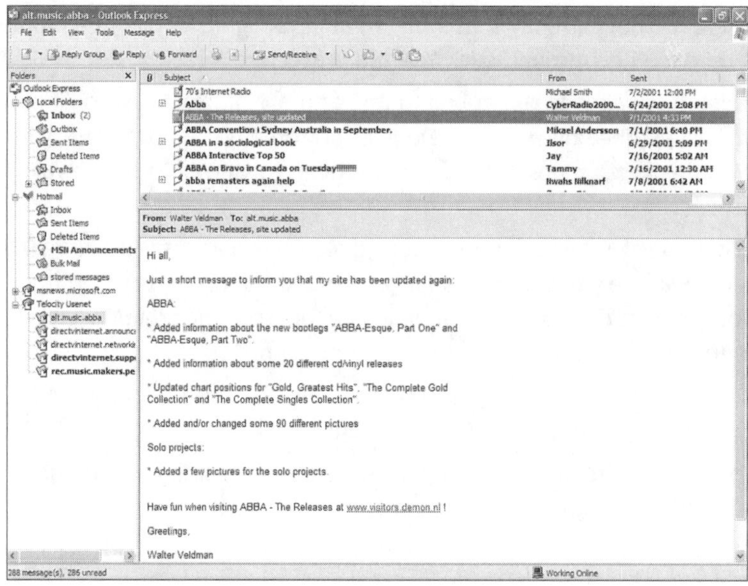

Figure 9.11

Reading newsgroup articles with Outlook Express.

If you'd rather read newsgroup articles offline (without typing up your phone line), you can choose to download all the articles from your favorite newsgroups. All you have to do is select a subscribed newsgroup, click the Settings button, and then select either All Messages or New Messages Only. When you click the Synchronize Account button, messages from your selected newsgroups will be downloaded for your offline reading pleasure.

Creating and Posting New Newsgroup Articles

To create and post new newsgroup articles with Outlook Express, follow these steps:

1. From within a specific newsgroup, click the New Post button.
2. When the New Message window appears, as shown in Figure 9.12, the selected newsgroup is displayed in the Newsgroups field.

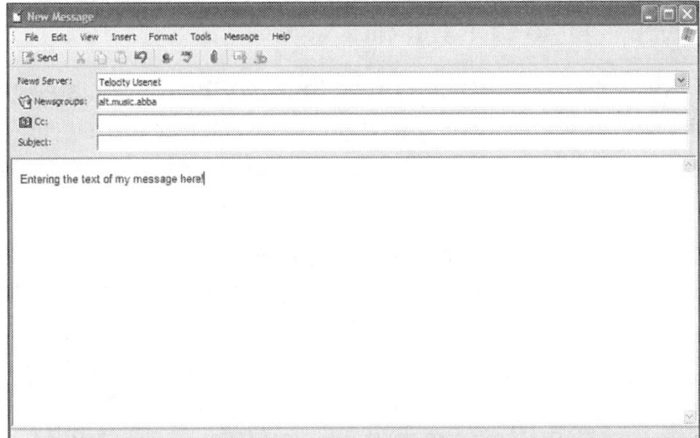

Figure 9.12

Composing a new newsgroup article in Outlook Express.

3. To post to other newsgroups, click the icon in the Newsgroups field. When the Pick Newsgroups dialog box appears, select one or more newsgroups from the list, click the Add button, then click OK. (To display all newsgroups, unclick the Show Only Subscribed Newsgroups button.)
4. Enter a subject in the Subject field, then type the text of your article in the main window.
5. Click the Send button to post this article to the selected newsgroup(s).

Take care before you click the Send button. Once an article is posted, it's out there for all the world to see!

Viewing, Saving, and Posting Attached Files

Like e-mail messages, newsgroup articles can also include attached files. Outlook Express lets you view the contents of attached files right in the Preview pane. You can also save attached files to your hard disk.

Unlike the way e-mail attachments work, Outlook Express does not automatically display the paperclip icon in a newsgroup article's header. The paperclip icon only appears after you've viewed the article's attachment.

Most attachments to newsgroup articles are graphics files. To view a graphics attachment, all you have to do is select the article header in the Message pane. The attached graphic should automatically display in the Preview pane.

To save an attachment to your hard disk, click the paperclip button in the Preview pane header, then select Save Attachments. When the Save Attachments dialog box appears, select the file(s) you want to save and click Save.

You can also choose to view attached files through their associated programs. Just click the paperclip icon in the Preview pane header and select the file you wish to view. The associated application will automatically launch and display the selected file.

Many newsgroups exist primarily for users to exchange graphics and sound files. These files are stored in binary format, and are typically located in newsgroups that start with alt.binaries.

You can also attach files to newsgroup articles you post. All you have to do is click the Attach button in the New Message window, and then select your file from the Insert Attachment dialog box.

ALTERNATIVE E-MAIL/NEWSREADER CLIENTS

Even though Outlook Express is a good e-mail/newsreader program, you don't have to use it if you don't want to. There are a number of other similar programs available, including:

- **Agent** and **Free Agent** (`www.forteinc.com/agent/`) are two versions of the most-popular non-Microsoft newsreader program. Agent is a commercial program that functions as a full-featured news and mail reader, including advanced features such as kill and watch filters, cross-post management, and so on. Free Agent is a free version of Agent, with a smaller, newsreader-specific, feature set.
- **Eudora** (`www.eudora.com`) is one of the oldest e-mail programs on the market. Eudora has similar features to Outlook Express, and is available in both free (advertiser-supported) and paid versions.
- **Microsoft Outlook** (`www.microsoft.com/office/outlook/`) is kind of the corporate version of Outlook Express. (Another way to think of Outlook is that it's like Outlook Express on steroids.) Outlook includes similar e-mail functionality as Outlook

Express, but adds more powerful contact management and a full-featured personal information manager (PIM) and scheduler. Since Outlook is included with Microsoft Office, it's the e-mail program of choice for many corporations.

- **Netscape Messenger** (`home.netscape.com/download/`) is the newsreader/e-mail program that comes with the Netscape Web browser. Netscape Messenger is free, and functions very similarly to Outlook Express.
- **News Rover** (`www.newsrover.com`) is a newsreader that automates message retrieval, with specific features for finding and downloading messages with MP3 and picture files attached.
- **NewsShark** (`www.wmhsoft.com`) is a high-performance newsreader optimized for downloading large binary files.
- **RoboNews** (`www.robonews.com`) is a sleek newsreader that automatically downloads specified types of binary files and displays picture files in either an image gallery or slide show.

JIM'S TOP TEN TIPS

Of all the auxiliary programs included with Windows XP, Outlook Express is probably the one you'll use most often. Just remember these ten important points:

1. You can use Outlook Express for both e-mail and Usenet newsgroups.
2. You don't have to settle for Outlook Express' default interface. Select View, Layout to make Outlook Express look more like Microsoft Outlook.
3. Outlook Express includes built-in protection against e-mail viruses. (You should still remember not to open any attachments with .EXE, .VBS, or .PIF extensions.)
4. If you want to block all e-mail from a spammer, select Message, Block Sender.
5. You can use Outlook Express' message rules to automatically sort incoming messages into separate folders.
6. Outlook Express can be configured to receive normal POP e-mail (from your ISP account) and Web-based e-mail, such as Hotmail.
7. When you get tired of plain-text messages, you can turn on Outlook Express' HTML function and send fancy formatted e-mails, complete with graphical stationery backgrounds.
8. An easy way to send a file to another user is to attach the file to an e-mail message. With Outlook Express, this is as easy as clicking the Attach button and selecting the file you want to attach.
9. Use the Address Book to store names and e-mail addresses of people you communicate with most often. You can add a recipient from your Address Book by clicking the To: or Cc: buttons when you're composing a new e-mail message.
10. When you're using Outlook Express to read newsgroup articles, you can view graphics attachments directly in the Preview pane.

CHAPTER 10

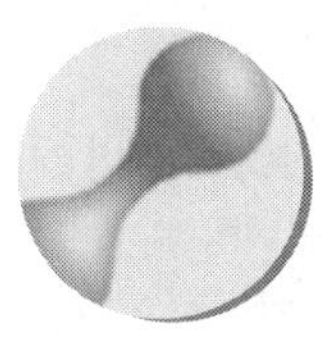

CHATTING ONLINE WITH WINDOWS MESSENGER

- Introducing Windows Messenger
- Getting Connected
- Finding New Contacts
- One-to-One Messaging
- Group Chats
- Making Internet Phone Calls
- Video Conferencing
- Jim's Top Ten Tips

If you're like a lot of Internet users, you like to chat online with other users. And if you like to chat, you probably do a lot of your chatting via instant messaging.

Instant messaging lets you communicate one-on-one, in real time, with your friends, family, and colleagues. It's faster than e-mail and less chaotic than chat rooms. It's just you and another user—and your instant messaging software.

Up until Windows XP, Microsoft's instant messaging software was MSN Messenger, and it was tied (somewhat) to Microsoft's MSN online service. MSN Messenger was a program pretty much like AOL Instant Messenger (AIM) and ICQ and Yahoo! Messenger, the other big players in the instant messaging market. In fact, it had become the number-two player, behind industry leader AIM.

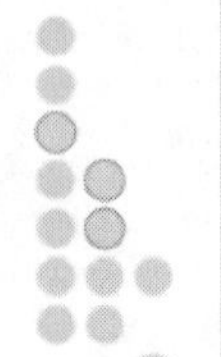

Microsoft also distributed a program called NetMeeting, which worked sort of like an instant messaging program, except that it did audio and video conferencing over the Web. (It was also a very complicated program to use.) Plus Microsoft had Internet telephony technology that kept popping up here and there—like in NetMeeting.

Well, with Windows XP, Microsoft has taken all those programs and technologies and combined them together into one very easy-to-use program called Windows Messenger. Like MSN Messenger, Windows Messenger does instant messaging. Like NetMeeting, Windows Messenger does audio and video conferencing. And it also lets you make Internet telephone calls to other computer users.

Windows Messenger does it all. Which is why many people are saying that it's the "killer app" in Windows XP.

INTRODUCING WINDOWS MESSENGER

Most users will use Windows Messenger as an instant messaging program. It's totally compatible with MSN Messenger, so you can talk online with anyone who's using either one of the two programs. (As is common with instant messaging services, you can't use Windows Messenger to talk to anyone using AIM, ICQ, or Yahoo! Messenger. None of these programs talk to one another.)

As you can see in Figure 10.1, Windows Messenger looks a lot like the old MSN Messenger. Almost all the commands and menus are similar, so if you're an MSN Messenger user, you'll be up and running with Windows Messenger in no time.

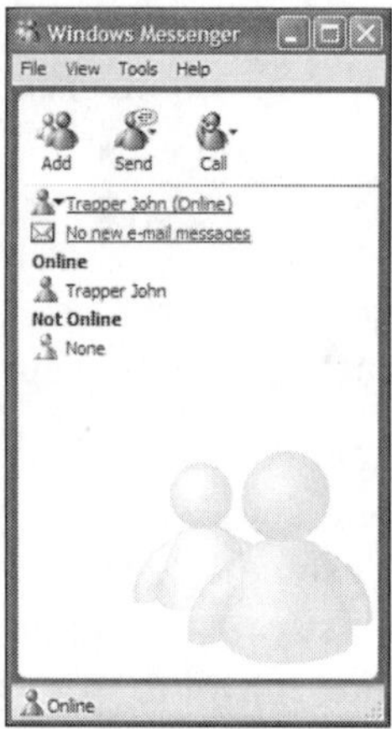

Figure 10.1

It may look like MSN Messenger, but it's really Windows Messenger, the so-called "killer app" of Windows XP.

What Windows Messenger Does

What can you do with Windows Messenger? Here's a short list:

- Send instant messages to other Windows Messenger and MSN Messenger users
- Conduct group conversations with other Messenger users
- Conduct live conversations—either one-on-one or in a group—using sound and video
- Create and track contacts lists of other Messenger users
- See who on your contact list is online at any given time
- Send and receive files to and from other Messenger users
- Make a phone call to another computer
- Make a phone call to anyone with a telephone (for an extra charge)
- Invite another Messenger user to play an online game
- Invite another Messenger user to operate your computer by remote control (using Windows XP's Remote Assistance feature, discussed in Chapter 20, "Getting Help")
- Receive a notice when you receive new Hotmail e-mail
- Receive notices regarding the status of your stocks and securities

What You Need to Use It

To use the basic instant messaging features, you don't need anything more than you already have—a computer, an Internet connection, and a copy of Windows XP. To use the telephony features, you need a full-duplex sound card and speakers, as well as a microphone of some sort connected to your computer. (You can substitute a headset for the speakers and microphone.) To make video calls or hold video conferences, add a PC camera to the mix.

In addition, if you want to use Windows Messenger, you need to sign up for a Microsoft Passport. Of course, if you subscribe to any other Microsoft service—such as Hotmail—you already have a Passport. It's Microsoft's way of keeping track of you, wherever you go. (Or, to be positive about it, it makes it easy to use multiple services with a single ID and password.)

Windows Messenger and Passport are parts of Microsoft's far-reaching .NET initiative. In fact, the Windows/MSN Messenger service is officially called the .NET Messenger Service.

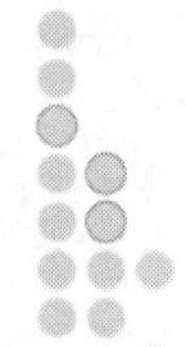

GETTING CONNECTED

To launch Windows Messenger and sign into the service, follow these steps:

1. Click the Start button and select All Programs, Windows Messenger.
2. When Windows Messenger opens, click the Click Here To Sign In link. (Once you've initially signed in, you won't have to repeat the sign-in process.)
3. When the .NET Messenger Service dialog box appears, enter your Passport (Hotmail) e-mail address and password, check the Sign Me In Automatically option, then click OK.

That's it. You're now signed in and logged in and connected to the service. You can now send messages to other users, or receive messages from other users.

Be aware that closing the Windows Messenger program does not sign you out of the service. Messenger stays running in the background, looking for messages and alerts, even when it's closed. Unless, that is, you manually sign out by selecting File, Sign Out. (You can also click the Windows Messenger icon in the Windows taskbar, and then click Sign Out from the pop-up menu.)

FINDING NEW CONTACTS

Windows Messenger is all about making contacts, and communicating with them. The best way to do this is to create a contact list of the people you talk to most often.

Adding Contacts

To add a contact to your list, follow these steps:

1. Click the Add button to open the Add a Contact Wizard, shown in Figure 10.2.

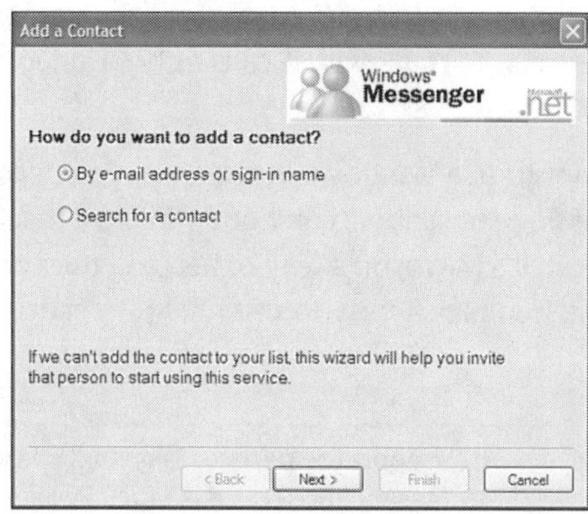

Figure 10.2

Use the Add a Contact Wizard to add names to your contact list.

2. If you know the user's sign-in name or e-mail address, check the By E-Mail Address or Sign-In Name option, then click the Next button. When the next screen appears, enter the name or address and click Finish.

3. If you don't know the name or address of the person, check the Search for a Contact option and click the Next button. When the next screen appear, enter as much information as you can, select where you want to search (either in your personal Address Book or in the Hotmail member directory), and click the Next button. The wizard will then return a list of matching names. Select the person you want, then click Next to finish adding them to your contact list.

When you search for another user, you're only searching through the list of Hotmail users. Because all Messenger users should have a Passport, and all Passport users should have a Hotmail address, this should be a good method to use. Just remember that you're not searching the entire Internet—just the universe of Hotmail users.

If you try to add a contact who isn't yet a Messenger user, you get a message telling you that Microsoft can't disclose a person's e-mail address to others. You then have the option of having Microsoft send an e-mail to that person inviting them to install Messenger, sign up for the service, and contact you.

Once you add contacts to your list, they appear in the main Messenger window. Contacts who are currently online are listed in the Online section. Those who aren't are listed as Not Online. To remove a contact from your list, all you have to do is right-click the name and then select Delete Contact.

Becoming Someone Else's Contact—or Not

If you'd like to see who has added you to their contact list, select Tools, Options to display the Options dialog box. Select the Privacy tab, and then click the View button. The Which Users Have Added You? dialog box will list all the other contact lists that you're a part of.

By default, you have to give approval before you can be added to another user's contact list. You can change this by going to the Options dialog box, selecting the Privacy tab (shown in Figure 10.3), and then *unchecking* the Alert Me When Other Users Add Me To Their Contact Lists option.

It's possible that you'll come across someone online who you don't want to talk to. Whether you're being stalked or just hiding from our boss, it's possible to block this person from seeing and contacting you.

To block this person, go to the Options dialog box, select the Privacy tab, and select that user's name in your Allow list. Click the Block button, and you've added this person to your Block list.

In a similar fashion, you can hide from *everyone* by clicking the All Other Users listing and then clicking the Block button. This blocks anyone on the service from seeing you or contacting you.

When you block a user (or all users), you become invisible. You don't appear as either online or offline, you just don't appear at all.

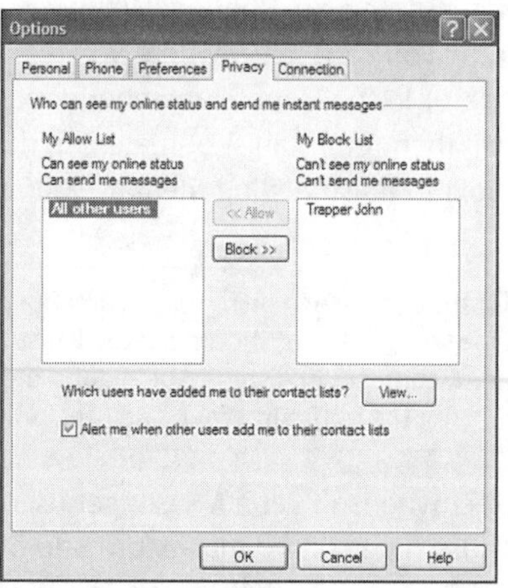

Figure 10.3

Use the Privacy tab to control who sees you and who doesn't.

If you'd rather appear as being offline when you're really online (so you can see others without being seen), go back to the main Messenger window and right-click the link for your name. Select Appear Offline from the pop-up menu, and everyone will think you're away from your computer—even though you're still there!

When you're "offline" like this, you can't send or receive messages from other users. You'll need to right-click your name again and select Online to go back online to communicate.

There are other options available when you right-click your name in the main window. You can choose to tell people that you're Busy, Away, On the Phone, Out to Lunch, or that you'll Be Right Back. These messages will appear next to your name in other user's contact lists.

ONE-TO-ONE MESSAGING

Windows Messenger lets you send basic one-to-one messages, or to use Messenger to send files and e-mails.

Send a Message

To send an instant message to another user, follow these steps:

1. Double-click the name of the contact you want to message.
2. When the Conversation window opens (see Figure 10.4), enter your message in the lower part of the window, then click the Send button (or press Enter).
3. Your message will appear in the top part of the window, as will your contact's reply.

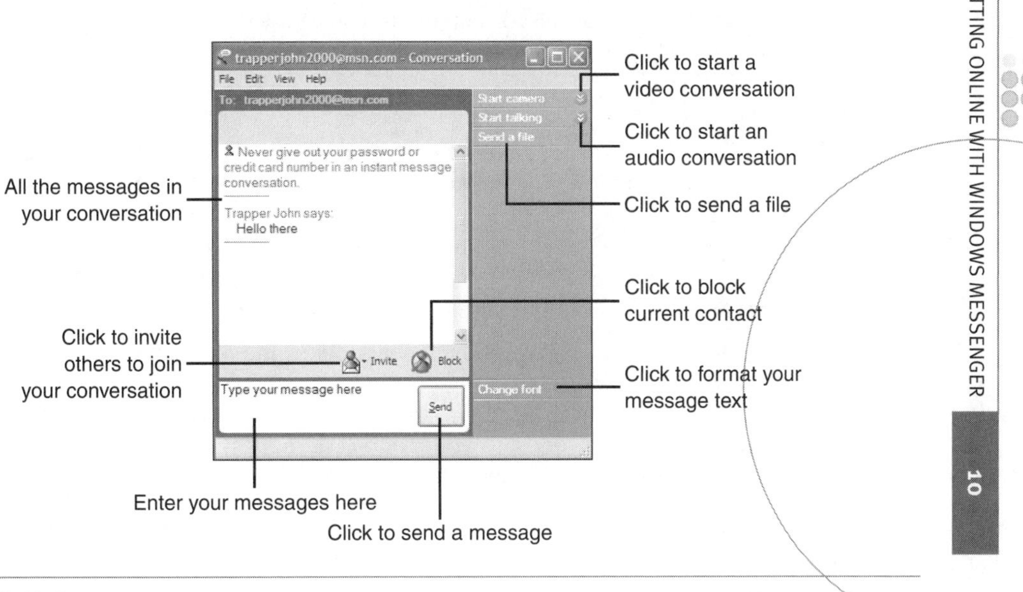

Figure 10.4

Carrying on a conversation via instant messages.

Continue talking like this, one message after another. Your entire conversation will be displayed in the top part of the window, and you can scroll up to reread earlier messages.

You can change the font face, color, style, and size of your message by clicking the Change Font link. When the Change My Message Font dialog box appears, select the settings you want, then click OK. The next message you send will reflect the new formatting you selected.

Receive a Message

When someone else sends you an instant message, Windows lets out with a little bleeping sound and then displays an alert in the lower-right corner of your screen. To open and reply to the message, click the alert.

If you happen to miss the alert, Windows will display a flashing message button in the taskbar. You can click this button to read your message.

Send an E-mail

You're not limited to sending instant messages to people on your contact list. You can also send e-mail messages directly from Windows Messenger.

Just right-click a name on your list and select Send Mail from the pop-up menu. This will launch Internet Explorer, send it to the Hotmail site, and load the Compose page. Write your message and send it as you would any Hotmail message.

If you don't have a Hotmail account, this technique will instead launch your normal e-mail program.

Send a File

Another feature of Windows Messenger is the ability to send a file direct to another user. It's easy to do:

1. Right-click a name in your contact list.
2. Select Send a File from the pop-up menu.
3. When the Send a File dialog box appears, select the file you want to send, and then click Open.

Windows Messenger now sends, to your contact, a request to transfer the file. When the contact accepts the file, you're notified.

Open a File

If one of your contacts sends you a file, you'll receive a message informing you that you have a file waiting. Click the link within the message to open the file.

Alternately, you can select File, Open Received Files from the main Messenger window. This will open a folder that contains all the files sent to you. Find the file you want to open, then click it.

GROUP CHATS

When you send instant messages back and forth between two users, it's called a conversation. Just as you can carry on real-world conversations with more than two people, Windows Messenger also lets you add other users to your conversation.

When you want to have a group conversation, you have to start with a one-on-one conversation. Once you've exchanged messages with one other person (and opened a Conversation window), you can then add other users to that conversation.

To add another user to an existing conversation, click Invite, To Join This Conversation, and then select a name. That's all there is to it. When the new user responds to your invitation, his or her messages will appear in the existing Conversation window.

Conversations can take place between a maximum of five people (that's four plus you).

MAKING INTERNET PHONE CALLS

It's easy to use Windows Messenger to make a PC-to-PC Internet phone call. As far as Messenger is concerned, a phone call is just a conversation with sound.

If you're already in a messaging conversation and want to add sound, click the Start Talking link in the Conversation window.

To start a new conversation with sound, click the Call button, then select the contact you want to call. Click Computer from the pop-up menu, and you're ready to start talking.

Alternately, you can right-click a contact in your Online list and select Call, Computer.

Naturally, both you and the other user must have speakers and microphones (or headsets) to carry on a voice conversation.

When you turn on Messenger's voice feature, a set of audio controls appears in the Conversation window's sidebar, as shown in Figure 10.5. You can use these controls to adjust the volume of the conversation, or to mute your microphone. To end the voice part of the conversation, click the Stop Talking button.

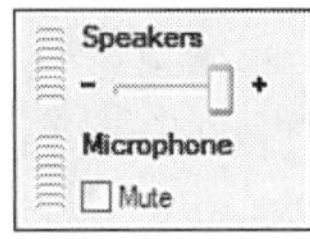

Figure 10.5

Use the audio controls to adjust your system for voice conversations.

The first time you try to make a voice call, Messenger will run a wizard to test and adjust your speakers and microphone.

VIDEO CONFERENCING

When you add sound to a text-based conversation you get an Internet phone call. When you add live video to a conversation, you get a video conference.

Put another way, a video conference is a normal Messenger conversation with video added.

To add video to an existing conversation, click the Start Camera link. This displays a monitor window, where the other user's picture will appear. Your picture will appear in a similar window in the other user's Conversation window. (Figure 10.6 shows a video conference in progress.) If you want to see your picture, too, click the Options link and check the Show My Video as Picture-in-Picture option.

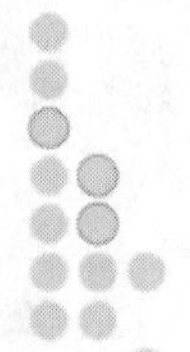

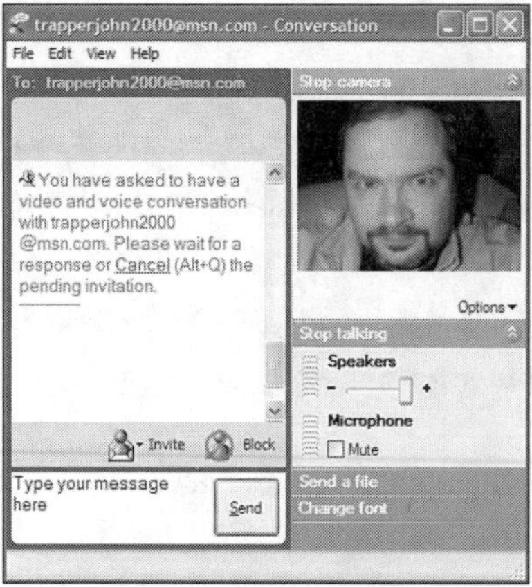

Figure 10.6

You and another user can conduct a video conference from within Windows Messenger.

JIM'S TOP TEN TIPS

The nice thing about Windows Messenger is how easy it makes everything. There's no big production about adding and configuring cameras and microphones. All you do is send a message, start a conversation, and then add sound and picture as desired.

It's a lot easier than the old NetMeeting, and no more difficult than the old MSN Messenger. Now if you could only use Windows Messenger to talk to AOL users!

That last wish is unlikely to be granted in the near future (not Microsoft's fault—AOL is the holdout, this time). Until then, remember these important points when you want to talk online:

1. Windows Messenger replaces both MSN Messenger and Microsoft NetMeeting. It's an instant messaging program that also offers Internet telephony and video conferencing.
2. Windows Messenger is compatible with MSN Messenger, so you can communicate with both Windows Messenger and MSN Messenger users.
3. To use Windows Messenger, you need a Microsoft Passport.
4. You create a list of contacts you want to talk to. You can fill this list by searching the contacts in your personal Address Book, or the Microsoft Hotmail subscriber list.
5. When you're online, your name appears in the Online section of the Messenger window. You can choose to display a message beside your name (Busy, At Lunch, and so on), or to appear offline when you're really online. This latter is a great way to hide from people, while still knowing whether they're online or not.
6. To send an instant message, double-click a name in your contact list.
7. You're not limited to sending instant messages to your contacts. You can also send files and e-mail messages.
8. To conduct a group chat, start a conversation with the first user, and then invite other users to join you.
9. To make a PC-to-PC phone call to another Messenger user, click the Call button, select the contact, and then click Computer. (Make sure your microphone and speakers are working!)
10. To start a video conference, initiate a normal text conversation and then click the Start Camera link. This opens a monitor window within Messenger, so you can see the person on the other end of the conference.

PART IV

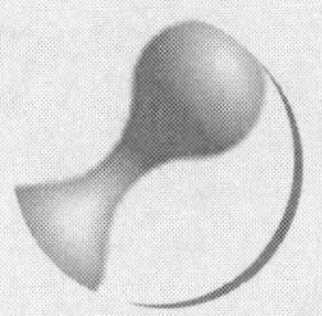

SOUNDS AND PICTURES

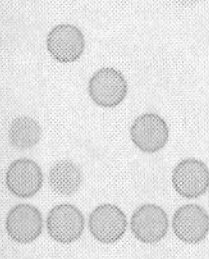

CHAPTER 11

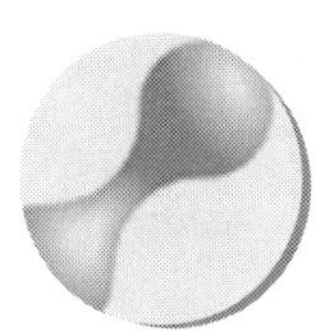

WORKING WITH PICTURES

- Working with My Pictures
- Tracking Details
- Different Views
- Editing Picture Files
- Working with Picture Files
- Jim's Top Ten Tips

If you're like me, you have a lot of pictures on your computer. I have a digital camera, and I transfer all the pictures I shoot to my hard drive. I also have a scanner, and I'm constantly scanning in old photos that I took before I bought my digital camera. Then there are the pictures I download from the Web, and the photos that friends and family send me via e-mail.

I have a *lot* of pictures on my computer.

Working with those pictures—editing them, storing them, sending them on to other users—takes up a lot of my time. And, prior to Windows XP, it wasn't easy. I had to use a ragtag assortment of third-party programs and utilities just to do the simplest tasks, and I didn't get any help from my operating system.

That all changes with Windows XP. Building on a handful of new features first introduced in Windows Me, Windows XP is Microsoft's first operating system to take digital pictures seriously.

Next chapter I'll tell you about how Windows XP works with scanners and digital cameras. This chapter I'll focus on the picture management capabilities of the operating system—how you can use Windows XP to view, store, and print your digital pictures.

WORKING WITH MY PICTURES

The key to Windows XP's picture management is the My Pictures folder. This is a file folder like My Documents, but customized for image-related operations.

The default My Pictures folder, shown in Figure 11.1, displays all your image files as thumbnails. This is *so* much better than displaying image files as stock icons or file listings—you can actually see the file that you're working with!

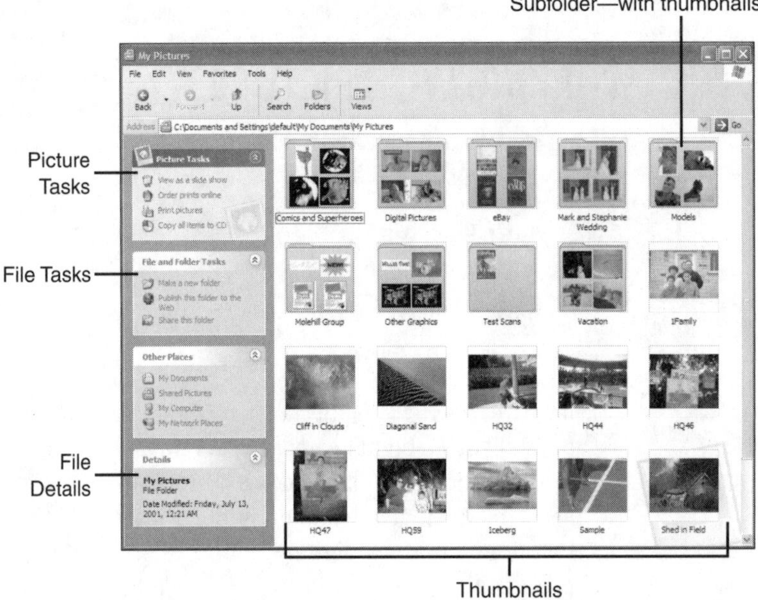

Figure 11.1

Windows XP's My Pictures folder—all your image files are displayed as thumbnails.

Naturally, the My Pictures folder includes a custom Tasks list, like the one found in every Windows XP folder. But it also includes a special Picture Tasks list. These Picture Tasks are operations specific to image management, such as ordering photo prints and viewing the image files as a slide show.

The My Pictures folder also includes a number of viewing options that should appeal to people who work a lot with digital pictures. I'll discuss the various My Picture views in the "Different Views" section, later in this chapter.

TRACKING DETAILS

If you're serious about digital photography, you'll appreciate all the image details that Windows XP tracks and displays. With a few clicks of your mouse, Windows XP will display an impressive amount of information about your image files, including when the photo was shot, with what kind of camera, at what settings, and so on.

Here are some of the details that Windows XP tracks for each of your digital images:

- File type (.JPG, .TIF, and so on)
- Image dimensions (in pixels)
- Horizontal and vertical resolution
- Bit (color) depth
- Make and model of camera used
- Lens aperture
- Subject distance
- Flash mode
- Focal length
- F-number
- Exposure time
- Date created

Windows XP can only track that information that was recorded by your digital camera. Most digital cameras collect this information (called EXIF information) and store it along with each individual picture file.

To display basic details about a file, all you have to do is hover your mouse over the file icon or thumbnail. XP will display a ToolTip-type pop-up that lists the image dimensions, the date the picture was taken, what camera was used, and the file size and type.

To display complete details about a specific file, right-click the file and select Properties from the pop-up menu. When the Properties dialog box appears, select the Summary tab, as shown in Figure 11.2. Here is where you'll find all the information you could ask for. (It's certainly a lot better than trying to remember what F-stop you used when you shot that one great photo!)

If the advanced details are not visible, click the Advanced button on the Summary tab.

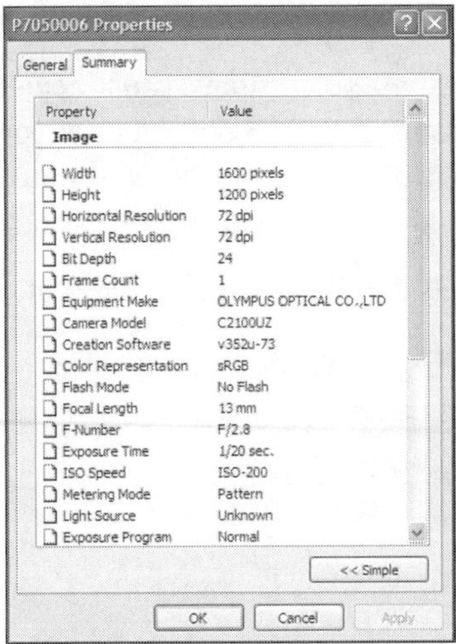

Figure 11.2

Windows XP stores an inordinate amount of information about the photos you shoot.

DIFFERENT VIEWS

While the default view in the My Pictures folder is perfect for most users, there are other viewing options you might want to check out. You can also access many of these viewing options in any folder that contains image files—including any subfolders you create within the My Pictures folder.

Displaying Thumbnails

If My Pictures is displaying icons instead of thumbnails, it's a simple job to switch back to the thumbnail view. Just select View, Thumbnails, and all your images will be thumbnailed within the folder.

If you prefer a more traditional file view, it's easy enough to switch to something other than the thumbnail view. Just pull down the View menu and select either Tiles, Icons, List, or Details.

TIP

If you choose to display your image files as tiles, icons, or filenames, the selected file will still be displayed as a thumbnail in the Details section of the activity center pane.

Displaying (and Sorting By) Details

If you choose the Details view for My Pictures, the details listed are specific to the types of files you're viewing. As you can see in Figure 11.3, My Pictures' Details view includes the

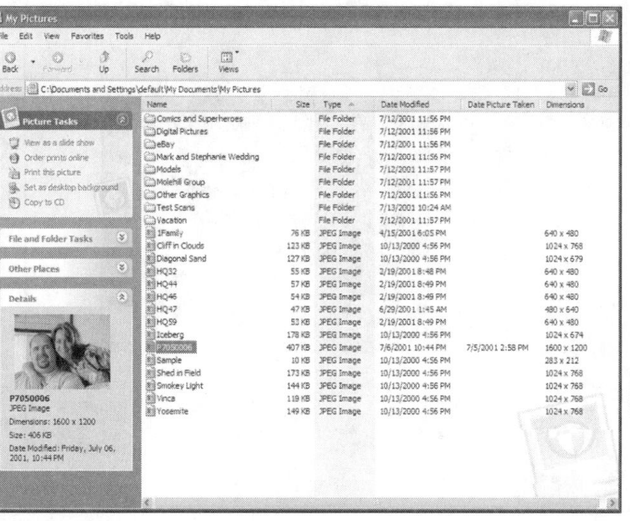

standard columns for file Name, Size, Type, and Modified. It also includes image-specific columns for Picture Taken On and Dimensions.

Figure 11.3

Use the Details view to display the dimensions of each picture, and when each picture was taken.

You can sort the files in Details view by clicking on any column header. Click a second time to reverse the order listed.

Even if you're not displaying in Details view, you can still sort your files by the Picture Taken On or Dimensions fields. Just select View, Arrange Icons By, and select either Picture Taken On or Dimensions. (This option works even better if you turn on the Show In Groups feature.)

Viewing a Filmstrip

If thumbnails are too small for you, there's another My Pictures viewing mode you ought to check out. Select View, Filmstrip to display My Pictures' Filmstrip mode. As you can see in Figure 11.4, the selected picture is displayed in a large window at the top of the pane, along with a selection of image-viewing controls.

Click the Next button to advance to the next image in the folder, or just hover over an image to display it in the large window.

Viewing a Slide Show

One cool though not particularly practical feature of the My Pictures folder is the ability to display the entire contents of the folders as an onscreen slide show. All you have to do is click the View As a Slide Show option in the Picture Tasks panel, and the first picture in the folder is displayed in full-screen mode. Every five seconds the picture will change, as the show cycles through all the pictures in the folder—and then starts again at the beginning.

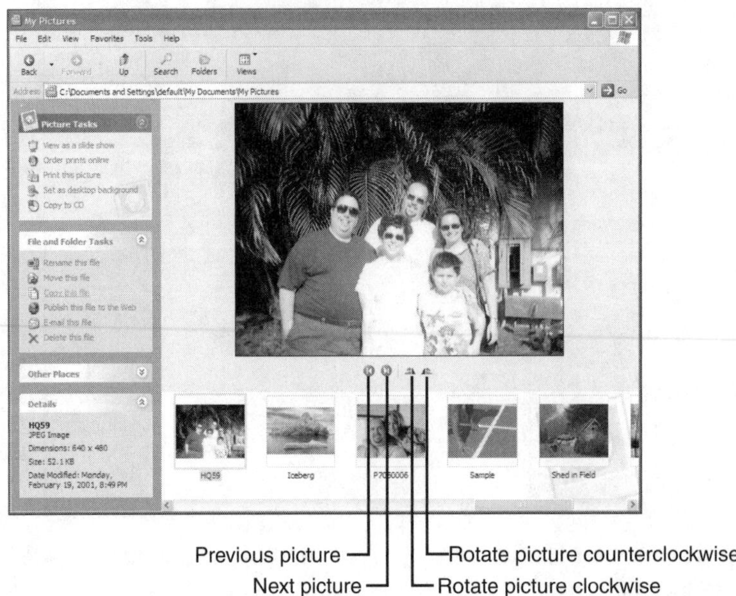

Figure 11.4

View your pictures big in My Pictures' Filmstrip mode.

If you want to manually run the show, all you have to do is move your mouse. This will display a small toolbar in the top-right corner of the screen. You can click the buttons on this toolbar to pause and restart the show, move back and forward manually, and exit the show and return to normal mode.

Previewing an Image

So far all the image viewing has taken place within the My Pictures Folder. What if you want to *really* view a picture, at full size?

Windows XP includes its own Windows Picture and Fax Viewer utility. Whenever you click a file in My Pictures, the Picture and Fax Viewer is launched and the selected picture is displayed. As you can see in Figure 11.5, the Picture and Fax Viewer includes the same functions as the Filmstrip viewer, with the addition of buttons for resizing, zooming, printing, editing picture info, saving the file (under a new name), and deleting the file.

NOTE

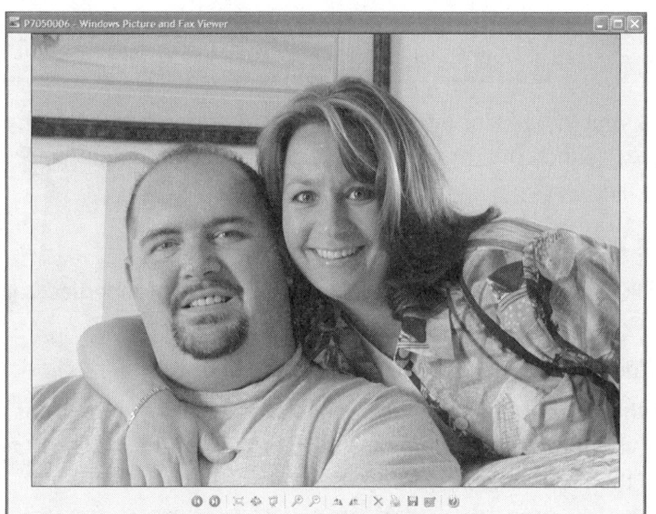

The Windows Picture and Fax Viewer replaces the somewhat-cranky Imaging for Windows utility included in previous versions of Windows.

Figure 11.5

View a full-size picture with the Windows Picture and Fax Viewer.

EDITING PICTURE FILES

Microsoft doesn't include an image-editing program in Windows XP. That's unless you count the old warhorse Microsoft Paint as an image-editing program—and I don't. (It's way too old and feature-poor for any practical use.)

This means that you'll have to use a third-party graphics program to edit your picture files. There are a lot of these programs on the market, and you probably have one or two already installed on your system. (Every digital camera or scanner you install invariably comes with its own image-editing utility.)

If you're in the market for graphics editor, my favorite programs include

- Adobe PhotoDeluxe (`www.adobe.com/products/photodeluxe/`)
- Adobe Photoshop (`www.adobe.com/products/photoshop/`)
- Corel Photo-Paint (`www.corel.com`)
- JASC Paint Shop Pro (`www.jasc.com`)
- MGI PhotoSuite (`www.mgisoft.com/photo/`)
- Micrografx Picture Publisher (`www.micrografx.com/mgxproducts/picturepublisher.asp`)
- Microsoft PictureIt! (`pictureitproducts.msn.com`)

If you have Microsoft Office 97 or above, it includes a simple little editor, called

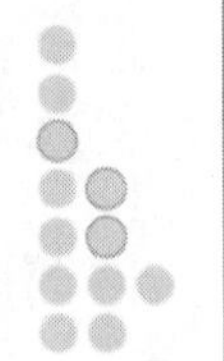

Microsoft Photo Editor. It's found in the Microsoft Tools folder. Typically not installed by default, you may have to add it in from your CD.

You can load your image files into any of these programs manually, or you can configure Windows XP to launch one of these programs instead of Image Preview when you click on an image file.

To reset what program opens a specific file, follow these steps:

1. Right-click any file of a specific type and then select Properties from the pop-up menu.
2. Select the General tab and click the Change button.
3. When the Open With dialog box appears, select a program to associate with this type of file. If the program you want isn't listed, click the Click Here link and navigate to the program you want to use.
4. Click OK when done.

This procedure affects all files of the selected type, not just the selected file.

The next time you click a file of this type, the program you selected will launch, with the selected file displayed.

Unfortunately, if you want to return to using the Image Preview utility, it's not a simple procedure. You have to select Tools, Folder Options to display the Folder Options dialog box, then select the File Types tab. Select the file type you want to edit, then click the Restore button. (Whew!) This should restore Image Preview as the default viewer for that file type.

WORKING WITH PICTURE FILES

We're not done yet—My Pictures has a few more functions up its sleeve. Read on and I'll tell you about some more image-specific tasks integrated into the My Pictures folder.

Printing Pictures

If you have a color printer, you can make good-quality prints of your image files. In fact, some manufacturers sell printers specifically designed for photographic prints. If you take a lot of digital photos, one of these printers might be a good investment.

Printing a picture from within the My Pictures folder is as easy as clicking a link. All you have to do is select the picture(s) you want to print, then click the Print Pictures link in the Picture Tasks pane. Windows XP now launches the Photo Printing Wizard, which walks you step-by-step through the printing process. You get to select which printer you want to use, what type of paper you'll be printing on, and how many (and what size) prints to print on a page (see Figure 11.6). When you complete the wizard, the printing starts, just as you specified.

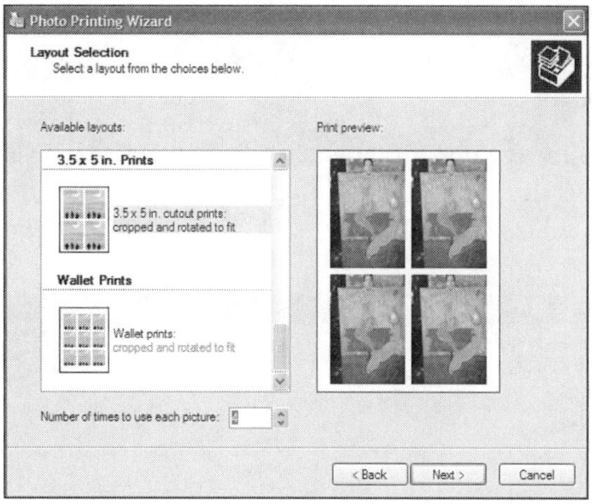

Figure 11.6

Use the Photo Printing Wizard to determine how and how many pictures to print on a page.

Ordering Prints

If you don't have your own photo-quality printer, you still need to use a professional photo-finishing service. There are a number of ways you can create prints from your digital photos:

- Copy your image files to disk and deliver the disk by hand to your local photo finisher
- Go to the Web site of an online photo-finishing service and transfer your image files over the Internet
- Use the Order Prints From the Internet option in Windows XP's My Pictures folder

The first option is the most traditional, and perhaps the most convenient for a lot of people. There also are no shipping charges involved.

The second option should appeal to those of you plugged into the online world. You may even find that prices are a tad cheaper, although you will have to pay to get your prints shipped back to you.

The third option is Microsoft's favorite, and perhaps the most convenient of all. Microsoft has arranged with a number of online photo-finishing sites to provide services to Windows users. Microsoft links to these sites from within the My Pictures folder—and receives a cut of the revenue generated. While that fee doesn't come out of your pocket (it's a kind of commission that the partner sites pay), if you're adverse to lining Microsoft's pockets any more than you have to, you might want to bypass the My Pictures option and deal directly with the sites, instead.

If you do want to order prints from within Windows XP, it's a simple procedure. All you have to do is select the files you want to print, and then click the Order Prints From the Internet option in the Picture Tasks panel. This launches the Internet Print Ordering Wizard.

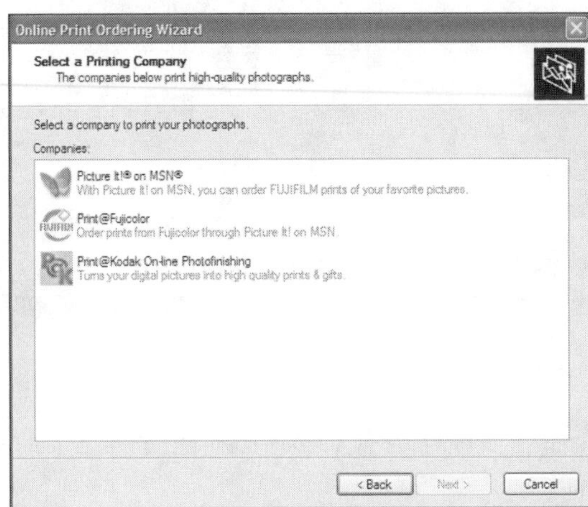

The wizard lets you pick which service you want to use (as shown in Figure 11.7), as well as what kind of and how many prints to make. You'll have to fill in all the normal shipping and payment information, of course. But then you'll receive your prints in a few days, just like you would if you ordered from that site without Microsoft's assistance.

Figure 11.7

Use the Internet Print Ordering Wizard to order photo-finishing services from within the My Pictures folder.

Turning a Picture into a Desktop Background

There's one final thing you can do from within the My Pictures folder. With a few clicks of your mouse, you can select any picture in the folder to be your Windows desktop background.

All you have to do is select a file, then click the Set As Desktop Background option in the Picture Tasks pane. Minimize the My Pictures window so you can see your desktop, and you can see that the selected file is now your desktop background.

(You can change the background to another image through the traditional Display Properties dialog box method, as discussed in Chapter 2, "Changing the Way Windows Looks—and Acts.")

JIM'S TOP TEN TIPS

As you can see, Windows XP makes it easy to work with your digital image files. Just remember these ten important tips:

1. Store all your picture files in the My Pictures folder, or in a subfolder within My Pictures.
2. You can configure My Pictures to display thumbnails of all your image files.
3. Display the Properties dialog box to view detailed information about the file—including when the photo was shot, what type of camera you used, and what its settings were.
4. To view a larger version of a selected file, switch to My Pictures' Filmstrip mode.
5. To view a full-size version of a file, click the file to launch the Windows Picture and Fax Viewer utility.
6. The Slide Show mode displays all the files in the My Pictures folder in a continuous full-screen slide show.
7. You can configure Windows XP to automatically launch a graphics-editing program by clicking the Change button in the Properties dialog box.
8. Printing digital photos is simplified by the Photo Printing Wizard.
9. If you want, you can order professional prints of your files from within My Pictures, by using the Internet Print Ordering Wizard.
10. Click the Set As Desktop Background option to use any image file as your Windows desktop background.

CHAPTER 12

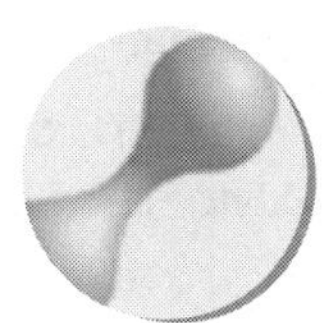

WORKING WITH DIGITAL CAMERAS AND SCANNERS

- Installing and Configuring a Digital Camera or Scanner
- Scanning Pictures
- Uploading Pictures from a Digital Camera
- Working With Pictures In the Camera
- Jim's Top Ten Tips

In the last chapter I told you about the new image-management functions of the My Pictures folder. In this chapter I'll show you how to fill up that folder with image files from digital cameras and scanners.

Windows XP incorporates a new standard, first available in Windows Me, called Windows Image Acquisition (WIA). WIA enables compatible imaging devices to integrate directly into the Windows shell. Under Windows XP, any WIA digital camera or scanner can be accessed from the Open dialog box of any application. So, for example, you could launch Microsoft Paint or Paint Shop Pro, select File, Open, and see the contents of your digital camera or scanner listed in the Open dialog box. This way you can work on digital images without first copying them to your PC's hard disk.

Any digital camera or scanner that is attached to your computer is visible from My Computer, and can be

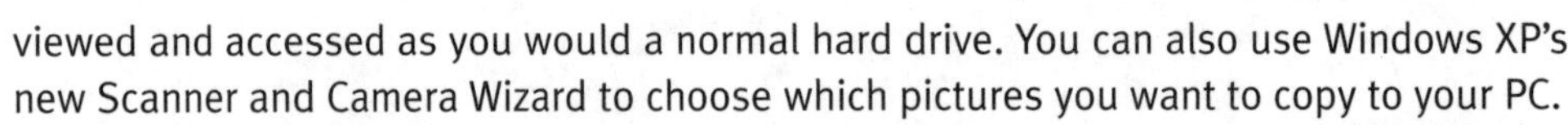

viewed and accessed as you would a normal hard drive. You can also use Windows XP's new Scanner and Camera Wizard to choose which pictures you want to copy to your PC.

INSTALLING AND CONFIGURING A DIGITAL CAMERA OR SCANNER

Installing a digital camera or scanner is extremely easy, especially if the device is Plug and Play-compatible and you use a USB connection. With this type of setup, Windows will recognize your camera or scanner as soon as you plug it in, and install the appropriate drivers automatically.

If Windows does *not* recognize your camera or scanner, you can use the Scanners and Cameras utility to install the new device on your system. Just follow these steps:

1. From the Control Panel, click the Scanners and Cameras icon.
2. When the Scanners and Cameras utility appears, click the Add Device icon.
3. When the Scanner and Camera Installation Wizard appears, follow the onscreen instructions to identify the make and manufacturer of your device (as shown in Figure 12.1), and install the proper drivers.

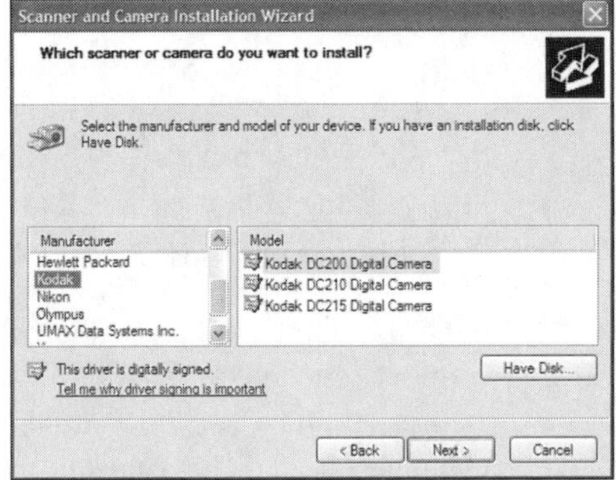

Figure 12.1

Use the Scanner and Camera Installation Wizard to manually install a new image capture device.

When you exit the wizard, your new camera or scanner will appear as a device in the Scanners and Cameras window.

If you want a particular graphics-editing program to launch whenever you copy pictures from your camera or scanner, right-click on the device's icon and select Properties from the pop-up menu. When the Properties dialog box appears, select the Events tab, select an event from the Select An Event list, click the Start This Program option, and then select the application you want to link to the event.

SCANNING PICTURES

The Microsoft engineers have fancy phrases for even the simplest activities. What you or I would call "scanning a picture," the engineers call a "scan event." (They call the act of connecting a digital camera to your PC a "connect event.")

Well, when Windows senses a scan event—that is, when you start a scan—it launches the Scanner and Camera Wizard. As you can see in Figure 12.2, the scanner part of this wizard lets you control how your picture is scanned. All you have to do is select one of the Picture Type options (Color Picture, Grayscale Picture, Black and White Picture or Text, or Custom), and the wizard will display a preview of what you're scanning.

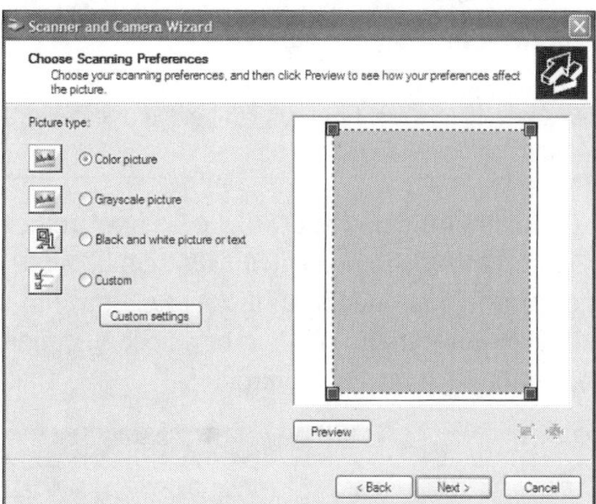

Figure 12.2

Using Windows XP to scan a photograph—preview your scan before you accept it.

If you like what you see, you can tell the wizard to finish the scan. If you don't like what you see, you can change the settings and look at another preview.

UPLOADING PICTURES FROM A DIGITAL CAMERA

Making your digital camera and PC work together used to be a pain in the rear. You were lucky if Windows even recognized your camera, and then you had to use the camera's proprietary software to copy all your pictures to your hard disk, all at once.

Well, Windows XP makes it easier. You can view the contents of your digital camera from My Computer, or you can use the Scanner and Camera Wizard to manage your photos for you.

When you connect your digital camera (or insert your camera's media card into a reader), Windows displays the Choose Pictures to Copy dialog box. At this point you can choose from four separate actions:

You can also display this dialog box by selecting the Get Pictures From Camera or Scanner task in the My Pictures folder.

- **Acquire Photos**—Choose this option to select photos to copy to your hard disk.
- **View a Slide Show of the Images**—Choose this option and Windows displays a full-screen slide show of the images currently stored in your camera. No copying of the images is necessary.
- **Print the Pictures**—This option lets you print individual photos without first copying them to your hard disk.
- **Open Folder to View Files**—Choose this option when you want to view, delete, rename, or otherwise manage the camera.

To perform the same action every time you connect your camera, check the Always Do the Selected Action option.

When you select Acquire Photos (and click OK), the Scanner and Camera Wizard launches. As you can see in Figure 12.3, you're presented with thumbnails of all the photos currently stored in your camera (or on your media card). You don't have to copy all these photos to your hard drive—although you can, by clicking the Select All option. Just select which photos you want to copy, then click the Next button.

Figure 12.3

Select which photos you want to copy to your hard disk.

Now you're presented with the Select a Picture Name and Destination screen, as shown in Figure 12.4. This is where you select the destination folder and filenames for your folders.

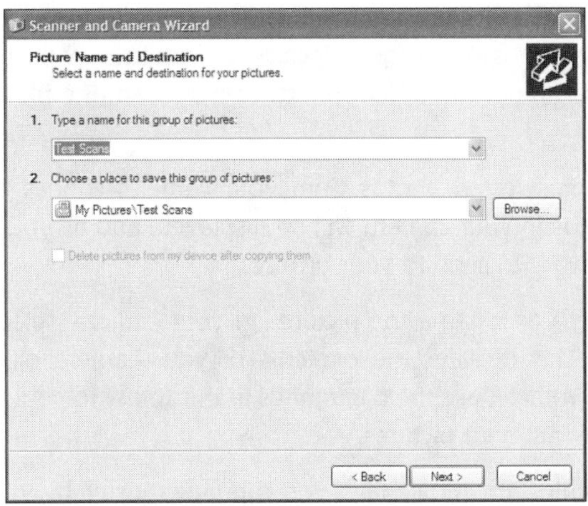

Figure 12.4

Select a name and location for your photos.

Windows XP names all your photos with a common filename, followed by a unique number. So, for example, if you entered Vacation as the picture name, your photos would be named Vacation 001, Vacation 002, Vacation 003, and so on.

You can also select which folder you want to copy these pictures to. By default, Windows XP will copy your pictures to the My Pictures folder. I recommend you create a subfolder within the My Pictures folder for each new group of pictures you copy. This will make it easier for you to keep track of all the different photos on your hard disk.

This screen also has two other interesting options. The first option is to copy your pictures to the Internet. Select this option if you want to post these photos as-is to your Web site.

The second option is to delete pictures from your camera after you've copied them to your hard disk. This is a good option to choose, as it automatically cleans up your digital camera storage, so you don't have to delete old pictures manually.

After you've entered all this information, click the Next button. The wizard will now copy your selected pictures to your hard disk. You can now use all the features of the My Pictures folder (discussed in Chapter 11, "Working with Pictures") to view, edit, and otherwise manage your pictures.

WORKING WITH PICTURES IN THE CAMERA

Interestingly, you don't have to copy photos from your camera to your hard disk to work with them. Windows XP includes some basic picture management functionality that can be used with the pictures currently stored in your digital camera.

As you recall, when you connected your camera to your computer you were presented with four different options. (You can also display these options by selecting the camera

icon in the Scanners and Cameras utility and clicking the Get Pictures option in the activity center pane.) You choose the Acquire Pictures option to copy pictures to your hard disk, but you can choose one of the other options to work with the pictures while they're still in your camera.

If you want to print selected photos from your camera, choose the Print the Pictures option. All the photos in your camera will be displayed, and all you have to do is choose which photos you want to send to your picture.

If you want to delete or rename the pictures in your camera, select the Open Folder to View Files option. This displays the contents of your camera or media card in a My Pictures-like folder. You can use the commands in this folder to perform a full range of file-management tasks with your pictures.

If your camera contains any movie files, you can play these movies on your PC by selecting the Play the Video Files option. Since many digital still cameras also let you record short MPEG movies, this option is a nice way to view your movies without first copying them to your hard disk.

JIM'S TOP TEN TIPS

You know, I wanted to make this chapter longer, but Windows XP makes working with cameras and scanners so easy, there wasn't that much to write about! It really is as simple as plugging in your device and working through the Scanner and Camera Wizard. Assuming you make the right choices in the wizard, it's tough to screw anything up.

Of course, it helps if you remember these ten key points:

1. Windows XP includes new Windows Image Acquisition technology that makes it easy to work with images from digital cameras and scanners.
2. The contents of your digital camera or scanner should appear in the Open dialog box of any image-editing software.
3. If Windows doesn't recognize your camera or scanner when you first connect it, open the Scanners and Cameras utility and click the Add Device icon to run the Scanner and Camera Installation Wizard.
4. When you scan an image with your scanner, Windows XP's Scanner and Camera Wizard lets you preview and configure the scanned image.
5. The Scanner and Camera Wizard also launches whenever you connect a digital camera to your PC. You can choose from a variety of tasks, including copying pictures to your PC (called "acquiring" pictures), printing pictures directly from your camera, running a full-screen slide show of your camera's photos, or performing typical file-management operations—while the pictures are still in the camera.
6. You use the Scanner and Camera Wizard to choose which photos to copy from your camera to your hard disk, what to name those photos, and where to copy them to.
7. By default, the Scanner and Camera Wizard copies your photos to the My Pictures folder. You probably want to create subfolders within the My Pictures folder to more easily manage all your different photographs
8. You can also use the Scanner and Camera Wizard to upload your pictures directly to your Web site.
9. When you check the Delete Pictures From My Camera After Copying Them option, you don't have to go back and manually delete pictures stored in your digital camera.
10. Once you've copied your photos to your hard disk, you can use the commands in the My Pictures folder to view, edit, and otherwise manage your pictures.

CHAPTER 13

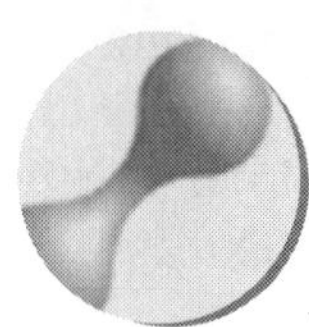

USING WINDOWS MEDIA PLAYER

- Understanding Digital Media Files
- Introducing Windows Media Player
- Configuring WMP
- Playing Audio Files
- Listening to Internet Radio
- Watching DVDs
- Organizing Your Media Files
- Using Other Media Players
- Jim's Top Ten Tips

You might not think of your PC as a full-featured audio/video playback and recording system, but it is. You can use your PC to listen to your favorite compact discs, tune in to radio broadcasts from around the world, watch movies on DVD, and record your own custom music collections.

There are lots of third-party software you can use for various playback and recording operations, Windows XP includes a single program that can perform all these tasks. Windows Media Player (WMP) is an all-in-one playback and recording utility that handles everything from CD and DVD playback to Internet radio and MP3 encoding.

And, if you've used a previous version of WMP, you'll be pleasantly surprised by the improvements in the

Windows XP player. New features include MP3 compatibility (for playback, you'll need to buy a $30 add-on pack to record MP3 files), a better looking interface, new visualizations, and improved information storage for your digital media files.

The version of WMP in Windows XP is technically version 8.0, but is more formally called Windows Media Player for Windows XP. (What a mouthful!)

I'll discuss basic player operation (for both audio and video) in this chapter. If you're interested in using WMP to record digital audio files, go straight to Chapter 14, "Playing and Recording MP3 and WMA Audio."

UNDERSTANDING DIGITAL MEDIA FILES

In the world of computers, all data has always been stored in digital format. (In a digital file, information is assembled from a series of 0 and 1 bits.) Digital is better than its counterpart (called analog) in that noise and distortion aren't introduced into the process. A digital copy, if recorded properly, can be an exact copy. It's impossible to make an exact copy using analog methods.

In the audio and video world, music and movies used to be stored non-digitally. (Vinyl records and VHS videotapes are both analog formats.) However, with the advent of compact discs (CDs) and digital video discs (DVDs), music and movies began to be stored digitally.

When music and movies are digital, it's easy to incorporate them into the computer environment. To a computer, one digital file is pretty much the same as another—especially when it comes to storage.

So if you can store digital music and movies on your PC, why not use your PC for playback, too? Well, you can—if you have the right media player software. There are many different file formats for storing digital audio and video, and different media players are compatible with different formats.

The Windows Media Player included with Windows XP can read and write the majority of today's most popular digital media files. To find out if your format of choice is compatible with WMP, check out Table 13.1. As you can see, there are only a handful of popular formats (chief among them Apple's QuickTime and RealNetwork's RealMedia) that can't be viewed with the Windows Media Player.

TABLE 13.1—Windows Media Player-compatible Digital File Formats

Format	File Extension(s)
CD audio	.CDA
Indeo (Intel) Video Technology	.IVF
Macintosh AIFF audio	.AIF, .AIFC, .AIFF
Windows Media (audio and video)	.ASF, .ASX, .WAX, .WMA, .WMV, .WVX, .WMP, .WMX
Native Windows formats (audio and video)	.AVI, .WAV

TABLE 13.1—CONTINUED

Format	File Extension(s)
Moving Picture Experts Group (audio and video)	.MPEG, .MPG, .M1V, .M3U, .MP2, .MP3, .MPA, .MPE, .MPV2
Musical Instrument Digital Interface (MIDI)	.MID, .MIDI, .RMI
UNIX AU audio	.AU, .SND

INTRODUCING WINDOWS MEDIA PLAYER

You launch the Windows Media Player by clicking the Start button and selecting All Programs, Windows Media Player. WMP starts in its Full mode, as shown in Figure 13.1.

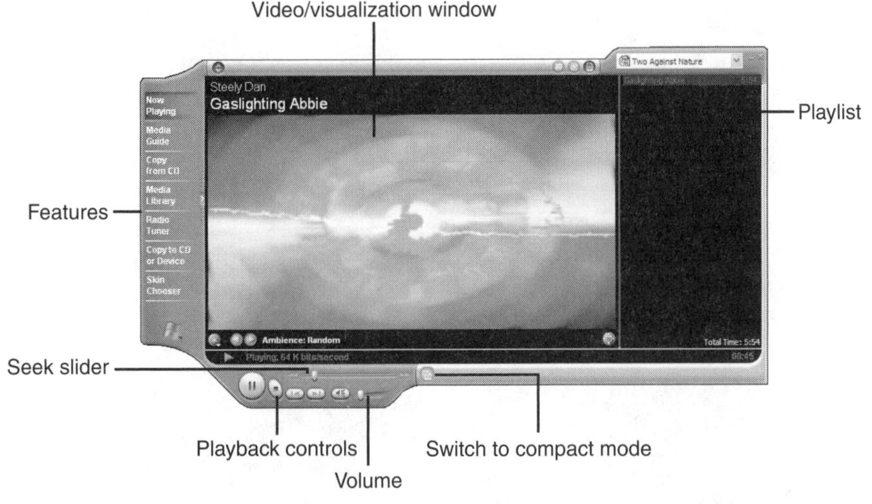

Figure 13.1

Windows Media Player for Windows XP—use WMP for all your audio and video playback and recording needs.

If you're using WMP to watch a movie or other video file, the picture displays in the video window in the center of the player. If you're using WMP to listen to music, this area can be used to display what Microsoft calls "visualizations." (Think of a visualization as a kind of "live" wallpaper that moves along with your music.)

WMP's playback controls are always at the bottom of the window. Here you'll find the normal transport buttons, including Play/Pause, Stop, Rewind, and Fast Forward. WMP also include Next and Previous track buttons, along with a volume control and mute button.

To the right of the window is the Playlist area. Individual tracks of a CD or DVD will be listed here. This area also displays the songs in any playlists that you create.

Between the playback controls and the video/visualization window is an area called the Now Playing Tools area. This area can display controls specific to the type of file you're playing. For example, if you're playing a DVD, this area can display the Variable Play Speed and Next Frame controls.

Finally, the seven buttons along the left of the window link to key features of the player. Click a button and the entire player interface changes to reflect the selected feature—Now Playing, Media Guide, CD Audio, Media Library, Radio Tuner, Portable Device, or Skin Chooser.

CONFIGURING WMP

WMP is a very customizable device. Not only can you resize it, as you can any Windows application, but you can also display it in a Compact mode, or with completely different looks and feels.

Changing the Size of the Player

The default display mode for WMP is the Full mode. If you'd rather display the player without all the extraneous controls, you can switch to Compact mode. As you can see in Figure 13.2, Compact mode focuses your attention on the video/visualization window. Some controls are shrunk and others are hidden.

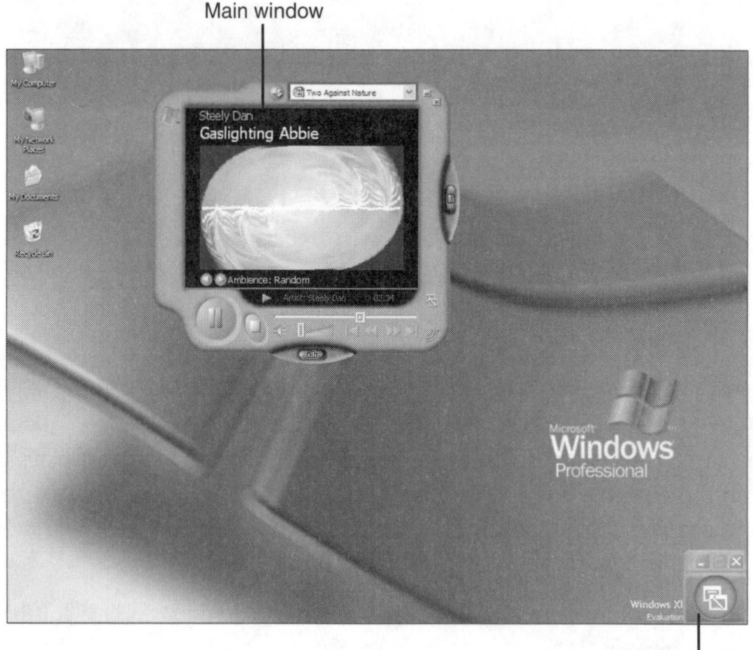

Figure 13.2

Windows Media Player in compact mode.

When you're in Compact mode, a small anchor window appears at the bottom left of your desktop. You can click the anchor window to return to Full mode, or to open a new file.

You switch to Compact mode by clicking the Switch to Compact Mode button at the lower-right of the WMP window, or by selecting View, Compact Mode.

Whether you're in Full or Compact modes, you can manually resize the main WMP window. When you resize the main window, the size of the video/visualization window also changes. All you have to do is use your mouse to grab any side or corner of the window, and then drag it to a new size.

Resize the WMP window to view a DVD movie at a larger size.

You can also resize the size of the video window when you're playing a DVD movie. Select View, Zoom, and then select a new zoom percentage.

Or, if you prefer, you can view a DVD using your entire computer screen. Just click the Full Screen button (at the lower-right corner of the video window) or select View, Full Screen, and the movie will fill your entire screen. Press Esc to return to normal viewing mode.

Changing Skins

If you don't like the default look and feel of WMP, you can change it. WMP lets you change its basic interface by applying new "skins." A *skin* is a complete interface that includes the window frame and background and all the controls. In fact, some skins have fewer controls than the default WMP interface.

Most skins are meant to be used in WMP's Compact mode.

To give you an idea of how different skins can change the way WMP looks and feels, check out Figures 13.3 and 13.4. Compare these two skins to WMP's default skin in Figure 13.2. It's a great way to put your personal stamp on your media player.

Figure 13.3

WMP with the Optik skin.

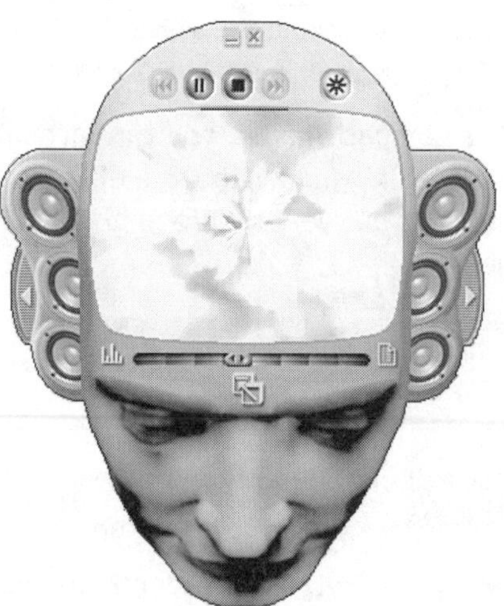

Figure 13.4

WMP with the Headspace skin.

To changes skins, follow these steps:

1. With WMP in Full mode, click the Skin Chooser button.
2. Select a skin from the left-hand list. The skin you choose will be previewed in the right-side window, as shown in Figure 13.5.
3. Click the Apply Skin button. WMP will now switch to Compact mode with the new skin applied.

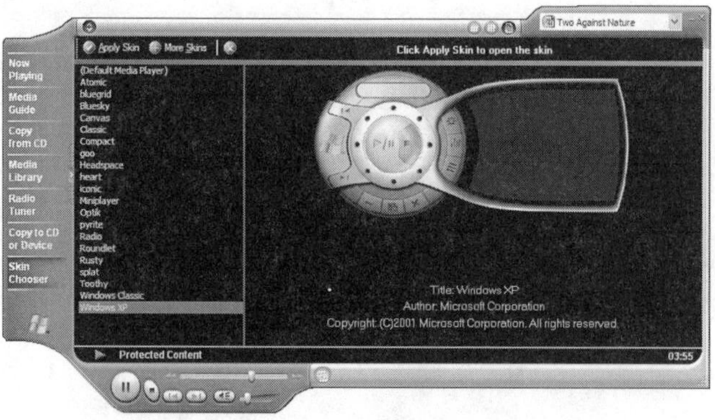

Figure 13.5

Choosing a new skin for the media player.

You change skins when you're in the Compact mode by clicking the Anchor window and selecting Select a New Skin from the pop-up window.

Windows XP includes a fair selection of skins built-in, but there are a lot more skins available from the Internet at Microsoft's WindowsMedia.com Web site. Just click the More Skins button (in the Skin Chooser window), and WMP will launch Internet Explorer and connect to the WindowsMedia.com Web site. Pick a new skin and follow the onscreen instructions to download it to your system.

Changing Visualizations

Microsoft apparently thinks that you'll get bored listening to plain old music without any visual stimulation. For that reason, it supplies a number of *visualizations* that play onscreen when you're listening to any audio-only file or broadcast.

A visualization is a splash of color and shapes that move to the beat of the music. Visualizations are displayed where the video picture would normally be displayed.

WMP includes a slew of visualizations you can watch while you're listening to music. The visualizations are grouped into collections based on specific themes. You can pick a specific visualization to watch, and even (for some visualizations) configure individual visualization properties.

To select a visualization, make sure you're in the Now Playing screen in Full mode, then select View, Visualizations. Choose a collection and then select an individual visualization.

You can cycle through all available visualizations by clicking the Previous Visualization and Next Visualization buttons directly underneath the visualization window.

As you might suspect, additional visualizations are available from the Internet. Just select Tools, Download Visualizations to go to the WindowsMedia.com Web site and browse for new visualization collections.

Some visualization collections let you personalize the way the look—colors used, speed, and so on. To customize a visualization, select Tools, Options to display the Options dialog box. Select the Visualizations tab, select the collection you want to customize, then click the Properties button. When the Properties dialog box appears, set the options as you like them.

Changing Audio and Video Settings

In addition to skins and visualizations, there are a number of useful settings in WMP that you might want to configure.

For example, you can use WMP's built-in graphic equalizer to fine-tune your PC's audio playback. Select View, Now Playing Tools, Graphic Equalizer to display the equalizer below the video/visualization window (see Figure 13.6). Make sure the equalizer is clicked On, then drag the equalizer controls to the shape the sound to your liking.

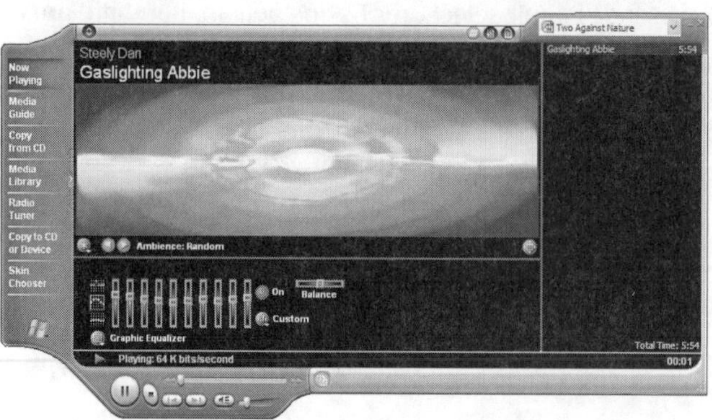

Figure 13.6

Fine-tune your bass and treble with WMP's graphic equalizer.

WMP also includes a variety of digitally processed audio effects—or what Microsoft calls SOS Wow Effects. (It sounds cooler.) You access these effects by selecting View, Now Playing Tools, SRS Wow Effects. Make sure the control is clicked On, then adjust the controls as follows:

- To enhance the bass, drag the TruBass slider to the right. To minimize the bass, drag the slider to the left.
- To widen the stereo effect, drag the WOW Effect slider to the right. To collapse the stereo effect, drag the slider to the left.
- To optimize the sound for your particular speakers or headphones, click the button under the On button and select from Headphones, Normal Speakers, or Large Speakers.

If you're playing a DVD, you can adjust the picture's brightness, contrast, and color hue and saturation. Just select View, Now Playing Tools, Video Settings to display these video controls, and adjust the sliders as appropriate.

Configuring Player Options

Finally, there are a bunch of general program options you can configure. These are available on separate tabs in the Options dialog box. (You open this dialog box by selecting Tools, Options.)

Table 13.2 details what configuration settings you can adjust.

TABLE 13.2—Windows Media Player Options, By Tab

Tab	Options
Player	Frequency of automatic software updates, Internet settings, and how the player is displayed on your desktop
Copy Music	Location of stored files, which file format (Windows Media or MP3) is used for copying/recording, and quality of copied music

TABLE 13.2—CONTINUED

Tab	Options
Devices	Playback and copy settings for audio CDs and portable audio devices
Performance	Connection speed and buffering for streaming media, as well as settings for video hardware acceleration
Media Library	Set access rights for Internet sites and applications
Visualizations	Add and configure WMP's visualizations
Formats	Sets which file formats WMP should be the default player for
DVD	Sets parental controls and language/audio settings for DVD playback
Network	Configures network protocols and proxy settings for streaming media playback

PLAYING AUDIO FILES

Now that we have all that messy configuration and customization out of the way, let's get down to the important stuff—using WMP to play audio files!

Normal Playback

You can use WMP to play audio files that are stored on your computer or downloaded from the Internet, or to play back songs from a normal audio CD.

CD playback should start automatically when you insert a CD into your PC's CD drive. To play back a digital audio file, you first have to load that file into the player (select File, Open).

The player's transport controls are located at the bottom of the main window. You start playback by clicking the Play button, or pause playback by clicking the Pause button. (It's the same button—it says Play when playback is paused or stopped, and Pause when a song is playing.) You stop playback completely by clicking the Stop button.

If you'd rather not use these transport controls, just pull down the Play menu and select either Play/Pause or Stop.

You don't have to play the entire song from start to finish. Where you're at in a song is indicated by the Seek slider. You can move the slider anywhere in the song, and playback will resume from the point you selected.

You can also choose to play the songs on a CD in a random order. Just select Play, Shuffle, and WMP will shuffle randomly through the tracks on the CD.

Adjust the Volume and Sound

If the sound is too loud (or not loud enough), you can change the volume by dragging the Volume slider to the right (louder) or left (softer). If you need to mute the sound quickly, click the Mute button to the left of the Volume slider. Click the Mute button again to unmute the sound.

Viewing File Information

Most audio files and CDs have information about their content embedded in the individual files. To view this information, select View, Now Playing Tools, Media Information. Details about the song currently playing will be displayed underneath the video/visualizations window.

To view detailed information about the current artist or album, go to the Media Library screen, select a track, and then click the Media Details button. This will display information about the selected album. Click Artist Profile to view information about the artist.

If you're listening to a CD, you can find more information on the CD Audio screen. Just select a track and click the Album Details button to display information about the current album. Click the Artist Profile button to view information about the artist.

To access any of this supplementary information, you must be connected to the Internet. WMP goes out to the Internet to retrieve information about any CD or DVD you're playing.

LISTENING TO INTERNET RADIO

Many real-world radio stations broadcast over the Internet using streaming audio. With streaming audio, playback can start before an entire file is downloaded. Since live radio has no files to download, it has to be streamed to your computer.

Some Internet radio programs are simulcasts of traditional radio stations. Other Internet radio programs are Web-only affairs. You can use WMP to listen to many Internet radio programs.

Internet radio streamed in the RealMedia (RealAudio or RealVideo) format can't be played with WMP. For these files, you'll need RealNetwork's RealMedia player, discussed in the "Other Media Players" section, later in this chapter.

The first step to listening to Internet radio is finding a station you want to listen to. WMP can access the Internet and display a Web page of compatible Internet radio stations, as shown in Figure 13.7. (This page is hosted by Microsoft's WindowsMedia.com site.) All you have to do is click the Radio Tuner button to display this screenful of listings, which is a good place to start when you want to listen to streaming audio broadcasts.

You can search for stations by format, band (AM or FM), language, location, callsign, frequency, or keyword. When you find a station you want to add to your list of presets, select the station and click the Add button. Your preset stations are displayed on the left side of the screen.

Figure 13.7

Go to the Radio Tuner page to view this listing of Internet radio stations.

There are also many Web sites that contain directories of and links to hundreds and thousands of Internet radio stations. The best of these Internet radio directories include:

- **Internet Radio List** (`www.internetradiolist.com`)
- **Live@** (`www.live-at.com`)
- **Radio-Locator** (`www.radio-locator.com`)
- **Web-Radio** (`www.web-radio.com`)
- **What's On Web Radio** (`www.whatsonwebradio.com`)

When you find a site on one of these pages that you want to add to your preset list, select File, Add to Media Library, Add Currently Playing Track. This adds this station to your Media Library (discussed later in this chapter). You can then go to the Media Library screen, find the station in the All Audio playlist, and add the song to a playlist of your own creation.

WATCHING DVDS

If you have a DVD-ROM drive in your computer and the proper DVD decoder software installed, you can use WMP to play DVD movies on your computer screen.

WMP does not include DVD decoder software. Chances are that if your PC came with a DVD-ROM drive, it also came with a DVD decoder. If not, you can purchase one of the DVD Decoder Pack add-ins (for about $30) from CyberLink (`www.gocyberlink.com`), InterVideo (`www.intervideo.com`), or Ravisent (`www.ravisentdirect.com/xppaks/`), that will add DVD playback capability to WMP.

Playing a DVD Video

When you put a DVD in your DVD drive, WMP starts playing it, automatically. You can also initiate playback by selecting Play, DVD or CD Audio.

As you can see in Figure 13.8, the DVD video displays in the video window. The individual tracks on the DVD are displayed in the Playlist area, and information about the DVD (including the DVD cover) is displayed beneath the video window.

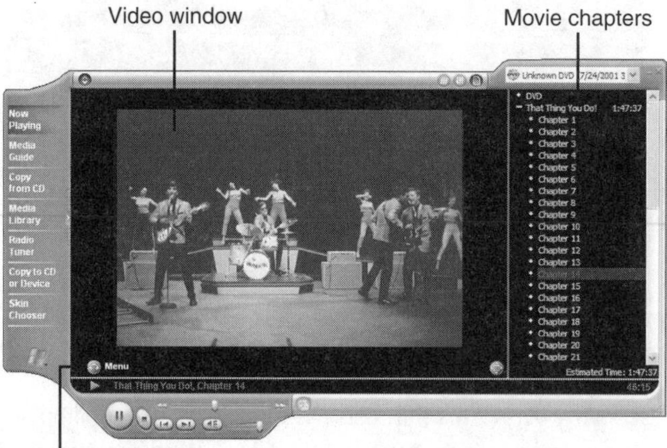

Figure 13.8

Watching a DVD movie with Windows Media Player.

You have to be connected to the Internet for WMP to find and display this DVD information and cover art.

Navigating DVD Menus

Almost all DVDs come with their own built-in menus. These menus typically lead you to special features on the disc, and allow you to select various playback options and jump to specific scenes.

To display the DVD's main menu, select View, DVD Features, Title Menu. To display the DVD's special features menu, select View, DVD Features, Top Menu. When the special features menu is displayed, you can click any of the options onscreen to jump to a particular feature.

You can also jump to the DVD's special features menu by clicking WMP's Menu button, located directly under the video window.

Changing Audio Options

Many DVDs come with an English-language soundtrack, as well as soundtracks in other languages. Some DVDs come with different types of audio—mono, Dolby Pro Logic surround,

Dolby Digital 5.1 surround, and so on. Other DVDs come with commentary from the film's director or stars on a separate audio track.

You can select which audio track you listen to by selecting View, DVD Features, Audio and Language Tracks. This displays a list of available audio options. Select the track you want to listen to, then settle back to enjoy the movie.

Playing in Slow Motion—or Fast Motion

WMP provides a variety of special playback features. You can pause a still frame, advance frame-by-frame, or play the movie in slow or fast motion.

To access these special playback features, you have to select View, Now Playing Tools, DVD Controls. This displays a set of special controls in the Now Playing Tools area of the WMP window, as shown in Figure 13.9.

Figure 13.9

Use the DVD controls for variable-speed playback.

To play the movie in slow motion, drag the Variable Play Speed slider to the left. To play the movie at a faster-than-normal speed, drag the slider to the right. To return to normal speed, click the Play button.

If you drag the slider to the left of the center mark, you'll actually start playing the movie *backwards*!

To pause the movie and display a still frame, click the Pause button. To advance one frame at a time, click the Next Frame button. Click the Play button to return to normal playback.

You can "shoot" a screen capture of any individual frame by selecting View, DVD Features, Capture Image. (If you pause the movie first, it's easier to select which frame to capture.) The still image is captured to the Windows clipboard, and can then be pasted into any graphics editing application.

Displaying Subtitles and Closed Captions

Many DVDs include subtitles in other languages. To turn on subtitles, select View, DVD Features, Subtitles and Captions, and then select which subtitles you want to view.

Other DVDs include closed captioning for the hearing impaired. You can view closed captions by selecting View, DVD Features, Subtitles and Captions, Closed Captions.

You can't display both subtitles and closed captions at the same time.

ORGANIZING YOUR MEDIA FILES

Windows Media Player functions not only as a media player, but also as a media manager. You can use WMP's Media Library feature to organize all the digital media files on your computer—as well as links to other digital content on the Internet.

Note that the Media Library is different from WMP's playlists. The Media Library contains *all* of your media files, where playlists contain lists of files that you personally create. (Thinking of it one way, playlists are subsets of the larger Media Library.)

You view and manage your files from WMP's Media Library screen, shown in Figure 13.10. Click the Media Library button to display this screen.

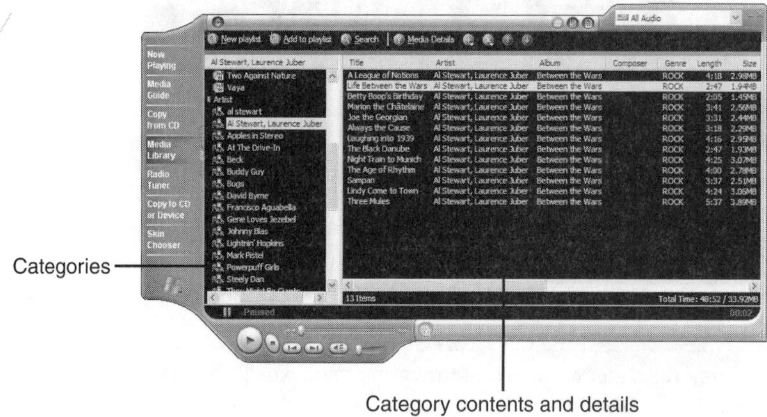

Figure 13.10

Manage your digital media files from WMP's Media Library.

Searching for Media Files

To add files to your Media Library, you first have to find them. One of the first places to look for files is on your PC's hard disk.

To search for media files on your computer, select Tools, Search for Media Files. When the Search for Media Files dialog box appears, select which drives and folders you want to search, then click the Search button. WMP will now begin the search, and add any digital media files it finds to either the All Audio or All Clips (for video files) categories.

If you add too many files to your Media Library, you may need to search the Library itself for specific files. To do this, click the Search button at the top of the Media Library screen. When the Search Library for Media dialog box appears (as shown in Figure 13.11), enter your search criteria and click the Search Now button. The results of your search will be displayed in the Search Results playlist.

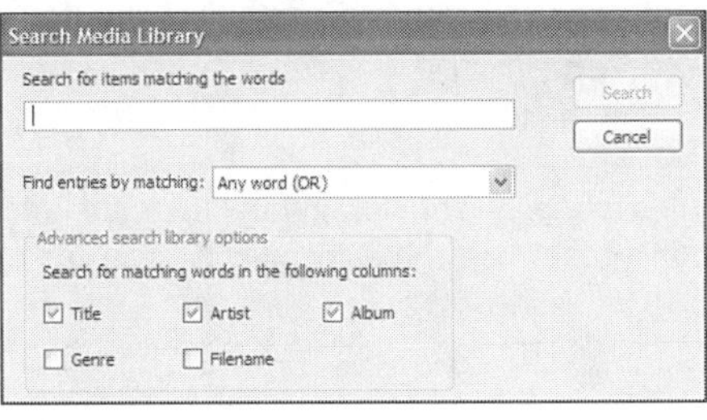

Figure 13.11

Searching for digital media files within the Media Library.

Adding Files to Your Media Library

You can add new files to your Media Library from compact discs, Internet sites, or other locations on your hard disk or network. Table 13.3 shows how to add various types of files.

TABLE 13.3—How to Add Files to Your Media Library

Type of file	Instructions
CD audio track	Select File, Add to Media Library, Add Currently Playing Track
File (on your PC or network)	Select File, Add to Media Library, Add File
File (on the Internet)	Select File, Add to Media Library, Add URL

After you add a file to your Media Library, you can play it by selecting it in the track list and then clicking the Play button. To delete a file from the Media Library, right-click the track and select Delete From Library from the pop-up menu.

Working with Playlists

An easier way to work with your favorite files is to create a customized playlist. You can play all the songs in a playlist with a single action, which is a lot easier than selecting all the songs individually.

To create a playlist, follow these steps:

1. From the Media Library screen, click the New Playlist button.
2. When the New Playlist dialog box appears, enter a name for your playlist, then click OK.
3. To add a file to your playlist, select the file from within a Media Library category, click the Add to Playlist button, and then select the playlist.

4. To rearrange items in a playlist, select the playlist in the Media Library list, then drag a file to a new position.
5. To remove a track from your playlist, right-click the item and select Delete From Playlist from the pop-up menu.

You can also add files to a playlist by dragging files within Media Library or My Computer and dropping them on a specific playlist. You can also right-click a specific file and select Add to Playlist.

Playing a Playlist

To play a playlist, go to the Now Playing screen, pull down the Playlist list, and select a playlist. The playlist should start playing automatically. If not, all you have to do is click the Play button. All the tracks in your playlist will play, one at a time, in the order listed.

To skip a track within a playlist, click the Next button or select Play, Next. To repeat a track you really like, select the track and then select Play, Repeat. You can also play the tracks in a playlist in random order by selecting Play, Shuffle.

USING OTHER MEDIA PLAYERS

I'll wrap up this chapter by noting that Windows Media Player isn't the only media player on the market. The reality is that Microsoft is in a bitter fight for the digital media market, and there are several strong competitors to WMP that you might want to check out.

RealPlayer

RealPlayer (available at `www.real.com/player/`) is the most-used streaming media player today. This is because the majority of Web sites use the RealMedia format to deliver their streaming media content. When you go to a Web site and click the link to start streaming audio or video playback, chances are that RealPlayer will launch automatically—it's probably already installed on your PC.

As with most media players, there are both free and paid versions of RealPlayer. For most users, the free version is more than adequate.

QuickTime Player

Apple's QuickTime Player is a media player used primarily for playing back QuickTime-format movies and video clips. While QuickTime movies aren't as common as Windows Media or RealMedia files, there are still a lot of QuickTime movies out there on the Web. You can download a copy of the player from `www.apple.com/quicktime/`.

Winamp

When it comes to playing digital audio files, MP3 is the most popular format, and Winamp is the most popular MP3 player. I'll talk more about MP3s in the next chapter, but if you want a good all-around MP3 player, you can't go wrong with Winamp. You can download a free copy of Winamp from `www.winamp.com`.

MusicMatch Jukebox

Where Winamp is the most popular MP3 player, MusicMatch Jukebox is the most popular MP3 encoder. (And my personal favorite.) It's actually a combination player/encounter, and it's incredibly easy to use. Not only is the playback process a push-button affair, but practically the entire ripping process is automated. You can download a free copy of MusicMatch Jukebox from `www.musicmatch.com`.

JIM'S TOP TEN TIPS

As users get more comfortable using their PCs to play audio and video files, Windows Media Player will become an even more essential part of Windows. (Well, I'm not convinced that it's actually a part of Windows. It still seems like a separate utility to me—even though the only way to get the latest version of WMP is by buying Windows XP.)

So you'll probably be using WMP a lot. Just make sure you remember these top ten tips:

1. The latest version of Windows Media Player includes a niftier interface, MP3 compatibility, DVD playback, and the ability to copy files to CDs and portable audio players. It's also not available as a freestanding application—only as part of Windows XP.
2. You can display WMP in either Full or Compact modes. Or, when you're watching DVD movies, you can switch to full-screen mode.
3. You can change the look-and-feel of WMP by selecting new skins. (Click the Skin Chooser button and choose away!)
4. To play a CD with WMP, all you have to do is insert the CD in your CD-ROM drive and click the Play button.
5. If you're connected to the Internet, WMP will go online and download detailed information about the CD or DVD that you're playing.
6. You can use WMP to listen to Internet radio stations. Just click the Radio Tuner button and search the type of station you want to listen to.
7. If you have a DVD-ROM drive in your PC, WMP will play back DVD movies. Disc chapters are displayed in the Playlist pane, and you can jump to the disc's main menu by selecting View, DVD Features, Title Menu.
8. To access WMP's special DVD playback controls (such as slow motion and frame advance), select View, Now Playing Tools, DVD Controls.
9. WMP lets you store and categorize all the digital media files on your computer—as well as CD tracks and selected files on the Internet. You organize your files in the Media Library; click the Media Library button to display your files.
10. To create a personalized playlist of files or tracks, go to the Media Library screen and click the New Playlist button. To add a file/track to your playlist, select the file/track in the Media Library, then click the Add to Playlist button.

CHAPTER 14

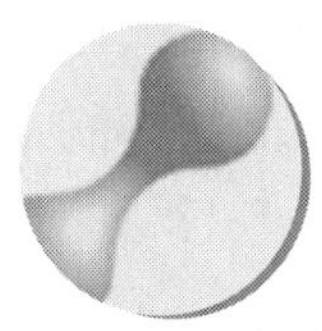

PLAYING AND RECORDING MP3 AND WMA AUDIO

- Introducing Digital Audio
- Finding and Downloading Digital Audio Files
- Copying (Ripping) CD Tracks to Your PC
- Burning Audio Files to a CD
- Other Rippers and Burners
- Jim's Top Ten Tips

Listening to and downloading music from the Web is a big deal. Instead of buying a CD at a traditional music store, you can download the music you like from the Internet. Then you can listen to your favorite songs directly from your hard disk, burn your own custom CD compilations, or copy the music you want to a portable audio player to listen to on the go.

There are any number of media player/recorder programs that can handle all these tasks for you. Windows Media Player (WMP) is one of them. And because it's included free-of-charge with Windows XP, why not us it?

I showed you the basic operations of WMP in Chapter 13, "Using Windows Media Player." In this chapter I'll show you specifically how to use WMP to download, store, and copy digital audio files.

One of the new features of the Windows XP version of WMP is the ability to record MP3-format audio files.

WMP could always play back MP3s, but this is the first Microsoft player that can also record MP3s—provided you purchase the MP3 Creation Pack. This add-on piece of software adds MP3 encoding capabilities to WMP. Without the MP3 Creation Pack, WMP will only encode WMA-format files.

INTRODUCING DIGITAL AUDIO

The advent of digital audio enables anyone with a personal computer to make reasonably acceptable (and, depending on the format, bit-for-bit perfect) digital copies of songs from compact discs, and to store these copies on their computer's hard disk. Digital audio also lets any PC user with an Internet connection trade songs with other users, and download copies of songs that other users have made. In addition, digital audio lets users download their favorite songs to portable audio players and listen to them while they're away from the computer. It's ultimate user control over the music you listen to.

In the last chapter I explained how music and movies are now recorded digitally. There are many different ways to make a digital recording, which results in many different file formats for digital audio.

Of all the available file formats, the one that has enjoyed almost universal popularity is the MP3 format. That's because MP3 was the first widely accepted format that combined good quality sound with reasonably small files.

But MP3 isn't the only digital audio file format in use today. Microsoft is waging a strong campaign for its Windows Media Audio (WMA) format, which offers similar quality to MP3 at half the file size.

I'll look at both these formats—MP3 and WMA—in the following sections.

MP3 Audio

MP3 is a digital audio file format that compresses music to fit within reasonably sized computer files—while maintaining near-CD quality sound. A typical three-minute song in MP3 format takes up about 3MB of disk space.

It's not an exaggeration to say that MP3 had taken the music industry by storm. Music fans love MP3s—even though most record companies (and many artists) despise it. In particular, they fear that unauthorized copying of their music will deprive them of revenues from traditional CD sales. Whether that's the case or not, MP3 has quickly become the standard for music on the Web—and there's no stopping it.

Developed (and patented) by Thomson Multimedia and the Fraunhofer Institute, the MP3 digital audio format is an extension of Motion Picture Experts Group (MPEG) Layer 3 technology. (The MP3 file extension itself is short for **MP**EG Layer **3**.) MP3 and other MPEG formats store music digitally, and in the process compress the original data to take up less space than it did originally. MP3's data compression reduces digital sound files by about a 12:1 ratio.

In addition to compressing the data in an audio file, MP3 also lets you choose the rate at which the original music is sampled. The lower the sampling rate, the smaller the filer size—and the lower the sound quality.

As an example, normal compact discs sample music at a 44.1kHz rate. In other words, the music is sampled, digitally, 44,100 times per second. Each sample is 16 bits long. When you multiply the sampling rate by the sample size and the number of channels (two for stereo), you end up with a *bit rate*. For CDs, you multiply 44,100×16×2, and end up with 1,400,000 bits per second (1,400Kbps).

The space taken up by these bits can add up quickly. If you take a typical three-minute song recorded at 44.1KHz, you end up using 32MB of disk space. While that song can easily fit on a 650MB CD, it's way too big to download over a 56.6Kbps dial-up Internet connection.

The appeal of the MP3 format is that it combines compression with lower bit-rate sampling. By recording at lower bit rates, you get smaller files—and faster downloads.

For example, if you choose to encode an MP3 file at a 128Kbps bit rate, that same 32MB three-minute song will compress down to just 3MB of storage. That's small enough to download easily, even on a dial-up connection.

The problem with shrinking files to this degree, of course, is that the sound quality suffers. The lower the bit rate, the worse the sound. The higher the bit rate, the bigger the file. It's a trade-off.

When you're recording an MP3 file, which bit rate should you use? Table 14.1 shows some of the more popular bit rates available, and describes the sound quality of each.

TABLE 14.1—Popular MP3 Bit Rates

Bit Rate	Sound Quality
56Kbps	Suitable for voice recording only. Extremely compressed sound, similar to AM radio.
64Kbps	Not noticeably different than 56Kbps. Still extremely compressed, not suitable for music.
96Kbps	Comparable to worst-case FM radio. Noticeable high-end loss, heavily compressed sound, lack of full dynamic range.
112Kbps	Noticeable improvement to 96Kbps. Still has poor definition and presence, with soft attacks.
128Kbps	Soft attacks, slightly compressed sound. Similar to normal FM radio, but still sub-CD quality. This is probably the most popular bit rate for encoding.
160Kbps	Sounds slightly softer and more compressed than the original, but less noticeably so than with lower bit rates.
192Kbps	Sounds similar to the original, but with less presence and somewhat restricted dynamic range.
256Kbps	Quality is approaching that of the original, but still has a slightly compressed sound.
320Kbps	Near CD-quality. This is the highest bit rate possible with the current MP3 standard.

If you're encoding MP3 files for use at your computer or with a portable MP3 player, the 128Kbps rate is probably good enough quality. If you're encoding MP3 files for playback on a high-fidelity audio system, you'll probably want to move up to at least a 256Kbps bit rate—although 192Kbps might be good enough. (Sound quality is highly subjective, as you can imagine—some "golden-eared" audiophiles find it difficult to listen to MP3s recorded at *any* bit rate!)

The basic Windows Media Player included with Windows XP will play back MP3s (at any recorded bit rate), but will not record MP3 files. That's because Microsoft doesn't want to pay a licensing fee for an MP3 encoder. (And, although Microsoft won't say so, it's also because they're pushing their competing WMA format, so anything they can do *not* to support MP3 only works to their advantage—or so they think….)

If you want to record MP3s with WMP, you have to buy an add-on software utility called the MP3 Creation Pack. This add-on pack will be available (for about $30) in three different versions, each using a different MP3 encoder. The three versions will be marketed by CyberLink, InterVideo, and Ravisent.

When you install one of the MP3 Creation Packs, you'll notice that WMP's Options dialog box (discussed later in this chapter) now lets you choose between WMA- and MP3-format recording. (Without the Creation Pack, you only have the WMA option.) You can then select from various bit rates, and use WMP as you would normally to rip MP3 files to your hard disk

Windows Media Audio

As I mentioned earlier, several competing audio formats have been introduced with the goal of providing listeners with either better sound quality or smaller file size (or both) than the current MP3 format. Microsoft's entrée in this competition is Windows Media Audio (WMA for short). WMA files offer similar sound quality as MP3 files, but at about half the size. (Or so Microsoft claims….)

WMA definitely offers better copyright protection than the MP3 format, which is a big issue for the music industry. Unlike MP3 files, you can protect WMA files from unlawful distribution, copying, and sharing. Which means no more downloading of your favorite songs—for free, anyway.

The way WMA copy protection works is that each CD track that you copy has a license. Theoretically, this license should deter people like you and me from stealing or copying the content.

When you use Windows Media Player to copy protected content from your computer to a CD or portable device, the license is copied along with the song. When you try to play the copy-protected song on another device, it won't play.

As you might suspect, consumers have not been overly supportive of the WMA format. On the other hand, the music industry loves it.

When you're making WMA recordings, you have a similar choice of bit rate that you do with MP3 files. The higher the bit rate, the higher the sound quality—and the larger the file size. Lower the bit rate and you lower the sound quality—but you also reduce the necessary disk space.

Some of this has to do with the fact that WMA files can be encoded at lower bit rates than MP3 files, with comparable sound quality. Table 14.2 compares bit-rate quality between the two formats.

TABLE 14.2—COMPARING BIT-RATE QUALITY BETWEEN WMA AND MP3 AUDIO FORMATS

MP3 Bit Rate	Comparable WMA Bit Rate	Sound Quality
64Kbps	48Kbps	Suitable for voice only
128Kbps	96Kbps	Similar to FM radio
192Kbps	128Kbps	Similar to the original
320Kbps	192Kbps	Near-CD quality

As with the MP3 format, you can really hear the difference between the different WMA bit rates. A 48Kbps recording sounds a lot like AM radio, while a 192Kbps recording is near CD-quality. Pick something in the middle, like 96 or 128Kbps, and you get a recording that sounds like decent FM radio.

MP3 Versus WMA: Which Format Is Best?

Microsoft would like you to think that WMA is a better format than MP3 because it delivers similar quality at half the file size. My problem with that argument is that I don't think it's true. In our experience at TechTV, it's possible to create somewhat smaller WMA files that sound similar to MP3 files. For example, a 128kpbs MP3 file is comparable to a 96kpbs WMA file—although, in our judgment, the WMA files still don't sound quite as good as the MP3 files. You should let your ears be the judge, of course, but my vote is for MP3.

The big difference, then, is the copy protection. WMA has it. MP3 doesn't.

You also have to deal with the popularity factor. Most song files that are being traded today are in MP3 format. Millions of users can't be wrong. MP3 is the king, and that's just the way it is.

The reality is that you'll probably use the MP3 format when making your own recordings. It's what all your friends use, and it's the format supported by all the latest portable audio players.

However, the songs you download from the Internet will be available in whatever format they're available in—whether MP3, WMA, or some newer, better format. Because Windows Media Player can play both these formats, it's a good all-around media player for all your digital audio needs.

There's a new audio format you should be on the lookout for. It's called AAC, it's from Dolby labs, and we actually like it better than either MP3 or WMA. Right now it's expensive, and as I write these words there hasn't been announcement of an AAC add-in for Windows Media Player. But keep your eye (or your ear!) on this format. It creates music files at 96Kbps that are better than 128Kbps MP3 files.

FINDING AND DOWNLOADING DIGITAL AUDIO FILES

With all those MP3 and WMA files floating around the Internet, how do you find the ones you want—and get them into your computer?

To download a digital audio file to your PC, connect to the Internet and follow these general steps:

1. Use Internet Explorer to navigate to a digital audio archive site (see the list in a few paragraphs).
2. Search the site to find the song you want to download, and then click the "download now" link.
3. Specify where on your hard disk you want to store the downloaded file, then click the Save button.

On a standard 56.6Kbps connection, it will take about 10 to 15 minutes to download a typical MP3-format song. The same file will only take a minute or two to download via a broadband connection.

Once you've downloaded the song, you'll want to add it to your WMP Media Library, and perhaps to a custom playlist. Follow the instructions in Chapter 13 to perform these tasks.

There are literally hundreds of Web sites devoted to the downloading of audio files. Most of these sites feature files in the MP3 format.

These digital music sites typically let you search by artist or song title, and some let you search or browse by genre. The majority of these sites store copies of files on their own servers. Some sites, however, search other sites on the Web for the music you're looking for.

Among the best of these digital music download sites are the following:

- **AMPCAST.COM** (`www.ampcast.com`)
- **ARTIST direct** (`www.artistdirect.com`)
- **Audiofind** (`www.audiofind.com`)
- **EMusic** (`www.emusic.com`)
- **GetMusic** (`www.getmusic.com`)
- **Liquid.com** (`www.liquid.com`)

- **Listen.com** (www.listen.com)
- **Lycos MP3 Search** (music.lycos.com)
- **MP3.com** (www.mp3.com)
- **MTV.com** (www.mtv.com)
- **MusicNet** (www.musicnet.com)
- **Musicseek** (www.musicseek.net)
- **passport** (www.passport.com)
- **sonicnet.com** (www.sonicnet.com)
- **Tunes.com** (www.tunes.com)

If you're looking for general information about playing and recording MP3s, check out MP3.com (www.mp3.com) and the askMP3 portal (www.mpeg.org/MPEG/mp3.html), which is part of the MPEG.ORG Web site.

In addition to these archives of digital music, there are also sites and software that let you swap digital audio files directly with other users. These file-swapping services, such as Napster, help you find other users who have the songs you want. You then connect directly to the user's computer, and copy the file you want from that computer to yours.

Among the most popular of these file-sharing services are

- **AIMster** (www.aimster.com)
- **Audio Galaxy Satellite** (www.audiogalaxy.com/satellite)
- **BearShare** (www.bearshare.com)
- **Gnutella** (gnutella.wego.com)
- **iMesh** (www.imesh.com)
- **KaZaA Media Desktop** (www.kazaa.com)
- **MusicCity Morpheus** (www.musiccity.com)
- **Napster** (www.napster.com)

COPYING (RIPPING) CD TRACKS TO YOUR PC

The next step in the digital audio revolution is learning how to copy tracks from your favorite CDs to your computer's hard disk. If you have a large-enough hard disk, you can store an entire library of CDs or individual tracks—and then choose from this library to burn your own custom CDs.

This process of copying files from a CD to your hard disk, in either MP3 or WMA format, is called "ripping." Windows Media Player makes it easy to rip your favorite songs.

Set the Format and Quality Level

Before you begin copying, you first have to tell WMP what format you want to use for your ripped files—MP3 or WMA. (Remember, the MP3 option will be there only if you've purchased and installed the MP3 Creation Pack.) You also have to choose the quality level for recording.

Here's how you set the format and quality:

1. From within Windows Media Player, select Tools, Options.
2. When the Options dialog box appears, select the Copy Music tab, as shown in Figure 14.1.

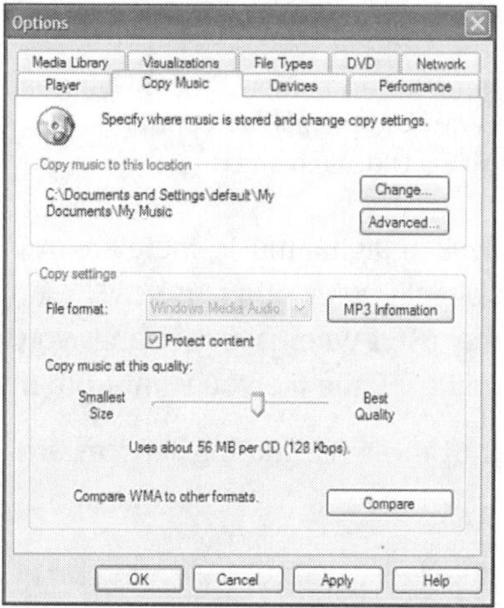

Figure 14.1

Before you copy a file, select which format and quality level you want to use.

3. In the Copy Settings section, pull down the File Format list and select either Windows Media Audio or MP3. (If you haven't installed the MP3 Creation Pack, you won't have a choice here—your only option will be Windows Media Audio.)
4. Unless you have some particular reason to want to copy protect the files you're ripping, uncheck the Protect Content option. (This option is available only with Windows Media files.)
5. Use the Copy Music At This Quality slider to set the bit rate for your ripped files. Move the slider to the left for smaller files and lower sound quality. Move the slider to the right for larger files and higher sound quality.
6. Click OK when done.

When you're copying in the WMA format, either the 96 or 128Kbps level should be a good compromise between file size and sound quality.

Rip the Files

Once your settings are set, it's time to start recording. (Technically, recording in a digital format is called *encoding*—although Microsoft calls it copying, and everybody else calls it ripping.)

Follow these steps:

1. Insert the CD you want to rip into your PC's CD-ROM drive.
2. Connect to the Internet so that WMP can download album and track details. (If you don't connect, you won't be able to encode track names or CD cover art.)
3. In Windows Media Player, select the Copy from CD tab to show the contents of the CD, a shown in Figure 14.2.

Figure 14.2

Getting ready to copy selected album tracks—just click the Copy Music button.

4. Put a check mark by the tracks you want to copy.
5. Click the Copy Music button.

WMP now begins to copy the tracks you selected, in the format you selected, and at the quality level you selected.

Unless you specify otherwise in the Options dialog box, the tracks are recorded into your My Music folder, into a subfolder for the artist, and within that in another subfolder for this particular CD. As you can see in Figure 14.3, the folder for the album displays the CD's cover graphics. (Assuming you connected to the Internet to download the cover art, that is.)

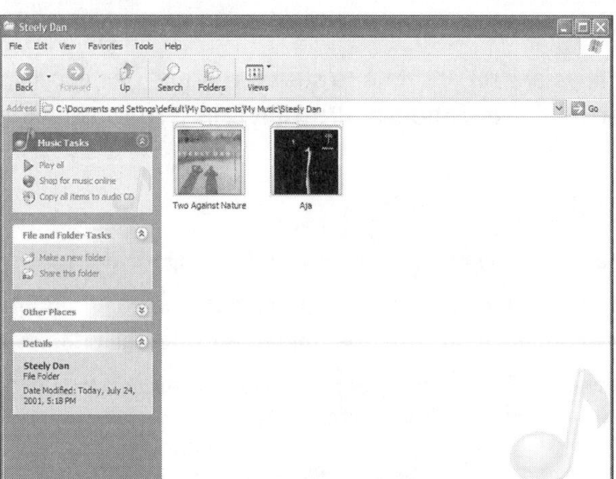

Figure 14.3

Your ripped files are stored in a subfolder for that particular CD.

BURNING AUDIO FILES TO A CD

If you can copy tracks from a CD to your hard disk, what's to stop you from going in the other direction—copying files from your hard disk to a recordable/rewritable CD?

Assuming that the tracks aren't copy protected, nothing.

This process of recording your own custom CDs is called *burning* a CD. And the Windows XP version of Windows Media Player makes it extremely easy to burn your own music CDs.

You can copy virtually any audio file from your hard disk to a blank CD. You can copy tracks you've ripped from other CDs, as well as MP3 or WMA files you've downloaded or swapped from the Internet. As long as the files are on your hard disk, they can be burned.

Naturally, to burn a CD, you need a CD-R or CD-RW drive in your PC. Many new PCs come with a CD-R/RW drive as standard. If you need to add a CD-R/RW drive, it won't cost you more than a few hundred bucks.

WMP lets you burn CDs in either CD-R (recordable) or CD-RW (rewritable) formats. CD-Rs can only be recorded once, but can play on any CD player. CD-RWs can be copied onto over and over, but can only be played in compatible CD-RW drives—CD-RW discs typically won't play in normal CD players. (Which means that you probably want to record in the CD-R format.)

The easiest way to record is to record an entire playlist. Assemble the playlist beforehand to get the timing right, and then send the entire playlist to your CD. You can record up to 74 minutes or 650MB worth of music, whichever comes first.

Unlike CD ripping, CD burning doesn't require you to set a lot of format options. That's because whatever format the original file is in, when it gets copied to CD it gets encoded into the CDA (CD Audio) format. All music CDs use the CDA format, so if you're burning an MP3 file, Windows Media Player translates it to CDA before the copy is made.

WMP lets you burn MP3, WAV, and WMA format files. The process of converting these files to CDA format is called transcoding.

There are no quality levels to set, either. All CDA-format files are encoded at the same bit rate. So you really don't have any configuration to do—other than deciding which songs you want to copy.

Here's what you have to do to burn a CD:

1. In Windows Media Player, select the Media Library tab and create a playlist of the songs you want to burn.
2. Click the Copy to CD or Device tab to display the Music to Copy list, as shown in Figure 14.4.

Figure 14.4

Getting ready to burn a CD with files from your hard disk.

3. Click the Music to Copy section to display all your playlists, then select the playlist or album you want to copy.
4. Insert a black CD in your CD-R/RW drive.
5. Select your CD-R/RW drive from WMP's Music On Device list.
6. Click the Copy Music button.
7. WMP now inspects the files you want to copy, converts them to CDA format, and copies them to your CD.
8. When the entire process is done, WMP displays a Closing Disk message for the last track on your playlist. The burning is not complete until this message is displayed.

If you're trying to copy too much music to the CD, WMP will display a "May Not Fit" message in the Status column of the final tracks. WMP will try to fit these tracks on the CD, but there may not be room for them.

You use a similar process to copy tracks to a portable audio player. Just connect your portable device, select the tracks or playlist you want to copy, select the device from the Music On Device List, and then click the Copy Music button.

OTHER RIPPERS AND BURNERS

While WMP is great for recording WMA-format files, it just doesn't cut it for recording MP3 files. (Think Microsoft is showing a bias here?) To rip MP3 files from a CD, you'll want an encoder that lets you record using the full range of available bit rates, without buying an expensive add-on program.

If you're serious about encoding MP3 files, here's a list of some of the most popular MP3 ripper software:

- AltoMP3 Maker (`www.yuansoft.com`)
- AudioCatalyst (`www.xingtech.com`)
- Grace Amp (`www.graceamp.musicdot.com`)
- Magix MP3 Maker (`www.magix.net`)
- MusicMatch Jukebox (`www.musicmatch.com`)
- RealJukebox (`www.real.com/jukebox/`)
- RioPort Audio Manager (`www.rioport.com/Software/`)
- SuperSonic (`www.gosupersonic.com`)

My favorite MP3 ripper is MusicMatch Jukebox, with RealJukebox a close second. They're both very good, very versatile MP3 encoding programs.

When it comes to burning audio files to CD, WMP does a good job—but it's not the best around. Here's a short list of my favorite CD audio burning software:

- Easy CD Creator (`www.roxio.com`)
- Nero (`www.ahead.de`)
- SIREN Jukebox (`www.sonicfoundry.com/products/`)

JIM'S TOP TEN TIPS

There's a ton of music on the Internet. A lot of it is available for free. Some of it will cost you. In either case, you can use Windows Media Player to manage and play your ripped and downloaded files—and to burn those files to CD. Just remember these ten key points:

1. MP3 is the most popular digital audio format today.
2. Microsoft's Windows Media Audio (WMA) competes with MP3, promising smaller file sizes and better copy protection at the same level of sound quality.
3. When you copy a song from CD to hard disk it's called *ripping*. When you copy a song from your hard disk to CD, it's called *burning*.
4. For most users, MP3 is the format of choice for ripping songs from CD. When downloading music from the Internet, you're likely to find files in both MP3 and WMA format.
5. The bit rate you choose for recording an MP3 or WMA file determines the trade-off between file size and sound quality.
6. If you're recording voices only, use MP3's 64Kbps bit rate or WMA's 48Kbps rate. If you want FM-quality music playback, use MP3's 128Kbps bit rate, or WMA's 96Kbps rate. If you want near-CD quality, go with MP3's 256Kbps rate, or WMA's 192Kbps rate.
7. You can find all types of songs at the big Internet digital music sites, such as MP3.com. You can also swap audio files directly with other users via a file-trading service such as Napster or Gnutella.
8. The standard Windows Media Player only includes WMA-format ripping. If you want to rip MP3 files with WMP, you'll need to purchase and install the MP3 Creation Pack add-in.
9. If you're serious about recording MP3 files, you'll want to use a player other than Windows Media Player—such as MusicMatch Jukebox. If you're serious about burning audio files to CD, check out SIREN Jukebox (formerly CD Architect).
10. When you burn audio files to CD, the original MP3, WAV, or WMA file is automatically translated into the standard CDA format for universal CD playback.

CHAPTER 15

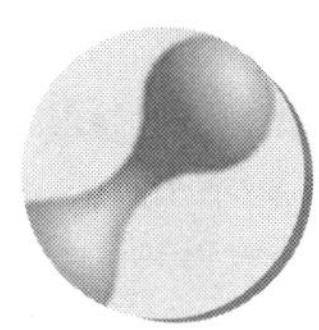

PLAYING AND EDITING DIGITAL MOVIES

- Introducing Windows Movie Maker
- Assembling Your Source Material
- Editing Your Video
- Saving Your Movie
- Jim's Top Ten Tips

If you're like most Americans, you have a camcorder, and a lot of videotapes. You use your camcorder to take what we used to call home movies. And most of your home movies sit, unwatched, somewhere in the back of your closet.

One reason Americans don't watch more home movies than they do is because the movies are—well, because they're not very good. You shoot and you shoot, and everything you shoot goes on tape. The only editing you do is "in camera," as the pros say. So you end up with a half hour's worth of good scenes scattered throughout a two-hour tape.

Wouldn't it be great if you could edit your home movies? If you could make them better?

You know, if you cut out all the dull sequences, insert some smoother transitions between scenes, maybe even add some titles and background music, you might have something worth watching. That sounds like a lot

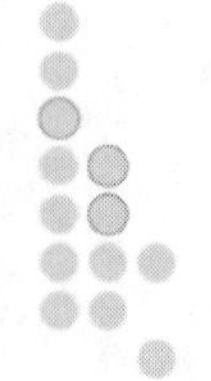

of work, though. And something that probably requires a few thousand dollars worth of professional video-editing equipment.

Except that it doesn't.

All those video-editing capabilities are now built into Windows XP. The Windows Movie Maker utility, first introduced in Windows Me, is an easy-to-use video editing program. All you have to do is hook your camcorder or VCR up to your PC, then you're ready to edit your home movies—on your personal computer, digitally.

The results will impress you.

INTRODUCING WINDOWS MOVIE MAKER

Windows Movie Maker really isn't a part of the operating system, in spite of what Microsoft says. It's a utility included with the OS, much the way Microsoft Calculator or Microsoft Paint have always been included with Windows. I don't think anyone could argue that video editing is a key operating system function, but since Apple started to include the iMovie video editor with all its iMacs, I'm sure Microsoft saw a competitive reason to add Windows Movie Maker to their Windows package.

In any case, if you use your camcorder a lot, you'll appreciate the fact that you have a free video-editing program sitting right on your Windows desktop. And, although it isn't the most fully featured video editor around, it has all the basic functions. For most users, it's more than good enough.

Learning the Interface

You start Windows Movie Maker by clicking the Start button and then selecting All Programs, Accessories, Windows Movie Maker. As you can see in Figure 15.1, the Movie Maker window is divided into four main parts:

- **Collections**—The Collections list displays all the audio, video, and still images included in your current project.
- **Clips**—This area displays the individual video clips in your project.
- **Workspace**—This area, at the bottom of the window, displays key scenes, and is used to edit your movie. The Workspace can be viewed in either Storyboard or Timeline view.
- **Monitor**—This window is used to preview your movie as you're editing it.

What You Need

Windows Movie Maker has more stringent equipment requirements than Windows XP does. The faster your processor, the more memory you have installed, and the larger your hard disk, the easier it will be to use Movie Maker to edit your home movies.

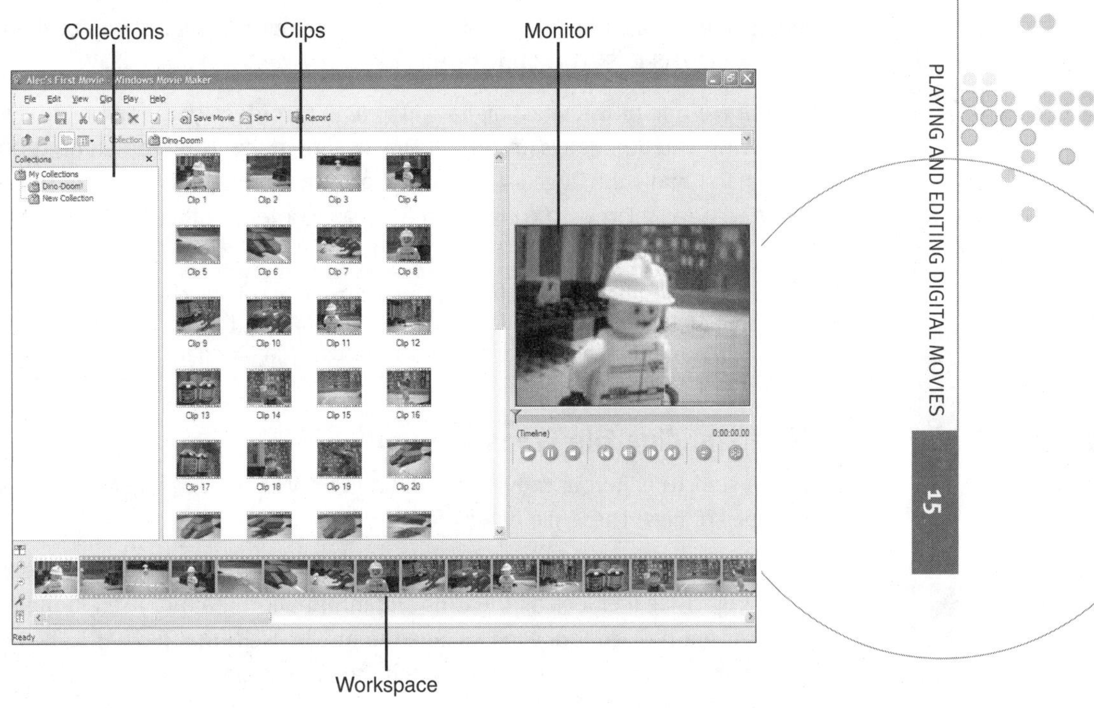

Figure 15.1

Windows Movie Maker—all your video editing needs in one easy-to-use program.

Here are the minimum system requirements that Microsoft specifies:

- 300MHz Pentium II or equivalent processor
- 64MB RAM
- 2GB free hard disk space
- Audio capture device (microphone)
- Video capture device (analog-to-digital video capture board)
- Internet connection and an e-mail program (not necessary, but recommended for posting and sending movie files over the Internet)

Personally, these requirements seem low. I'd recommend at least a 600MHz Pentium III, at least 256MB memory, and at least a 40GB hard disk. Anything less will be *very* sluggish when you start editing longer movies.

A key consideration is what kind of camcorder or VCR you have, as this determines how your source material (your videotaped movie) gets into your PC.

If you have an older non-digital recorder, you'll need to install an analog-to-digital video capture card in your PC. You'll plug your recorder into the jacks in this card. It will convert the analog signals from your recorder into the digital audio and video that your computer understands. You'll need to install this board if your recorder is one of the following formats: VHS, VHS-C, SVHS, 8mm, or Hi8.

If you have one of the latest digital video (DV) recorders, you don't need a video capture card. What you do need is an IE1394 FireWire interface. This type of the connection is fast enough to handle the huge stream of digital data pouring from your DV recorder into your PC. You'll need a FireWire connection if your recorder is either Digital8 or MiniDV format.

For best results, you should strive for a completely digital chain. Start with digital video shot on Digital8 or MiniDV, edit the video digitally with Windows Movie Maker, and then output the completed movie to a CD or DVD in WMV format.

Understanding File Types

As you start to edit your movies, you'll find that Windows Movie Maker uses three different types of files. These file types are

- **Project file**—This is kind of a "container" file, with the .MSWMM file extension. The project file includes all the clips and information that are used in the editing of the current project. It doesn't include the movie itself—that file has to be created after you've done all your editing within the project file.
- **Movie file**—When you're done cutting and pasting and inserting, you assemble all the pieces and parts together and save them as a single finished movie file. Your movies are created in Windows Media Video format, with a .WMV extension.
- **Collections file**—This is a database file that stores information about your collections and clips. It doesn't contain the clips themselves, but rather serves as a pointer to all those pieces and parts. This file has a .COL extension.

ASSEMBLING YOUR SOURCE MATERIAL

Before you can edit your movie, you have to have something to edit. This means importing whatever video and audio that you want to include in your finished movie.

For most movies, your main source material will be your original videotape(s). You'll use Windows Movie Maker to record the tape as you play it back on your VCR or camcorder. You can import material from more than one videotape, in case you want to edit several shorter tapes together into a longer movie.

If you want to add background music or voiceover narration, those are other elements you need to assemble. In addition, any title cards you want to include must be created (in a graphics editing program) and then imported into Windows Movie Maker.

Each item you assemble goes into your collection for this project. The movies you record are included as clips, which you can rearrange and delete and otherwise manipulate to edit your project. (You can also split big clips into several little clips, as I'll explain later.)

Once you have all your elements assembled, then you can proceed with editing. But before we get into the tough job of editing, I'll show you how to assemble various types of source material.

Starting a New Project

Before you import any source material, you have to have something to import it into. That thing is called a project, and you start a new one by selecting File, New, Project. You can open an existing project by selecting File, Open Project.

Recording from a Camcorder or VCR

If you have an analog camcorder or VCR, you have to connect it to the video capture board installed in your PC. (If your PC doesn't have a video capture board—and few new PCs do—then you'll have to purchase and install one.) If you have a DV camcorder or VCR, you connect it through your PC's FireWire connection.

Once you have the camcorder or VCR connected and turned on, follow these steps:

1. Select File, Record.
2. When the Record dialog box appears, as shown in Figure 15.2, make sure you're recording from the right device. If not, click the Change Device button and select the proper device.

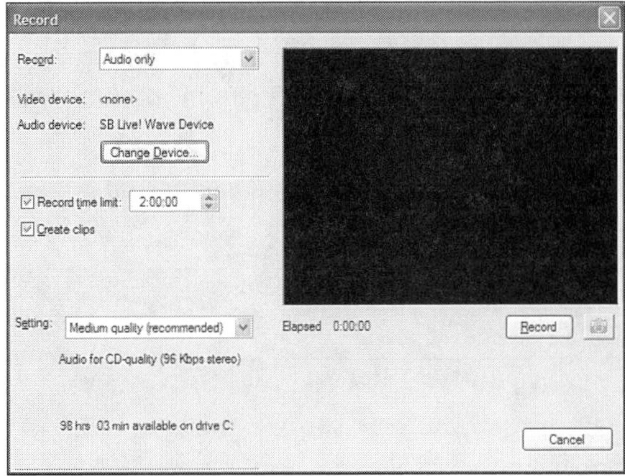

Figure 15.2

Selecting what to record and at what quality level.

You can also use the Record dialog box to record audio-only material from microphones and CDs.

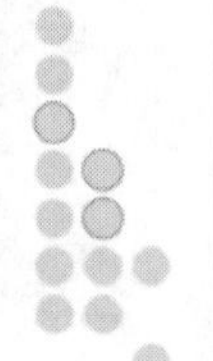

3. Pull down the Record list and select the type of source material you want to record.
4. Pull down the Setting list and select the level of recording quality you want. For most purposes, Medium Quality represents a good compromise between audio/video quality and file size. (The higher the quality, the larger the resulting movie files.)
5. Check the Record Time Limit and Create Clips options. When you choose to create clips, Movie Maker breaks up large videos into smaller, more manageable parts. (A new clip is created each time an entirely different frame is detected in the source video—such as when you switch from pause to begin recording.)
6. Click the Record button.
7. Press the play button on your VCR or camcorder.
8. Recording will automatically stop after two hours, or when you click the Stop button.
9. When recording is stopped, the Save Windows Media File dialog box appears. Enter a name and location for this file, then click Save.

The new clips you create will now appear in the Clips area of the Movie Maker window.

Importing Other Files

While most of your projects will consist primarily of movies recorded from videotape, you can include several other types of source material. For example, you can edit in movie clips you download from the Internet, or songs you rip from your favorite CDs, or title slides you create in a graphic editing program.

In case you're curious, Table 15.1 lists all the different file types that can be imported into Windows Movie Maker.

TABLE 15.1—Acceptable File Types for Importing into Windows Movie Maker

Type of File	File Types
Video	ASF, AVI, M1V, MP2, MPA, MPE, MPEG, MPG, WMV
Audio	AIF, AIFC, AIFF, AU, MP3, SND, WAV, WMA
Still images	BMP, DIB, GIF, JFIF, JPE, JPEG, JPG

There are a few eccentricities you should know about when you import some of these files into Movie Maker. These include

- When you import a file, the file itself doesn't actually move or get copied. Instead, Movie Maker creates a Clip that points to the original file. That means that if you move or delete the original file, Movie Maker won't be pointing to the right place anymore.

- When you import a video file, Movie Maker will break it into multiple clips based on scene transitions. So don't freak out when you import a single file and see multiple Clips appear in the Movie Maker window.
- When you import a still image that's taller than it's wide, it will be resized or framed to fit within a standard 4:3 ratio television screen.

All that said, importing a file is a piece of cake. Just follow these instructions:

1. Select the collection you want to import into.
2. Select File, Import.
3. When the Select File to Import dialog box appears, navigate to and select the file you want to import.
4. Click the Open button.

The file you imported will now appear as one or more clips in Movie Maker's Clips area.

EDITING YOUR VIDEO

The creation of your movie is accomplished in the Workspace area at the bottom of the Movie Maker window. You create a movie by dragging clips down into the Workspace. You can insert clips in any order, and more than once if you want to. Once the clips are in the Workspace, you can drag them around in a different order. This is how you edit the flow of your movie.

By default, the Workspace is shown in Storyboard view. This view is easiest for seeing how all your clips fit together.

When you get the basic flow of your movie in place, you can switch the Workspace to Timeline view, shown in Figure 15.3. In this view you see the timing of each segment, and can overlay background music and narration.

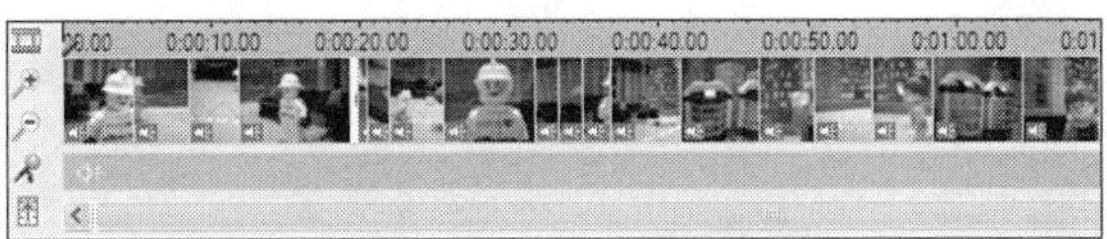

Figure 15.3

Displaying the Workspace in Timeline view.

(You switch views by clicking the Timeline/Storyboard button at the top left of the Workspace.)

As you work, you can preview your project-in-process with the Movie Maker Monitor. Just select one or more clips in the Workspace, then click the Play button on the Monitor.

Working with Clips

Working with Movie Maker's clips is fairly intuitive. Just drag things into place and move them around as you like, and you have 90% of it mastered.

Add a Clip

To add a clip to your project, use your mouse to drag it into position in the Workspace. You can add a clip more than once, to repeat it in different sections of your movie.

Move a Clip

To move a clip from one position to another, grab it with your mouse and drag it to the new position. The surrounding clips will be rearranged when the clip is dropped into its new position.

Remove a Clip

If you end up with a clip that you no longer want to include, just select it and then select Edit, Delete.

Trim a Clip

Sometimes a clip contains more footage than you really want. You can remove excess parts from a clip by *trimming* it from the beginning or end.

You trim a clip by setting its *trim points*. There's a start trim point and a end trim point, and everything outside these two points will be trimmed.

The easiest way to set the trim points is to display the Workspace in Timeline view and then select the clip to trim. Two trim handles appear above the selected clip (as shown in Figure 15.4), and you can use your mouse to move the handles to make your trim.

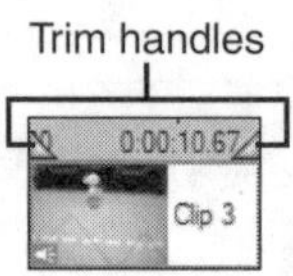

Figure 15.4

Adjust the trim handles with your mouse when you're in Timeline view.

Trim handles are easier to work with when you expand the Timeline by clicking the Zoom In button.

You can also trim a clip in real time by playing the clip on the Monitor. While the clip is playing, select Clip, Set Start Trim Point to set the beginning of the area to be trimmed. Select Clip, Set End Trim Point to set the end of the area to be trimmed.

Split a Clip

As you start to edit your movie, you'll probably find that the cuts and edits you want to make sometimes fall in the middle of a clip. When this is the case, you can split the clip in two and then work with each half of the clip separately.

To split a clip, follow these steps:

1. From the Clips area, select the clip you want to split and begin playing it on the Monitor.
2. When you reach the point where you want to make the split, click the Pause button. (You can then reverse and forward the clip to find the exact split point.)
3. Select Clip, Split.

You've now created two separate clips. The first clip retains the name of the original clip. The second clip has the original name with the number one in parentheses (1).

Combine Multiple Clips

You may want to combine two or more contiguous clips into a single clip, to make them easier to work with in the Workspace. To do this, select the clips (by holding down Ctrl while clicking each clip) and then select Clip, Combine. The combined clip retains the name of the first clip you selected.

Working with Transitions

Once you've assembled all your clips, you can see how your movie plays by selecting all the clips and playing them on the Monitor. What you'll see is the "rough cut" of your movie, with very abrupt cuts between clips.

To make a more pleasing movie, you can add professional transitions between each scene in your movie. Windows Media Player lets you create cross-fade transitions, where the last frames in the first clip fade out as the initial frames of the second clip fade in.

To create a transition, the Workspace must be in Timeline view. Then all you have to do is drag the second clip so that it overlaps the first clip. The shaded area indicates the length of the transition.

You can change the length of the transition by dragging the second clip left or right in small increments. If you drag the second clip far enough to the right, you remove the transition.

Working with Audio

Most of your video clips will also have accompanying audio. You can overlay additional audio on top of the original audio by inserting audio clips into the timeline.

To work with audio clips, the Workspace must be in Timeline mode.

Insert Audio

You insert an audio clip the same way you insert a video clip. The difference is that the audio clip is displayed below the video clip in the Workspace, in what is called the audio bar. (You can see an audio clip in the audio bar in Figure 15.5.)

Figure 15.5

Insert background audio clips into the Workspace's audio bar.

Mix Audio Levels

When you insert an audio clip, it plays simultaneously with the audio from the current video clip. Actually, the audio is mixed 50/50 for each clip. You can even insert overlapping audio clips—as long as the two clips do not start and stop at precisely the same points. Again, the sound from each clip will be equally mixed.

If you don't like the automatic level mixing, you can adjust the sound levels for each clip manually. This way you can set your audio clip for background music or ambient sound, and set your video clip for foreground dialog.

To set audio levels manually, select Edit, Audio Levels. When the Audio Levels dialog box appears (see Figure 15.6), adjust the slider to the left or to the right. To bring the video track's audio up in the mix, move the slider more toward Video Track. To bring the audio track up in the mix, move the slider more toward Audio Track. When you move the slider all the way to one end, the other track is effectively muted.

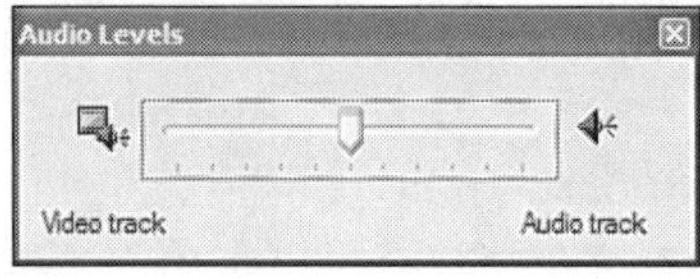

Figure 15.6

Use the Audio Levels dialog box to adjust the mix between background and foreground sound.

The audio mix that you set in the Audio Levels dialog box affect the sound throughout the entire movie.

Record Narration

If you have a microphone connected to your computer, you can add a personal narration to your movie. Just put the Workspace into Timeline view and follow these steps:

1. Select File, Record Narration.
2. When the Record Narration dialog box appears (as shown in Figure 15.7), make sure your microphone is selected as the recording device. If not, click the Change button and select your microphone from the Configure Audio dialog box.

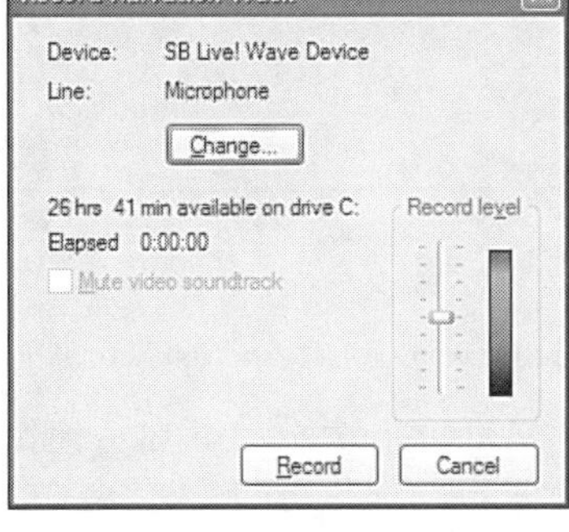

Figure 15.7

Get ready to record your own narration!

3. If you want to mute the video sound while your narration plays, check the Mute Video Soundtrack option. If you want your narration to play above the regular soundtrack, leave this option unchecked.
4. Drag the Record Level slider to increase or decrease the volume of your narration.
5. Click the Record button and start talking. Click Stop when you're done.
6. When the Save Narration Track Sound File dialog box appears, enter a name for your narration file and click Save.

Your narration is now saved as an audio clip and automatically inserted into the Workspace. You can now edit and move the narration track as you would any audio track.

SAVING YOUR MOVIE

You save your project by selecting File, Save Project. This does not save a movie file, however—it only saves the component parts of your project.

When your project is absolutely, positively finished is when you actually make the movie. Select File, Save Movie and the Save Movie dialog box (shown in Figure 15.8) is displayed. From here you have to select the playback quality, enter a title, and click OK. Windows Movie Maker then creates your movie and saves it as a WMV-format file. (Be patient—creating a movie can take some time!)

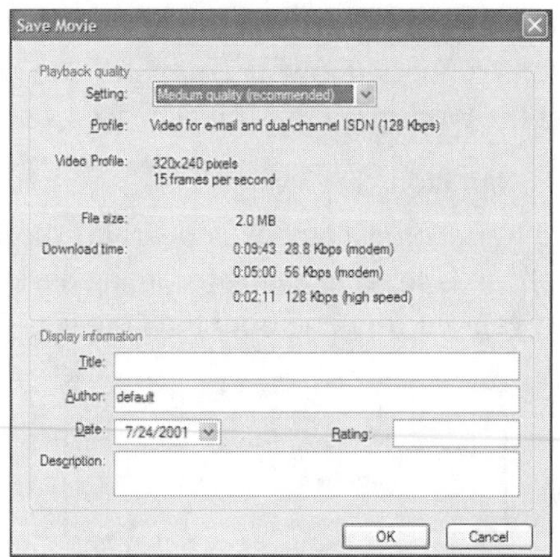

Figure 15.8

Choose a playback quality level and save your project as a WMV-format movie.

Choosing the right quality level is important. The higher the quality, the larger the file size. (And movie files can get really big, really fast!) You can create smaller files by lowering the quality, but if the quality is too low, viewers might not be able to fully enjoy the movie.

That's why it's important to match the playback quality to the intended use. When you pull down the Setting list, you're presented with three quality levels (Low, Medium, and High), as well as an Other option. When you select Other you can pull down the Profile list, which provides seven quality options—the original three, plus four more.

Which quality setting should you use? Table 15.2 details Movie Maker's quality settings, and their intended uses.

TABLE 15.2—Windows Movie Maker Playback Quality Options

Quality Setting	Recommended Uses	Video Bit Rate	Video Display Size (in pixels)	Audio Properties
Other: Video for Web Servers (28.8Kbps)	Web pages over slow dial-up connections	20Kbps	160 × 120	8kHz
Other: Video for Web Servers (56Kbps)	Web page over normal dial-up connections	30Kbps	176 × 144	11kHz
Other: Video for Single-Channel ISDN (64Kbps)	Web pages over fast connections	50Kbps	240 × 176	11kHz
Medium: Video for E-Mail and Dual-Channel ISDN (128Kbps)	Web pages over fast connections; e-mail distribution	100Kbps	320 × 240	16kHz

TABLE 15.2—CONTINUED

Quality Setting	Recommended Uses	Video Bit Rate	Video Display Size (in pixels)	Audio Properties
High: Video for Broadband NTSC (256Kbps)	Web pages over broadband; e-mail distribution	225Kbps	320 × 240	32kHz
Other: Video for Broadband (384Kbps)	Web pages over broadband; e-mail distribution	350Kbps	320 × 240	32kHz
Other: Video for Broadband NTSC (768Kbps)	CD/DVD distribution; Web pages over broadband; e-mail distribution	700Kbps	320 × 240	44kHz

Here's the bottom line. If you want to show your movie on a Web page where most users are connecting via dial-up, use the Other: Video for Web Servers (56Kbps) setting. If you intend for your movie to be viewed from recordable/rewritable CD or DVD, or if you want to output your movie to videotape, use the Other: Video for Broadband NTSC (768Kbps) setting. The other settings are compromises that really don't have any value.

After you've saved your movie, you can use Windows Media Player to watch it. Just open the My Videos folder and click the movie you want to watch. WMP will automatically launch and begin playing the movie.

JIM'S TOP TEN TIPS

As you can see, Windows Movie Maker is a decent little digital video editing program. It isn't as full featured as some other programs on the market, though. If your needs are more sophisticated, check out Adobe Premiere (`www.adobe.com/products/premiere/`) or Ulead MediaStudio Pro (`www.ulead.com/msp/`). Both of these programs offer a lot more in the way of professional transitions, titling, special effects, and the like.

When you're using Windows Movie Maker, remember these ten key points:

1. Windows Movie Maker is a digital video editing program that you can use to edit your home movies originally recorded on videotape.
2. For the best results, stay all-digital throughout the entire process. This means recording your original movie in Digital8 or MiniDV format.
3. When you use a Digital8 or MiniDV camcorder, you connect the camcorder to your PC via an IE1394 FireWire connection. When you use an analog camcorder, you have to install an analog-to-digital video capture board in your PC, and connect to that board.
4. In addition to your videotaped movies, you can also import audio files, still images, and other video files into your project.
5. The bits and pieces of your project are called *clips*.
6. You put together your movie by dragging clips into the Workspace area at the bottom of the Movie Maker window.
7. To create a cross-fade transition between clips, drag the second clip so that it overlaps the end of the first clip.
8. You add background music by dragging an audio clip on top of the video clips. Audio from both your audio and video clips will play simultaneously, mixed 50/50.
9. You can plug in a microphone and record your own narration. You can choose to layer your narration on top of the existing soundtrack, or mute the soundtrack while your narration plays.
10. When saving your project as a movie file, choose the Other: Video for Web Servers (56Kbps) setting if you intend to upload the movie to your Web page. Choose the Other: Video for Broadband NTSC (768Kbps) setting if you intend to distribute the movie via CD or DVD.

PART V

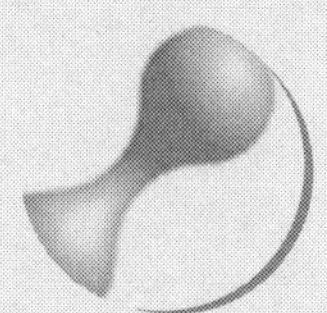

IN THE HOME AND ON THE ROAD

CHAPTER 16

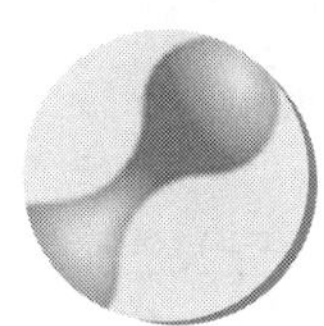

WORKING WITH MULTIPLE USERS

- Planning for Multiple Users
- Types of Users
- Setting Up New Users
- Editing User Settings
- Switching Users
- Sharing—or Not Sharing—Files and Folders
- Jim's Top Ten Tips

If you're using your personal computer at home, chances are you're not the only person using it. When you're not pounding the keys, chances are that either your spouse or your children are perched in front of the screen. This makes your PC a multiple-user machine, whether you like it or not.

The Windows 9X/Me operating system was really built as a single-user operating system. Yes, you could use it with multiple users, but it just didn't feel right.

In contrast, Windows NT/2000 has always been a multiple-user operating system. It had to be. This industrial-grade OS was built to handle multiple users on multiple computers over a corporate network. Handling multiple users was essential for NT/2000, from day one.

Because Windows XP is built on the Windows 2000 engine, it goes to figure that it inherits the multiple-user functionality of the corporate OS. XP even adds some new wrinkles to how multiple users are handled, so that it's easier than ever to share one PC among several people.

PLANNING FOR MULTIPLE USERS

Why would you want to set up your computer for multiple users? Why can't each user just sit down at the keyboard and start using the computer without all this logging in business?

Well, you *could* have multiple users use your computer under a single user name. The problem with this approach is that all your files are accessible to everybody else using your PC—which may not be a good thing, depending. In addition, you'll have to live with any changes to the interface made by other users, or take the trouble to reconfigure things back to the way you like them. As you can see, while communal computing is possible, it isn't ideal.

A better situation is one where every user gets to configure Windows to his or her own personal tastes. When each user logs in, Windows displays the settings specific to that user. Plus, each user has his or her own private files, which other users can't access. This type of multiple-user setup is better for both personalization and privacy.

In addition, the chief user of the system (called the *computer administrator*) can control what the other users can do when they're logged on. For example, you might want to restrict some users (like your kids) from installing their own software on the machine. As the administrator, you have that power.

TYPES OF USERS

Windows XP lets you create multiple user accounts. Each user gets to choose his or her own account name, picture, and password. In addition, whatever interface and file personalization one user makes sticks with that user. Each user even gets his or her own My Documents folder, separate from other users' My Documents.

Each user account can be protected with a password. Anyone trying to access that user's account and files without the password is denied access. Unless, that is, the user has marked his or her files and folders as shared. Anyone can access shared folders, no password required.

There are three different types of user accounts you can establish on your computer:

- **Computer administrator account**—This is the main account on your PC. The computer administrator is the one account that can make system-wide changes to the computer, install software, and access all the files on the system—even files created by another account. The computer administrator can also create, delete, and edit other users' accounts.

There can be more than one computer administrator account per computer.

- **Limited account**—A limited account is for someone who uses a computer but doesn't manage it. A user with a limited account cannot install software or hardware, but can access programs that are already on the computer. A limited user can edit his or her account settings, but can't change the password.
- **Guest account**—A guest account is intended for use by people who have no formal user account on your computer. Guests don't get passwords, can't install software or hardware, and don't get their own My Documents folder. They can, of course, access software already installed on the computer. Guest accounts are great for guests (of course!) who just want to check their e-mail or do a little Web surfing while they're visiting.

When you're setting up Windows XP for home use, the first thing you want to do is set yourself up with a computer administrator account. Then, after you've set up your own account, you can set up the accounts for everybody else in your household.

To avoid undue marital stress, you should probably set up your spouse with a computer administrator account, as well. Then you can set up your kids with limited accounts. (This will keep them from installing new software without your permission.)

If you're one of several housemates sharing a computer, it's probably a good idea to configure each user as a computer administrator. Just make sure you set up your personal files with file sharing turned off, so your roomies can't get into your private stuff.

In either situation, any household visitors can access your PC via the guest account. They won't be able to mess around with any of Windows' settings, of course, but they can use what's there—your software, and your Internet connection.

SETTING UP NEW USERS

Only the computer administrator can add a new user to your system. Here's how it's done:

1. From the Control Panel, click the User Accounts icon.
2. When the User Accounts utility opens (see Figure 16.1), select Create a New Account.
3. When the next screen appears, enter a name for the account and click Next.
4. On the next screen, check either the Computer Administrator or Limited options, then click the Create Account button.

Windows XP now creates the new account, and randomly assigns a picture that will appear next to the user name. You or the user can change this picture at any time. (See "Editing User Settings," next.)

You can also assign a password to this new account. By default, no password is assigned. But if you follow the instructions in the "Changing Another User's Settings" section of this chapter, you can create a password and force the user to enter it whenever he or she wants to use the computer.

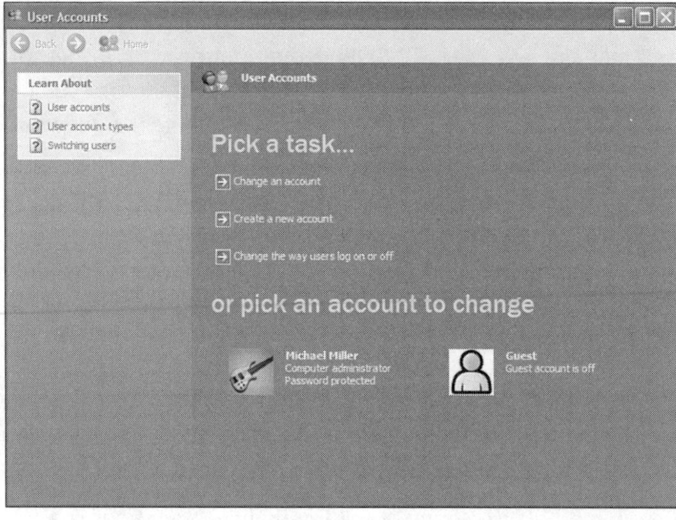

Figure 16.1

Use the User Accounts utility to create and change user accounts.

When you turn on your computer, you're greeted with Windows XP's Welcome screen. All registered users are listed on this screen. Click your user name or picture and enter your password (if necessary), and you launch Windows as the selected user, with access to your own personal files and settings.

EDITING USER SETTINGS

Nothing is set in stone. If you don't like the way a user account is set up, you can change it.

Changing Another User's Settings

As the computer administrator you can change anything you want about any limited user's account. You can change the account name or picture, or even the password and account type. You can even delete the account, if you want. (That'll show 'em!)

Limited users can only change their own accounts. They can't change anyone else's account.

To change another user's settings, follow these steps:

1. From the Control Panel, click the User Accounts icon.
2. When the User Accounts utility opens, select Change an Account.
3. When the Pick an Account to Change screen appears, select the account you want to edit.

4. When the What Do You Want to Change screen appears (shown in Figure 16.2), select one of the following options: Change the Name, Change the Password, Remove the Password, Change the Picture, Change the Account Type, or Delete The Account.

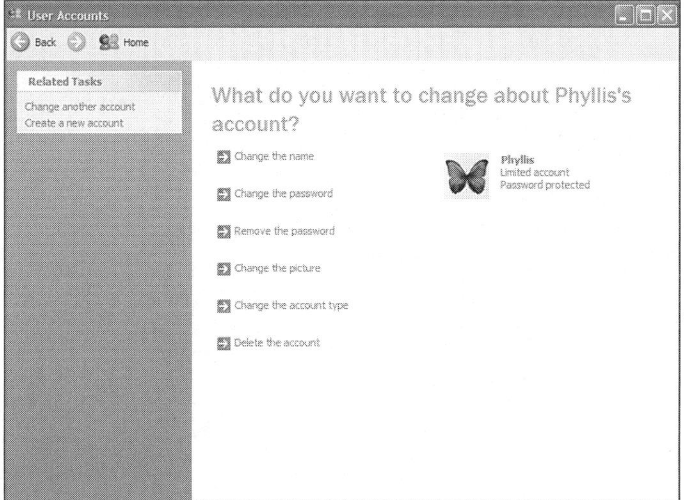

Figure 16.2

The computer administrator can change anything about any other user's account.

The Change a Password option only appears if this user has already created a password. If no password has yet been created, this option is changed to Create a Password.

5. Follow the onscreen instructions to change the setting that you selected.

Changing Your Own Settings

If you're not the computer administrator, you can still change certain of your own user settings. You can change the picture associated with your user name, you can create or change your password, and you can create a Microsoft Passport account.

You make the changes from the User Accounts utility, which looks different if you're a limited user than if you're a computer administrator. (See Figure 16.3 to see how the limited user utility looks.)

To change a setting, all you have to do is select in on this main screen, and then follow the onscreen instructions.

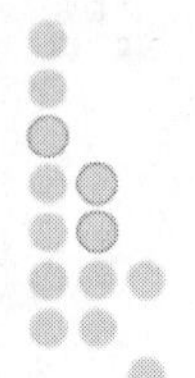

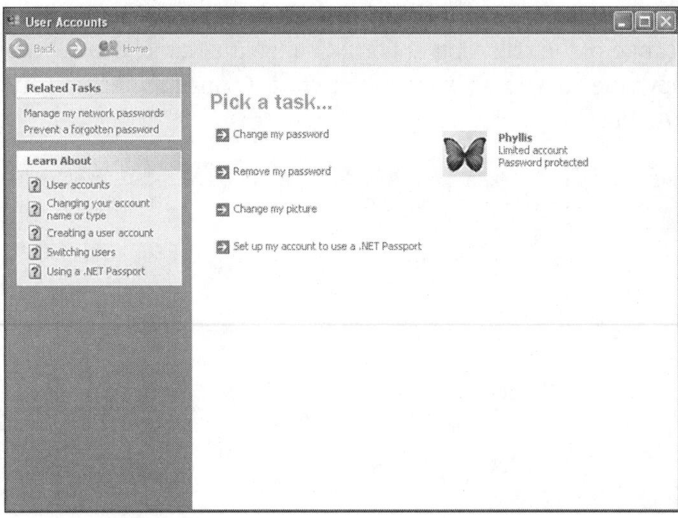

Figure 16.3

Even limited user accounts can change their basic settings.

Change Your Picture

If you don't like the picture Windows assigned to your user name, it's easy to change it. In fact, you can even choose to have your own personal photograph appear next to your name.

Here's how you do it:

1. From the User Accounts utility, select Change My Picture.
2. When the next screen appears, as shown in Figure 16.4, select one of the pictures listed and click the Change Picture button, or....
3. Click the Browse for More Pictures button. The Open dialog box will now display the contents of your My Pictures folder. Select any picture you want (even a picture of yourself!), then click the Open button. When you return to the previous screen, make sure this new picture is selected, then click the Change Picture button.

Create or Change Your Password

If you have multiple users accessing the same PC, it's a good idea for each user to have their own password. This way other users can't access their personal data or settings. Since users have to enter a password to log into their account, if you don't know a password, you can't log in.

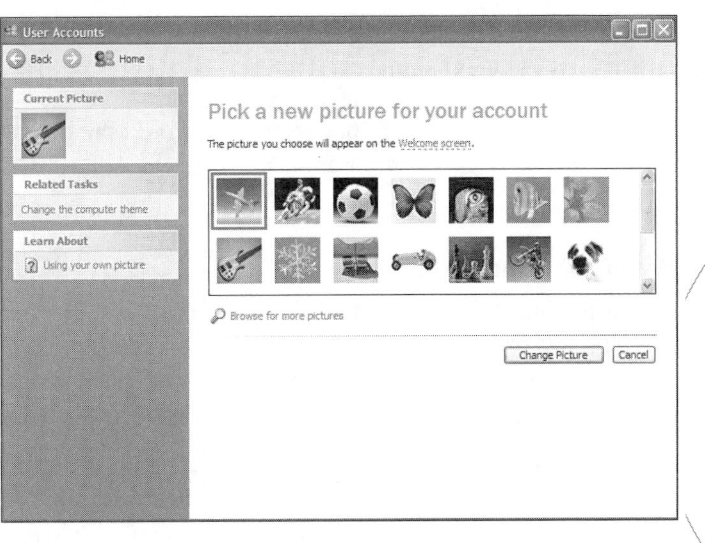

Figure 16.4

Don't like your user account picture? Then change it!

To create a new password for your account, follow these steps:

1. From the User Accounts utility, select the Create a Password option.
2. When the Create a Password for Your Account screen appears, as shown in Figure 16.5, enter your new password in the first box, then again in the second box.

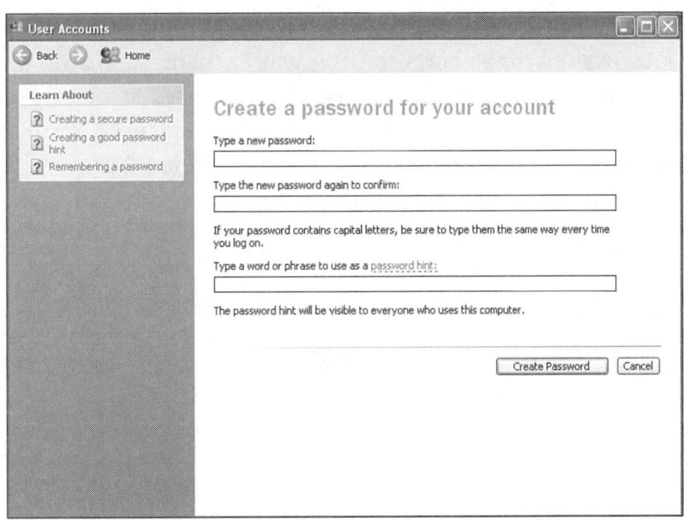

Figure 16.5

Create a password to keep other users out of your account.

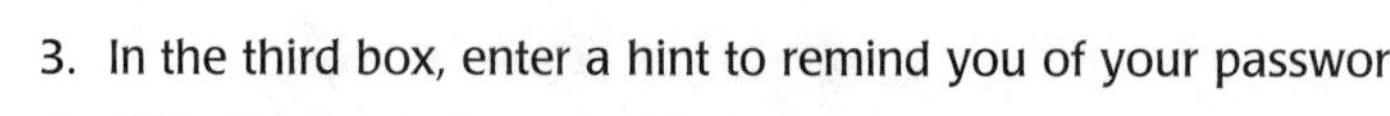

3. In the third box, enter a hint to remind you of your password.
4. Click the Create Password button.

To change your password, select the Change My Password option, enter your old password, then enter your new password information. Click the Change Password button to register the change.

Create a Passport Account

Microsoft is really pushing the notion of having a Passport account. This account assigns you a single user name and password that is then used across a range of Microsoft services. For example, your Password account is used to access your Hotmail account, your Windows Messenger account, and just about any other account you have on any MSN-related Web site.

If you want to create a Passport account—and you have to, if you want to access any of Microsoft's services—all you have to do is open the User Accounts utility and click the Create a Passport option. This launches the Passport Wizard. Follow the wizard's instructions to enter the appropriate personal information and create your account.

You have to be connected to the Internet to create your Microsoft Passport.

SWITCHING USERS

One neat new feature of Windows XP is that you don't have to reboot your computer to switch users.

Under previous versions of Windows, the only way to change users was to restart the computer and log on as a different user. Windows XP uses something called Fast User Switching to change users without rebooting. In fact, when you switch to another user and then back again, all your open programs and documents are still there, still open and running. It's almost like have multiple users logged on at the same time!

When you have Fast User Switching activated, programs do not automatically shut down when users log off the computer. For example, if you're working in a Word document and one of your kids wants to check their e-mail, you can switch users for a few minutes, then switch back to your account. when you switch back, your Word document will still be open on your desktop.

Activating Fast User Switching

For Fast User Switching to work, you have to turn it on. (And only a computer administrator can do this.) Follow these steps:

1. From the User Accounts utility, select the Change the Way Users Log On or Off option.

2. When the next screen appears, check both the Use the Welcome Screen and Use Fast User Switching options.
3. Click OK.

The only downside to using Fast User Switching is that it causes your computer to run slower when multiple users are logged on. (That's because everyone's programs keep running in the background.) If your system is too sluggish, turn off Fast User Switching and make everyone log on and off like they used to in previous versions of Windows. I can't stress this point enough—Fast User Switching eats up a lot of RAM. Beyond the basic 256MB of RAM recommended by TechTV Labs, you should plan on adding another 64MB of RAM for each user that will be using Fast User Switching.

Switching Users

To switch users under Fast User Switching, all you have to do is click the Start button, click the Log Off button, and then select Switch User from the Log Off Windows dialog box. When the Welcome screen appears, click the user to switch to and enter the password (if assigned).

That's it. Windows will now log on the next user, with all that user's settings active. Which means that this instance of Windows could look and feel quite different from what was just on the screen mere seconds ago.

That's because Windows XP automatically saves the settings for each user and activates that user's settings when the user logs on. So if you'd selected one wallpaper and the next user had selected another, the wallpaper would change. As would all the customization options discussed in Chapter 2, "Changing the Way Windows Looks–and Acts," including folder settings, display settings, special effects, and so on.

When you switch back over to your account, all the settings change again. Which is a heck of a lot better than reconfiguring Windows every time a new user logs on!

Now, if you'd rather just log off permanently, that's a different deal. When you log off permanently, all your open documents and applications close, and won't be there waiting for you when you next log on. To log off in this fashion, without necessarily switching users, click the Start button, click the Log Off button, and then select Log Off.

SHARING—OR NOT SHARING—FILES AND FOLDERS

Just because you're sharing your PC with other users doesn't mean you want to share all your documents, too. Windows XP gives you the option of sharing your key files and folders, or not sharing them. (If your files are in the least bit personal, I recommend *not* sharing them.)

To make a folder private, follow these steps:

1. Using My Computer or My Documents, right-click any of the following folders: Desktop, Start Menu, Favorites, or My Documents (and any its subfolders).

2. Select Properties from the pop-up menu, then select the Sharing tab, as shown in Figure 16.6.

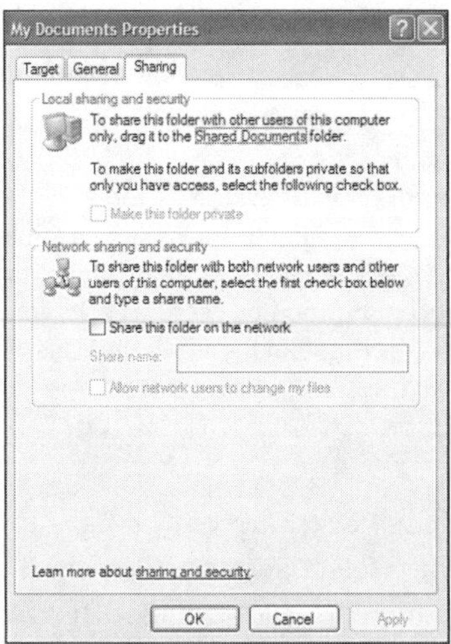

Figure 16.6

Sharing—or not sharing—folders is an important decision to make when you have multiple users on the same PC.

3. Uncheck the Share This Folder On the Network option, or....
4. If you want to share this folder, check the Share this Folder On the Network option. If you want the contents of the folder to be read-only, uncheck the Allow Network Users to Change My Files option. If not, uncheck this option.
5. Click OK.

A few things about this option. First, only certain folders can be shared–in particular, the Desktop, Start Menu, Favorites, and My Documents folders. (Any subfolder in the My Documents folder can also be shared.)

Second, when you make a folder private, all of its subfolders are made private, too. For example, if you make My Documents private, then My Music and My Pictures are also private.

The same is almost true for sharing. That is, when you share the main folder, you also turn on sharing for all the subfolders. The difference is, you can then go in and turn off sharing for each subfolder, individually.

JIM'S TOP TEN TIPS

The way Windows XP handles multiple users is great. It's easy to use, it's intuitive, and it isn't terribly intrusive. You can use passwords if your want to, or not. And your personal settings are always there waiting for you whenever you log on.

All you have to remember are the following key points:

1. Unlike previous versions of Windows, Windows XP's Fast User Switching lets you switch users without rebooting your PC.
2. However, Fast User Switching uses a lot of system memory. Plan on having at least 256MB of RAM for basic use, and another 64MB for each additional user using Fast User Switching.
3. There are three types of user accounts in Windows XP: computer administrator account, limited account, and guest account.
4. Only the computer administrator can create new accounts.
5. While limited users can edit their own account settings, the computer administrator can edit *every* user's settings. (And even delete users, if they want to!)
6. Each user can choose his or her own password and user picture.
7. However a user configures Windows, those settings are always applied when they log in.
8. To switch users without logging off, click the Start button, click the Log Off button, and then select Switch User. If you want to log off permanently, click the Start button, click the Log Off button, and then select Log Off.
9. When you switch users without logging off, all your open programs and documents stay open (in the background), and are there waiting for you when you switch back to your account.
10. You can choose whether or not to share your personal files and folders. When you turn off file and folder sharing, no other user can access your selected folders.

CHAPTER 17

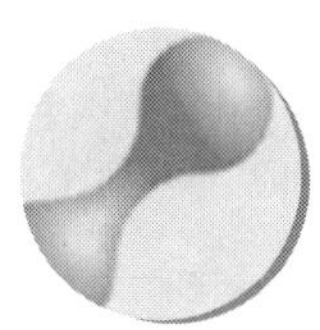

PLAYING GAMES

- Installing and Configuring Game Controllers
- Building a Better Gaming System
- Embracing DirectX
- Troubleshooting Games Problems
- Jim's Top Ten Tips

You might find this hard to believe, but one of the most technically demanding applications for your personal computer is playing games.

That's right. Playing games.

There are a few very logical reasons for this.

First, the newest PC games feature sound and graphics that are nothing short of stunning. Very realistic, very high quality. It's very demanding on your hardware and operating system to create these graphics and move them around in real time.

Second, the *oldest* PC games were based on the old DOS platform. Maintaining compatibility with DOS-based games is a huge challenge for the operating system. Especially one, such as Windows XP, that wasn't built on that old 16-bit platform. And doesn't claim to have 100% perfect legacy support.

Given these challenges, I was pleasantly surprised to discover what a good job Windows XP does with both the oldest and the newest PC games. The OS incorporates all the latest DirectX standards used by the newest games, and has an extremely high compatibility with the older games.

I'll go out on a limb and say that Windows XP is the best PC-based operating system yet for game playing—which is something I didn't expect to be saying.

INSTALLING AND CONFIGURING GAME CONTROLLERS

The first step in preparing Windows XP for game playing is to plug in and set up all your favorite game controllers. Whether you use a joystick or a button controller or a steering wheel and foot pedals, getting everything connected is a relatively easy task.

USB Controllers

The easiest types of controllers to connect are those that connect via a USB port. All you have to do is plug in the controller, and Windows should recognize the new device and install the proper drivers automatically.

That's Plug and Play at work, for you.

If XP doesn't recognize the new controller, then you can install the controller manually via the Add Hardware Wizard. See Chapter 6, "Adding New Hardware," for more information.

Game Port and Serial Port Controllers

Many game controllers are designed to hook up to your PC's dedicated game port, or into a spare serial port. This type of connection is a little less automatic than a USB connection, but still not a show stopper.

Just follow these steps:

1. From the Control Panel, click the Game Controllers icon.
2. When the Game Controllers utility opens, click the Add button.
3. When the Add Game Controller dialog box appears (see Figure 17.1), select the type of device that you're installing. (If the device isn't listed here, click the Custom button and custom-configure Windows XP for your new device.)
4. Now pull down the Port list and select the port that the controller is connected to.
5. Click OK when done.

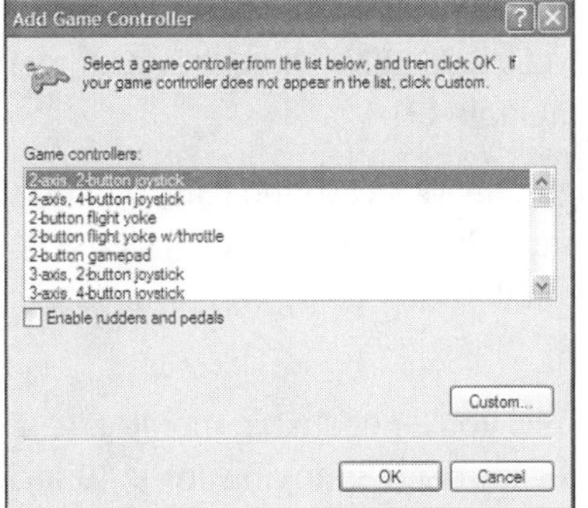

Figure 17.1

Installing a new game controller, manually.

Test a Controller

After you've installed a new game controller, you can test it by following these steps:

1. From the Game Controllers utility, select the controller you want to test.
2. Click the Properties button, and then select the Test tab.
3. Follow the onscreen instructions to move or press each control, including the all the pads and buttons.

If your controller doesn't check out 100%, you may need to calibrate it—which I'll discuss next.

Calibrate a Controller

To calibrate a game controller, follow these steps:

1. From the Game Controllers utility, select the controller you want to calibrate.
2. Click the Properties button, then select the Settings tab.
3. Click the Calibrate button.
4. Follow the onscreen instructions to calibrate that particular device.

BUILDING A BETTER GAMING SYSTEM

To play today's technically demanding PC games, you need a truly state-of-the-art computer system. In fact, it takes a more powerful system to play games than it does to perform more traditional computer applications, such as word processing and number crunching.

If you're buying a new PC for your game play, expect to shell out some big bucks. For the system you want, you'll probably be in the $2,000 range—or possibly more, if you really want to go first-class.

The first thing you want is a fairly powerful processor. Think Pentium 4 or AMD Athlon, running at 1GHz or more. You'll also need a bunch of memory, at least 256MB.

Because games take up a lot of disk space, go for at least a 40GB hard disk. You should also make sure you get a CD/DVD-ROM drive, because many new games are coming on single DVDs rather than multiple CDs.

You'll definitely want a high-quality 3-D sound card, and either a 32MB or 64MB 3-D video card with graphics accelerator. You'll also want a kick-ass speaker system with a powerful subwoofer. You should even consider going with four satellite speakers instead of two, for true surround sound.

Finally, to play the big games you'll need a big monitor. A 17-inch monitor is the bare minimum, and I'd seriously recommend springing for a 19-inch model. The price difference isn't that much, these days.

Obviously, any PC with these specs is more than capable of running Windows XP without any problems. Your main concern is making sure your system has enough horsepower to run the latest and greatest games.

EMBRACING DIRECTX

Part of the horsepower comes from the technology support necessary to reproduce a game's dazzling graphics and full-range sound. Windows XP supports DirectX 8.0, which is a set of APIs that provide full access to the advanced features of high-performance hardware. DirectX works to create hardware-accelerated 3-D images and engrossing music and sound effects.

DirectX works in the background to match the game's parameters with your PC's hardware capabilities. This way even the most multimedia-laden games can take full advantage of the latest video and audio chips and cards.

There are seven key components of DirectX:

- **DirectDraw**—Works with your PC's video card to display 2-D graphics.
- **Direct3D**—Works with your video card to render 3-D graphics.
- **DirectSound**—Works with your audio card to provide sound mixing and other functions related to digital audio playback.
- **DirectMusic**—Works with your audio card to deliver high-quality MIDI music for your game's background soundtrack.
- **DirectInput**—Provides direct input for joysticks and other input devices—including the latest force-feedback game controllers.
- **DirectPlay**—Supports game connections over a modem, LAN, or the Internet—and is essential for multiple-player online/network games.
- **DirectShow**—Provides capture and playback of multimedia files in a variety of formats, including ASF, AVI, DV, MPEG, MP3, WAV, WMA, and WMV; DirectShow also enables video capture, DVD playback, video editing and mixing, and the reception of broadcast television signals.

As you might suspect, these DirectX components are used for more than just playing games. Any multimedia application can tap into DirectX for improved audio and video performance. Games, however, really utilize what DirectX has to offer. And because Windows XP supports the latest version of DirectX, you should be able to run the newest games on the newest hardware with maximum effect.

TROUBLESHOOTING GAME PROBLEMS

If anything is going to test the capabilities of your system, it's going to be a game. Systems that work perfectly with every other type of application will show their weaknesses when tested with the latest, most demanding PC games. In other words, if you want to try to break your system, you need to play some games!

Compatibility Issues

Every time Microsoft issues a new operating system, the same question gets asked—which games won't work on it?

Given the poor track record Windows 2000 had with playing games, I fully expected a boatload of compatibility issues with Windows XP. Imagine my surprise when I discovered that Windows XP was as strong a game platform as Windows 98—and perhaps even stronger.

This application robustness is due primarily to the efforts of Microsoft's Application Compatibility Experience (ACE) group. ACE was formed at about the same time Windows XP went into development, with the goal of making as many applications as possible run as smoothly as possible under the new operating system.

The ACE group did their job. Not only does Windows XP run every Windows 2000-compatible application, it also runs the vast majority of Windows 9X/Me applications, and an amazing number of older DOS-based applications.

This means that whether you have a new copy of Diablo 2 or the original version of Doom, your games stand a very good chance of working just fine under Windows XP.

There are several factors behind this high level of compatibility with older games and applications. First off, Microsoft added SoundBlaster-compatible sound support to Windows XP, as well as high-resolution VESA video support, which are necessary for some older games to run.

Second, XP includes a new compatibility mode, which can trick games and other applications into thinking that they're running on an older operating system. So if a game is designed to run only on Windows 95, you can rev up the compatibility mode and make the game think that Windows XP is really Windows 95. You'd be surprised at how effective this is!

If you're having trouble running an older game, here's what you should do:

1. From within My Computer, create a shortcut to the problematic program. (Or, if a shortcut to the program already exists in the Programs menu, navigate to that shortcut.)
2. Right-click on the shortcut icon and select Properties from the pop-up menu.

3. When the Properties dialog box appears, select the Compatibility tab (shown in Figure 17.2).

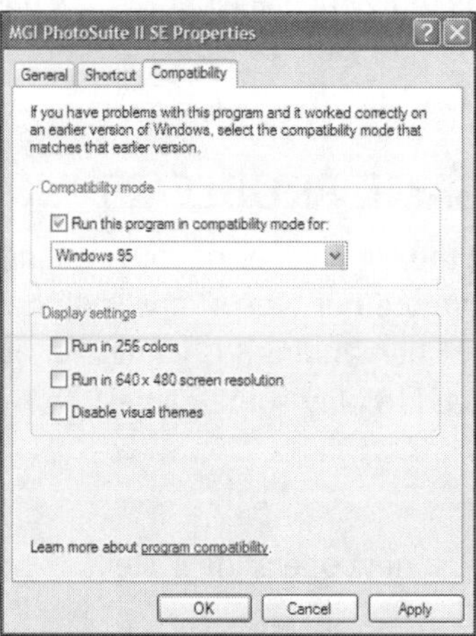

Figure 17.2

If you're having trouble running an older game, configure it to run in compatibility mode.

4. Check the Run This Program in Compatibility Mode For option, then pull down the list and select which operating system you want to emulate. (You can choose to emulate Windows 95, Windows 98, Windows NT4, or Windows 2000.)
5. If you need to run the program at a lesser color depth or lower screen resolution, check the Run in 256 Colors and/or Run in 640×480 Screen Resolution options.
6. Click OK.

If this doesn't get that old game up and running, all hope isn't lost—yet. You should search the Microsoft Knowledge Base (`support.microsoft.com/directory/`) to see if there has been a reported issue with your particular game, and if so, what kinds of fixes are available.

You can also check with Microsoft's Compatibility Center to see if a particular game is compatible with your computer. You can connect to the Compatibility Center by opening XP's Help and Support Services and clicking the Compatible Hardware and Software Link. (You'll need to open an Internet connection to check this database.)

Another good place to check for compatibility issues is at the NT Compatible Web site (`www.ntcompatible.com/0.shtml`). This site lists hundreds of different games, and whether they're compatible with various versions of Windows.

Our experience at TechTV Labs is that if you're running newer games on newer hardware, you probably won't run into any problems. For that matter, older games in and of themselves don't seem to cause a lot of problems.

Any problems you encounter are more likely to be related to older or more obscure hardware installations. If you have an old, out-of-date sound card from a defunct manufacturer, for example, you might have trouble playing some older games under Windows XP. Replace the sound card with a newer model and your problems will probably go away.

In other words, when you're playing games, hardware compatibility will probably be a bigger issue than software compatibility. Even if you think it's a game problem, it very well could be a hardware problem.

Which is just one more reason why Microsoft says that Windows XP is really intended for new installations, and not to upgrade older PCs.

Hardware Issues

Speaking of hardware problems, Windows XP includes some very good built-in troubleshooters to help you track down any problems that may develop with your game hardware:

- If you have game controller problems, you should run the Windows XP Hardware Troubleshooter. (From the Help and Support Services window, click the Fixing a Problem link, then click Hardware and System Device Problems, then Hardware Troubleshooter.)
- If you're having more general problems getting a game to run properly, you should run the Multimedia and Games Troubleshooter. (From the Help and Support Services window, click the Fixing a Problem link, then click Games, Sound, and Video Problems, then Games and Multimedia Troubleshooter.)
- If you're having DirectX-related problems, you should run the DirectX Diagnostic Tool. (From the Help and Support Services window, click the Fixing a Problem link, then click Games, Sound, and Video Problems, then Troubleshooting DirectX.)

You should also check out Microsoft's Compatibility Center, as discussed previously, to see if there might be a compatibility issue with a particular audio, video, or controller device on your system.

JIM'S TOP TEN TIPS

The best way to see if a game works under Windows XP is to install it and try to play it. If it works—great! If not, then you can run through the various compatibility and troubleshooting options available to you.

When it's time for games, just remember these ten key points:

1. You can connect your game controller via a USB port, game port, or serial port—although the USB connection is probably easiest.
2. You can test and calibrate your game controller in the Game Controller utility, accessible from the Control Panel.
3. For best game play, you need a fairly high-powered system with a fast processor, lots of memory and hard disk space, a CD/DVD-ROM drive, and 3-D sound and video cards.
4. Windows XP supports the latest version of DirectX (version 8) for hardware-accelerated game play.
5. For compatibility with older 16-bit games, Windows XP includes SoundBlaster and VESA video support.
6. If you're having trouble running an older game, open its Properties dialog box and select an older compatibility mode—this will trick the game into thinking that it's running on an older version of Windows.
7. If you're unsure whether a particular game or hardware component is compatible with Windows XP, open the Help and Support Services and click the Compatible Hardware and Software link to access Microsoft's Compatibility Center.
8. Another good place to check for game compatibility is NT Compatible (`www.ntcompatible.com/0.shtml`).
9. If you're going to have problems, it's more likely to be caused by older or nonstandard hardware than it is by the games you try to play.
10. To track down hardware-related problems, use either the Hardware Troubleshooter, Multimedia and Games Troubleshooter, or DirectX Diagnostic Tool.

CHAPTER 18

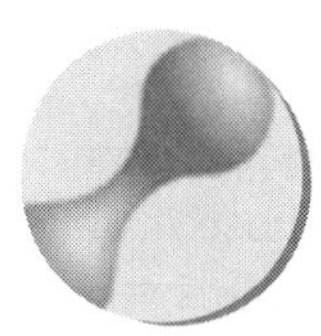

SETTING UP A HOME OR SMALL BUSINESS NETWORK

- Understanding Different Types of Networks
- Setting Up Your Network
- Running the Network Setup Wizard
- Setting Up Network Sharing
- Accessing Files, Printers, and Other Computers on Your Network
- Jim's Top Ten Tips

If your home is like mine, you have more than one computer in use. Maybe you have one computer for your work, and another for your spouse to use. Maybe there's a third computer that your kids use. Maybe you even have a laptop that you plug in from time to time.

In addition to all these computers, you probably have a bunch of peripherals sitting around. Probably a printer, maybe two, possibly a scanner and a PC camera. Maybe even a digital still camera or an external Zip drive.

And then there's the Internet. You have one connection, and all those computers. And everybody wants to be online at the same time.

When you need to share files, or printers, or an Internet connection, you need to hook all your computers together into a network. A local area network (LAN), to be precise.

A LAN, whether in your house, in a small business, or in a large corporation, used to be a big hairy very technical thing to set up and configure. You had to deal with routers and switches and hubs and all sorts of protocols and configurations. Not to mention what seemed like miles and miles of coaxial or twisted-pair cable, and network cards that you had to install in every PC.

In other words, setting up a network used to be beyond most of us.

Fortunately, things have changed.

With the advent of affordable network cards, hubs, and cables—not to mention easy-to-install networking kits—the physical part of putting a network together has become much easier than it used to be. And, thanks to Windows XP, installing each PC on the network is now a piece of cake.

Really. Anyone can do it. All you have to do is connect everything together, and then run Windows XP's Network Setup Wizard. XP's Universal Plug and Play technology is smart enough to recognize which devices are installed where (even those installed on other PCs!), and does almost all the configuration for you. You have to answer a question or two—and you still have to plug in all the cards and cables, of course—but that's about it.

With Windows XP, there's not reason *not* to set up a multiple-PC network in your home or small business.

UNDERSTANDING DIFFERENT TYPES OF NETWORKS

A computer network is, quite simply, two or more computers connected to each other. When the computers are connected, they can send electronic signals back and forth. This lets them communicate with each other (via e-mail, typically), or share things. The computers on a network can share files–that is, one computer can access the files stored on another computer. They can share printers, by sending their print requests over the network to the PC that is physically connected to the printer. They can share a single Internet connection, whether that's via a traditional modem or some sort of broadband connection. They can even share software applications. (Think multiple-player games here.)

When you have multiple computers connected like this, it's almost like all your users are working on one really big computer. When you're connected together in this way, does it matter where a file resides, or to which computer a printer is connected to? You just do your work, and access the resources you need, wherever they may be.

Network Basics

Connecting all these computers together is actually fairly simple. Each computer has to have a *network interface card* (NIC) installed and configured. If you're connecting more than two computers in your network, each network card then has to be connected to a *hub*, which is a simple device that functions like the hub of a wheel, and functions as the central point in your network. And each computer has to configured to function as part of the network, and to share designated files, folders, and peripherals.

The physical part of connecting a network is something beyond the scope of this book, but it's really pretty easy. You can choose from wired or wireless types of networks. You can probably find everything you need for either type of network in a pre-assembled "networking kit." These kits typically contain all the cards and cables and hubs you need to create your network, along with easy-to-follow instructions. (And if you don't want to open up your computer, you can even find kits that include external network "cards" that connect via USB!)

The configuration part of setting up a network is handled by the operating system. Prior to Windows XP, it wasn't terribly easy. With Windows XP, however, it *is* easy. Very easy. Running-a-wizard type easy.

Windows XP's Network Setup Wizard guides you through the setup and configuration of your network. You run the wizard on each PC that's connected to the network, and tell it about anything else you have connected—such as a printer, or an Internet connection you want to share.

The wizard does all the hard work, and when it's done, your network is up and running and ready to use.

The Network Setup Wizard is compatible with computers running Windows XP, Windows Me, Windows 98, and Windows 2000. If you have a computer running any other operating system, you'll need to use third-party networking software instead.

Connection Options

When it comes to physically connecting your network, you have a handful of choices. Here's a brief overview of the major types of networks to consider.

Ethernet Networks

An *Ethernet network* is a traditional wired network. You install Ethernet NICs in each PC, and connect the cards via Ethernet cable. While this type of network is very easy to set up and probably the lowest-cost alternative, you have to deal with all that cable. Which can be a hassle if your computers are in far different areas of your house. Data is transferred at either 10Mbps or 100Mbps, depending on what equipment you install.

A 100Mbps Ethernet network is called *Fast Ethernet*. Some cards and hubs are labeled 10/100 because they can handle either 10Mbps or 100Mbps data transmission, depending on the capability of the other equipment on the network.

If you're connecting your network to a DSL or cable modem connection, you'll need at least part of your network to be an Ethernet network. That's because most DSL and cable modems are designed to connect to an Ethernet card in your PC. (You can then create a *bridge* between the Ethernet connection and another type of network, if you need to.)

Wireless Networks

A *wireless network* uses radio frequency (RF) signals to connect one computer to another. The big advantage of wireless, of course, is that you don't have to run any cables—a big plus if you have a big house with computers on either end.

Windows XP supports the IEEE 802.11b wireless networking standard, which is capable of speeds up to 11Mbps. This is the same type of wireless network that is used in large corporations, and is very stable and robust. It's also fairly costly.

The official marketing name for 802.11 wireless networking is *WiFi*, for *wired fidelity*. WiFi lets you connect to wireless network access points up to 150 feet away from your PC.

Another reason to consider installing an 802.11b wireless network is that WiFi network access points are being installed in a number of public locations. (Your local Starbucks is at the top of the list, and your local airport won't be far behind.) Windows XP's implementation of 802.11b is such that you can walk from one coverage area to another, and your PC will be configured on the fly for the new access point, totally automatically. This means that you can switch wireless networks without rebooting, which isn't a bad deal.

Another type of wireless network, also supported by Windows XP, is called HomeRF. HomeRF networks are typically lower-priced than 802.11b wireless networks, but also slower. For example, Diamond's HomeFree wireless system transfers data at 1Mbps, and Intel's AnyPoint Wireless system will go all the way up to 1.6Mbps. That's not that fast, especially if you transfer large amounts of data back and forth. (It is fast enough for sharing a broadband Internet connection, though.)

Phone Line Networks

When you don't want to run cables but also don't want the high cost of an 802.11 wireless network (or the low speed of a HomeRF system), consider connecting your network via your home's telephone lines.

A *phone line network* provides a similar level of convenience as a wireless network, but with higher data transfer rates and greater reliability. With telephone line networking (commonly referred to as HomePNA, based on the specifications developed by the Home Phone Networking Alliance), you connect each computer to an adapter that plugs into a standard phone jack. Data signals are sent from your computer through the adapter into your home phone line, and received by another adapter and PC elsewhere on the network.

Because each adapter on a HomePNA network sends its signal at a different frequency, your computer network can share the phone line with other voice and data traffic.

There are many HomePNA products on the market, the most popular of which is Intel's AnyPoint Home Network kit. The standard AnyPoint adapter plugs into a parallel or USB port on your PC, and then connects to the nearest phone line. (No hub necessary.)

Where the earliest HomePNA networks transferred data at just 1Mbps, most current phone line networks offer 10Mbps transfer rates. Some newer (and more expensive) HomePNA networks even get up into the 100Mbps range. So if you need decent speed without the hassle of running lots of cable, this may be the way to go.

SETTING UP YOUR NETWORK

Before you run the Network Setup Wizard, you have to plan out and then physically connect all the pieces and parts of your network. Here are some general guidelines on how best to proceed.

First, sketch out a diagram of your network. Include everything that you want connected, including printers, scanners, phone lines, or DSL/cable modems.

Next to each computer on your diagram, indicate what hardware is connected to that PC. For example, one PC might be connected to a printer, another to a dial-up modem. If any of your computers already have network cards installed, note that.

If you intend to share an Internet connection, determine which PC will be the *host* for the connection. This will typically be the PC nearest the dial-up or broadband modem. (Note that this host computer must have *two* network cards installed, for Windows XP's Internet Connection Sharing to work.)

Determine which type of network adapters you're going to be using: Ethernet, wireless, or phone line. Then make a list of all the hardware you'll need to purchase. Include network cards, a hub (if you're running an Ethernet network), and cables. And make sure you buy cables that are long enough to run where they need to run.

Even if you're connecting a wireless or phone line network, your host PC must still have an Ethernet card installed to activate Internet connection sharing. The Ethernet card will connect to your Internet connection, while the wireless or phone line card will connect to the rest of your network.

Next, head out to your local computer store and buy all the hardware and cables you need. Make sure you check out the various networking kits available for purchase. You might be able to find a kit that includes some or all the equipment you need, often at a discounted price.

The next step is the tough one—installing all the hardware. You'll need to install a network card in each of your PCs (and two in your host PC). With Plug and Play, this is normally as easy as turning off your PC, installing the card, and then turning your PC back on again. Windows XP should recognize the new card, and install the appropriate drivers automatically.

If you want to avoid messing around inside your PC's system unit, you can get USB-based Ethernet and 802.11b adapters. They're more expensive than the traditional internal cards (and they don't run at 100Mbps), but they are very easy to install and configure.

For more information on installing new hardware in your PC, see Chapter 6, "Adding New Hardware."

Before you perform the next step, you have to power down and turn off all your computers and printers. Once the power is off, run all the cables you need to run, and connect them to each computer and hub in your network. Once all the computers are connected, you can power them back on again.

Make sure the host PC has an active Internet connection, then run the Network Setup Wizard on that PC. Once the host PC is configured, run the wizard on the other PCs, one at a time.

Once the last PC is configured, your network is set up—and running. You can then configure individual peripherals and folders for sharing (or not) across the network, and get back to whatever it was you were doing before you embarked on this little chore.

Table 18.1 shows the specific equipment you'll need for each PC on each type of network.

TABLE 18.1—Equipment Needed for Each Type of Network

Type of Network	Host PC	Other PCs
Ethernet	Ethernet network cards (2) Ethernet network hub (1 for the entire network) Modem (dial-up or broadband)	Ethernet network card (1)
Wireless	Wireless network adapter (1) Ethernet network card (1) Modem (dial-up or broadband)	Wireless network adapter (1)
Phone line	HomePNA network adapter (1) Ethernet network card (1) Modem (dial-up or broadband)	HomePNA network adapter (1)

If you're connecting an Ethernet network, you'll also need one Ethernet cable to go from the hub to the host computer, and additional cables to connect each of your other PCs to the hub. If you're connecting a phone line network, you'll need telephone cables to connect each PC (including the host) to the nearest telephone jack. And, no matter which type of networking you're installing, if you're connecting a broadband modem, you'll need an Ethernet cable to run from the modem to your host PC.

RUNNING THE NETWORK SETUP WIZARD

After you've physically connected your computers together, Windows XP's Network Setup Wizard guides you through setting up your home network. Once the wizard is run, you can share resources such as files, printers, and an Internet connection with all of the computers on your network.

The Network Setup Wizard must be run on each computer on your network. You start by running the wizard on your host computer.

Follow these steps:

1. Click the Start button and then select All Programs, Accessories, Communications, Network Setup Wizard.
2. Click the Next button to move through the introductory screens. When you come to the Select a Connection Method screen (shown in Figure 18.1), select the first option, This Computer Connects Directly to the Internet—The Other Computers In My Home Network Connect to the Internet Through This Computer. Click Next.

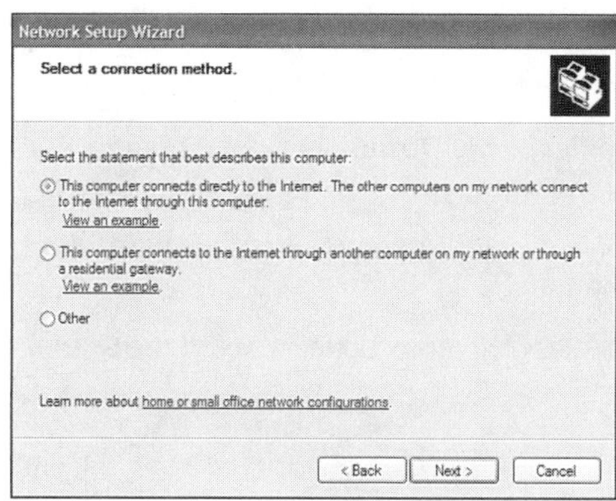

Figure 18.1

Using the Home Network Wizard to configure the PC you have connected to the Internet.

3. When the Select Your Internet Connection screen appears, select the Internet connection that you'll be using for your network. Click Next.
4. When the Give This Computer a Description and Name screen appears, enter a description for this PC (make and model is good), along with a unique name (such as "Main Computer"). Click Next.
5. When the Ready to Apply Network Settings screen appears, click the Next button, then follow the onscreen instructions to complete the configuration of your network.

Once you've rut n he Network Setup Wizard on your host PC, you have to run it on all the other PCs on your network. If a computer is running Windows XP, you can run the wizard as previously described. If a computer is running Windows 98, Windows Me, or Windows 2000, you need to run the wizard from the Windows XP installation CD. (Insert the CD and then, after the main screen appears, select Use Windows Support Tools, and then select Tools, Network Setup Wizard.)

When you run the wizard on a non-host PC, you'll want to select the This Computer Connects to the Internet Through Another Computer In My Home Network option. Then you'll follow the onscreen instructions and let XP finish the network configuration for you.

Once all your computers are configured, your network is now fully functional. You can now share files between PCs, play multiple-player games (on two PCs), send documents to your printer, and connect to the Internet—from any PC on your network.

SETTING UP NETWORK SHARING

One of the main reasons you set up a network is to share things—files, printers, even your Internet connection.

Sharing Files and Folders

To share files with other users on your network, you have to enable Windows XP's file sharing. You do this by putting the folders and files you want to share in a shared network folder. You can make these files editable by other users, or read-only.

To share a file or folder, follow these steps:

1. From My Computer or My Documents, open the drive or folder that contains the file or folder you want to share.
2. Right-click the file or folder that you want to share, and select Sharing and Security from the pop-up menu.
3. When the Properties dialog box appears, select the Sharing tab (shown in Figure 18.2).

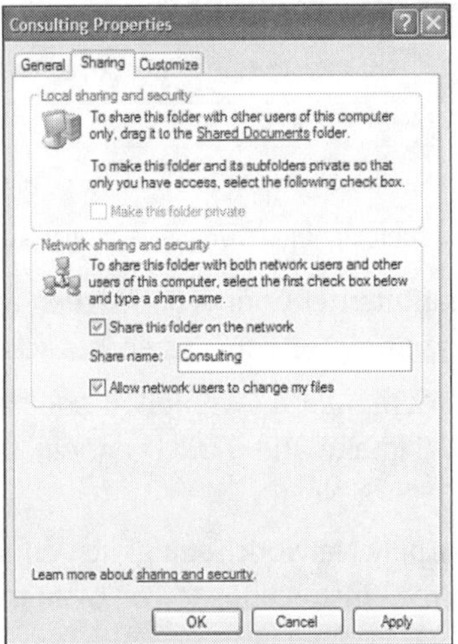

Figure 18.2

Configuring file sharing over your network.

4. Check the Share This Folder On the Network option.
5. If you want this file to be read-only, *uncheck* the Allow Network Users to Change My Files option. If you want your files to be fully editable by all users, check this option.
6. Click OK.

You'll need to do this for each folder or file you want to share. If you choose to share a folder, all the files and subfolders within that folder are also marked for sharing.

Sharing Drives and Devices

Not only can you share individual files and folders, you can also share complete disk drives—including hard disk drives, CD-ROM or DVD drives, and removable disk drives, such as Zip disks. Just follow these steps:

1. From within My Computer, select the drive or device you want to share.
2. From the activity center Tasks list, select either Share This Disk Drive, Share This CD, or Share This Disk.

Sharing Printers

Sharing one printer between several computers is a very cost-effective measure. Very seldom do you need dedicated printers for every PC in your home.

To share a printer with all the other computers on the network, you need to configure the PC that the printer is connected to. Follow these steps:

1. From the Control Panel, click the Printers and Faxes icon.
2. When the Printers and Faxes utility opens, right-click the printer you want to share, and then select Sharing from the pop-up menu.
3. When the printer's Properties dialog box appears (shown in Figure 18.3), select the Sharing tab.

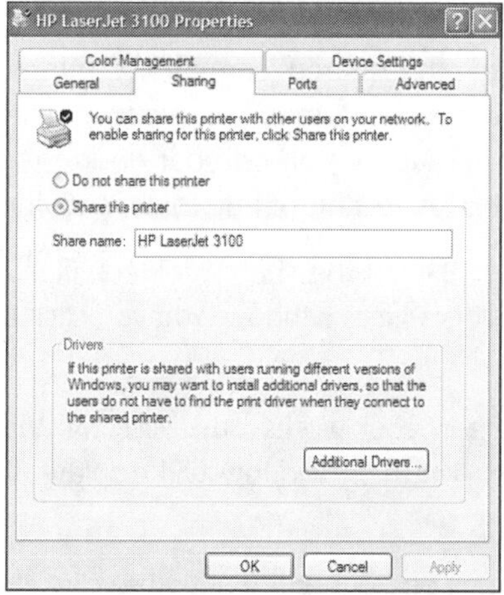

Figure 18.3

Configure the printer's host PC to share the printer with the rest of your network.

4. Check the Share Name option and enter a name for the printer. (Make and model number is always good.)
5. If any other computer on your network is running something other than Windows XP, you'll need to install printer drivers for that operating system. Click the

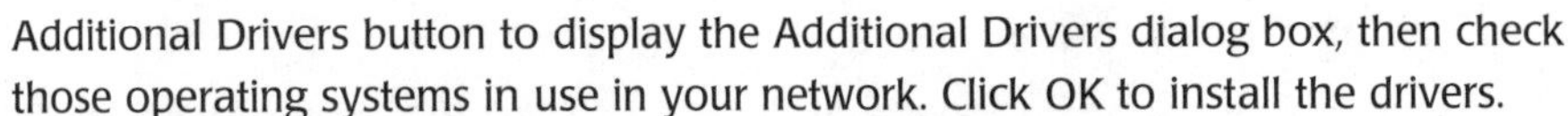

Additional Drivers button to display the Additional Drivers dialog box, then check those operating systems in use in your network. Click OK to install the drivers.

6. When you return to the Properties dialog box, click OK.

Once the printer's host PC is configured, this printer should now appear automatically on the other PCs on your network. You can check this by opening the Printers and Faxes utility on the other PCs and looking for the newly networked printer. If the printer *doesn't* appear, you may have to click the Add Printer icon to add the network printer to that PC.

Sharing an Internet Connection

When you ran the Network Setup Wizard, you activated Internet Connection Sharing for your network. As long as your host computer is connected to the Internet, all your other computers have simultaneous Internet access.

To learn more about sharing an Internet connection, turn to Chapter 7, "Making the Connection."

ACCESSING FILES, PRINTERS, AND OTHER COMPUTERS ON YOUR NETWORK

Once you've set up all your computers for file, folder, and printer sharing, how do you access all those files, folders, and computers? It's really quite easy—as long as you know where to look.

Windows XP displays all the shared computers, printers, drives, folders, and other resources available on your network in the My Network Places folder. You open this folder by clicking the My Network Places icon on your desktop, or by clicking the My Network Places link in the Other Places section of any folder activity center pane.

As you can see in Figure 18.4, all the shared folders, files, and devices are automatically displayed in the My Network Places window. You can click any of these icons to open that particular resource.

To view all the computers in your workgroup, click the View Network Computers link in the Network Tasks panel. The next window will display all the computers that this computer is connected to.

To display all the computers on your entire network, click the Microsoft Windows Network link in the Other Places panel. The next window will display all the networks that this computer is connected to. Click a network icon to display all currently connected computers. (Your home network probably is labeled Mshome.)

A computer will be displayed only if it is turned on and connected to the network. Any computer connected to the network but powered down will not be displayed.

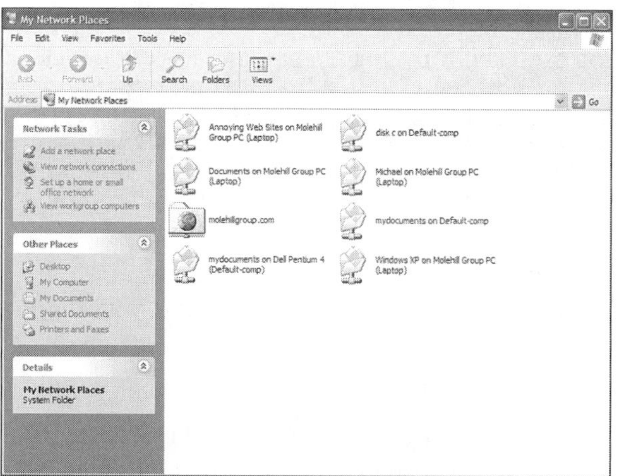

Figure 18.4

Use My Network Places to access all the shared resources on your network.

You can also create shortcuts in the My Network Places folder to files and folders within shared folders. (This makes it easier to go directly to a file or folder, rather than clicking through a bunch of subfolders.) Just click the Add a Network Place link in the Network Tasks panel, and follow the instructions in the Add Network Place Wizard.

Finding Other Computers on Your Network

If your computer is connected to a large network, only those computers in your local workgroup are displayed in the My Network Places window. You can view all computers on the network by clicking the Entire Network icon, or you can search for specific computers by using Windows XP's Search Companion. Just follow these steps:

1. Click the Search button on the My Network Places toolbar.
2. When the Search Companion opens, enter the name of the computer you want to find into the Computer Name box.
3. Click the Search button to list all computers with that name on your network.

You can use *wildcard* characters in the computer name if you are not exactly sure of the computer's name. For example, to search for any combination of multiple characters, use an *; searching for BOB* will return BOBS, BOBBIE, or BOBBY.

Accessing a Shared File or Folder

If a file or folder has been marked for sharing, it's really easy to access that item from another computer on the network. All you have to do is open the My Network Places folder and tunnel down through the shared drives and folders until you get to the item you want.

Once you find that file or folder, you can work on it just as you would a file or folder on your own PC. You can even copy that file or folder to your own PC.

You can't edit any files that have been marked as read-only over the network.

Printing to a Network Printer

If you've configured your PCs to share a specific printer, you can print to that printer from any PC on your network. The shared network printer will appear as a printer choice in all the applications on all your PCs.

When you go to print a document from an application, select File, Print. When the Print dialog box appears, select the network printer from the Name list.

When you click OK to start printing, your print job will be sent from the current PC, over your network, to the PC connected to the printer, and then to the printer for printing. All with the click of a single button!

JIM'S TOP TEN TIPS

With previous versions of Windows, a chapter like this about networking would have been at least twice as long. That's because with those older Windows, you had to set up all sorts of complicated network protocols (such as TCP/IP and IPX), pretty much by hand. Windows didn't do a good job of recognizing all your network devices, and the network configuration was a long, drawn-out process. (More trial and error than anything else, to be truthful.)

One of the true joys of Windows XP is how easy it makes home networking. Network devices are recognized automatically, and configuration takes place in the background. You still have to make the physical connections, of course, as well as click a few options in the various wizards. But all things being equal, connecting a network under Windows XP is relatively painless.

When you're planning and connecting your network, keep these points in mind:

1. When you want to share information, files, printers, or an Internet connection between two or more computers, you need to connect those computers in a network.
2. You can choose to create an Ethernet (wired) network, a wireless network (using RF signals), or a network that connects via your home phone lines. An Ethernet network is fastest and cheapest, although you may have to deal with running a lot of cable.
3. When you connect an Ethernet network, you have to install a network interface card in each computer, and then connect each card to a network hub.
4. Windows XP's Home Network Wizard greatly simplifies the process of installing and configuring your network. Just install your hardware and run the wizard (on each computer), and you'll be up and ready to go.
5. To share an Internet connection, the computer connected to the Internet (called the host PC) must have two network cards installed—one going to your modem, and the other going to your network hub.
6. Once your network is installed, you can configure individual disk drives, folders, and files to be shared with other computers on your network. (Use the Shared tab in the file/folder dialog box.)
7. To share a printer with other computers on the network, you have to turn on printer sharing on the PC that the printer is connected to. You also have to add that printer (using the Add Printer Wizard) to each PC on your network.
8. All the contents of your network—all the computers, all the shared files and folders, and all the shared printers—are displayed in the My Network Places folder.

9. If a device or computer doesn't appear in the My Network Places folder, click the Entire Network icon. You can also search for individual computers on a large network by clicking the Search For Computers link.
10. When you access a shared file or folder over the network, it's just like accessing that item on your own PC. You can even copy or move that file or folder to your PC.

CHAPTER 19

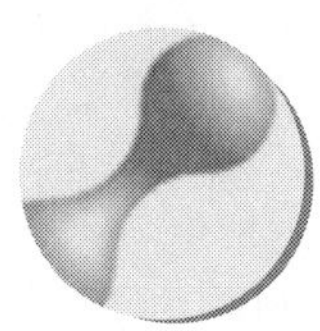

USING WINDOWS XP ON PORTABLE PCs

- Improving Your Display with ClearType
- Optimizing Battery Life
- Connecting Two PCs with a Direct Network Connection
- Controlling Another Computer with Remote Desktop Connection
- Using Briefcase to Synchronize Files
- Working with Offline Files
- Jim's Top Ten Tips

Windows XP includes several new or improved features that should be of interest to portable computer users. These features make it easier to see what you're doing, maximize how long your batteries last, and help you share and synchronize files with your home PC or network. There's even a new remote desktop feature included with Windows XP Professional (not Home, sorry) that lets you access your desktop PC when you're on the road.

These features may be little things, but sometimes the little things add up.

Take ClearType, for example. It's a little thing, hardly mentioned in Microsoft's marketing materials and buried a few layers deep in the Display Properties dialog box. But this little feature improves the typical laptop display so much I can't even describe it. It's like somebody adjusted the fine-tuning control on my screen, automatically smoothing all the jagged edges. A little thing, but a big impact.

The only issue I find with XP's mobile features is that too many of them aren't available in the Home Edition. Two of the most useful new features, Remote Desktop Connection and offline files, are only available on Windows XP Professional. That might make some sense, as XP Professional is targeted to corporations, where the majority of road warriors work. But a lot of home and small business users have portable PCs, and they might not want to spend the extra money for XP Professional. (They probably don't need all the advanced networking and security features, either.)

So if you're a heavy notebook user, examine the Professional-only mobile features, and decide for yourself whether you can live with the Home Edition, or need to spring for XP Professional.

IMPROVING YOUR DISPLAY WITH CLEARTYPE

Take a look at Figure 19.1. This shows a page of type as displayed on a typical LCD computer screen. You probably don't notice anything strange or wrong with this screen, because that's what you've been used to seeing since the advent of full-color screens.

But compare that screen with the one in Figure 19.2. All of a sudden you can see the ragged shapes and jagged edges of the first screen, especially when compared to the smooth letters and perfectly rounded edges of the second screen.

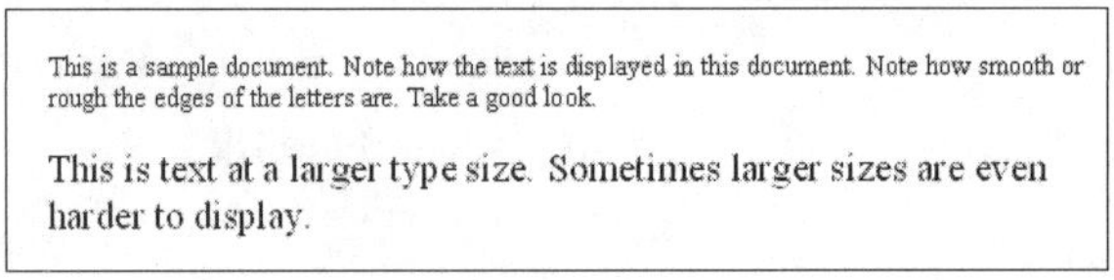

This is a sample document. Note how the text is displayed in this document. Note how smooth or rough the edges of the letters are. Take a good look.

This is text at a larger type size. Sometimes larger sizes are even harder to display.

Figure 19.1

Text displayed on a typical LCD computer screen...

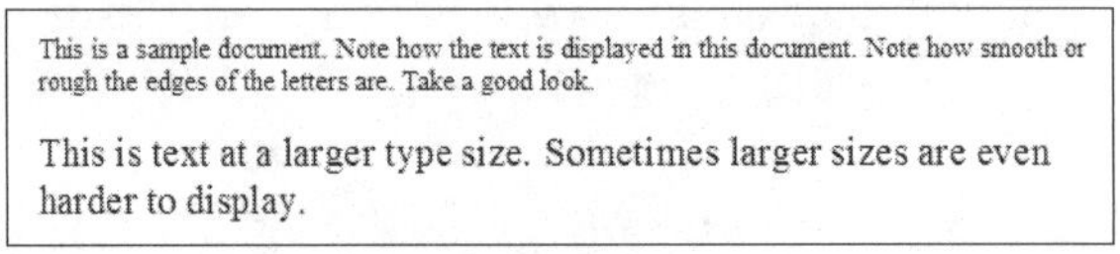

This is a sample document. Note how the text is displayed in this document. Note how smooth or rough the edges of the letters are. Take a good look.

This is text at a larger type size. Sometimes larger sizes are even harder to display.

Figure 19.2

...and text displayed on an LCD screen with ClearType enabled.

The first screen is a computer display without ClearType. The second screen has ClearType enabled.

The two figures printed in this book give you a taste of how ClearType improves the look of LCD displays. Trust me, the real-world difference is even more impressive.

As I explained in Chapter 2, "Changing the Way Windows Looks—and Acts," ClearType is a new display technology that effectively triples the horizontal display resolution on LCD displays. If you're using a portable PC of any make or model, you'll definitely what to turn on ClearType. You'll wonder how you ever lived without it.

To turn on ClearType, follow these steps:

1. From the Control Panel, click the Display icon.
2. When the Display Properties utility opens, select the Appearance tab.
3. Click the Effects button.
4. When the Effects dialog box appears (as shown in Figure 19.3), check the Use the Following Method to Smooth Edges of Screen Fonts option, and select ClearType from the pull-down list.

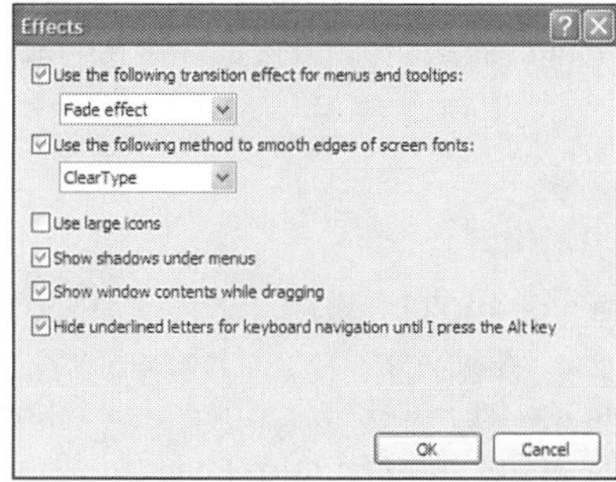

Figure 19.3

Turn on ClearType from the Effects dialog box.

5. Click OK, then click OK again.

That's all there is to it—and you'll never turn it off.

Microsoft says that ClearType is designed for LCD screens only, such as the ones in portable PCs and flat-screen monitors. Activating ClearType on a tube-type monitor might make text and other onscreen elements appear slightly blurry. Or, depending on your monitor, it might smooth out some of the roughness you typically get with some screen fonts. In other words, YMMV (your mileage may vary). The best thing to do is try it yourself, and see if you like it!

OPTIMIZING BATTERY LIFE

Now that you've improved your notebook's display by about a gazillion percent, let's turn our attention to your PC's battery life. Because there's nothing more frustrating than having your portable computer go dead in the middle of a cross-country flight (or in the middle of a long meeting!), you know how important it is to squeeze every last second of life out of your PC's battery.

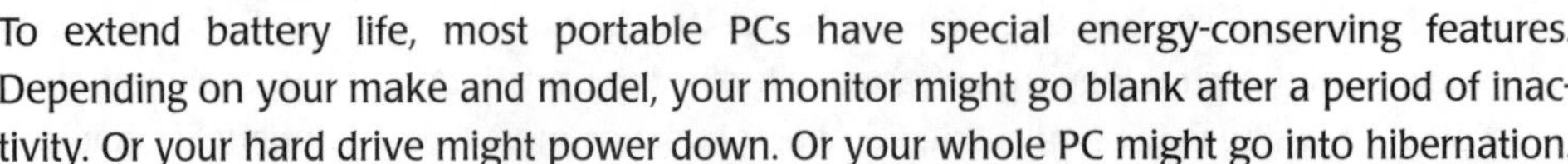

To extend battery life, most portable PCs have special energy-conserving features. Depending on your make and model, your monitor might go blank after a period of inactivity. Or your hard drive might power down. Or your whole PC might go into hibernation.

Windows XP includes a Power Options utility that helps you manage the power consumption of your portable computer. With the Power Options utility you can configure monitor and hard disk use, set alarms to go off when your battery power drops too low, display power meters for each battery in your PC, and set standby and hibernation settings.

To display the Power Options utility, all you have to do is click the Power Options icon in the Control Panel.

The Power Options available will vary depending on your exact hardware configuration. It's also possible that the manufacturer of your portable PC has included its own power management utilities. You should use these utilities either in addition to or in place of Windows XP's power management features, as they are most often tailored to your specific hardware.

Setting Up Power Schemes

The easiest way to manage your notebook's power consumption is through the use of what Microsoft calls *power schemes*. A power scheme is a collection of settings that manage the activity of your computer's monitor and hard drive, as well as the computer's standby and hibernation modes. (I'll talk about standby and hibernation in a few pages—be patient!)

To change power schemes, follow these steps:

1. From the Control Panel, click the Power Options icon.
2. When the Power options utility opens, select the Power Schemes tab (as shown in Figure 19.4).

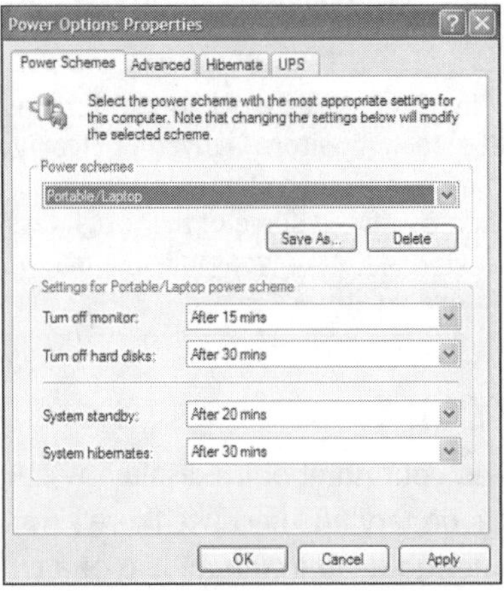

Figure 19.4

Choose a power scheme to manage your battery usage.

3. Pull down the Power Schemes list and select a new scheme. (The available schemes are detailed in Table 19.1.)
4. Click OK.

Table 19.1 shows the key settings for each power scheme.

TABLE 19.1—KEY POWER SCHEME SETTINGS FOR BATTERY USAGE

Power Scheme	Turn Off Monitor After	Turn Off Hard Disks After	Initiate Standby Mode After	Initiate Hibernate Mode After
Home/Office Desk	2 mins	10 mins	1 min	10 mins
Portable/Laptop	15 mins	20 mins	30 mins	Never
Presentation	Never	5 mins	15 mins	Never
Always On	2 mins	3 mins	5 mins	Never
Minimal Power Management	5 mins	15 mins	5 mins	Never
Max Battery	1 min	3 mins	2 mins	Never

You can edit any of these schemes, or create your own schemes. Just make the appropriate changes to the various settings, then click the Save As button.

Typically, you want to turn off your monitor or hard disk if you're not using them, to conserve battery power. If you plan to be away from your computer for a while, you put your computer into the low-power standby mode. If you're going to be away from your computer for an extended period of time, you activate hibernation mode.

Both standby and hibernation modes are more convenient than turning your computer completely off. When you restart your PC from one of these power-saving modes, your desktop is restored exactly as you left it—open programs and all.

Setting a Low-Battery Alarm

It helps if you know when your battery is about to run out of juice. Otherwise you'll keep working up to the point of no return, and you won't get a chance to save your work and shut down properly before your computer turns off.

You can configure Windows XP to sound one of two different low-battery alarms. The Low Battery Alarm typically alerts you via a dialog box that your battery is running low. The Critical Battery Alarm typically throws your system into hibernation mode, which at least preserves your current work until you can plug into a power outlet and recharge your battery.

This option is only available if you have a battery-operated portable computer.

To configure either of the two alarms, follow these steps:

1. From the Power Options utility, select the Alarms tab.
2. To activate either of the alarms, check the appropriate option.
3. Adjust the sliders to determine when the alarm will sound. The sliders represent how much power your battery has left when the alarm is activated.
4. To change what happens when an alarm is activated, click the Alarm Action button. You can choose to generate an alarm sound, display an onscreen message, send your PC into hibernation or sleep mode, shut down, or run a program.
5. Click OK when done.

Working with Standby Mode

Standby mode—sometimes called *sleep* mode—helps you reduce power usage without actually shutting off your computer. When your PC is in standby mode, your monitor and hard disks are turned off, even though power is kept to the rest of your system. When you come out of standby mode, your system appears exactly as you left it.

You can configure Windows XP to send your PC into standby mode whenever you close your notebook's lid or press the power button. All you have to do is select the Advanced tab in the Power Options utility (shown in Figure 19.5), and select the appropriate options in the Power Buttons section.

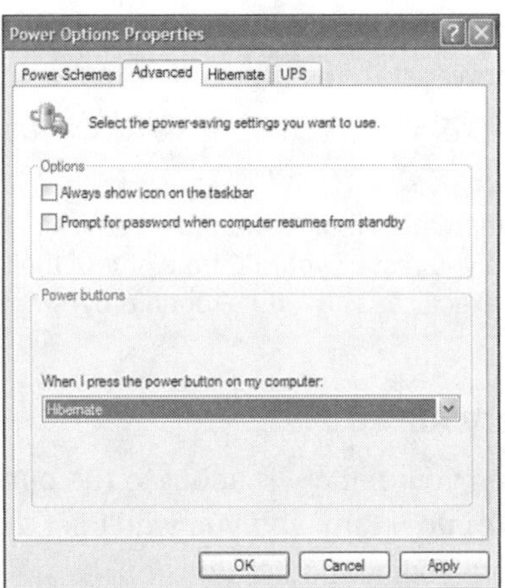

Figure 19.5

Make your PC go into either hibernation or standby mode when you close the lid or press the power button.

By the way, Windows XP can take advantage of BIOS tweaks found on some newer notebooks, which lets them resume from standby mode in under a second. (You can't believe how fast this is until you see it!) This is almost a good-enough reason to buy a new notebook with XP pre-installed!

You probably want to save your work before putting your computer in standby mode. That's because information in your computer's memory is not saved to your hard disk while the computer is on standby. If there is an interruption in power, all your work will be lost.

Working with Hibernation Mode

Hibernation mode is even more extreme than standby mode. When your PC is in hibernation mode, your monitor and hard disk turn off, Windows saves everything that's currently in memory to your hard disk, and actually turns off the computer. When you come out of hibernation, the information in memory is restored to your desktop, and you're back in business just like nothing happened.

Make sure you have enough free disk space to create the hibernation file. If you're running 256MB of memory, the hibernation file will be a little over 256MB in size.

You can configure Windows XP to automatically send your computer into hibernation mode whenever you close the lid or press the power button. Open the Power Options utility, select the Advanced tab, and select the appropriate options in the Power Buttons section.

CONNECTING TWO PCS WITH A DIRECT NETWORK CONNECTION

If your portable PC is part of a network, it's easy to send files back and forth. If your PC is *not* part of a network, you can still share files with another computer—you just have to set up a direct connection between the two PCs, manually.

With Windows XP you can connect any two PCs by using either a serial cable or a DirectParallel cable. (I recommend the DirectParallel method—it's faster.) This method is also useful for connecting Windows CE devices to your desktop or portable PC.

Microsoft calls this sort of connection a *direct network connection*. To make it work, you first need to connect the cable between the two PCs, and then follow these steps:

1. From the Control Panel, click the Network Connections icon.
2. When the Network Connections utility opens, click the Create a New Connection link in the Network Tasks panel to open the New Connection Wizard. Click the Next button to get things going.
3. When the Network Connection Type screen appears, check the Advanced Connection option, then click Next.
4. When the Advanced Connection Options screen appears (as shown in Figure 19.6), check the Connect Directly to Another Computer option. Click Next.

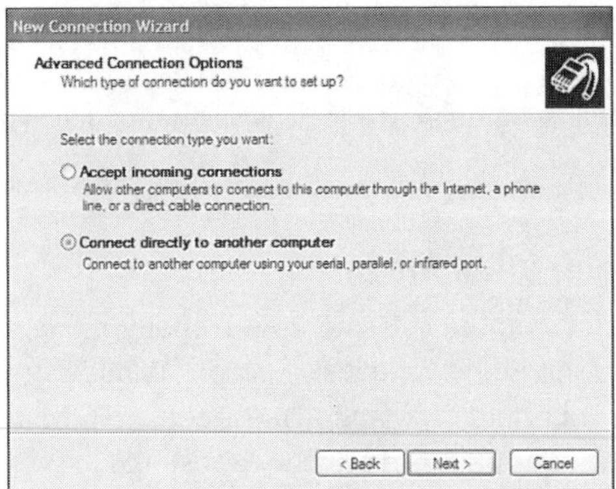

Figure 19.6

Configure your PC to connect directly to another computer, no network required.

5. When the Host or Guest? screen appears, check the Guest option if you're configuring the PC that will be accessing information on the other machine. Check the Host option if you're configuring that contains the information you need to access. In most cases, your portable PC will be the guest, and a desktop PC will be the host. Click Next whenever you're ready.
6. When the Connection Device screen appears, select how the two computers will be connected, then click Next.
7. When the Default Connection screen appears, ignore everything and click Next.
8. When the final screen appears, enter a name for this connection and then click the Finish button.

Once your two PCs are connected, you can transfer files back and forth as if you were on a regular network.

CONTROLLING ANOTHER COMPUTER WITH REMOTE DESKTOP CONNECTION

What do you do if you're on the road but need to access a file on your home or office PC? If you have Windows XP Professional installed on your notebook you can open a Remote Desktop Connection, and use your main PC by remote control—over a standard dial-up connection, or via the Internet.

The PC doing the remote controlling has to be running Windows XP Professional. This feature is not available in Windows XP Home Edition—although the machine being controlled can be running either the Home Edition or Professional.

By the way, for me this feature is a good reason to move up to Windows XP Professional. I often have to help my dad work through his various and assorted computer problems, and it's a lot easier for me to take control of his PC by remote control than it is to try and talk him through this or that procedure. If I'm running his computer, I *know* his problems will be fixed!

Configure the Remote Computer

Before you can use Remote Desktop Connection, you first have to configure your home computer—what Microsoft calls the *remote* computer—to accept this type of remote control. You do this by opening the System Properties utility (click the System icon in the Control Panel), selecting the Remote tab, and checking the Allow Remote Assistance option.

Establish a Remote Connection

Now you have to create a new connection on the controlling PC. (Microsoft calls this the *local* computer.) Here's how you do it:

1. Click the Start button, then select All Programs, Accessories, Communications, Remote Desktop Connection.
2. When the Remote Desktop Connection utility opens, as shown in Figure 19.7, enter the name or IP address of the remote computer into the Computer box. (If you've already created a connection, pull down this list and select the computer you want to connect to.)

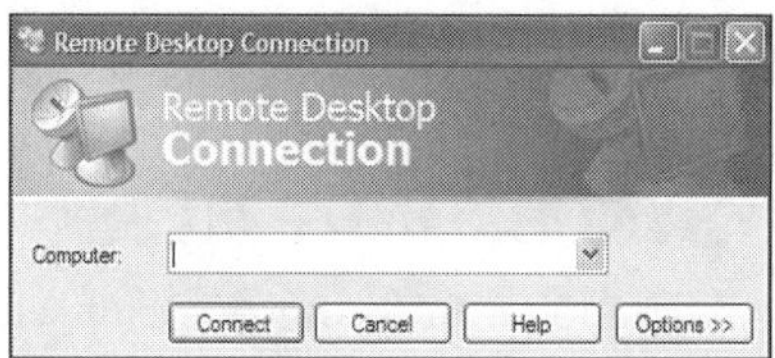

Figure 19.7

Configure your local computer to connect to a remote PC.

3. Click the Connect button. If you're trying to connect to a computer over the Internet and you're not yet connected, you'll be prompted to do so.
4. Windows XP will now locate the computer you specified, and then initiate the log on process. When the Log On to Windows dialog box appears, enter your user name, password, and domain (if required).
5. Click OK.

The screen from the remote computer now appears on your local PC. You can now use your local machine to do anything you want on the remote computer.

Configure the Local Computer

Exactly how the remote computer appears on your local PC is up to you. There are a number of viewing and control options you can configure, all from the Remote Desktop

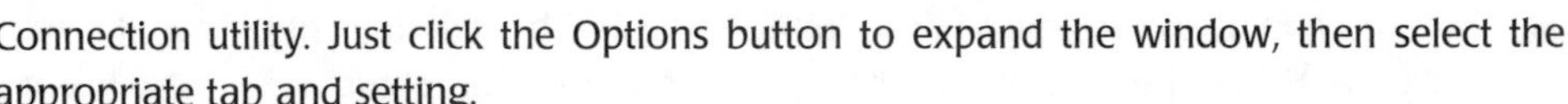

Connection utility. Just click the Options button to expand the window, then select the appropriate tab and setting.

Here's what you can configure with each tab:

- **General**—Use this tab to automate your log on to the remote computer, as well as to save your configuration settings.
- **Display**—Use this tab to configure how much screen space the remote desktop takes up on your local PC, as well as the number of colors displayed. (You can run the remote PC in full-screen mode, or have it take up only a portion of your local screen.)
- **Local Resources**—Use this tab to determine whether or not you hear the sound from the remote computer, which Windows hotkeys you can use, and whether you want to make your local devices (printers, disk drives, and so on) available to the remote computer.
- **Run**—Use this tab to set a program you want to automatically run when you connect to the remote PC.
- **Advanced**—This tab lets you set bitmap caching and compression options that can speed up your remote connection.

Remote Desktop Connection is also used by technical support personnel to troubleshoot PC problems remotely, as discussed in Chapter 20, "Getting Help."

USING BRIEFCASE TO SYNCHRONIZE FILES

Whether you're bringing work home from the office or writing some personal letters at your local coffeeshop, the time will come when you need to share files between your portable PC and a desktop computer. When you're working on the same file from multiple PCs, figuring out which is the most recent version of the file can be a challenge.

One way to deal with this problem is to use Windows XP's Briefcase feature to synchronize your files. Briefcase has been around for several versions of Windows, and remains essentially unchanged in Windows XP. With Briefcase you simply pop the files from your primary PC into a Briefcase folder. You can copy the Briefcase folder to another PC or work on its files from a notebook. When you copy the Briefcase back to your main PC or reconnect your notebook to the network, Briefcase automatically updates the original files with your latest changes.

To be honest, I've never much used Briefcase. It's kind of awkward, and not very intuitive. Still, it works as promised, and is there if you need it. (It's also available in Windows XP Home Edition, which offline files—discussed later in this chapter—are not.)

Using Briefcase on a Floppy

If you're not connected to a network, you can copy the files you want to share to a floppy disk, and then use that floppy disk on another PC. It's the old-fashioned way to do it, but it's also a darned convenient way to take a few files home from the office without a lot of hassle.

To use Briefcase on a floppy, follow these steps:

1. Create a Briefcase icon on your desktop (or in a specific folder) by right-clicking the desktop and selecting New, Briefcase from the pop-up menu.
2. To add a file to your Briefcase, use My Computer or My Documents to navigate to the folder that contains the file you want. Drag the file from its current location and drop it onto the Briefcase icon. Repeat this step to add multiple files to your briefcase.
3. Copy your Briefcase to a floppy disk by opening My Computer, dragging the Briefcase icon from your desktop, and dropping it onto the selected floppy drive. (The desktop icon won't disappear.)
4. To use your Briefcase folder on another computer, simply insert the floppy that contains Briefcase into your secondary PC. Open the Briefcase folder (shown in Figure 19.8) directly from the Briefcase floppy disk. You can then open, work on, and save the files in the Briefcase folder.

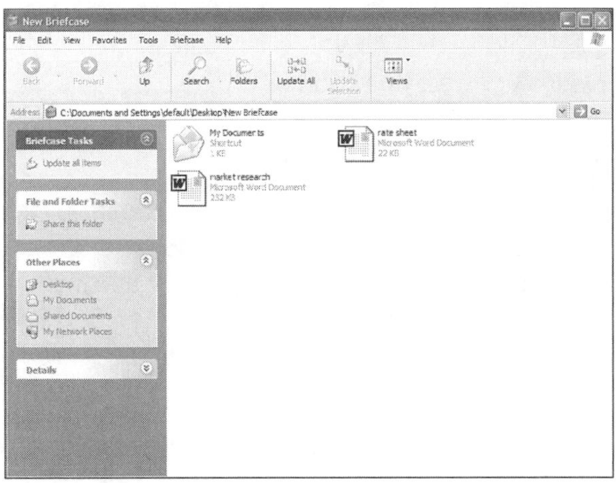

Figure 19.8

Copy files to your Briefcase folder to use them on another PC.

Do *not* copy the briefcase folder to your second PC! The folder must remain on the floppy disk for the synchronization feature to work.

5. To synchronize your Briefcase files with the originals on your primary PC, insert the Briefcase floppy disk into your main PC's floppy disk drive. Start My Computer and open the specified floppy disk drive. Drag the Briefcase icon from the floppy drive and drop it onto the Briefcase icon on your desktop. Briefcase will automatically synchronize your files so that you are always using the most current version.

Using Briefcase on a Network

If your laptop is connected to a network, you can use Briefcase to copy files from another computer to your laptop. You can then work on the files when you're on the road, and use Briefcase to synch up the files when you get back to the office.

Here's what you do:

1. Create a Briefcase icon on your portable PC's desktop (or in a specific folder) by right-clicking the desktop and selecting New, Briefcase from the pop-up menu.
2. To add a file to your Briefcase, use My Network Places to navigate to the PC and folder that contains the file you want. Drag the file from its current location and drop it onto the Briefcase icon on your notebook. Repeat this step to add multiple files to your briefcase.
3. Disconnect from the network and go on the road. You can work on the files that are stored in the Briefcase folder as you would any other files.
4. When you return to your office, connect to the network. Open the Briefcase folder and select Briefcase, Update All. This will update the original files with the changes you made while you were on the road.

WORKING WITH OFFLINE FILES

As clunky as Briefcase is, it's no surprise that Microsoft came up with a new way to work with network files when you're on the road. Windows XP Professional lets you store shared network files on your portable PC (or any PC, for that matter) so that they're available even when you're not connected to the network. The next time you reconnect, any changes you've made to the files are synchronized with the version of the files still on the network.

Microsoft calls this working with *offline files*. I call it a neat way to do what you need to do when you're on the road.

The big disappointment is that this new method is available only if you're running Windows XP Professional. (And even then, you can't use offline files if you have Fast User Switching turned on—you have to choose one or the other, not both.)

If you're using Windows XP Home Edition, you're stuck with using Briefcase. Offline files are available only on XP Professional.

Configure Your PC for Offline Files

To set up your computer to use offline files, follow these steps:

1. From the Control Panel, click the Folder Options icon.
2. When the Folder Options utility opens, select the Offline Files tab.
3. Make sure that the Enable Offline Files option is checked.
4. Check the Synchronize All Offline Files Before Logging Off option.
5. Click OK.

Make a File Available Offline

Once your computer is properly set up, you can select which files or folders you want to work on offline. Follow these steps:

1. From My Computer, open the network drive and folder that contains the file or subfolder you want to take offline.
2. Select the file or folder, then select File, Make Available Offline.

Manually Synchronize Offline Files

By default, your offline files will be automatically synchronized the next time you connect to your network. If you want to manually synchronize a file—or configure the basic synchronization settings—you use Windows XP's Synchronization Manager. (You open the Synchronization Manager by clicking the Start button, then selecting All Programs, Accessories, Synchronization Manager.) All you have to do is select the item(s) you want to synchronize, and then click the Synchronize button.

If you and another user both make offline changes to the same file, you can choose to save your version, the other version, or both versions.

JIM'S TOP TEN TIPS

When you're getting ready to hit the road, make sure the batter on your portable PC is charged up, and that you remember these ten key points:

1. You can dramatically improve the look of your laptop's display by turning on ClearType. (Open the Display Properties utility, select the Appearance tab, and click the Effects button.)
2. You can manage the power usage of your laptop by using one of Windows XP's pre-selected power schemes—or by creating one of your own. (Windows' power schemes control how long your computer sits inactive before it shuts down your monitor and hard drives.)
3. When you're going to be away from your computer for a few minutes, send it into standby mode. If you're going to be away for quite awhile, send it into hibernation mode.
4. If you buy a newer notebook PC with Windows XP pre-installed, XP will wake your notebook from standby mode in under a second!
5. Make sure you configure your computer's Power Options to sound an alarm when your battery starts to run low.
6. If your laptop isn't connected to a network, you can connect it to another PC with a DirectParallel cable and Windows' Direct Network Connection. Once connected, you can transfer files just as you would over a network.
7. If you want to access your home computer while you're on the road, set up your system for a Remote Desktop Connection. This new utility lets you completely run another computer by remote control—just as if you were sitting behind the keyboard.
8. While the local computer in a Remote Desktop Connection has to be running XP Professional, it can control computers running either XP Professional or the Home Edition.
9. If you're running Windows XP Home Edition, you can use Briefcase to transfer files to another PC. Briefcase will then synchronize the changes you make with the original files on the main PC.
10. If you're running Windows XP Professional (with Fast User Switching turned off), you can use offline folders to work on files when you're away from the network, and then resynchronize the files when you next connect.

PART VI

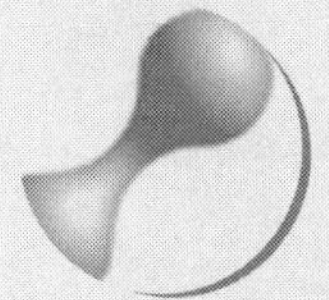

MAINTENANCE AND TROUBLESHOOTING

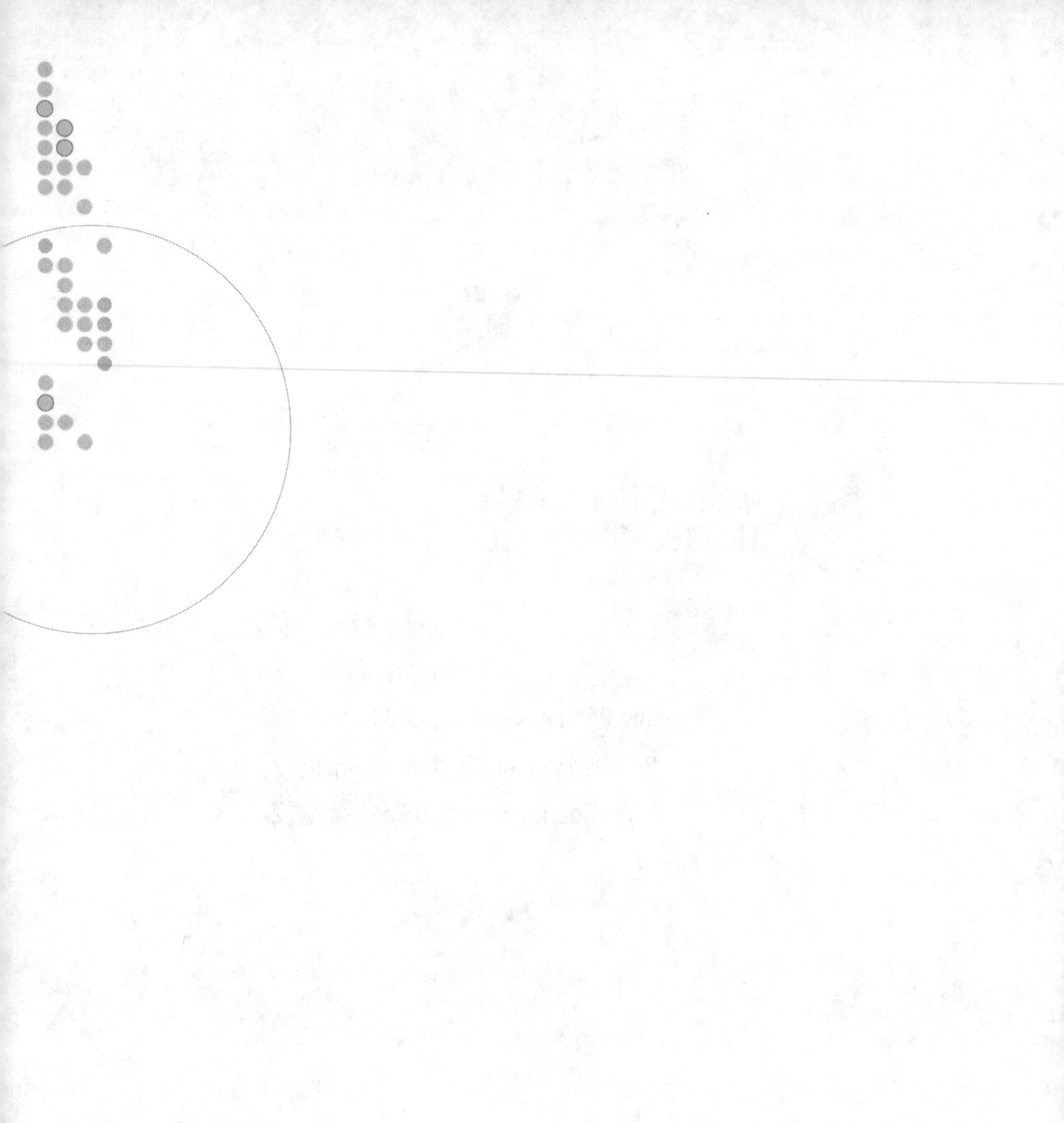

CHAPTER 20

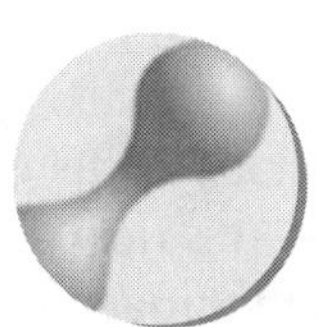

GETTING HELP

- Introducing Windows XP's New Help and Support Center
- Finding More Help Online
- Getting Remote Assistance
- Jim's Top Ten Tips

The Help system in Windows has never been great. In fact, Windows Help has typically been about the weakest part of the entire operating system. Not only was it hard to find answers to any particular question, but when the Help system finally displayed a useful page, it was written in something just this side of techie geek-speak

Made me wonder if the guys and gals out in Seattle ever took a high school or college English class.

I'd like to say that the Help system in Windows XP is light years ahead of all those older Help systems.

I'd like to say that, but I can't.

What I *can* say is that the Help system (now called the Help and Support Center) is much improved, and actually useful in places. The underlying Help text, however, is still somewhat cryptic, and it's still not terribly easy to find the exact information you're looking for.

But I'll give Microsoft credit for trying. The new Help and Support Center interface is much friendlier than

the old Help system. Microsoft has also done a good job incorporating various troubleshooting tools alongside the standard Help contents. They've even made it relatively easy to go online for more help, which is great for all those times when the built-in Help system doesn't help.

Best of all, Microsoft added a feature called Remote Assistance, which lets you turn control of your computer over to another user. This way you can have a friend or a tech support person take a look at your system and see if they can figure out what's wrong. This feature alone might be worth the price of admission—especially if you have a hard-to-track-down problem.

INTRODUCING WINDOWS XP'S NEW HELP AND SUPPORT CENTER

The Windows XP Help and Support Center is accessed directly from the Start menu. Just click the Start button and select Help and Support.

As you can see in Figure 20.1, the Help and Support Center doesn't look anything at all like the intimidating Help system found on older versions of Windows. This Help Center looks and acts just like a Web page, so you can click Back and Forward through the relevant resources. (See the buttons at the top of the window–the same ones you have on Internet Explorer.)

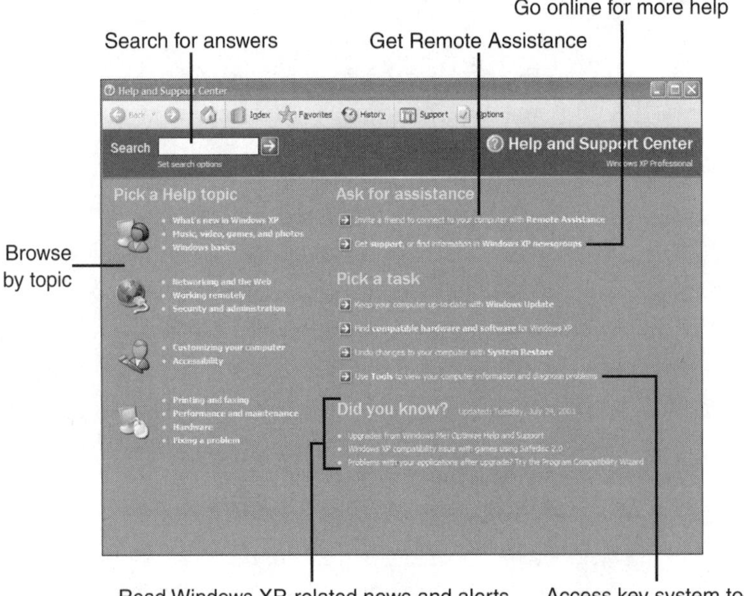

Figure 20.1

Microsoft's new and improved Help and Support Center.

The Help and Support Center is divided into five main areas, each offering a slightly different type of help.

Search for Help

At the top of the window, below the browser toolbar, is a big Search box. You can use this Search box to search XP's built-in Help database—and more.

When you enter a query, you not only search Windows XP's built-in Help, you also (if you're connected to the Internet) search the Microsoft Knowledge Base. (I'll discuss the Knowledge Base a little later in this chapter. Suffice to say that it's Microsoft's premier online database of technical information.)

The results of your search, as shown in Figure 20.2, are displayed in a Search Results pane. There are three categories of results:

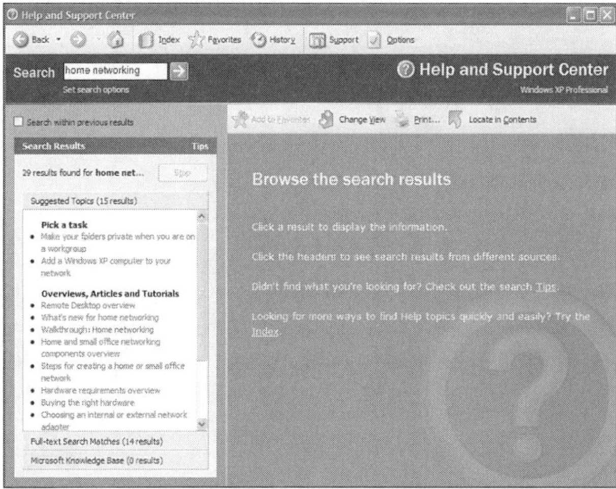

Figure 20.2

The results of a typical Help search in Windows XP.

- Click the Suggested Topics header and you see those topics in the built-in Help system that directly pertain to your query.
- Click the Full-Text Search Matches header and you see all articles that contain a reference to the words in your query.
- Click the Microsoft Knowledge Base header and you'll see those Knowledge Base articles that are relevant to your query.

Click a Search Results link to read the entire Help article in the right-hand pane.

Browse for Help

The entire left side of the Help and Support Center window is titled Pick a Help Topic. This is where you can browse through specific topics, such as Networking and the Web and Customizing Your Computer. The help in this area consists of the typical shorter Help files, as well as a few longer overview articles.

Of particular note in this section is the link for Fixing a Problem. Click this link and you access all of Windows XP's Troubleshooters. These are semi-interactive procedures that walk you through troubleshooting specific problems.

For example, if you have a problem with your home network, you'd start the Networking Troubleshooter (shown in Figure 20.3). The Troubleshooter will ask you a series of questions, suggestion various things to try at each step. You continue stepping through the screens and answering the questions until you fix your problem or you run out of options, whichever comes first.

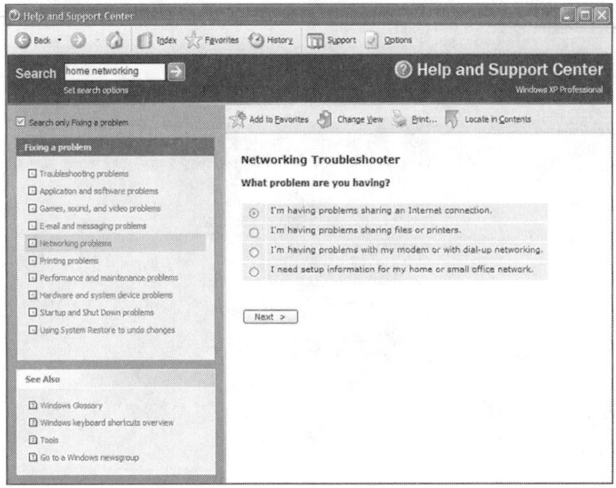

Figure 20.3

Use Windows XP's troubleshooters to step through potential solutions to common problems.

For more information on figuring out Windows XP problems, turn to Chapter 24, "Troubleshooting Common Problems."

Go Online for Help

At the top right of the Help and Support Center window is a section labeled Ask for Assistance. There are two links in this section, each of which calls up a different type of help.

The first link invites you to invite a "friend" to connect to your computer with Remote Assistance. This is how you let other users take over your computer via remote control to look for hard-to-find problems. I'll talk a lot more about this feature in the "Getting Remote Assistance" section, later in this chapter.

The second link, when clicked, opens the Support part of the Help and Support Center—which is, essentially, online support. From here you can go online to Microsoft's Web site for additional information, or link to one of Microsoft's official newsgroups.

Being able to supplement the built-in help with various online resources is an important feature of Windows XP. Despite the improved interface, the amount of text-based help that Microsoft builds into Windows XP isn't a whole lot more (or better) than the help in previous versions of the operating system. Which means that what's available is fairly thin, hard to understand, and not always the most up-to-date information.

If you want more—and more up-to-date—information, you need to go online. There are a wealth of useful resources available at Microsoft's Web site. (As well as at third-party sites and in various Usenet newsgroups, as you'll shortly see.)

Once you open the Support window (from the link in the main Help and Support Center window, or by clicking the Support button in the window's toolbar), you have three options in the Support pane. The first option opens the Remote Assistance utility (discussed later in this chapter). The second option takes you online to the Microsoft Personal Support Center. The third option takes you to one of Microsoft's official newsgroups.

Microsoft's online support isn't the only help you can find on the Internet. I'll talk more about online help resources in the "Finding More Help Online" section, later in this chapter.

The Microsoft Personal Support Center

Your first choice should always be the Get Help From Microsoft option. Assuming that you're connected to the Internet, clicking this option turns the right side of the Help window into a Web browser, and directs you to the Microsoft Personal Support Center Web site.

You can access the Microsoft Personal Support Center directly by entering the `support.microsoft.com/directory/` URL into Internet Explorer.

This site, shown in Figure 20.4, serves as the gateway to all of Microsoft's support services, including the indispensable Microsoft Knowledge Base. This site is a great clearinghouse for a ton of FAQs, service releases, patches, and program updates. (The updates are found in the Microsoft Download Center, accessible from the main Support Center page or directly at `www.microsoft.com/downloads/`.)

Here's some of what you can find on Microsoft's product support site:

- Product FAQs (Frequently Asked Questions)
- Software updates, patches, and service packs
- New and updated device drivers
- Utilities and add-ons for Microsoft software
- Links to Microsoft's Usenet newsgroups
- Webcasts of product presentations by Microsoft support professionals

- Forms to send support questions direct to Microsoft technical support
- Listing of Microsoft technical support phone numbers

Plus, of course, the Microsoft Knowledge Base.

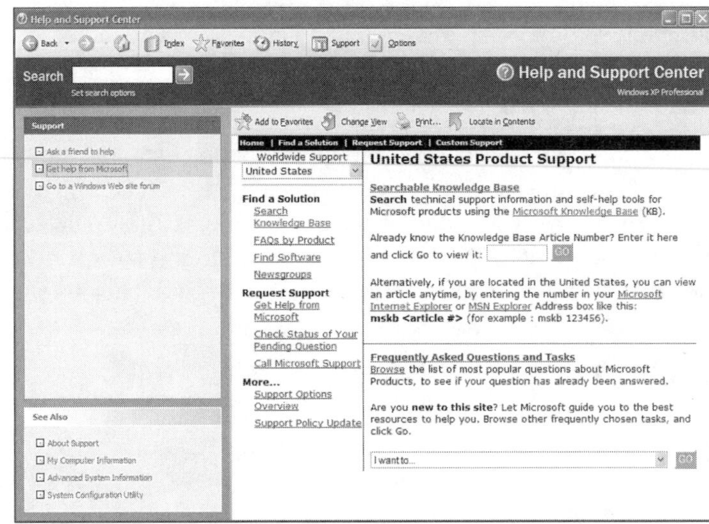

Figure 20.4

The Microsoft Personal Support Center—the gateway for all of Microsoft's online technical support.

The Microsoft Knowledge Base

The Microsoft Knowledge Base is a database of thousands of articles describing various technical problems and issues for all of Microsoft's software products. It is *the* place to look for solutions to your most troubling Windows XP problems.

If you can't find it anywhere else, it's probably in the Knowledge Base.

You can use your browser to go directly to the Knowledge Base Search page at `search.support.microsoft.com/kb/`.

As you can see in Figure 20.5, the Knowledge Base Search page lets you search by a number of key parameters. You start by selecting which product you're having trouble with, choose to conduct a Keyword Search, and then enter your question in the My Question Is box. Click the Go icon, and your query is sent to the Knowledge Base.

Microsoft now displays a list of Knowledge Base articles that match your query. Click an article's header to read the full article.

The articles in the Knowledge Base are written by and for technical professionals. As such they can sometimes be a little dry and jargony. Try to ignore the geek speak and drill down to the specific solutions suggested. Since these solutions come direct from Microsoft's staff, they're of particularly high quality.

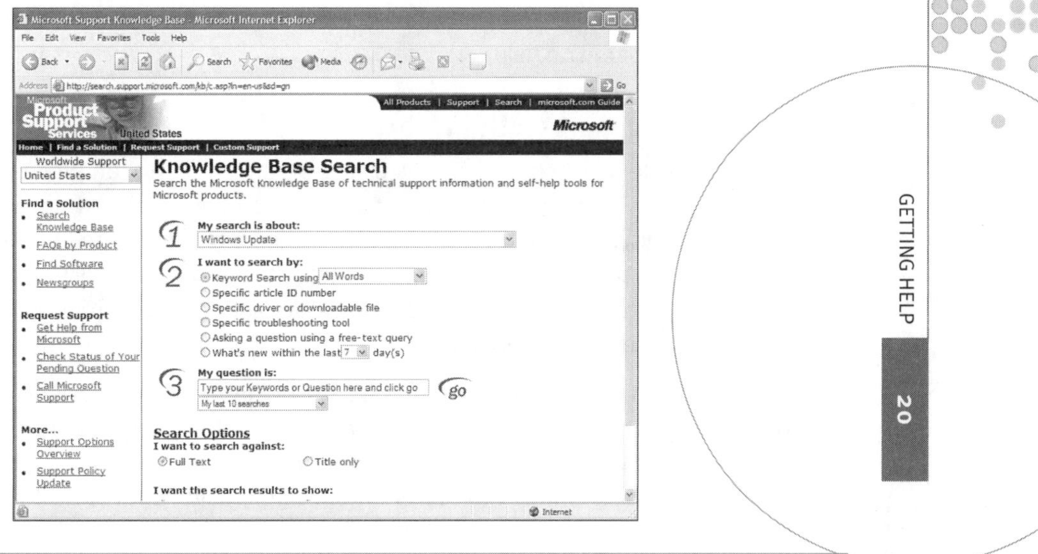

Figure 20.5

Find technical answers to technical problems in the Microsoft Knowledge Base.

I'd go so far as to say that the Knowledge Base is your best bet for finding solutions for most Windows problems. This is particularly true if you're somewhat familiar with technical issues, and don't mind getting your hands dirty with technical solutions to these technical problems.

Access Windows System Tools

In the middle of the right side of the Help and Support Center Window is the Pick A Task section. This section doesn't offer the traditional text-based help that you're used to. Instead, it links to various Windows XP system tools that you can use to troubleshoot and fix problems, as well as restore and configure your system. See Chapter 22, "Keeping Windows Healthy and Happy," for more information on these useful utilities.

Read News and Alerts

Finally we come to the bottom right of the Help and Support Center window. This section doesn't offer help, per se, but rather displays the latest news and announcements regarding the operation of Windows XP. These listings get updated whenever you connect to the Internet, and link to various online stories and resources. Click a link to read the article or alert.

FINDING MORE HELP ONLINE

As good as Microsoft's online technical support is (and it's pretty good, I must admit), it's not the only technical support available on the Internet. Read on and I'll tell you about my favorite sites for online help.

Technical Support on the Web

There are quite a few computer-related sites on the Web that can prove useful when you need help with Windows XP. Some of these sites offer news and reviews, while others incorporate discussion forums where you can post questions, get answers, and maybe even help out someone else. Still more sites offer drivers and utilities for downloading, deliver online tutorials and How-Tos, or provide free or fee-based technical support from experts (both real and self-professed).

I'd be remiss to my employer if I didn't single out the TechTV site (`www.techtv.com`) as one of the best of these sites. Our site offers a nice mix of current tech news stories, in-depth overviews and reviews, and pure, sound, technical advice. Plus, you can watch various TechTV broadcasts through the links on our home page. It's a site I'd frequent even if I didn't work for them!

Learn more about TechTV's Web site in Appendix D, "A Tour of TechTV."

That self promotion out of the way, here's a short list of some of the other technical sites on the Web:

- **Active-Hardware** (`www.active-hardware.com`). This is a PC hardware-oriented site, complete with tech news, reviews, and a large selection of downloadable device drivers.
- **Click & Learn** (`www.mkdata.dk/click/`). This easy-to-use site offers hundreds of illustrated guides and tutorials for all manner of technical topics, from adapters to ZIP drives.
- **CMPnet** (`www.cmpnet.com`). CMPnet is one of the larger networks of technical sites on the Web, offering news and information from the CMP magazine group.
- **CNET** (`www.cnet.com`). I have to reveal that CNET is the number-one competitor to TechTV in broadcast media, and hope that that doesn't bias me when it comes to their online efforts. I have lots of good things to say about CNET's network of Web sites, which is where the company really shines. CNET is really a tech portal, with a network of sites that offer tech news, file and driver downloads, hardware and software reviews, and how-to and help information.
- **Computing.Net** (`www.computing.net`). This site does a good job of centralizing technical support for all operating systems and types of computers. The best part of the site is the support forums, organized by operating system (Windows 9x,

Windows XP, Linux, and so on). Also useful are the numerous FAQs that contain answers to the most common questions asked in the forums, a huge listing of downloadable hardware drivers, a number of How-Tos for solving common problems, and a section just for novices.

- **DriverGuide.com** (`www.driverguide.com`). This is *the* place to look for updated device drivers—which you'll need if you're upgrading an older system to Windows XP. The site consists of a massive database of drivers, compiled from the site's users.
- **Experts Exchange** (`www.experts-exchange.com`). This site is billed as "the #1 professional collaboration network." It works on a type of bonus system, where you answer questions on a topic for another user, and then earn points towards getting *your* questions answered by other experts.
- **FixWindows** (`www.fixwindows.com`). If you're having problems with any version of Windows, then FixWindows (`www.fixwindows.com`) is the site for you. This is a great site for finding and fixing all manner of Windows-related problems. Especially useful are the site's numerous Troubleshooting Flowcharts.
- **PCsupport.com** (`www.pcsupport.com`). This site offers a combination of automated online support tools, searchable "knowledge directories" of more than 2200 hardware and software products, and 24/7 live support from certified technical experts. Some of this is free, some is fee-based. (This site recently acquired MyHelpDesk, another of my favorite tech support sites, and integrated that site's content and services into the PCsupport.com site.)
- **SuperSite for Windows** (`www.winsupersite.com`). Hosted by technical author Paul Thurrott, this is one of the top sites for news, reviews, tips, and advice regarding all versions of Microsoft's Windows operating system.
- **Tom's Hardware Guide** (`www.tomshardware.com`). This is simply one of the best PC hardware sites on the Internet. It features tons of information you can use to either troubleshoot or soup up your system.
- **WinDrivers.com** (`www.windrivers.com`). The main feature of this site is its huge library of downloadable Windows device drivers from practically every vendor in existence. Also features Windows-related hardware support.
- **ZDNet** (`www.zdnet.com`). This tech portal, now owned by CNET, combines all the technology news and information from *PC Magazine, Macworld,* and other Ziff-Davis magazines. (Disclaimer: TechTV used to be part of the old Ziff-Davis organization, and I used to write for various Ziff-Davis magazines.)

Technical Newsgroups

When you have a particular technical question you need answered, you can try searching through Windows XP's Help system, or browsing through the various technical Web sites I just listed. You may have better luck, however, in a Usenet newsgroup devoted to your particular technical issue. Usenet is where the real techno-geeks hang out, and posting a question in a newsgroup can bring surprisingly fast (and surprisingly insightful) answers.

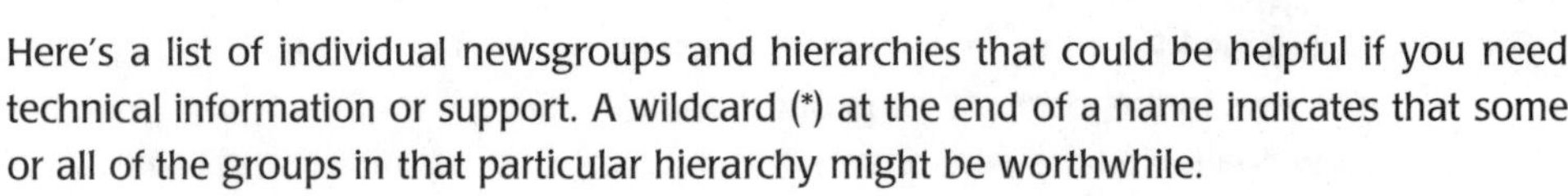

Here's a list of individual newsgroups and hierarchies that could be helpful if you need technical information or support. A wildcard (*) at the end of a name indicates that some or all of the groups in that particular hierarchy might be worthwhile.

- `alt.comp`
- `alt.comp.hardware.*`
- `alt.comp.periphs.*`
- `alt.computer`
- `comp.misc`
- `comp.os.ms-windows.*`
- `comp.periphs`
- `comp.periphs.*`
- `comp.sys.ibm.pc.hardware.*`
- `microsoft.public.windowsxp.*`

This last hierarchy might not be found on every public newsgroup server. These are the newsgroups that Microsoft hosts on its own msnews.microsoft.com newsgroup server. You can also access these newsgroups by clicking the Go to a Windows Web Site Forum link in the Support window.

You can sometimes find the answers to your questions in older newsgroup articles. When you want to search the Usenet archives, go to Google Groups (`groups.google.com`). Google recently purchased the old Deja.com/DejaNews site, which had been archiving Usenet articles almost from day one. If somebody posted it, you can find it here!

GETTING REMOTE ASSISTANCE

For many users, the best source of technical help isn't found within Windows, nor is it found online. The best help, more often than not, is provided by someone you know—someone more technical than you who can help you walk through the steps it takes to solve your PC problems.

I know about this kind of help because I'm often a provider of it. I've mentioned earlier in this book that my dad depends on me to help him fix any computer problems he runs into. Well, my dad isn't the only one—and I'm not the only guy who serves the role of unofficial technical support specialist.

Asking a friend for help is great if your friend is nearby and can stop by for a few beers and a little keyboard punching. But what do you do if your technical friend lives halfway across town—or halfway across the country?

Microsoft added a neat little feature to Windows XP that lets your own personal tech support guy do his thing, from wherever he happens to be today. Remote Assistance, as

Microsoft calls it, essentially lets you hand over control of your computer to another user. Assuming that you're both connected to the Internet (or to the same local area network), the tech support person can fully operate your computer from his own desktop, which makes it easier to track down and solve truly vexing problems.

Naturally, this feature can be used not only by technical friends and family, but also by professional technical support staff. If your computer is part of a large corporate network, your corporate tech support folks can now do their thing remotely. If you need a Microsoft support person to troubleshoot a Windows-specific problem, that can also be arranged.

Any Windows XP user (Home Edition or Professional) can be the recipient of Remote Assistance. The user performing Remote Assistance, however, has to have Windows XP Professional installed on their machine.

The first step to using Remote Assistance is to ask for help—literally. You have to open the Help and Support Center and click the Remote Assistance link in the Ask for Assistance section. When the Remote Assistance screen appears, click the Invite Someone to Help You link. When the next screen appears (as shown in Figure 20.6), you get to pick how you want to contact your "assistant." (That's Microsoft's word. I like to think of myself as a "technoslave.")

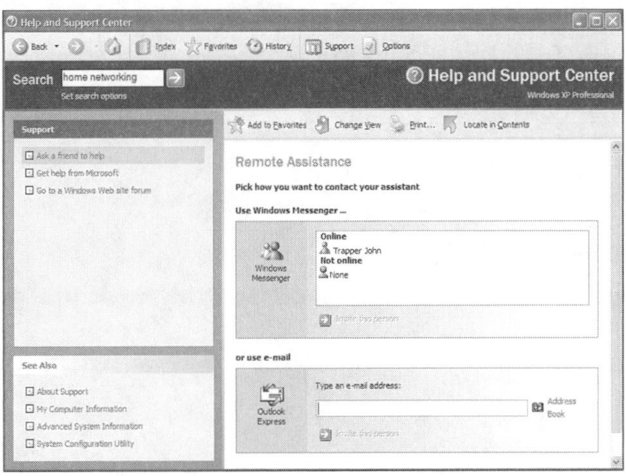

Figure 20.6

Ask a more technical user to help you via Remote Assistance.

You can choose to contact your assistant with Windows Messenger, or via e-mail. Messenger is good if your assistant is also a Messenger user and happens to be online at the time. E-mail is a more sure-fire way to get in touch with them.

As you proceed through the screens, you'll be asked to set a time where your invitation can be accepted. (In other words, when you want your helper to perform his or her magic.) You'll also provide your assistant with a password, which is necessary to gain remote access to your system.

Be extremely careful when handing out permissions and passwords to access your system remotely. Make sure it's either someone you know, or a certified professional from Microsoft or some similar responsible organization.

When the time comes, make sure your computer is connected to the Internet. (Or, if you're getting corporate help, that it's connected to the office LAN.) Your assistant will use the Windows XP Professional version of Remote Assistance (called Remote Access, as discussed in Chapter 19, "Using Windows XP on Portable PCs") to gain access to your PC. You must be logged out at the time, as Remote Assistance treats your remote assistant as a separate user—and only one user can be logged in at a time.

Your remote assistant will now have total control over your computer. Your desktop will appear on his screen, and his keyboard and mouse will provide input to your system. He can launch programs, run system diagnostic tools, and upgrade and install device drivers.

If you picked the right assistant, you'll have your problems fixed in short order. If not—well, there are other technoslaves out there....

JIM'S TOP TEN TIPS

Probably the most important thing Microsoft did in regards to improving user help in Windows XP was to make the operating system itself more robust. Fewer crashes and fewer problems mean less need for technical support of all types. If it don't break, you don't need help to fix it.

Still, Windows XP *is* a Microsoft product, so it probably will break, at some point in time. When you need help with Windows, then, remember these ten tips:

1. Microsoft has totally revamped its old Help system, which is now called the Help and Support Center.
2. For traditional text-based help, you can search for specific information (using the Search box) or browse through general topics (in the Pick a Help Topic section.)
3. If you don't know the cause of a problem, click the Fixing a Problem link to open one of Windows XP's interactive Troubleshooters. Walk through the questions and suggestions to try and isolate the cause of your current problem.
4. The Help and Resource Center also functions as a central access point for Windows XP's key system maintenance and troubleshooting utilities. The best of these utilities are listed in the Pick a Task section.
5. If you can't find your answer in the built-in Help files, click the Support button to go online and search Microsoft's vast repository of Internet-based help resources.
6. If you want to access Microsoft's online help through your browser, go directly to the Microsoft Personal Support Center at `support.microsoft.com/directory/`.
7. Microsoft also offers a number of company-supported Usenet newsgroups for technical support issues. You can find them in the microsoft.public.windowsxp.* hierarchy, at the msnews.microsoft.com newsgroup server.
8. You don't have to limit yourself to Microsoft's technical resources. There are a ton of computer-oriented sites on the Web that can help you with various technical problems—including the official site of TechTV at `www.techtv.com`.
9. If there's no way you can figure out your problems on your own, use XP's Remote Assistance feature to let a technical professional (or just a savvy friend) take control of your entire system by remote control. While connected, a remote assistant can launch programs, run troubleshooting utilities, and even download and install new and updated device drivers.
10. To be on the receiving end of Remote Assistance, all you need is a copy of Windows XP Home Edition and an Internet connection. To control another computer, you need to be running Windows XP Professional.

CHAPTER 21

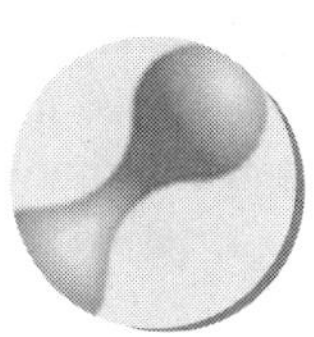

UPDATING WINDOWS

- Picking and Choosing Windows Components
- Downloading and Extracting Device Drivers
- Updating Windows Online
- Transferring Files and Settings
- Creating an Emergency Startup Disk—or Not
- Jim's Top Ten Tips

Keeping Windows updated is a full-time job. Up until recently, Microsoft saved up all its bug fixes, program patches, and driver updates and threw them all into annual "service packs." Installing a service pack was a big deal, as it ended up being a rather major update. It also took a lot of time, and had to be planned for.

Thanks to Microsoft's assuming that every single customer has a persistent Internet connection, we're now spared the huge hassle of those enormous service packs. Instead, Windows XP goes online and updates itself on a regular basis, downloading much smaller files and fixing bugs much quicker than was possible before.

Of course, you still have your Windows XP installation CD. (You do, don't you? You should—as you'll learn in this chapter, it's important.) And on that CD are additional utilities and applications that probably weren't installed when you first installed Windows XP.

That's because XP's default installation doesn't install everything that's available. Microsoft figures that there are some utilities that only a few users will need, so it doesn't install them. They're still available, of course, from the Windows XP installation CD. But if you want them, you have to install them manually, after the fact.

(I like the way Microsoft assumes that it knows precisely how I use my computer. I don't know how I could get by without Microsoft doing my thinking for me!)

In this chapter I'll cover a lot of odds and ends that all have something to do with supplementing the basic Windows XP installation. If you pick up anything from this chapter it should be this: Hang on to your Windows XP installation CD!

PICKING AND CHOOSING WINDOWS COMPONENTS

There may come an occasion where you go to use a particular aspect of Windows XP, and find that it isn't installed on your system. Windows may ask you to insert your installation CD and install the missing component automatically. Or you may have to manually install these components that weren't part of the default installation.

As long as you have your original Windows XP installation CD, this is an easy thing to do. Just follow these steps:

1. From the Control Panel, click the Add or Remove Programs icon.
2. When the Add or Remove Programs utility opens, click the Add/Remove Windows Components button.
3. This launches the Windows Components Wizard, shown in Figure 21.1. Components already installed are marked with a checkmark. Components not installed are not checked.

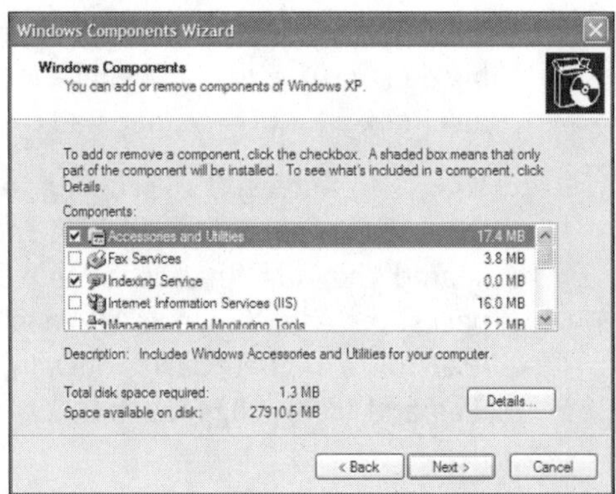

Figure 21.1

Use the Windows Components Wizard to install any components not installed as part of the default Windows XP installation.

4. Check those new components you want to install. If a component has optional subcomponents, click the Details button to check or uncheck those individual items.
5. Click the Next button, make sure your installation CD is inserted, and follow the onscreen instructions to complete the installation.

DOWNLOADING AND EXTRACTING DEVICE DRIVERS

Sometimes the new component you need is actually a device driver. This is particularly true if you install a new piece of hardware, and Windows can't locate a driver for the hardware through its normal means.

Extracting from a .CAB File

Microsoft stores many of its key Windows system files, pre-installation, in compressed *cabinet* files. These files are kind of like Zip files, except they have the .CAB extension.

One key .CAB file that Windows downloads to your hard disk during the installation process is the **driver.cab** file. This compressed file, typically located in the **\windows\driver cache\i386** folder, contains thousands of smaller driver files. Chances are if you need a new driver, it's in the **driver.cab** file.

Because .CAB files are hidden files in hidden directories, you have to reset your Folder options to show hidden and system files. You do this by opening the Folder Options utility (from within the Control Panel), selecting the View tab, and then checking the Show Hidden and Files Option and *unchecking* the Hide Protected Operating System Files option.

If you know which driver file you're looking for, it's relatively easy to extract it from the **driver.cab** file. Just follow these steps:

1. From within My Computer, navigate to the folder that contains the **driver.cab** file.
2. Right-click the **driver.cab** file and select Explore from the pop-up menu.
3. My Computer now displays the entire contents of the **driver.cab** file. Find the file you want to extract and click it.
4. When the Select a Destination dialog box appears, select where you want to extract the file to, then click the Extract button.

The file you selected will now be extracted, and used for whatever purposes you need.

In some older versions of Windows, the operating system downloaded the entire contents of the installation CD (or installation disks) into .CAB files on your computer's hard drive. It was possible, then, to create a copy of the installation CD by extracting all the .CAB files and burning them to a blank CD-R. Unfortunately, this trick is not possible with Windows XP. (Microsoft doesn't want you making illegal copies of its installation CDs!)

Downloading from the Internet

If you need a new device driver for a particular piece of hardware, there are several places you can look for that driver. First, Windows might have its own driver for that device. Second, a driver might exist in the Windows' **drivers.cab** file, as just discussed. Third, a driver might exist on any installation CD or disk that came with the hardware. Fourth, the hardware manufacturer might have new drivers available for downloading from its official Web site. Fifth, Microsoft might have drivers available at its Web site. And sixth, there may be other sites on the Web that might have the necessary file.

When it comes to finding drivers online, you can't go wrong with DriverGuide.com (`www.driverguide.com`). This site, which requires (free) membership, offers you several different ways to find the drivers you need, including links to the manufacturer's official site, as well as links to other official and unofficial sites. Even better is the mammoth user-created driver database. All you have to do is search for a particular manufacturer and model number, and you'll see a list of drivers that helpful users have uploaded for your downloading pleasure.

Even though going to the official site is certainly the recommended way to proceed, I've found that I can almost always find the right drivers faster on DriverGuide.com.

UPDATING WINDOWS ONLINE

If you want to keep your operating system up-to-date, you can go online to Microsoft's official Web site every few days and look for bug fixes, patches, and other updates, then manually download and install the new items as they come available.

Or you can let Windows do it for you.

Windows Update is the online extension of Windows XP that helps you to keep your operating system up-to-date. When Windows Update is activated, it will periodically go online and check in with the main Windows Update Web site. It will notify if you if any new updates are available. You can choose to download the updates, and install them.

Getting Automatic Updates

By default, Windows Update will run in the background and use the Internet to check for updated system files. It will then automatically download and install those files on your PC.

Windows Update runs once a day, when it goes online and checks the Microsoft Web site for updates to the basic operating system. If it finds an update, it downloads the files automatically. Once the files are downloaded, you'll be prompted to install them. (So it's not totally automatic—it's good to have at least a little choice in the matter!)

You can turn off the automatic updating by opening the System Properties dialog box (click System in the Control Panel), selecting the Automatic Updates tab, and making the appropriate changes.

Updating Manually

You can also choose to use Windows Update manually. From the Help and Support Center, go to the Pick a Task section and click the Keep Your Computer Up-to-Date with Windows Update link. You'll now be connected to the Internet and taken to the Windows Update Web site, shown in Figure 21.2.

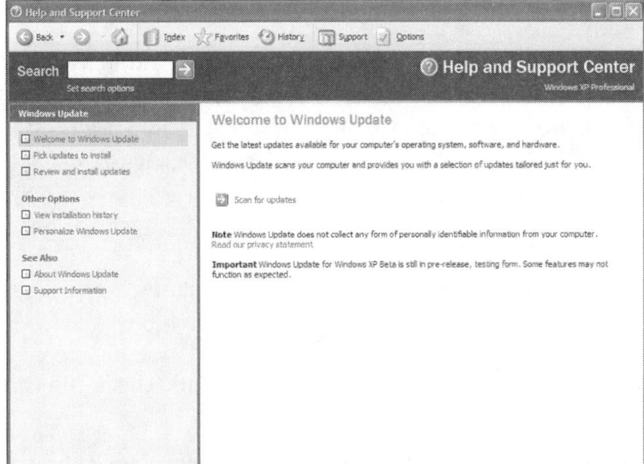

Figure 21.2

Use Windows Update to keep your copy of Windows XP up-to-date.

The site will install the latest version of its software on your PC, and then proceed to scan your computer. Click the Scan for Updates option and you'll then be provided with a list of updates that are available for your particular system. Follow the onscreen instructions to install specific updates.

TRANSFERRING FILES AND SETTINGS

Have you ever bought a new PC, and then spent days—and *days*—trying to get your new PC configured the same way your old one was? Have you ever had to manually add all your Internet Explorer favorites and Address Book contacts to a new installation? Have you ever searched all through your old hard disk, hunting for all the document files you created in the past few years that absolutely, positively have to be copied to your new system? Have you ever wished you'd just stuck with the old PC, since you'd spent so much time getting it configured *just so*?

Microsoft felt your pain.

Windows XP includes a new Files and Settings Transfer Wizard. This wizard lets you pick and choose which files and configuration settings you want to keep when you move to a new machine. It then copies those files, templates, and settings to some form of removable

storage (you can burn a CD or use a Zip disk, or beam the files and settings across a network), which you can take with you to your new machine. Then you run the wizard on the new machine, and copy your old files and settings to the new PC.

So, with a minimum of fuss and muss, your new PC will assume all the personalization of your old PC—complete with all your personal files.

Not a bad deal, eh?

You can run the Files and Settings Transfer Wizard from within Windows XP, or from the Windows XP installation CD (for those older systems running a different version of Windows). Within Windows XP, you launch the wizard by clicking the Start button and then selecting All Programs, Accessories, System Tools, Files and Settings Transfer Wizard.

Copying Your Old Files and Settings

Here's how you copy the files and settings from your old PC.

1. When the wizard launches, click the Next button.
2. When the Which Computer Is This? screen appears, check the Old Computer option, then click Next.
3. When the Select a Transfer Method window appears, select how you want to transfer the files—over a home network, on multiple floppy disks, or from some other removable drive (such as a Zip disk). Click Next.
4. When the What Do You Want to Transfer? screen appears (as shown in Figure 21.3), select whether you want to copy settings, files, or both.

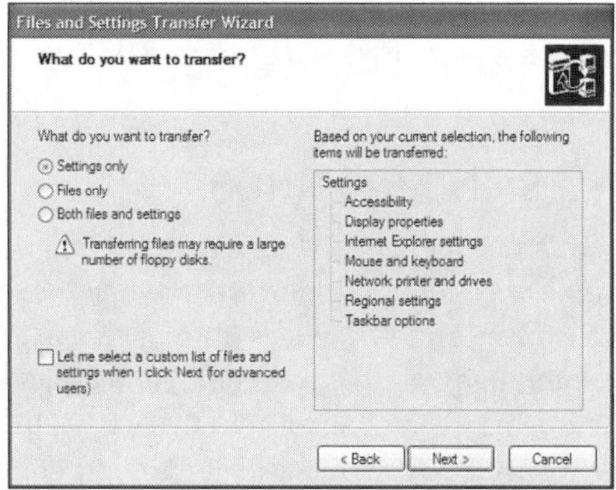

Figure 21.3

Use the Files and Settings Transfer Wizard to copy all the important stuff from your old PC to your new PC.

5. If you want to select specific files and settings to copy, check the Let Me Select a Custom List of Files and Settings option. When you click Next, you'll be able to select specific items to copy.

6. The wizard now collects everything it needs to copy to the new PC. This will take several minutes.
7. You'll now be prompted to insert a disk in your disk drive, or connect to the network, or do whatever is necessary to begin the transfer. Follow the onscreen instructions to complete the procedure.

Transferring Your Files and Settings to a New PC

Now you have to transfer all those files and settings to your new computer. Launch the Files and Transfer Settings Wizard on your new PC, then follow these steps:

1. When the wizard launches, click the Next button.
2. When the Which Computer Is This? screen appears, check the New Computer option, then click Next.
3. When the Where Are the Files and Settings screen appears, select how you've stored the files, then click Next.

The wizard will now transfer the files and settings to your new computer. If you're asked to insert disks, do so. Otherwise, set back and wait for the whole thing to finish. When it's done you may have to reboot your computer, but then it will be up-and-running—and looking and acting just like you're used to!

CREATING AN EMERGENCY STARTUP DISK—OR NOT

In previous versions of Windows you were prompted to create a system disk (sometimes called a startup disk) before you installed the operating system. You would use this disk to boot your system just in case Windows came crashing down around your shoulders and wouldn't start on its own. You'd insert your system disk in your PC's drive A:, and thus get up and running in a minimal fashion. (Enough to start fixing your big Windows problems, in any case.)

Booting from CD

When you install Windows XP, you're *not* asked to create a startup disk. That's because you don't need it anymore. As long as you have your original Windows XP installation CD, you can actually boot from the CD in case you can't start Windows or access your hard disk.

I'll talk more about what to do if you're having trouble starting your system in Chapter 23, "Recovering from System Crashes." Until then, just remember that you'll need your XP installation CD in case you can't start your system any other way.

Another good reason to hold onto that CD!

Booting from MS-DOS

While Windows no longer prompts you to create a Windows startup disk, and provides no obvious means to do so, you can still run into problems that would make it impossible to

boot your system. For example, what do you do when your hard disk is trashed—or you can't use your CD drive for booting?

For these reasons, I still like to have a system disk that I insert into drive A: and boot my system. This is kind of a last resort disk. When nothing else works, I can always boot my system from this disk.

You can use Windows XP's format command to create a bootable MS-DOS floppy disk. Then, if you can't start your PC any other way, you can insert this disk into drive A: and boot into DOS—and use basic DOS commands to access your hard disk and other parts of your system.

To create an MS-DOS startup disk, follow these steps:

1. Insert a blank floppy disk into your PC's floppy drive.
2. From My Computer, right-click your floppy drive icon and select Format from the pop-up menu.
3. When the Format Floppy dialog box appears (shown in Figure 21.4), check the Create an MS-DOS Startup Disk option.
4. Click the Start button to format the disk.

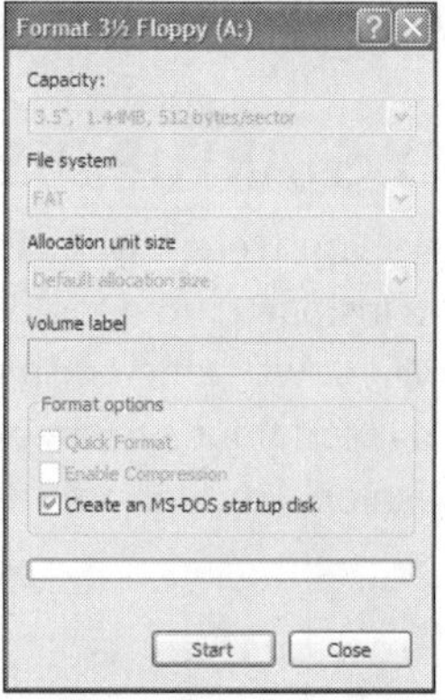

Figure 21.4

Create your own MS-DOS startup disk with Windows XP's format command.

Label this disk something like "MS-DOS Startup" and keep it in a safe place—just in case you ever need it!

JIM'S TOP TEN TIPS

As you've no doubt realized, just because you've completed the formal installation procedure doesn't mean that you're done installing Windows. Keeping Windows XP fresh and up-to-date is a constant process!

Just keep these key points in mind, and you'll always have the latest, greatest version of Windows XP installed on your computer:

1. Whatever you do, you should make sure to *never lose your Windows XP installation CD!* You should store this CD in a safe place, along with the CD key necessary to reinstall the software.
2. Not all of Windows is installed in a default installation. There are other, less-used, components available on the Windows XP installation CD.
3. You install new Windows components by using the Add or Remove Programs utility and the Windows Components Wizard.
4. Additional device drivers are available in the **drivers.cab** file, which Windows should have downloaded to your hard disk. To use one of these drivers, open the **drivers.cab** file, find the driver file you need, and click to extract it.
5. There are more drivers available online, at a variety of sites. Your hardware manufacturer's Web site is a good place to look, as is DriverGuide.com.
6. Windows XP includes the Windows Update utility, which automatically goes online to find updates and patches for your operating system. (You can activate the utility manually by clicking the Windows Update link in the Help and Support Center window.)
7. When you're moving to a new PC, you can transfer all your personal files and settings from your old PC by using the Files and Settings Transfer Wizard. (Make sure you pick a storage medium that's large enough to hold all the files—or hook your two computers up to a network to transfer files directly.)
8. If your old PC doesn't have Windows XP installed, you can run the Files and Setting Transfer Wizard directly from the Windows XP installation CD.
9. Windows XP doesn't require you to make an emergency startup disk, because the operating system can boot from the installation CD.
10. You still should have a bootable floppy disk, however—just in case you can't boot at all from your hard disk or CD drive. You can create an MS-DOS system disk when you format a blank floppy disk.

CHAPTER 22

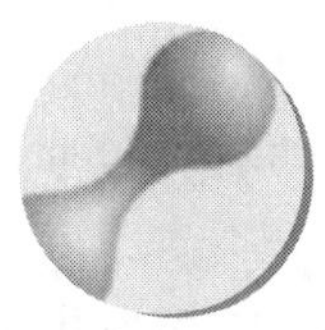

KEEPING WINDOWS HEALTHY AND HAPPY

- Cleaning Up Unnecessary Files
- Defragging Your Disk
- Perform a Hard Disk Checkup with ScanDisk
- Viewing System Performance
- Viewing More System Information
- Displaying Key System Properties
- Managing Your Devices
- Accessing More System Information—and Utilities
- Scheduling Your Maintenance
- Backing Up and Restoring Critical Files
- Managing the Windows Registry
- Jim's Top Ten Tips

Windows XP includes several utilities to help you keep your system running smoothly. These utilities are mainly unchanged since Windows 98, when Microsoft completely overhauled almost all of Windows' system maintenance features.

One thing that has changed in XP is that some of these system tools are a little easier to get to. While you can still find most of these tools by clicking Start, All Programs, Accessories, System Tools, you can also find some of the key tools in the Help and Support Center

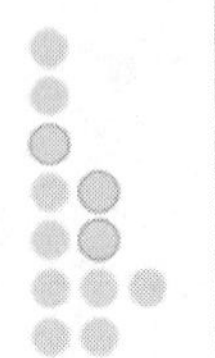

(as discussed in Chapter 20, "Getting Help"). When you click the Use Tools to View Your Computer Information link in the main Help and Support window, Windows displays a list of the most popular support tools. Click any of these links to launch the tool.

(In fact, this is the *only* place to find some of the most popular tools. If you're looking for a tool or utility that used to be on the System Tools menu and isn't there anymore, open the Help and Support Center and look for it there.)

In this chapter I'll discuss the most important the system maintenance utilities found in Windows XP. You should use these tools not only when your system is having problems, but also as part of a regular maintenance routine. A little preventive medicine now can save you from costly computer problems in the future!

CLEANING UP UNNECESSARY FILES

Even with today's humongous hard disks, you can still end up with too many useless files taking up too much hard disk space. Fortunately, Windows XP includes a utility that helps you identify and delete unused files on your hard disk.

Disk Cleanup is a great tool to use when you want to free up extra hard disk space for more frequently used files. When you run Disk Cleanup it identifies unused files and, with your permission, deletes them.

To use Disk Cleanup, click the Start button, then select All Programs, Accessories, System Tools, Disk Cleanup. Disk Cleanup will now start and automatically analyze the contents of your hard disk drive. When it is finished analyzing, it presents the dialog box shown in Figure 22.1.

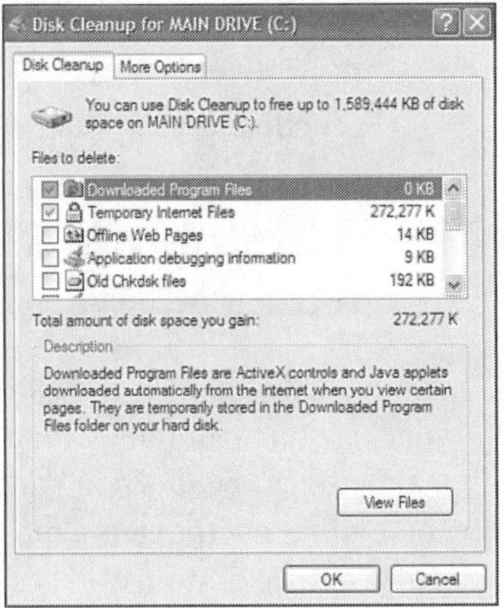

Figure 22.1

Use Disk Cleanup to identify and delete unused files from your hard disk.

Start by selecting the Disk Cleanup tab. You can have Disk Cleanup delete the following types of files:

- **Downloaded Program Files**—These are ActiveX controls and Java applets associated with Web pages you've recently visited. It's normally okay to delete these files. If you need them again, they'll be automatically downloaded at that time.
- **Temporary Internet Files**—These are Web pages cached by your Web browser for faster reloading. It's normally okay to delete these.
- **Offline Web pages**—These are Web pages you've downloaded for offline viewing. If you're done with them, you might as well delete them.
- **Recycle Bin**—This clears all recently deleted files from the Windows Recycle Bin. Check this one if you're sure you won't need to undelete any of these files. (Remember—once you clear a file from the Recycle Bin, it's really truly deleted. You can't get it back!)
- **Temporary Files**—These are hidden files that Windows creates while running various programs. It's normally okay to delete these.
- **Catalog Files for the Content Indexer**—These are files left over from a previous indexing operation that are no longer necessary.

If you want to remove infrequently used programs, Windows components, or older restore points for the System Restore utility, select the More Options tab and make those choices. Otherwise, click OK to begin cleaning up your hard disk.

DEFRAGGING YOUR DISK

If you think that your computer is taking longer than usual to open files, or notice that your hard drive light stays on longer then usual, you may need to defragment your hard drive.

Any time you run an application or when you edit, move, copy, or delete a file, you create file fragments on your hard drive. This type of file fragmentation makes your hard drive work harder to find specific files, and slows down the operation of your entire system.

Fragmentation is sort of like taking the pieces of a jigsaw puzzle and storing them in different boxes along with pieces from other puzzles. The more dispersed the pieces are, the longer it takes to put the puzzle together. So if you notice your system takes longer and longer to open and close files or run applications, you probably need to defragment your drive—in effect, putting all the pieces of the puzzle in one box.

Windows XP's Disk Defragmenter not only defragments your hard drive, it also rearranges files on the drive according to how often you use them. In essence, Disk Defragmenter places those files you use most frequently together near the front of your hard drive, so that they can be accessed more quickly.

To defragment your hard drive, click the Start button, then select All Programs, Accessories, System Tools, Disk Defragmenter. When the Disk Defragmenter utility opens (as shown in Figure 22.2), choose the drive you want to defragment and then click the Defragment button.

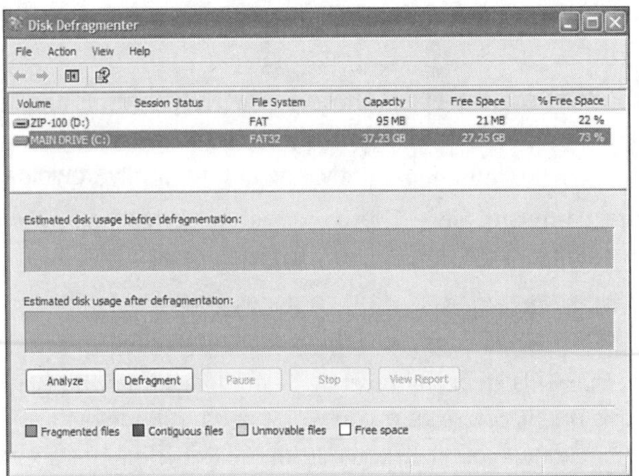

Figure 22.2

Use Disk Defragmenter to improve the efficiency of your hard disk drive.

Defragmenting your drive can take awhile, especially if you have a large hard drive or your drive is really fragmented. So you might want to start the utility and let it run while you are at lunch.

You should close all applications and stop working on your system while Disk Defragmenter is running. This includes disabling your screen saver, deactivating your anti-virus program, and turning off power management's standby mode.

PERFORMING A HARD DISK CHECKUP WITH SCANDISK

Any time you run an application, move or delete a file, or accidentally turn the power off while the system is running, you run the risk of introducing errors to your hard disk. You can find and fix most of these errors from within Windows XP.

Previous versions of Windows included a utility called ScanDisk, which was available in the System Tools folder. This utility has now been built into the tasks available for your system's hard drive. (So don't go looking for it on the System Tools folder—and don't look for it by the ScanDisk name!)

To find and fix errors on any hard drive, open My Computer and right-click on the drive you want to work from. When the pop-up menu appears, select the Properties option, and then select the Tools tab. As you can see in Figure 22.3, there are three tools available to you—Error-Checking, Defragmentation (the Disk Defragmenter utility), and Backup.

(This last option is only available if you're running XP Professional, or if you've manually installed the Backup utility. See the "Backing Up and Restoring Critical Files" section later in this chapter.)

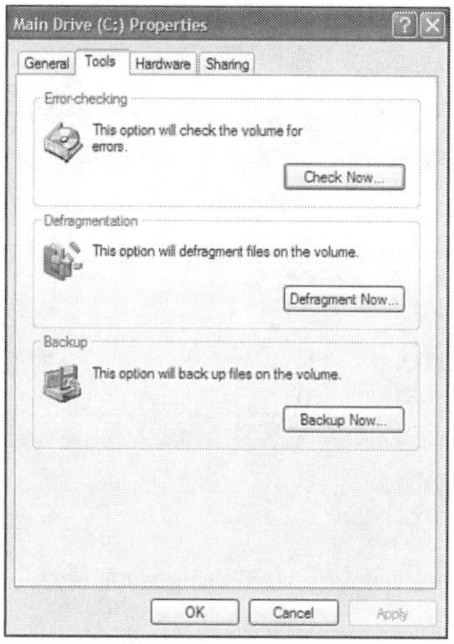

Figure 22.3

Right-click a hard drive to check it for errors.

Click the Check Now button and you'll see the Check Disk dialog box. Check both the options (Automatically Fix File System Errors and Scan For and Attempt Recover of Bad Sectors), then click Start. Windows will now scan your hard disk and try to fix any errors it encounters.

You should run this utility any time you think you're having difficulty with a hard drive. What kind of difficulties should you look for? Some of the more common symptoms are slow disk access, the inability to open a file, and when your system hangs if you're opening or saving a file.

VIEWING SYSTEM PERFORMANCE

The Windows Task Manager, which you now use to shut down unruly applications, also can be used to view the performance of your system. (You open the Task Manager by right-clicking any open portion of the Taskbar, then selecting Task Manager from the pop-up menu.)

As you can see in Figure 22.4, the Task Manager has five tabs. The first tab, Applications, is the one you use when you need to shut down a frozen application. The second tab, Processes, shows every system process that is currently running in memory.

The third tab, Performance, is the one that's really interesting—visually, at least. This tab displays graphs of your system CPU and memory usage. It also displays numerical information about various system parameters, such as physical and kernel memory. It's a fun little tab to watch, if nothing else.

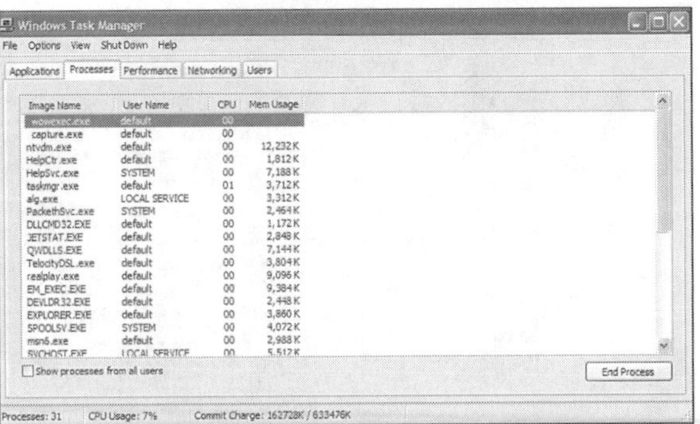

Figure 22.4

Use the Windows Task Manager to view your system's processor and memory usage.

The fourth tab, Networking, displays similar usage graphs for the connections on your network. The fifth tab, Users, simply lists the users current logged on to your PC. (It also lets you log them off or disconnect them.)

VIEWING MORE SYSTEM INFORMATION

Fore even more detailed information about your system, check out the tools available in Windows XP's Help and Support Center. There are two tools here, each offering a different level of system detail.

My Computer Information

Begin by opening the Help and Support Center, clicking the Use Tools link (in the Pick a Task section), and then clicking the My Computer Information link. The My Computer Information tool lets you look at four different reports:

- General system information
- System hardware and software status
- Installed hardware
- Installed Microsoft software

Figure 22.5 shows the General System Information report. The other reports appear in a similar format, and provide a similar depth of information.

Advanced System Information

When you click the Advanced System Information (in the Tools panel), you're presented with five options:

- View detailed system information
- View running services

- View Group Policy settings applied
- View the error log
- View information for another computer

The first option opens the System Information utility, discussed later in this chapter. The other options provide more specific reports regarding the selected function.

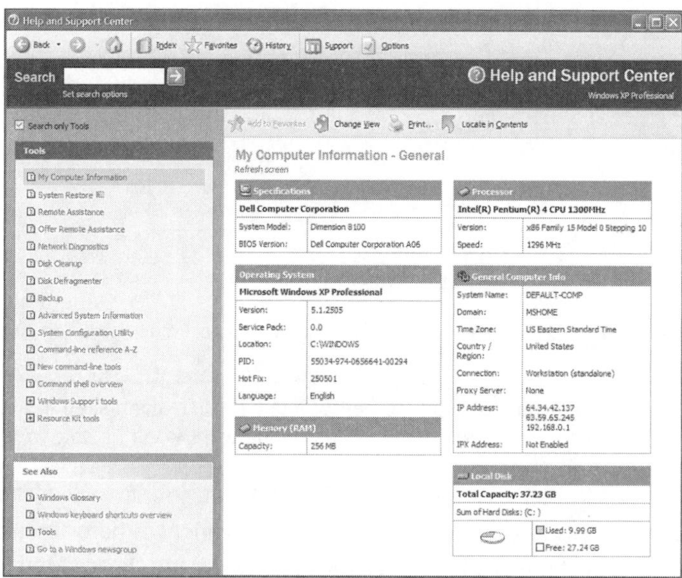

Figure 22.5

View the status of your computer's hardware and software with the My Computer Information tool.

DISPLAYING KEY SYSTEM PROPERTIES

Another place to turn when you want to know more about the pieces and parts of your system is the System Properties utility. You can open this utility from the Control Panel (click the System icon) or by right-clicking My Computer on your desktop and then selecting Properties from the pop-up menu.

In Windows XP there are now seven tabs in the System Properties window. Here's what you'll find on each:

- **General**—This tab (shown in Figure 22.6) displays very basic information about your system—what type of computer you're using, what version of Windows you're running, and your user name.
- **Computer Name**—This tab displays the name and description of your PC as it appears to other computers on your network. Click the Change button to change this information.

Figure 22.6

Access a variety of system properties and information from the System Properties dialog box.

You should avoid changing your computer name if you're connected to network. If you change the name, the other computers on the network won't be able to recognize your computer!

- **Hardware**—This tab serves as a gateway to a variety of hardware-related tools and utilities, including the Add New Hardware Wizard, the Device Manager (discussed next), and Hardware Profiles.
- **Advanced**—This tab serves as a gateway to performance, user profile, and startup and recovery settings.
- **System Restore**—This tab lets you turn off and on and configure the System Restore tool.
- **Automatic Updates**—This tab lets you configure how Windows Update works in the background to find and download updates to the operating system.
- **Remote**—This tab is where you configure the settings for the Remote Assistance feature.

MANAGING YOUR DEVICES

When you open the System Properties dialog box, select the Hardware tab, and click the Device Manager button, you open one of Windows' most important utilities—the Device Manager. You use the Device Manager to view key properties for any device installed on your PC, and change those properties as necessary.

If you're familiar with the Device Manager from Windows 9X/Me, you might be surprised at its slightly different look in Windows XP—as well as its new location. (It used to be a tab on the System Properties dialog box, now you have to click a button to get to it.)

As you can see in Figure 22.7, the Device Manager lists all the devices currently installed on your system. Click a listed device type that has a plus sign beside it, and it displays a list of all the devices that are in that category.

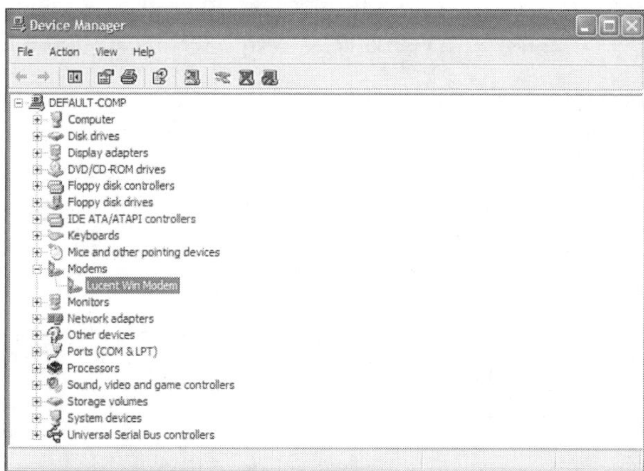

Figure 22.7

Use the Device manager to display and change the properties of any device installed on your system.

For example, when you click the Ports category, you'll see a list of all the ports on your system, including your serial ports and parallel ports. The serial ports are called Communications ports, and the parallel ports are called Printer ports.

Viewing Device Properties—and Conflicts

There are two ways you can organize the devices in the Device Manager–by device type or by connection. Generally, it's easier to organize them by type because it organizes the devices by *what* they are, not *where* they are. You can change the way your devices are displayed by clicking the View menu and selecting an alternate view.

If Windows is reporting a problem with a specific device driver, you'll see a special symbol next to that device. A black exclamation point (!) on a yellow background indicates that the device is in what Microsoft calls a "problem state." A red "X" indicates that the device is currently disabled–probably because the correct driver isn't loaded. A blue "i" on a white background indicates that the device is using a manual configuration instead of the default settings. (This isn't necessarily a bad thing.)

To look at the properties of a device, double-click the device's icon. This opens a Properties window that shows the device specifications and the driver that's running it.

For some devices, you can look at and set which port, IRQ, and memory it uses. However, it's generally a bad idea to mess with those settings because it prevents Windows from reassigning resources should you decide to add or remove devices later.

Resolving Conflicts

If you have a device conflict, open that device's Properties window and select the General tab. You'll now see a message that explains the basic problem and presents the steps Windows recommends to solve it. The message may also display a problem code and number that can be useful when consulting with a technical support specialist.

Sometimes you can resolve a resource conflict by choosing an alternate IRQ and/or memory configuration for the problem device. For example, suppose you have two devices that both want to use IRQ11, and one of them isn't working because of it. You can display the properties for one of the devices by double-clicking it in Device Manager and displaying its Resources tab. At the bottom of the screen, it will report the conflict with the other device.

To fix the conflict, deselect the Use Automatic Settings check box and choose a different configuration from the Settings Based On list. Make sure to choose a configuration that results in No Conflicts being reported in the Conflicting Device List.

If there aren't any suitable configurations to choose from in the Settings Based On list, you can assign an IRQ or memory address manually. To do so, click the one you want (IRQ or Input/Output Range) and then click Change Setting. A box appears in which you can make your selection.

If you see a message that the resource cannot be modified, try the other side of the equation. That is, try to change the resources for the other device involved in the conflict.

Updating Drivers

In some cases you may need to update to a newer version of a device driver. To do this, go to the device's Properties window, select the Driver tab, and then click the Update Driver button. this starts the Update Device Driver Wizard. Click the Next button and then select Search for a Better Driver. Click Next and you'll now be prompted as to *where* you want to search for an upgraded driver. If you have the driver on disk (hard, floppy, or CD-ROM), select the appropriate option. If you prefer to go out on the Internet and search Microsoft's Web site for an updated driver, select Microsoft Windows Update. Once a new driver is found, you can use the rest of the Wizard to install and configure the new driver.

If you install a new driver and things all of a sudden stop working properly, there's something wrong with the new driver. Maybe it's the wrong driver, or maybe the driver file is corrupt. Whatever the cause, you need to abandon the new driver and revert back to the previous one—the one that was working okay. You can do this easily by clicking the Roll Back Driver button. This "rolls back" the driver to the previous version, which should get your system up and running again.

ACCESSING MORE SYSTEM INFORMATION—AND UTILITIES

There's one more utility you need to be familiar with. That's because it displays even more valuable system information—and serves as a gateway to even *more* system tools that you can't find anyplace else.

System Information

The utility I'm talking about is called System Information. You open it by clicking the Start button, and then selecting All Programs, Accessories, System Tools, System Information.

As you can see in Figure 22.8, the left pane of the System Information window displays information about the five key parts of your system: Hardware Resources, Components, Software Environment, Internet Explorer, and Applications. Click the "+" next to one of the categories to display additional subcategories. When you highlight a specific subcategory, information about that topic appears in the right pane.

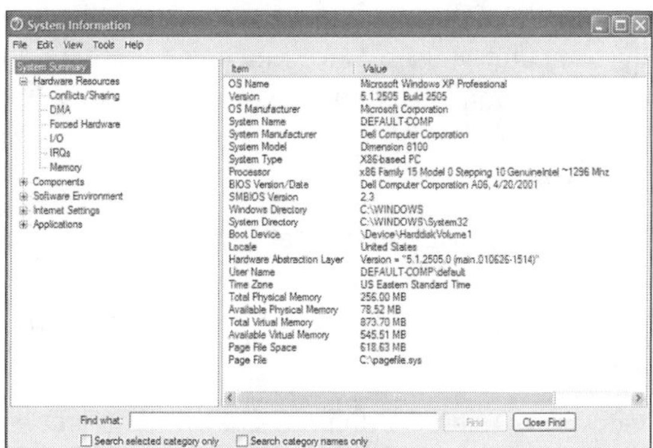

Figure 22.8

Use System Information to view more detailed information about your system—and to access a variety of technical tools.

System Information is particularly useful for finding device conflicts. Open the Hardware Resources category and then select Conflicts/Sharing. The right pane will now display a list of all shared IRQs—one of which is probably causing your current problem. Identify the problem IRQ, and then use the Device Manager to either reconfigure or reinstall the device to use a different IRQ.

Windows XP uses System Information not only as a utility onto itself, but also as a kind of gateway to a number of other system utilities. Many of the so-called "hidden" tools (which I discuss next) are accessible from the Tools menu in the System Information window. Some of these utilities are a bit technical in terms of what they monitor or do, but if you're having problems with some new piece of hardware you've installed, you'll probably find at least some of these utilities useful when you go to troubleshoot your problem.

Net Diagnostics

The Network Diagnostics utility scans your system and gathers information about the network connections you've set up. This tool is designed to provide technical personnel with the information necessary to troubleshoot a variety of network-related problems.

System Restore

This starts the System Restore utility that I discuss in Chapter 23, "Recovering from System Crashes."

File Signature Verification Utility

Windows XP's File Signature Verification Utility locates signed and unsigned files on your system. Digitally signed files have been granted a Microsoft digital signature that states that the file is an unaltered copy of the original file. Unsigned files are less trustworthy.

To be honest, I can't find a lot of use for this particular utility, outside the occasional hunt for files altered by computer viruses. Since antivirus programs do a much better job of hunting down these files, I don't know when you'd actually use this utility.

DirectX Diagnostic Tool

The DirectX Diagnostic Tool provides information about any DirectX components and drivers installed on your system. It also provides a way to test their sound and graphics output, and you also use the tool to disable or adjust particularly problematic hardware acceleration features.

Like many of Windows' so-called hidden tools, this one is probably more useful to tech support personnel than it is to normal users. The information gathered by this utility can provide useful technical information about any problems you encounter when running DirectX applications.

As you can see in Figure 22.9, information about different DirectX components and drivers are displayed on separate tabs in the DirectX Diagnostic Tool window. For example, the System tab displays basic system information, while the DirectX Files tab displays the properties for each DirectX file installed on your system.

If you're having trouble running DirectX applications on your system, examine the file listings on these tabs for any obvious discrepancies. For example, if an input device (such as a joystick) isn't working, go to the Input tab and make sure that that particular device is listed. You might also want to go to the DirectX Files tab and look in the Attributes column for any file that is not labeled *Final Retail*. (It's possible that a specific application has gotten out the door without all the final files in place, which can cause the application to run slower than normal, erratically, or not at all.) In other words, examine the listings on each tab, and look for any items that aren't like the others—chances are that's the file that's causing your current problem.

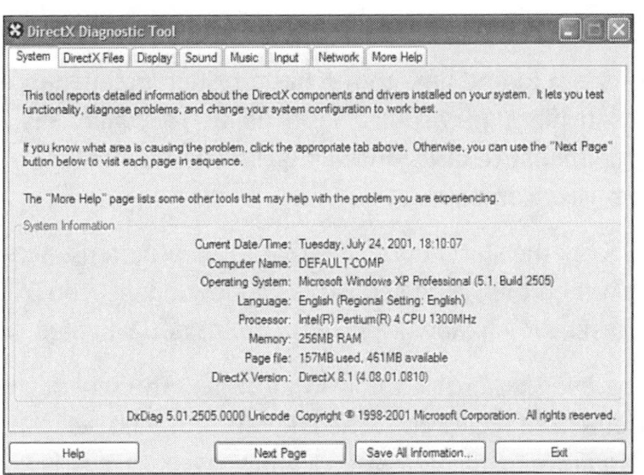

Figure 22.9

Use the DirectX Diagnostic Tool to test and configure your system's DirectX components.

Dr. Watson

Dr. Watson, shown in Figure 22.10, is a familiar tool to experienced Windows users. It takes a snapshot of your system whenever a system fault occurs, which aids in the diagnosis of tricky problems.

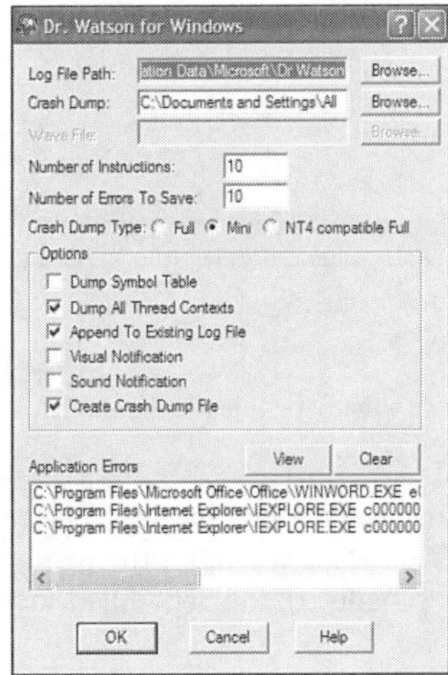

Figure 22.10

Use Dr. Watson to help you diagnose problems with your system.

By intercepting software faults, Dr. Watson identifies the software that failed, and offers a general description of the cause. In some cases, Dr. Watson will diagnosis the problem and offer a suggested course of action. You can also feed the information that Dr. Watson collects to tech support personnel; it will often provide the detailed technical information they need to find and fix tricky system problems.

SCHEDULING YOUR MAINTENANCE

If you can never seem to find time to run basic system maintenance, you should be glad that Windows XP includes a Scheduled Tasks utility. This utility lets you automatically run various system maintenance tasks—including Disk Defragmenter and Disk Cleanup—while you're away from your computer.

To use this utility, click the Start button, then select All Programs, Accessories, System Tools, Scheduled Tasks. When the Scheduled Tasks window opens, you'll find that several maintenance-related tasks are already displayed. They're not activated, but they're displayed.

To turn on a scheduled task, click the icon to display the scheduling dialog box, like the one shown in Figure 22.11. Click the Schedule tab, and then select how often you want to run the task. If you're scheduling a disk cleanup, once a week is good. If you're scheduling disk defragmenting, once a month should be sufficient. Click OK to schedule the task.

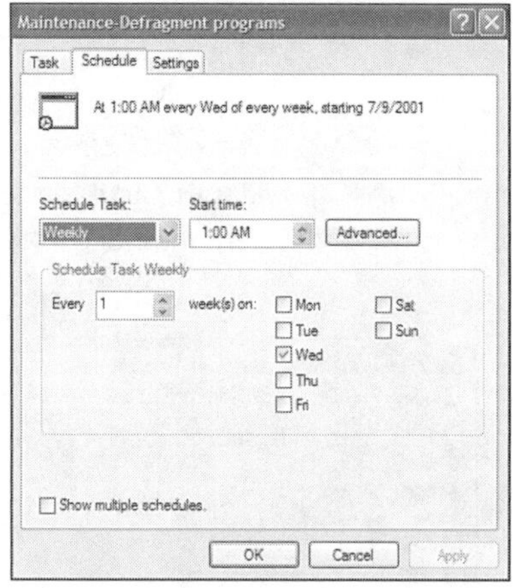

Figure 22.11

Schedule key maintenance activities with the Scheduled Tasks utility.

For a scheduled task to run, your computer has to be turned on during the scheduled maintenance periods. Windows XP will *not* turn on your PC for you! If your PC is turned off when maintenance is scheduled, the Scheduled Task utility simply skips that scheduled activity.

If you want to schedule a task that hasn't already been created, click the Add Scheduled Task icon. This launches the Scheduled Task Wizard, which walks you through the selection and scheduling of a particular activity.

BACKING UP AND RESTORING CRITICAL FILES

I always tell my friends that they need to back up the critical files on their PC on a regular basis. They don't always listen to me (to be honest, they seldom—if *ever*—listen to me!), but it's still good advice. Even if it's advice I don't always follow myself.

If you're running Windows XP Home Edition, you may think that Microsoft took the tried-and-true Microsoft Backup utility out of the new operating system. This isn't the case. It's still there, it's just not installed by default. (In the Home Edition, that is. Microsoft Backup *is* installed by default in XP Professional.)

To use the Backup utility, you'll need to install it from your Windows XP Installation CD. I told you how to install additional Windows components back in Chapter 21, "Updating Windows." I won't repeat that information here, so turn back to that section if you need instructions.

Once you have Microsoft Backup installed, you can use the utility to back up your personal files and settings. The entire operation is run from the Backup or Restore Wizard, which makes this somewhat dull task just a little easier.

Microsoft Backup lets you store your backup files on diskettes, backup tapes, Zip disks, or CD-R/RW discs. If you ever happen to have a hard drive crash, you can restore your backed-up files from your backup copies, and thus minimize your data loss. Even if you've never had a hard drive fail or become corrupted, you should always make regular backup copies of your critical files—*just in case*.

How often you need to back up your files depends on how often the files change and how critical the changes are. For many users, once a month is often enough. If your system crashes, you'll lose some information, but nothing you can't reproduce with a little time and effort. If you store critical information that changes rapidly, however, you should consider backing up more regularly.

You start the Backup or Restore Wizard by right-clicking the drive you want to backup and selecting Properties from the pop-up menu. When the Properties dialog box appears, select the Tools tab, then click the Backup Now button.

When the wizard launches, follow the onscreen instructions to select where you want to back up your files, what files to back up, and what kind of backup to make. Insert the backup media as directed, and make sure you keep your backup copies in a safe place.

If you ever need to restore files from a backup, you do it from the same Backup or Restore Wizard. Just tell the wizard that you want to restore your files and settings, and follow the onscreen instructions to copy your backup files back to their original locations.

Remember that restored files might not be the most recent versions, especially if the files were used any time after your most recent backup. Still, recovering a slightly older version of a file is better than not having any version of that file at all.

MANAGING THE WINDOWS REGISTRY

The majority of your system's configuration is stored in a huge database of information called the Windows Registry. The Registry contains all the properties you set via the Control Panel, settings for each of the applications installed on your system, and configuration information for all your system's hardware and peripherals.

The Registry is updated automatically whenever you change a configuration through normal means. You can also make changes directly to the Registry, using a utility called the Registry Editor.

You need to know, however, that editing the Registry directly is a tricky proposition. If you do something wrong, you could make your system totally inoperable. For that reason, you should only edit the Registry if it's absolutely necessary to correct an otherwise hard-to-fix problem—and you should back it up before attempting any edits.

Understanding the Registry

Why have a Registry? Well, in the old days of computing, when you wanted to install a new software program, you just copied the files for the program onto your hard disk and ran them. The problem is, as programs got larger, they had to be broken into task-specific modules. As time went by, programmers found that they could maintain a library of certain modules that did certain tasks, so that they could reuse a module over and over in different programs.

Eventually, this led to the concept of object-oriented programming, or OOP. With OOP, each object in a program has a set of qualities or capabilities that defines it, as well as a number of component modules or resources. In many cases, these resources are stored in different folders on your hard disk. The Registry keeps track of all the pieces of your programs so Windows can find them when it needs them.

Back in the prehistoric days of windows, before Windows 95, there were two files that kept track of much of this information—**win.ini** and **sys.ini**. But as more objects became installed, and All Programs added, these files became huge and unwieldy—and contributed significantly to slowing Windows. Starting with Windows 95, all the information formerly stored in these two files (and more) was moved to the Registry, which is much more organized and easier-to-manage than the previous files. (By the way, **win.ini** still exists in Windows XP, mainly for compatibility with any older programs that still write to that file.)

Backing Up and Restoring the Registry

Because editing the Registry is risky—even for experienced computer users—you should back up the Registry files before you commence making any changes. This will give you the option of restoring the pre-edited Registry, just in case anything goes wrong.

Fortunately, Windows XP's System Restore feature automatically backs up your Registry whenever a restore point is created. If you're going to edit your Registry, make sure you create a new restore point immediately prior to making any changes. If anything goes wrong in the editing process, you can use System Restore to restore your system back to the previous restore point. (See Chapter 23 for more information about System Restore and restore points.)

If you want to be extra safe, you can make a backup copy of your Registry and store it on some form of removable media, such as a Zip disk or CD-RW. The Registry is actually composed of two hidden files, SYSTEM.DAT and USER.DAT, located in the `\windows` folder. All you have to do is unhide these files and copy them to another location. (You can copy them back later if you totally trash your system in the meantime.)

Editing the Registry

Most of the time you won't need to bother with the Registry—it operates in the background, automatically updated whenever you change a Windows setting or install a new piece of software or hardware. However, there will come the occasion when you experience a particularly vexing system problem that can fixed only by editing a particular value in the Registry.

Typically, you'll be instructed to edit the Registry by a tech support person working for the company whose product is causing you problems. (Trust me, it happens.) When worse comes to worst, you need to know how to edit the Registry—which you do via the Registry Editor utility.

The Registry Editor is a powerful utility that lets you edit individual values in the Registry. You start Registry Editor by clicking the Start button and selecting Run to display the Run window. Enter `regedit` in the Open box and then click OK.

The Registry Editor window has two panes, as shown in Figure 22.12. The left pane displays the different parameters or settings, called *keys*. All keys have numerous *subkeys*. The right pane displays the values, or configuration information, for each key or subkey.

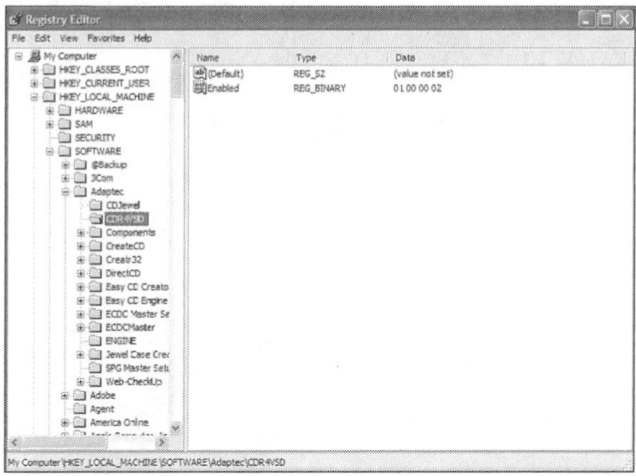

Figure 22.12

When worse comes to worst, you can also edit the (highly technical) values in the Windows Registry.

You display the different levels of subkeys by clicking on the "+" next to a specific item. You edit a particular value by highlighting the subkey in the left pane and then double-clicking the value in the right pane. This displays the Edit Value (or Edit String) window. Enter a new value in the Value Data box, then click OK.

Registry settings are changed *as you make the changes*. There is no "save" command in the Registry Editor. There is also no "undo" command. So be very careful about the changes you make—they're final!

To add a new value to a subkey, right-click the subkey and select one of the New, Value options from the pop-up menu. Type a name for the new value, then double-click the value to display the Edit Value (or Edit String) window. Enter the new value in the Value Data box, then click OK.

You can also add new subkeys to the Registry. Just right-click the key where you want to add the subkey, then select New, Key from the popup menu. A new subkey (with a temporary name) appears. Type a name for the new subkey, and then press Enter.

To delete a subkey or value, right-click the item and select Delete. Remember, however, that all changes are final. Once a subkey is deleted, it's gone!

JIM'S TOP TEN TIPS

Most users don't like to mess with system maintenance and troubleshooting tools. I don't blame you. This stuff really isn't any fun, and it's often too technical and confusing to truly understand.

Still, you need to perform periodic maintenance on your system. And you may eventually run into a problem that requires the use of some of the more technical system tools. For those reasons, it pays to familiarize yourself with these tools and utilities. If nothing else, remember these ten key points:

1. You need to perform periodic maintenance to keep your hard disk running at maximum efficiency.
2. Microsoft has moved a lot of its maintenance utilities from the System Tools folder to the Help and Support Center. If you can't find a specific tool in one place, look in the other!
3. The two essential hard disk maintenance activities are cleaning up unused files and defragmenting the disk.
4. Even though ScanDisk no longer exists as a standalone program, the function of finding and fixing hard disk errors is still around. In Windows XP this disk fixing is accessible by right-clicking a hard disk icon in My Computer, selecting Properties, selecting the Tools tab, and clicking the Check Now button.
5. Many new system reports are available in the Tools section of the Help and Support Center. Click My Computer Information to display basic hardware and software reports, or click Advanced System Information to display more detailed information.
6. The System Properties dialog box also displays a lot of key system information, and serves as a gateway to other tools and utilities—including the Device Manager.
7. You use the Device Manager to view and reconfigure all the devices that are attached to or installed in your computer. (You can also use the Device Manager to install new device drivers, or roll back your system to use a previously installed version of a driver.)
8. If you think you have a device conflict, use the System Information utility to display all the shared resources on your system. (You also use System Information to access several "hidden" utilities, including the Windows Report Tool, DirectX Diagnostic Tool, and Dr. Watson.)
9. Even though it isn't installed by default, Windows XP Home Edition *does* include the Microsoft Backup tool. You'll need to install Backup manually from your installation CD, and then you can use it to back up important files and settings.
10. The Windows Registry is where Windows stores all its configuration information. You can edit the Registry with the Registry Editor utility.

CHAPTER 23

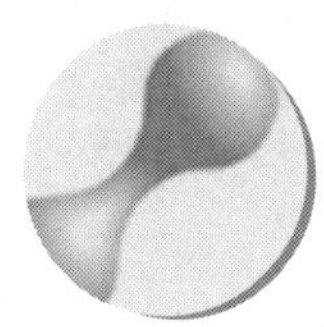

RECOVERING FROM SYSTEM CRASHES

- Starting in Safe Mode
- Tracking Down Problems With the System Configuration Utility
- Undoing Something Bad with System Restore
- Avoiding and Recovering from Computer Viruses
- Jim's Top Ten Tips

It happens.

You go to turn on or reboot your computer, and something bad happens. Either your system doesn't start at all, or it hangs in mid-startup, or it issues forth with some incomprehensible error message. It's then that you know that you have a bit of detective work ahead of you to track down and fix the problem.

This chapter is for you. There are some very precise things you can do to get your system up-and-running again after a crash, and I'll tell you about them. (I'll also remind you, right now, how important it is to back up your important files and settings—*just in case* this sort of disaster happens to you!)

STARTING IN SAFE MODE

If you're having trouble getting Windows to start, it's probably because some setting is set wrong or some driver is malfunctioning. The problem is, how do you get into Windows to fix what's wrong, when you can't even start Windows?

The answer is to hijack your computer before Windows gets hold of it, and force it to start *without* whatever is causing the problem.

You hijack your computer by watching the screen as your computer boots up, and pressing the F8 key just before Windows starts to load. (You'll probably see some of onscreen message about Windows starting, or pressing F8 for startup options, or selecting the operating system to start.)

When you press F8 your computer will display the Windows startup menu. This menu lists a number of different ways that you can start Windows. I'll discuss all these modes in a minute. For now, use your up and down arrow keys to select Safe mode, and then press Enter.

Understanding Safe Mode

Safe mode is a special mode of operation that loads Windows in a minimal configuration, without a bunch of pesky device drivers. This means the screen will be low-resolution VGA, and you won't be able to use a lot of your peripherals (such as your modem or your printer). But Windows will load, which it might not have, otherwise.

Any time you can't load Windows normally, you should revert to Safe mode. In fact, Windows will automatically start in Safe mode if it encounters major problems while loading. Safe mode is a great mode for troubleshooting, because Windows still works and you can make whatever changes you need to make to get it up-and-running again in normal mode.

Once in Safe mode, you can look for device conflicts, restore incorrect or corrupted device drivers, troubleshoot your startup with the System Configuration Utility (discussed later in this chapter), or restore your system to a prior working configuration (using the System Restore utility, also discussed later).

Other Startup Options

When you press the F8 key when Windows is starting, Safe mode is just one of the options available on the Windows startup menu. Here are some of the other options:

- **Normal**—This starts Windows in its normal mode—as if you hadn't pressed F8 to begin with.
- **Safe Mode**—Starts Windows with a minimal number of device drivers loaded.
- **Safe Mode with Networking**—A version of Safe mode that also loads key network drivers, you can still connect the ailing computer to your network.

- **Safe Mode with Command Prompt**—Boots to the old DOS command prompt instead of to the Windows interface.
- **Enable Boot Logging**—This logs all remaining startup operations to the BOOTLOG.TXT file.
- **Enable VGA Mode**—Loads Windows as normal, but with a generic VGA video driver. (This is a good mode if you think you're having trouble with your video driver.)
- **Last Known Good Configuration**—Uses the Windows Registry information and drivers that were saved the last time you shut down your system—presumably before your system got screwed up.

Depending on your system configuration, you may have more, fewer, or just different options available on the Windows startup menu. The basic Safe mode option should be available on all systems, however.

TRACKING DOWN PROBLEMS WITH THE SYSTEM CONFIGURATION UTILITY

The System Configuration Utility is the tool you turn to when you know you have a startup problem but you don't know what's causing it. This utility troubleshoots your system by duplicating the procedures used by Microsoft's tech support staff when they try to diagnose system configuration problems. This utility leads you through a series of steps that, one-by-one, disable various components of your system on startup, until you're able to isolate the item that's causing your specific problem.

You find the System Configuration Utility in the Tools section of the Help and Support Center. (See Chapter 20, "Getting Help," for more information about Windows XP's Help system, and Chapter 22, "Keeping Windows Healthy and Happy," for more information about Windows XP's other diagnostic tools.)

The easiest way to check your system is to perform a *diagnostic startup*. This routine enables you to interactively load specific device drivers and software when you start your system.

You perform a diagnostic startup by selecting to the General tab (shown in Figure 23.1) and selecting the Diagnostic Startup option. When you click OK, your computer will restart and you'll be shown the Windows Startup Menu. Select Step-by-Step Confirmation, and then choose to process all files.

Windows will now start, but with only the most basic devices and services loaded. If you find that your problem is no longer present, you know that the problem was caused by one of drivers or services that you *didn't* load.

From here you need to return to the General tab and check the Selective Startup option. Then, starting with the first available option, enable each option (one at a time) and restart your system. By going through this admittedly time-consuming process, you should be able to determine which file or service is causing your problem.

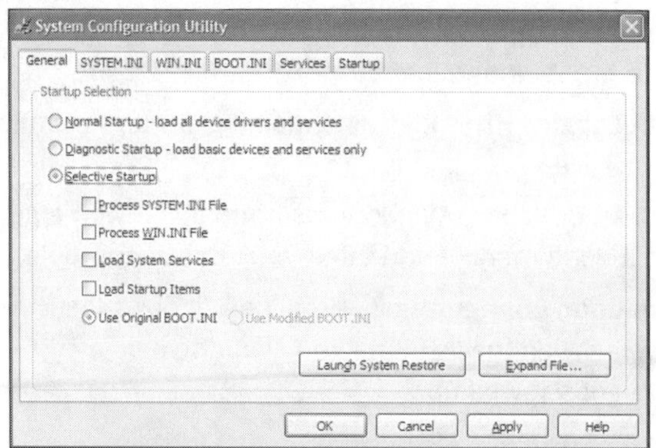

Figure 23.1

Use the System Configuration Utility to track down startup problems.

Your job isn't done yet, however. You now have to find the item within that file—the specific driver, in most cases—that is causing your problem. Click the tab that corresponds to the problematic file or service, and work through one item at a time, rebooting your computer after enabling each item.

Again, working through one item at a time is very time-consuming, but this is the exact same procedure that the tech professionals use. Working methodically, you can isolate the precise item that is causing your problem.

If, after working through these steps, your computer still acts up, select the Startup tab. Here you see a list of all the programs that get launched every time you start Windows. Work through this list, line-by-line (rebooting your computer after each change, of course), to determine if one of these programs is causing your system problem.

Even though this process is time-consuming, more often or not it *will* help you isolate your problem. Of course, once the problem is isolated, you still have to fix it—normally by reinstalling a missing or corrupted driver file.

UNDOING SOMETHING BAD WITH SYSTEM RESTORE

Perhaps the best course of action when your system crashes is to use Microsoft's System Restore utility. This is a relatively new utility, first introduced in Windows Me, that can automatically restores your system to the state it was in before your problems cropped up.

Even though it's sometimes a little shaky (an earlier version blew up one of my systems!), System Restore is basically a good idea. Prior to Windows Me, it wasn't uncommon to run into problems that required you to reinstall your entire operating system. With System Restore, reinstallations are a thing of the past—because it can automatically restore your system to a prior working state.

Think of System Restore as a safety net for your essential system files. It isn't a backup program per se, because it doesn't make copies of your personal files. It simply keeps track of all the system-level changes that are made to your computer, and (when activated) reverses those changes.

Setting System Restore Points

How does System Restore work?

It's quite simple, actually. System Restore actively monitors your system and notes any changes that are made when you install new applications. Each time it notes a change, it automatically creates what it calls a *restore point*. A restore point is basically a "snapshot" of the Windows Registry and selected system files just before the new application is installed.

Just to be safe, System Restore also creates a new restore point after every ten hours of system use. You can also chose to manually create a new restore point at any point in time. Which is a good idea whenever you make any major system change—such as installing a new peripheral or piece of hardware.

To set a manual restore point, click the Start menu and then select All Programs, Accessories, System Tools, System Restore. When the System Restore window opens (shown in Figure 23.2), select Create a Restore Point and click Next. You'll be prompted to enter a description for this new restore point. Do this and then click the Create button.

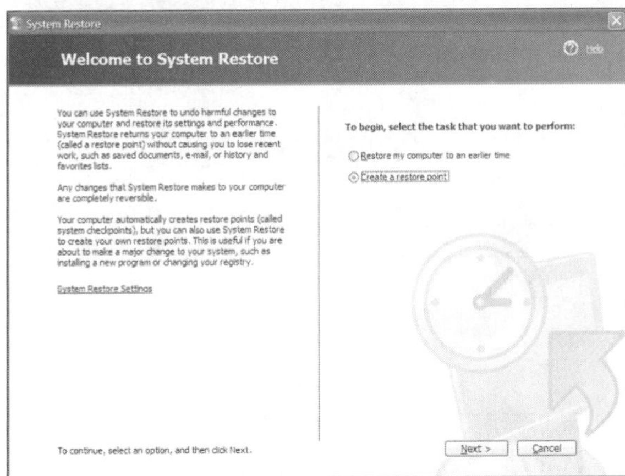

Figure 23.2

Use System Restore to create a new restore point before you install a new piece of hardware or software.

That's all you have to do. Windows notes the appropriate system settings, and stores them in its System Restore database.

Because System Restore only monitors system files and Registry settings, you cannot use it to restore changed or damaged data files. For complete protection, you'll still need to back up your important data files manually.

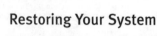

Restoring Your System

If something in your system goes bad, you can run System Restore to set things right. Pick a restore point before the problem occurred (such as right before a new installation), and System Restore will then undo any changes made to monitored files since the restore point was created. It also replaces the current Registry with the one captured at the restore point. This will restore your system to its pre-installation—that is, *working*—condition.

To restore your system from a restore point, all you have to do is follow these steps:

1. Click the Start button, and then select All Programs, Accessories, System Tools, System Restore.
2. When the System Restore window opens, check the Restore My Computer To An Earlier Time option, then click Next.
3. When the Select a Restore Point screen appears (as shown in Figure 23.3), you'll see a calendar showing the current month. (You can move back and forward through the months by clicking the left and right arrows.) Any date highlighted in bold contains a restore point. Select a restore point, then click the Next button.
4. When the confirmation screen appears, click Next.

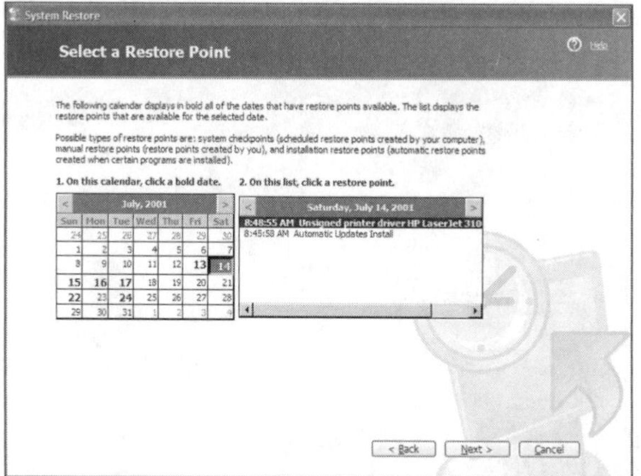

Figure 23.3

Pick a restore point to restore your system to the way it used to be—before it started acting up.

Windows now starts to restore your system. You should make sure that all open programs are closed down, because Windows will need to be restarted during this process.

When the process is complete, your system should be back in tip-top shape. Note, however, that it might take a half-hour or more to complete a system restore—so you'll have time to order a pizza and eat dinner before the operation is done!

AVOIDING AND RECOVERING FROM COMPUTER VIRUSES

While we're on the topic of recovering from system crashes, it makes sense to talk about one of the most frequent causes of these crashes—the computer virus.

A computer virus actually is similar in many ways to a biological virus. A biological virus invades your body's system and replicates itself, causing all sorts of damage to the host (you!). Likewise, a computer virus invades your computer's system, also replicates itself, and also causes untold damage to the host (your computer).

Like biological viruses, computer viruses can be destructive, or they can simply be annoying. Just as you try to protect your own body from biological viruses and find a cure when you become infected, you want to protect your computer from computer viruses—and find a cure if its system ever becomes infected.

How Viruses Work

A computer virus is a computer program that places copies of itself in other programs on your system, or somehow manipulates other files on your system.

Viruses can infect program files, the macro code found in some data files, or the HTML code used to create a Web page. Plain-text e-mail messages are not capable of being infected—although HTML e-mail and e-mail attachments *can* contain viruses.

How do you know whether your computer system has been infected with a virus? You may notice one or more of the following symptoms:

- Strange messages appear on your computer screen.
- Strange graphics appear on your computer screen, such as bouncing balls or a simulation of your screen "melting."
- Strange noises ("beeps," "boops," "squeals," "phfffts," and so on) emanate from your computer speaker.
- Normally well-behaved programs start operating erratically or crash intermittently.
- Friends report that they've received a strange e-mail message from you—and the message came with a suspicious file attached.
- Files you know you haven't erased turn up missing.
- Common program files appear to have grown in size since your last analysis.
- Your system begins to act sluggish.
- Your system fails to boot.

If your computer exhibits one or more of these symptoms—especially if you've just downloaded a file or received a suspicious e-mail message—the prognosis is not good. Your computer is probably infected.

How to Catch a Virus

Whenever you share data with another computer or computer user, you risk exposing your computer to potential viruses. There are many ways you can share data, and many ways a virus can be transmitted, including

- Sharing a data diskette
- Sharing a file with someone else on your network
- Opening a file that was downloaded from the Internet
- Opening files attached to an e-mail message
- Reading an HTML e-mail message
- Viewing a Web page in your Web browser

In other words, practically anything you do with your computer on a regular basis can be a means to transmit a virus.

Scary, isn't it?

Practicing Safe Computing

Because you're not going to completely quit doing any of these activities, you'll never be 100% safe from the threat of computer viruses. There are, however, some steps you can take to reduce your risk:

- **Share disks and files only with users you know and trust**—If you don't know where a disk comes from, don't stick it in your computer's disk drive. The same with files sent over your network. Unless you know for sure that the file is safe, delete it.
- **Download programs only from reliable sites**—If you're connecting to a non-commercial Web site run out of some guy's basement, avoid the temptation to download any files from that site. If you must download files from the Internet, use only those established and reliable Web sites (such as CNET's Download.com or the ZDNet Software Library) that actually check their files for viruses before they post them for downloading.
- **Don't open e-mail attachments from people you don't know**—If you get an unsolicited e-mail message from someone you've never heard of before, and that message includes an attachment (a Word document, or an executable program), *don't open the attachment!* The attached Word file could contain a macro virus, and the attached program could wipe out your entire hard disk! In fact, I would even caution against opening unsolicited attachments from people you *do* know, because some viruses are set up to replicate themselves through e-mail messages that are sent out without the user's knowledge. And if you want to be even more safe, configure Outlook Express to reject any potentially virus-bearing attachments.

- **Don't execute programs you find in Usenet newsgroups**—Newsgroup postings often contain attachments of various types. Executing a program "blind" from an anonymous newsgroup poster is just asking for trouble.
- **Use antivirus software**—Antivirus programs protect you against all types of viruses—including both executable and macro viruses. Purchase, install, and run a program such as Norton AntiVirus or McAfee VirusScan. Then let the antivirus program check all new files downloaded to or copied to your system.

These precautions, taken together, should provide good insurance against the threat of computer viruses.

Using an Antivirus Program

Antivirus software programs are capable of detecting known viruses and protecting your system against new, unknown viruses. These programs check your system for viruses each time your system is booted, and can be configured to check any programs you download from the Internet.

Unfortunately, Windows XP doesn't include a built-in antivirus utility. (It includes everything else—and I'd much rather have antivirus protection than online photo finishing!) Fortunately, you can find several popular antivirus programs at your local computer software retailer, or online. My favorites are McAfee VirusScan and Norton AntiVirus.

Recovering From a Virus Attack

What should you do if a virus has infected your computer? A lot depends on the type of virus you've been blessed with, and the damage that it's done.

If your system is still working and you have full access to your hard disk, you can use one of the antivirus programs to "clean" infected files on your system. If specific files can't be cleaned, then they should be deleted.

If you can't start your system or access your hard disk, then you'll have to boot your system from the Windows XP installation CD. From there you can use a hard disk utility program to repair/rebuild/restore your hard disk. Once your system is up and running again, run an antivirus program to perform additional cleaning.

Even if you can get your system up and running again, you still run the risk of losing key data files. If your system has been hit, you may have to essentially start from scratch with a "fresh" system. Which means you'd lose any data that wasn't previously backed up.

Which is one of the main reasons everyone hates viruses.

JIM'S TOP TEN TIPS

I hope the information in this chapter will be of help if you're ever the victim of a bad system crash. I'd also advise you to read Chapter 24, "Troubleshooting Common Problems," for more information finding and fixing operating system problems.

And, of course, you should always keep in mind these ten important tips:

1. You can select which mode Windows starts in by pressing F8 while your computer is booting (and before Windows loads).
2. When Windows encounters a major problem, it tries to restart in Safe mode, with minimal drivers and services loaded.
3. You can use Safe mode to reinstall bad drivers, reset incorrect settings, and troubleshoot startup problems.
4. Another option is to select the Last Known Configuration option, which should start Windows the way it was when you last shut down your system.
5. Most startup problems are caused by bad or incorrect device drivers. You can use the System Configuration Utility to selectively load drivers, one at a time, to see which is causing your current problem.
6. If you think a problem was caused by something (hardware or software) that you recently installed, you can use the System Restore utility to restore your system to the state it was in before the installation.
7. It's a good idea to use System Restore to set a manual restore point any time you install a new piece of hardware or software.
8. Another frequent cause of computer crashes is becoming infected with a computer virus.
9. Just about any way you communicate or transfer data with other computer users can also be used to transmit computer viruses.
10. Because there's no sure-fire way to completely protect your system from viruses, you should use caution when dealing with strange files and attachments, and religiously use an antivirus program.

CHAPTER 24

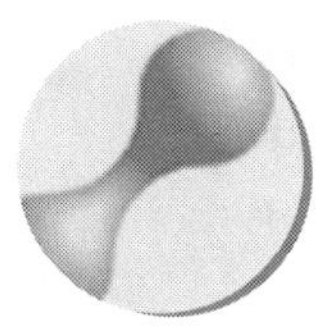

TROUBLESHOOTING COMMON PROBLEMS

- Basic Troubleshooting Tips
- Troubleshooting Technical Problems with Technical Tools
- Simple Solutions to Common Problems
- Jim's Top Ten Tips

Well, you've made it this far. Now it's time to get down the nitty gritty, and talk about what to do if your copy of Windows XP starts causing you problems.

The reality is that Windows XP is a much more robust operating system than Windows 9X/Me. It's built on the 32-bit Windows NT/2000 engine, which is designed to keep a licking and keep on ticking. This means that it should crash a whole lot less than what you're used to—even frozen and crashed applications shouldn't bring down the whole operating system.

Still, things don't always run as they're supposed to. If you start experiencing problems after you've installed Windows XP, use the advice in this chapter to try and track down your problem. Chances are it's something simple, and something you can fix yourself—without calling in a technical support person.

BASIC TROUBLESHOOTING TIPS

No matter what kind of computer-related problem you're experiencing, there are six basic steps you should take to track down the cause of the problem.

Here are the key steps you should take in troubleshooting most PC problems (while remembering to stay calm and positive). Several of these steps occur before you ever power down and remove the case.

1. Check for operator errors—something *you've* done wrong. Maybe you've clicked the wrong button, or pressed the wrong key, or plugged something into the wrong jack or port. Retrace your steps and try to duplicate your problem. Chances are the problem won't recur if you don't make the same mistake twice.
2. Check that everything is plugged in to the proper place, and that the PC itself is getting power. Take special care to ensure that all your cables are *securely* connected—loose connections can cause all sorts of strange results!
3. Make sure that you have the latest versions installed for all the software on your system. While you're at it, make sure you have the latest versions of device drivers installed for all the peripherals on your system.
4. Run the appropriate Windows diagnostic tools. If you have them, use third-party tools, as well.
5. Try to isolate the problem by *when* and *how* it occurs. Walk through each step of the startup process to see if you can identify which driver or service might be causing the problem.
6. When all else fails, call in professional help. Contact Microsoft's technical support department and tell them about your problem. Use Windows XP's Remote Assitance utility to let a remote technician examine your system. Or just break down and take your machine into the shop. The pros are there for a reason. When you need technical support, go and get it!

I should probably add a seventh step, before step number one:

Don't panic!

Just because there's something wrong with your PC is no reason to fly off the handle. Keep your wits about you and proceed logically, and you can probably find what's causing your problem, and get it fixed. React irrationally, and you'll never figure out what's wrong—and you'll get a few gray hairs, in the bargain!

TROUBLESHOOTING TECHNICAL PROBLEMS WITH TECHNICAL TOOLS

Remember all those technical tools I told you about back in Chapters 20, 21, 22, and 23? Well, now's the time to use them.

Find and Fix Easy Problems with Windows Troubleshooters

As you learned back in Chapter 20, "Getting Help," Windows XP includes several Troubleshooters that can walk through various problems with your system. These Troubleshooters are like wizards, in that you're led step-by-step through a series of questions. All you have to do is answer the interactive questions in the Troubleshooter, and you'll be led to the probable solution to your problem.

In most cases, Windows XP's Troubleshooters can help you diagnose and fix common system problems. It's a good idea to try the Troubleshooters before you pick up the phone and dial Microsoft's Technical Support line—or start trying to track down problems manually.

To run a Troubleshooter, open the Help and Support Center and click the Fixing a Problem link. When the next page appears (shown in Figure 24.1), click the link for the type of problem you're having, and then click the link to start a specific Troubleshooter. All you have to do now is follow the interactive directions to troubleshoot your particular hardware problems.

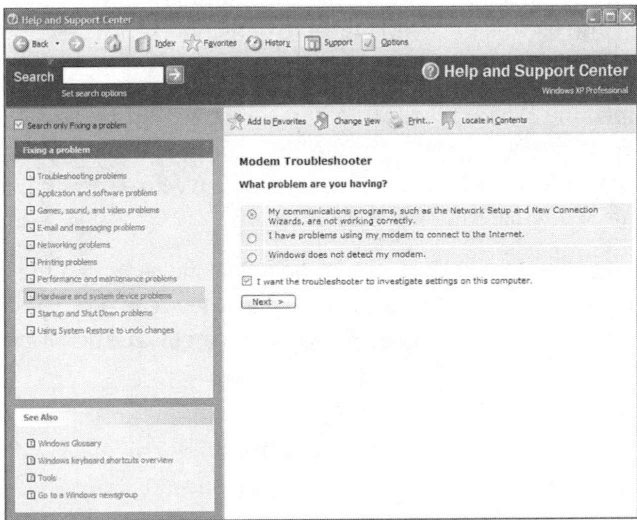

Figure 24.1

Working through a modem-related problem with the Modem Troubleshooter.

Find and Fix Shared IRQs with System Information

Sometimes a new piece of hardware will inadvertently try to share an IRQ with another previously-installed component, with predictably bad results. In Windows XP you can use the System Information utility to examine any and all shared IRQs on your system.

To open this utility, click the Start button, then select All Programs, Accessories, System Tools, System Information. When the System Information window opens, open the

Hardware Resources section of the System Summary, then select Conflicts/Sharing. This displays a list of all shared IRQs on your system. Identify the device causing your problem, and either reconfigure or reinstall the device to use a different IRQ.

Find and Fix Driver Problems with the Device Manager

For any piece of hardware to work with Windows, Windows has to install and configure a device driver file. Windows XP includes drivers for most popular hardware devices. If you have a newer or less widely-used peripheral, however, the manufacturer may have to provide its own drivers for Windows to use.

In most cases, Windows XP automatically recognizes your new device and installs the proper drivers. Even when that doesn't work, the Add Hardware Wizard can be used to install the proper drivers for new devices. Still, these methods can't add new and improved drivers if those drivers aren't physically available.

Windows XP's Device Manager (select the Hardware tab in the System Properties utility and click the Device Manager button) is where you can review your various hardware settings. You can also use the Device Manager to determine which devices may have conflicts or other problems.

When you open the Device Manager, any resource conflict on your system will be highlighted within the problematic Class group. Click the "+" next to the hardware device type to view all corresponding devices. If there is a problem with a specific device, it will be identified with one of the following symbols:

- A black exclamation point (!) on a yellow field indicates that the device is in what Windows calls a "problem state." Note that a device in a problem state can still be functioning, even though it has some sort of problem. The problem will be explained by the accompanying problem code.
- A red "X" indicates that the device is currently disabled. This usually means that the device is physically present in your system, but doesn't have a driver loaded—although it could also mean that a driver is loaded but not functioning properly.
- A blue "i" on a white field indicates that the device is not using the automatic settings, but has a manual configuration instead. (This icon isn't necessarily bad, because it doesn't indicate a problem, only a different type of configuration.)

If you have a device conflict, right-click that device and select Properties from the pop-up menu. This displays the Properties dialog box. When you select the General tab you'll see a message indicating the basic problem and the steps Windows recommends to solve the problem. The message may also display a problem code and number that can be useful when consulting with a technical support specialist.

To reconfigure a device, select the Resources tab in the Properties dialog box. (If this device doesn't have a Resources tab, either you can't change its resources or it isn't using any resource settings.) Select the resource you want to change, uncheck the Use Automatic

Settings option, and then click the Change Setting button. When the Edit Resource dialog box appears, edit the system resources as necessary. Click OK when done

To update a device driver, select the Driver tab in the Properties dialog box, and then click the Update Driver button. When the Hardware Update Wizard appears, select where you want to search for an upgraded driver. If you have new driver software from your hardware's manufacturer, check the Install From a List or Specific Location option, then insert the disk or CD-ROM and follow the onscreen instructions to install the specific driver.

If you'd rather have Windows search for a better driver, check the Install the Software Automatically option. Windows will now search for an updated device driver. If it finds one, follow the onscreen instructions to install it. If it doesn't find one, choose to keep your present driver. (And then go online yourself to try to find an updated version, if one exists.)

Find and Fix Memory Problems with Virtual Memory

Windows XP augments your system's random access memory (RAM) with *virtual memory*. Virtual memory is hard disk space that Windows treats as RAM. When Windows runs low on conventional memory, it simply begins to store temporary data on your hard drive.

Most of the time you don't have to worry about virtual memory, because Windows does the configuration automatically. If you're running low on hard drive space, however, you can decrease the amount of hard drive used for virtual memory and give yourself more storage room for your permanent data.

To change Windows' virtual memory settings, go to the Control Panel and click the System icon. When the System Properties dialog box appears, select the Advanced tab and click the Settings button in the Performance section.

When the Performance Options dialog box appears, select the Advanced tab and then click the Change button. When the Virtual Memory dialog box appears, choose the hard disk you want to use for virtual memory, and then specify the Initial and Maximum number of megabytes you want Windows to use for virtual memory. Click the OK button when done.

Find and Fix Big Problems with the System Configuration Utility

If your problem is so major that you can't fix it with the Troubleshooters or the Device Manager, you need to turn to a more powerful tool. That tool is the System Configuration Utility.

I discussed the System Configuration Utility in depth in Chapter 23, "Recovering from System Crashes." Go back and read that section if you need more information. (And while you're there, brush up on Windows Safe mode, just to be safe.)

SIMPLE SOLUTIONS TO COMMON PROBLEMS

Now that the preliminaries are out of the way, let's get down to the main event.

You have a problem, and you need it fixed!

The following sections present the most common Windows-related problems you're likely to encounter. I've provided some advice on the probable causes of each problem, and the steps you can take to fix the problem.

I can't guarantee that I've presented *every* possible problem or solution. I only hope that *your* particular problem is included, and that my advice is sound!

Your Computer Doesn't Start—You Hear No Noises and See No Lights

(To be fair, this isn't likely to be a Windows-related problem. I'm presenting it here just to be helpful!)

First things first–*don't panic*!

Now, very calmly, look at the back of your system unit. Is the power cable plugged into the right connector? Now follow the power cord to the other end. Is it firmly connected to a power outlet? Now check the wall switch. Is it turned on? Now walk to your fuse or circuit-breaker box. Is the fuse good or the circuit breaker set? Now go back to your computer. If it still isn't working, unplug the computer from the power outlet and plug in something that you know works–a lamp or a radio, perhaps. If the appliance doesn't work, you have a bad power outlet. If the appliance *does* work, you really do have computer problems.

If you're positive that your computer is getting power and that you're turning it on correctly, you probably have a hardware problem. The most likely suspect is the power supply in the system unit. To determine the culprit and fix the problem, however, you'll need to call in professional help at this point. Take your system to a certified repair center and let its technicians get to work.

Your Computer Doesn't Start, But It Makes the Normal Startup Noises

(Also not likely to be a problem caused by Windows–but it's still important enough to mention here.)

If your system is making noise, at least you know that it's getting power. Because you can rule out a bad power cord, the most common things to look for are poorly connected cables or a nonfunctioning monitor.

Begin by checking your monitor. Is it turned on? Is it plugged into a power outlet? Is the power outlet turned on? Is the monitor connected to the correct port on your system unit? Is the connection solid? Is the connection solid in the back of the monitor? Are the brightness and contrast controls turned up so that you can actually see a picture?

If everything is connected and adjusted properly, you might have a monitor that needs repair. Is the monitor's power light on? If not, your monitor may have power supply problems that need attention from a professional. If your monitor's little green light is on but nothing shows on-screen, the video card in your system unit may be loose or set up incorrectly. Turn off your system, open the computer case, and check the video card to make sure it's installed, seated, and connected properly.

It's also possible that your keyboard isn't plugged in properly, or that you have some other internal problem that causes your system to halt during start-up. Check *all* your connections before you try rebooting again.

Your Computer Starts, But the Monitor Displays an Error Message (*Before* Loading Windows)

(The last non-Windows problem, I promise. How do I know this isn't caused by Windows? Because Windows hasn't loaded yet, that's why!)

Your system uses error messages to communicate with you when it encounters certain problems. Table 24.1 details some of the most common error messages you may encounter on startup (*before* Windows loads), their causes, and how to fix the problem.

TABLE 24.1—STARTUP ERROR MESSAGES

Error Message	Causes/Solutions
Non-system disk or disk error Replace and press any key when ready	You see this message when you have a nonbootable disk in drive A. Check the floppy disk drive and remove the disk, and then press any key to restart your computer using your hard disk drive. (You *can* boot from drive A, of course, but you must have a *bootable* disk in that drive—such as the MS-DOS system disk discussed in Chapter 21, "Updating Windows."
Keyboard error, press F2 to continue	It sounds kind of silly to ask you to use your keyboard to confirm that your keyboard isn't working, doesn't it? This message is generated when the rest of your system works but the PC can't find the keyboard. If you receive this message, your keyboard probably is disconnected, has a loose connection, or has a stuck key. Check the connecting cable (at both ends) and reboot. If you still receive this message, you have a keyboard problem. Verify this fact by plugging in a keyboard from a friend's machine. If you do have a keyboard problem, it's probably cheaper to buy a new keyboard than to get your old one fixed.
File allocation table bad, drive *x*:	This message is not good. Something has messed up your FAT (File Allocation Table), the part of your hard disk that holds vital information necessary for your system to operate. One of the most common causes of this problem is a computer virus. Another cause is some sort of physical damage to your hard disk, caused by contaminants or plain old wear and tear. If you have actual physical damage to your disk, you may need to use a third-party utility program, such as Norton Disk Doctor, to repair the damage—or you may want to drop back ten and punt by letting a technical professional handle the situation from here.

TABLE 24.1—CONTINUED

Error Message	Causes/Solutions
General failure reading drive x General failure writing drive x	These very serious messages mean that something is wrong with your computer—but it has no idea what the trouble is. Try shutting down your system for a few minutes and then rebooting; sometimes this message is generated when your system gets a little cranky. More likely, however, is that you have something seriously wrong with your hard disk, which means it's time to hop in the car and drop your PC off at your local computer repair center. The pros there have diagnostic software and equipment that can pinpoint problems much easier than you or I can.
Invalid drive specification Drive not ready	Either of these error messages indicates that you're having problems with the drive you're trying to boot from. If you're booting from a floppy disk drive, your bootable floppy may be bad. Try using another bootable disk. If the problem persists, or if you're booting from a hard disk drive, the problem may reside in the drive mechanism itself. Sometimes an older drive can operate too slowly to always boot properly; try rebooting your system. If the problem persists, have a professional check out your system. The drive in question may need to be replaced.
CMOS RAM error	This message appears when something is bad in the setup held in memory by your system's CMOS RAM chip. (This chip holds important system information in permanent, battery-powered memory.) When you see this or any similar message, you are given the opportunity to press the F1 key to continue. Do this, and adjust your CMOS setup accordingly. (See your system's documentation for information on how to do the latter.) If this message persists, you may have a dead CMOS battery; see your repair center to replace the battery.
Memory size error Memory size mismatch Not enough memory Insufficient memory Parity check xxx Parity error x	Any of these messages indicate that something is wrong with your computer's memory. Your CMOS setup may be incorrect, or you could have some bad or improperly seated memory chips. It's also possible that you recently added extra memory to your system and it isn't configured correctly. If this is the case, enter your CMOS setup menu and reconfigure your system for the new memory. If you can't fix this problem via the setup routine, you should probably consult a computer professional for further assistance.

Your Computer Starts, But Windows Doesn't—and You Receive an Error Message

(Okay, this is really a Windows problem!)

If Windows doesn't load–if your system, after the standard boot procedure, just "hangs" in place–then there is probably something wrong with the way Windows is installed or configured. This typically happens after you add something new (hardware or software) to your system. The new thing changes the settings that *used to* work okay to a configuration that doesn't work okay anymore.

It's also possible for Windows to have trouble loading even when you've done nothing new or different to your system. Even the 32-bit Windows XP can be finicky at times, and can surprise you with what it does or doesn't do.

If you receive an error message while Windows is loading, it's likely that Windows is trying to load a bad or incorrect device driver of some sort. In fact, the error message will more often than not tell you exactly which driver it's having trouble with. Once you know which driver is causing problems, you can either reinstall that driver, or eliminate that driver from the loading process—by using the options in the System Configuration Utility.

If the error message doesn't tell you which driver is causing the problem, you can determine that yourself by using the System Configuration Utility to perform a selective startup. Restart Windows in Safe mode, then run the System Configuration Utility and follow the instructions I gave in Chapter 23.

If you'd rather not go through the entire selective startup business, just launch the System Restore utility. Choose to restore your system to some prior restore point, and get on with your business. (Of course, you might not figure out what was actually causing the problem—but at least you'll be up and running!)

Your Computer Starts, But Windows Doesn't—and You *Don't* Receive an Error Message

What if you can't load Windows and *don't* receive an error message? In this instance you want to start Windows in Safe mode, and then disable any other programs that may be loading when Windows starts up. Click the Start button and select All Programs, Startup. Use your mouse to move all items in the Startup menu to another menu (any menu will do, as long as you remember which one it is!). Now restart Windows again and see what happens.

If Windows now starts properly, that means that one of the programs that *used to* start up when Windows started is causing you problems. One at a time, drag those programs back to the Startup menu (using the same procedure as before), then restart Windows. Each time Windows starts properly, you know that particular program is okay. When Windows *doesn't* start properly, you know that particular program is a problem—so leave it out of your Startup folder.

If, on the other hand, removing the programs from your Startup folder *didn't* fix your problem, then you have a problem with a specific device driver. If you're technically minded (and very patient), you can use the System Configuration Utility's startup diagnostics to try and isolate the problem driver.

A better bet for most of us is to run the System Restore utility and restore your system back to an earlier state—presumably before you installed or updated the driver that is causing your problems.

If even this doesn't work, it's time to reinstall Windows. Use your Windows XP installation CD to initiate a complete installation and setup—and if *this* doesn't fix your problem, it's time to contact a technical professional.

Your Computer Starts, But Windows Doesn't—and You Can't Enter Safe Mode

Sometimes Safe mode isn't safe enough. Any number of conditions can cause Windows not to start in Safe mode:

- **Your system is infected with a computer virus**—You may need to reinstall Windows to eliminate the effect of the virus, then use an anti-virus program to initiate a more complete cleansing of your system.
- **Your computer's CMOS settings are incorrect**—During boot-up, check your CMOS settings, and make corrections as necessary. If your CMOS battery is weak and not holding its settings, replace the battery.
- **You have a hardware conflict**—Some device in your system is conflicting with some other device; the most common conflicts are IRQ conflicts. Ask a technical professional (or just an old geek who knows how to use DOS) to hunt down the errant device with the Safe Mode with Command Prompt option.

If you have persistent problems starting in Safe mode, try choosing the Last Known Good Configuration startup option. If even this doesn't work, you may need to reinstall Windows XP from scratch.

Your Computer Starts, and Windows Enters Safe Mode Automatically

Windows starts up in Safe mode automatically when it senses a major driver problem or conflict. Follow the steps in the "Your Computer Starts, But Windows Doesn't—and You Receive an Error Message" section to track down the source of the problem. (Or just launch System Restore and restore your system to some prior condition.)

Your Computer Starts, Windows Starts—and So Does Another Program or Utility That You *Don't* Want to Start

Many programs, when first installed, have the audacity to think that you want them to run whenever you start up your PC. So they configure themselves to launch when Windows launches—whether you want them to or not.

If you want to *stop* a program from launching automatically when Windows starts, you first have to find out from *where* it is being launched. The first place to check is the Startup menu. Click the Start button, then select All Programs, Startup. If the offending program is here, right-click it and select Delete from the pop-up menu. (This doesn't delete the program itself—it just removes it from the Startup menu.)

If the offending program isn't in the Startup menu, it's probably being loaded via a setting in the Windows Registry. There are several keys in the Registry that can contain autoload instructions. If you find the offending program in any one of these, delete it!

Here are the keys to check, using the Registry Editor:

- HKEY_LOCAL_MACHINE\SOFTWARE\Microsoft\Windows\CurrentVersion\RUN
- HKEY_USERS\.DEFAULT\SOFTWARE\Microsoft\Windows\CurrentVersion\RUN
- HKEY_CURRENT_USER\SOFTWARE\Microsoft\Windows\CurrentVersion\RUN

Windows Freezes—Your System Unit Has Power, But Your Keyboard and/or Mouse Isn't Working

If no error messages appear onscreen but you can't type a thing, you probably face a simple problem: Your keyboard is unplugged. So plug it back in.

Same thing if your mouse quits working. Check to see if it's firmly connected, then try rolling it again.

Of course, the solution might not be quite that simple. If replugging your keyboard or mouse doesn't work, you might have to reboot your computer to recognize the replug. (You'll probably have to turn off your system with the main power switch or button–if you can't click or type, you can't exit Windows normally!)

If you still experience difficulties after rebooting, you actually may be the not-so-proud possessor of a bad keyboard or mouse. Try plugging another keyboard or mouse into your PC, or your keyboard or mouse into another PC, to determine whether device failure is at the root of your problem.

Windows Freezes—and Displays an Error Message

Windows XP can sometimes exhibit perplexing behavior. Computer people refer to this as "unstable" behavior. I prefer to call it "screwy."

When Windows freezes up, it sometimes displays some sort of error message. These messages are just nice ways to say that something (who knows what) has bombed.

More often than not, it's just your current program that has frozen, and not all of Windows. In this case you get a Program Not Responding error message. Try pressing Ctrl+Alt+Del to bring up the Windows Task Manager, and then manually shut down any unresponsive program.

If the error message you get is displayed on a blue screen (known in the industry as the "blue screen of death"), follow the onscreen instructions to get rid of the blue screen. You may have to press Enter to close the program causing the error, or press Ctrl+Alt+Del to reboot your computer. Once you encounter the blue screen, your system typically gets unstable, so I recommend rebooting your entire system, even if you're able to close that particular program manually.

Blue screen messages are often caused when you start running out of space on your hard disk. This might sound odd, but Windows uses a disk cache to supplement conventional memory. (That's the virtual memory that I talked about earlier in this chapter.) If you don't have enough free hard disk space, Windows thinks that it's low on memory, and start acting flaky.

The blue screen error messages can also be caused by errors on your hard disk. If you get a lot of these error messages, it wouldn't hurt to check for disk errors before proceeding.

Windows Freezes—and No Error Message Appears

Sometimes Windows freezes without displaying an error message. One of two things has happened: (1) Windows itself has locked up, or (2) Your current Windows application has locked up.

In either case, the solution is the same: Press Ctrl+Alt+Del.

If Windows itself has frozen, either nothing will happen or you'll start hearing a beep every time you press a key on your keyboard. In which case you'll need to press Ctrl+Alt+Del again to fully reboot, or you may have to turn your PC off at the On/Off button (or at the power source).

If, on the other hand, it's an errant program that freezes up, you should see the Windows Task Manager when you first press Ctrl+Alt+Del. Select the "not responding" program and click End Task. If and when the Wait/Shutdown dialog box appears, go ahead and shut down the offending program.

If the Task Manager doesn't appear, or if you try to shut down a program but your system is still locked up, it's time to fully reboot by pressing Ctrl+Alt+Del twice in a row.

What causes Windows to freeze? There can be many different causes of a Windows freeze, including the following:

- You may be running an application that isn't compatible with Windows XP. If so, upgrade the program.
- You may not have enough memory to run Windows effectively. Upgrade the amount of RAM in your PC.
- A memory conflict may exist between applications or between an application and Windows itself. Try running fewer programs at once, or running problematic programs one at a time to avoid potential memory conflicts.
- You may not have enough free hard disk space for Windows to use for temporary files. Delete any unnecessary files from your hard drive.
- Your hard disk may be developing errors or bad sectors. Check your hard disk for errors.

If your system crashes or freezes frequently, call in a pro. These kinds of problems can be tough to track down by yourself when you're dealing with Windows.

Windows Won't Let You Exit

The most common cause for this situation is that you have a misbehaving program. Try closing all your open programs, one at a time. If any individual program is frozen, use Ctrl+Alt+Del to close that "not responding" program.

Beyond a single misbehaving problem, a number of things can cause Windows to not shut down. Believe it or not, one of these things can be a bad sound file! It's that stupid sound you hear every time you go to shut down Windows. If that file is corrupted, the shutdown sequence stops there, leaving Windows running. To fix this problem open the Control Panel and select the Sounds and Audio Devices icon. When the Sounds and Audio Devices Properties utility appears, select the Sounds tab, then pull down the Sounds list and select None. Now click OK and try shutting down your system again. (If you do have a corrupted sound file, you can reinstall this particular file from your Windows installation CD.)

It's also possible that Windows' Power Management technology is keeping you from closing Windows. Disable Power Management by opening the Control Panel and selecting the Power Options icon. When the Power Options Properties utility appears, select the Power Schemes tab, pull down the Power Schemes list, and select Always On. You can even go the extra step and configure each of the individual settings to always stay on.

If you still can't shut down Windows after trying all these actions, there is probably a "fragment" of a program still running somewhere in your system's memory. It's near impossible to track down that fragment. Instead, you need to reboot via the double Ctrl+Alt+Del procedure.

Windows Won't Wake Up from Standby Mode

What do you do when Windows doesn't wake up from standby mode? Normally you "wake up" your computer by moving your mouse, or pressing any key on your keyboard. Some keyboards have special "wake up" keys that need to be pressed to exit sleep mode. In any event, if you move and click your mouse a bit and then type furiously on your keyboard and Windows stays fast asleep, you have problems. (Make sure, however, that your monitor is actually plugged in and turned on. A switched-off monitor looks suspiciously like standby mode!)

The solution here is to reboot your computer—*somehow*. Try the Ctrl+Alt+Del method first. However, if your system is in a really deep sleep, it might not recognize any keyboard input. So you'll probably have to turn your system off at the main power switch/button, wait a few seconds, and then turn it back on again.

If you're using a notebook computer and this happens, you may have to remove *all* your power sources. This means unplugging the computer from the wall *and* removing the battery. Wait a few seconds, and then plug your notebook back in. That should do the trick!

In addition to this type of oversleeping, standby mode can sometimes cause other problems. I've had standby mode screw up my video display (dropping me down to a lower-resolution mode!) and cause some programs not to run at all post-wake up. It's fair to say that I've found standby mode to be the most bug-ridden of all Windows features.

If you experience constant standby mode-related problems—*disable it!* Go to the Power Options Properties dialog box, select the Power Schemes tab, and set every option so that all the parts of your computer will always be on. Then take the extra step and disable your system's screen savers, too. They're another big cause of wake-up problems.

It's possible that your system has a different kind of "sleep" function built into the PC's BIOS. If so, you'll need to enter the CMOS BIOS setup during system startup and disable the sleep mode there.

Finally, it's possible that your system woke up but your *monitor* stayed asleep! Yes, some monitors have their own sleep modes, and if they get stuck in that mode, you won't know if your system is awake or not. It doesn't hurt to turn your monitor off and then back on (which definitely wakes it up!) just in case the sleep problem is the fault of your monitor, not your PC. (If this problem persists, of course, you may need to repair or replace your monitor.)

Windows Runs Slower Than Normal

The most likely culprit behind a system slowdown is memory—or rather, the lack of it.

Are you running any new applications—or upgrades of older applications—that may consume more memory? Are you running All Programs than usual at the same time? Are you running any programs in the "background" during a heavy computing session—programs such as Windows Messenger or ICQ? Do you have any "hidden" utilities taking up space in the system tray? Any of these factors consumes more memory and forces Windows to slow down. If you're dissatisfied with the performance of Windows on your system, the answer is simple: *Add more memory!*

I find that Windows XP runs best when you get up to 256MB of memory. Anything below this can be problematic, especially if you have multiple users logged in simultaneously.

You Accidentally Deleted an Important File

Deleting an important file can be one of the most disconcerting errors you will make in the course of using your computer. How could you do that?

In Windows XP, all deleted files are temporarily stored in the Recycle Bin. To undelete a file in the Recycle Bin, select the Recycle Bin icon on your desktop, then when the Recycle Bin window opens, select the item you want to undelete and select Restore This Item from Recycle Bin Tasks panel.

If a file has been "permanently" deleted from the Recycle Bin, there still might be a way to bring the missing file back from the dead. You see, just because a file isn't accessible doesn't mean that it's been physically deleted from your hard disk. In fact, all deleted files continue to reside on your hard disk, although all reference to the data in the file allocation table (FAT) has been removed—at least until the reference data has been overwritten by newer data. There are several third-party programs—including Norton Utilities, my favorite—that include special "undelete" utilities. These utilities will recover any existing data from the FAT and thus "restore" the deleted file back to your hard disk.

You Can't Delete a File

You tried to delete a file, but it won't delete. This problem can occur for one of three reasons:

- **The file is currently in use by another program**—Try closing that program and then deleting the file.
- **You're trying to delete a file from a floppy disk that is write-protected**—If you're trying to delete a file on a floppy disk, slide the tab in the lower-left corner so that the hole is closed, then try the procedure again.
- **The attributes of the file have been set so that you can't delete it**—Every file has multiple attributes. One such attribute makes a file read-only, meaning that you can't delete it or write to it. To change a file's attributes, right-click the file in My Computer and select Properties from the pop-up menu. When the Properties dialog box appears, *uncheck* the Read-Only attribute, then click OK.

You Attempt a File Operation and Get a Windows Error Message

Windows error messages often appear to let you know that you incorrectly clicked or typed something. So if you get such a message, the first action is always to try the operation again, more carefully this time. However, even when you do whatever it is you're doing more carefully, you can still get error messages. Table 24.2 presents those you're most likely to encounter when working with files.

TABLE 24.2—WINDOWS FILE-RELATED ERROR MESSAGES

Error Message	Probable Cause and Solution
Cannot find file	The most common cause for this message is that the file in question is either missing or corrupted. Use the Search utility to search for the file. Reinstall the file in question if necessary.
Cannot read from drive *x*	Windows is looking for a file on drive *x:* (probably drive A:) and there isn't a disk in the drive. Insert any disk to end the Windows look loop. If a disk *is* in drive *x:* and you get this error message, you either have a bad (or unformatted) disk, or something wrong with your disk drive.
Folder xxx does not exist	You have specified a folder that does not exist. Check the spelling of the folder and path name. You might also try selecting View, Refresh to refresh the file/folder display.

TABLE 24.2—CONTINUED

Error Message	Probable Cause and Solution
File already exists. Overwrite?	You're trying to create or save a file with a name that already exists. Windows is asking if you wish to overwrite the existing file. If so, answer yes. If no, answer no, and assign a new name to your file.
File is missing	When Windows loads, it tries to load any programs that are included in the Startup folder. This message is generated when one of these files no longer exists or has been entered incorrectly. Use My Computer to open the Startup folder and check all programs and associations, removing or editing those that are not correct.
Not a valid filename	You typed an invalid filename. Try again.
The specified path is invalid	You typed an incorrect path for a file operation. Check the path and retype the command.
Write protected disk	You're trying to perform a file operation on a disk that is write protected. Change disks, or slide the write-protect tab into the down position.

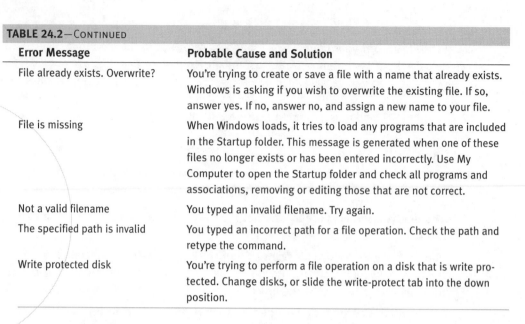

A Particular Software Application Won't Run

Several factors can cause a Windows application to refuse to run:

- **The program may not be compatible with your version of Windows**—Some older Windows programs are incompatible with Windows XP. If an older Windows application won't run and gives you an error message, you probably have an incompatible program. You'll need to upgrade this software to a Windows 2000 or Windows XP version—or activate Windows XP's Compatibility Mode. Right-click the program's icon and select Properties, then select the Shortcut tab. Check the Run In Compatibility Mode option, then select another version of Windows that you know the program is compatible with. This will trick the program into thinking it's running on an older version of Windows, and might just fix your problem.
- **Your system may not have enough memory available to run the program**—Try closing other Windows applications before you start this one, or try adding more memory to your system.
- **Your computer may not have enough disk space to run the program**—Windows employs extra disk space as virtual memory. If there isn't enough free disk space available, you may not be able to run some programs. Try deleting unused files from your hard disk before you restart the program.

If you can't get a certain program to run, first make sure that the program is referenced properly from the menu item or icon you selected. Right-click on the item or icon and select Properties from the pop-up menu. When the Properties dialog box appears (see Figure 24.2), select the Shortcut tab and note the file and path entered in the Target box. Now use My Computer to go to that location, and confirm that the target file actually is where it's supposed to be. If the target file *isn't* there, use the Search utility command to find the file, and then enter the correct location in the shortcut's Target box.

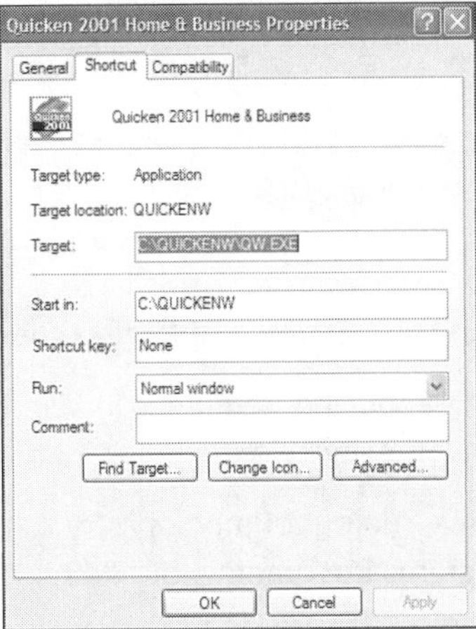

Figure 24.2

Use the Properties dialog box to make sure the right target file is referenced by any given shortcut—or to run this program in Compatibility mode.

If the file is where it's supposed to be but doesn't launch when selected, exit Windows, restart your computer, and try launching the program again. This "fixes" your problem quite often, surprisingly.

If your program still doesn't launch, make sure that the program is installed correctly. If you have your doubts, uninstall the program (by selecting the Add or Remove Programs icon from the Control Panel) and then reinstall it. (You'd be surprised how many problems get solved by reinstalling the software!)

You should also be certain that this particular program is compatible with your computer's particular hardware configuration. Your machine may need more memory, a faster microprocessor, or a higher-resolution video card before your finicky new program consents to run on it.

If all else fails, consult the instruction manual or Web site for this particular piece of software, or call the software publisher's technical support line.

A Software Application Crashes or Freezes

Everything works fine, but then—all of a sudden—your software bombs!

Fortunately, Windows XP is an exceptionally safe environment. When an individual application crashes or freezes, it seldom messes up your entire system. You can use the Windows Task Manager to close the problem application without affecting other Windows programs.

When a Windows application blows up, follow these steps:

1. Press Ctrl+Alt+Del.
2. When the Windows Task manager opens, select the Applications tab, then select application that is frozen from the list. Now click the End Task button.
3. After a few seconds, a Wait/Shutdown window appears; confirm that you want to shut down the selected application.
4. Click the End Task button.

This will close the offending application and let you continue your work in Windows.

Some programs crash with annoying frequency in Windows. The causes are myriad and often difficult to pin down. They include the following:

- Your system may have run out of memory. Try running the program while no other Windows programs are running, or add more memory to your system.
- The program may be getting caught in a memory conflict with another Windows program. Try running the program by itself.
- The program may be an older version that's incompatible with your version of Windows. Upgrade the program to its latest version, or activate Windows XP's compatibility mode for that program.
- Windows was just feeling cantankerous. Start the program again and hope for the best.
- You have a bug in your software—or even a corrupted program file. If nothing else pans out, try reinstalling your program from scratch. If this doesn't fix the problem, call the knowledgeable folks at the software publisher's technical support line for assistance. After all, that's what they're there for.

If you have multiple applications that crash on a regular basis, the situation probably can be attributed to insufficient memory. See your computer dealer about adding more RAM to your system.

You Can't Launch a Document File

The likely cause for this program is that the document's file type is not associated with a program type—or with the right program type. When you select a document file, it should launch the associated program, with the selected document pre-loaded. If, instead of launching the program, Windows displays the Open With dialog box, you need to select an application to associate with the file.

You can also associate files with applications manually. See Chapter 3, "Managing Files," for more information.

A Newly Installed Peripheral Doesn't Work

This could be one of a number of things. If you installed a new card, it may not be properly seated in the slot. You may not have all your cables connected properly. You may have broken something while you were diddling about inside your PC. You may have a bad part. You may not have *completed* the installation or setup. Windows XP might not have recognized your new hardware—or may have installed the wrong driver by mistake. The driver installed may be corrupted, or may need to be updated.

Whew! That's a lot that can go wrong!

It's also possible that your system doesn't recognize your new component. Depending on what you installed, you may have to do one of several things:

- Change CMOS settings (most common for memory and disk drives)
- Load new drivers via the Add Hardware Wizard
- Adjust specific jumpers or switches on your motherboard or other specific component

Remember, after you make any of these changes you'll need to reboot your system in order for the changes to take effect.

The important thing to remember is to retrace your steps *backwards* through your installation, and try to determine if everything was done correctly. If all else fails, call the technical support line for your new component, or consult with a technical professional.

After You Add a New Peripheral, Something Else on Your System No Longer Works Properly

This is probably caused by some sort of resource conflict between your new and old components. The most common resource conflicts involve IRQ and/or port settings.

The fastest and easiest solution to this problem is to run System Restore, and restore all your drivers and settings to a point before you added the new peripheral. You can also use the Device Manager to roll back a driver that you think may have been overwritten by the latest installation.

If you want to troubleshoot the cause of this problem, I'd recommend that you start by changing ports. (Many of these types of problems are actually port or IRQ conflicts.) If this doesn't fix it (or if you installed an internal device), you'll need to change IRQ settings for one or both of the devices in conflict.

Also know that conflicts can occur when devices hooked up to two *nonconsecutive* ports are used at the same time. In other words, if you have two devices trying to use COM1 and COM3 (or COM2 and COM4) simultaneously, both could freeze up. (I've had this happen with a mouse hooked up to COM1 and a modem hooked up to COM3.) If this is your problem, change the port for one of the devices.

Still, it's easier to restore your system and then work out these problems.

Your Modem Doesn't Work—Nothing Happens

If you attempt to use your modem but it does nothing at all, start by checking all your connections–especially the connection to the phone line. A malfunctioning modem usually results from a bad connection. If you use an external modem, make sure that it's hooked to the correct port in the back of your PC. Make certain, too, that the modem is plugged into a power source (if necessary) and connected to a phone line. If you use an internal modem, check to ensure that the card is firmly seated in its slot. You should also try hooking a normal phone to the line hooked to your computer, just to make sure that you have a dial tone. After you've taken care of a poor or overlooked connection, you may need to reboot your system to recover from the problem.

Next, you should check to see if your modem is communicating with your computer. In Windows XP you can do this by going to the modem's Properties dialog box, selecting the General tab, and then clicking the Troubleshoot button. This will initiate a troubleshooting sequence that, more often than not, will identify your problem.

Your Modem Is Working, But It Doesn't Dial

After you've confirmed that your modem is working and communicating with your computer–but you still can't dial a number–you should confirm that you're not trying to make one Internet connection while a previous connection is still open. (You can't dial two places at the same time!). Then make sure that the phone line your modem is connected to is working by disconnecting your modem and hooking a working telephone to the same phone line. If the phone doesn't pick up a dial tone, neither will your modem. Try another phone line, or call the phone company for repairs.

If you have voice mail on your phone line, some voice mail systems change the dial tone to indicate when you have messages waiting. This modified dial tone may not be recognized as a real dial tone by some modems. Answer your voice mail to change the tone back to normal, then try dialing again.

It's also possible that you have your phone line plugged into the wrong jack at your modem. Most modems have two jacks–one labeled "line" and the other labeled "phone." Make sure that the phone line is plugged into the one labeled "line."

If your problem persists and it clearly isn't caused by a bad connection, an inoperable phone line, or a defective modem, the most likely source of your woes is an incorrect configuration within Windows. Make certain that you've selected the correct COM port and check the modem initialization string. (Your modem's documentation should the correct commands to use for your device.) Also check the Maximum Port Speed setting in the Modem tab of the modem's Properties dialog box. You might try *reducing* this setting if your modem is having difficulty communicating with your computer. And check for any COM port conflicts between your modem and another device, such as a mouse.

You should always check the port settings from within Windows to make sure that they're configured correctly. You can do this from the Device Manager utility, where it pays to examine the Properties for ports COM1 through COM4.

If Windows appears to be configured correctly (or it wasn't and you've fixed it) but your modem still doesn't dial, check your hardware. Many modems have physical switches that must be set in certain positions for the device to operate. Refer to your modem's documentation for the correct switch settings for your system.

Your Modem Dials, But It Doesn't Connect

Many common causes for this problem are the same as for the previous problem—either your hardware or software is set up incorrectly. If you think this is the case, see the previous problem for troubleshooting instructions.

It's also possible that your modem is dialing an incorrect phone number, or that something is screwy at your ISP. Make sure that your modem's speaker is enabled, then listen to the connection in process. If you hear your modem dialing, dialing, dialing—and it receives no answer from your ISP—then check the phone number you entered for your ISP. If the phone number is correct, then it's possible that your ISP is having problems and temporarily can't accept incoming calls. (Dial your ISP's voice support line to confirm or report this problem.) If you hear a busy signal after dialing, that means that too many people are trying to dial in at one time, and your ISP can't accept any more incoming calls right now. Wait a few minutes and try dialing in again.

You Connect to Your ISP, But at a Slower Speed Than Desired

There are many factors that determine which speed you actually connect at. The most common cause of slower-than-expected connections is line noise. I run into this problem a lot when traveling. Many older hotels have very noisy phone systems, which cause my modem to connect at speeds as slow as 14.4Kbps. (Man! That's slow!)

In addition, the busier your ISP is, the more likely that you'll connect at a slower speed. If you try to connect during "prime time" (from just after dinner to bed time in your specific time zone) chances are you'll get a slower connection than if you try to connect after midnight.

If you want to speed up your Internet connections, the obvious solution is to upgrade to broadband! Still, sometimes the Internet *is* slow, no matter what you do or how you connect. That's why the WWW is sometimes referred to as the World Wide *Wait*.

Your Session Gets Unexpectedly Disconnected

You can get disconnected in the middle of a session if you have more than one phone in your house hooked to the same phone line. If someone picks up an extension while your modem is online, the resulting interruption can scramble the connection. Sometimes the problem can be rectified simply by hanging up the extension; other times, you must cancel the current modem session and start over again.

Call Waiting can also be the cause of disconnect problems. When the Call Waiting signal comes down the line it stands a good chance of either scrambling your modem session or disconnecting your modem completely. While you can simply abstain from ordering the Call Waiting service, you can also turn it off while you're online by editing the settings on the Dialing Rules tab in the Phone and Modem Options utility.

Some ISPs and commercial online services (AOL is notorious for this) will disconnect you if you've been idle for too long. (They don't like users staying connected without actually doing anything.) If you want to stay connected, do *something* every few minutes, even if it's just checking your e-mail inbox or clicking to a different Web site.

Sometimes a Windows-related problem can cause your modem session to shut down. If Windows is low on memory, it may not have enough resources to let your modem do its thing. If you think this is the problem, try closing a few Windows applications and then restarting your modem. If you have continual modem problems under Windows, you may need to add more memory to your system.

Another increasingly common cause of this problem is a noisy phone line. If you have frequent trouble connecting or staying connected, it might not hurt to have your local phone company check your line for excess noise.

Using Your Modem Causes Your Mouse to Act Funny—or Vice Versa

This is actually a common problem. It results from weird hardware bugs that force two different COM ports to use some of the same system resources. As the following paragraphs explain, however, resolving the conflict is simple.

First, check the port settings for your mouse and your modem. If they're both configured for the same COM port, change one of the devices' settings so that it can use a different port.

Now, check that they're not both set for COM ports with even numbers (COM2 and COM4). If so, reconfigure one of the devices to use an odd numbered port.

At the same time, check that the two devices aren't both configured for COM ports with odd numbers (COM1 and COM3). If so, reset one of the devices to use an even number.

If you're running your modem on COM2–and there is no COM1 on your system–you may not be able to get your modem to work at all. This is because Windows looks for COM ports in order, and if COM1 doesn't exist–well, you've got problems. Reassign your modem–or some other accessory–to COM1, and you'll fix your problem.

Your Computer Acts Oddly Soon After You've Downloaded a File or Opened an E-mail Attachment

What now? You've just pulled several files–including a great new game–from this new Internet site you found, and now your computer acts as though it needs to be decked out in an electronic straitjacket. It doesn't seem to have any problems with loose connections, incorrect settings, or excess line noise. In fact, your online session went without a hitch. So what's wrong?

Well, along with your nice new files, you have probably downloaded a not-so-nice computer virus! Any time you download a file, run the file, and then find your computer starting to do strange things (running more slowly, mysteriously losing files, displaying unusual messages onscreen), you may have accidentally infected it with a virus. If the symptoms seem to match, refer to the section on viruses I wrote in Chapter 23.

You Can't Find Another Computer on Your Network

You open up My Network Places looking for another computer on your network, but it isn't there. Where did it go?

First, try looking a little harder. Click the View Network Computers link in the Network Tasks panel. This *should* display all connected computers.

If the missing computer isn't there, click the Search button in the My Network Places toolbar. When the Search Companion appears, enter the name of the computer, then click Search. If you don't know the name of the computer, enter an asterisk (*). This should search for (and then display) all the computers on the network.

If you still can't see the missing computer, it's time to check the obvious. Is the other computer turned on? (Sleeping computers don't show up on the network.) Is it connected to the network? (Double-check both ends of the cable.) If you're on an Ethernet network, are *both* your computers connected to the hub, and does the hub have power?

More basics: Have you run the Home Networking Wizard on the second computer? If not, run it now, from the Windows XP installation PC. (And don't assume that because your network worked pre-XP everything will show up after you install XP on your main PC. You'll probably have to run the XP Home Networking Wizard on all your network PCs.) Try running the wizard *again*. (Sometimes it takes two tries to get everything recognized.) Now reboot both your PCs and see if they recognize each other.

Now for some serious troubleshooting. Open the Help and Support Center, click the Fixing Problem link, click Networking Problems, and then run the Home and Small Office Networking Troubleshooter. Chances are this will fix most simple networking problems.

You may have a bad network connection on either one of the two computers. To repair a host of connection problems, open the Network Connections utility (from the Control Panel). Right-click the problem connection, then select Repair from the pop-up menu.

If worse comes to worst, delete the problematic connection from the second PC, and then rerun the Home Networking Wizard to reinstall the network. You may also have to rerun the wizard on your host PC (to recognize the new PC).

JIM'S TOP TEN TIPS

Well, that just about does it. I hope you've enjoyed this book, and learned at least a little more about Windows XP than you did before you started.

From this chapter, you should have learned how to systematically track down any Windows XP problems you might encounter. When worse comes to worst (as it often will), remember these key points:

1. The main cause for most computer problems is—*you!* Make sure that you haven't clicked the wrong button, hit the wrong key, or connected something to the wrong port. Whatever you were doing, try it again—and get it right, this time!
2. Make sure that all your cables are plugged in firmly—and to the right place.
3. Make sure that your software is compatible with Windows XP. If not, try running the program in Windows XP's Compatibility Mode, or upgrade the program to a Windows XP version. While you're at it, make sure that you have the latest versions of all your key device drivers. Old or bad drivers can cause a lot of problems.
4. Don't guess blind. Use all of Windows XP's diagnostic tools to help you track down the cause of the problem.
5. Think through your problems logically. What happened when? Did you do something new or different just before the problem occurred? Is the problem somehow related to a new piece of hardware or software you just installed? Think calmly and systematically to figure out what may be causing your current problems.
6. If you want a simple solution, run Windows XP's System Restore utility. This tool can restore your system to a point *before* your problem popped up. (It's great for when a new peripheral causes new problems!)
7. Don't be afraid to call in professional help. Contact Microsoft's technical support, or the technical support department at your local computer dealer.
8. If you have a friend or a colleague who's a technical wiz, let them do your troubleshooting for you with Windows XP's Remote Assistance utility.
9. Whatever else, don't be afraid of Windows. Windows XP is a good little operating system, a significant improvement over Windows 98 or Windows Me, and will serve you well. Use the information and advice I've given you to get the most out of the operating system—and start having fun with Windows XP!
10. Finally, for all the latest technical tips, news, and information, tune in to TechTV on your local cable or satellite system. My colleagues and I are there every day, bringing you technical information you can really use—including a lot of Windows XP tips!

PART VII

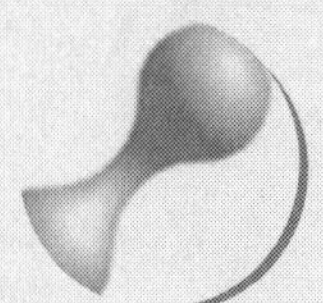

APPENDIXES

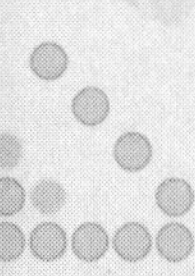

APPENDIX A

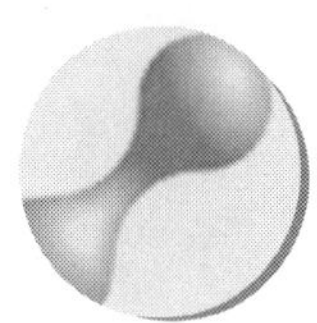

UPGRADING TO WINDOWS XP

- The Typical Upgrade Installation
- The "Clean" Installation
- Activating and Registering Windows
- Uninstalling Windows XP

Installing Windows XP is much easier than installing any previous version of Windows. If you received Windows XP as part of a new computer purchase, you don't have to worry about installing it at all—it's already installed. If you're upgrading an existing computer to Windows XP, you have the choice of an *upgrade* installation or a *clean* installation. For most users, the upgrade installation is the easiest way to go. I'll discuss both types of installations over the next few pages.

Whichever type of installation you choose, you'll find that it takes an hour or so to install the Windows XP software. You don't have to stand by your PC for the entire process, fortunately. Once you get past the initial decision-making, you can walk away and let the installation program do its thing.

To install Windows XP, you'll need a working CD-ROM drive hooked up to your PC, as the entire installation is done from CD. It also helps if you're connected to the Internet, as the software needs to activate itself in order to operate. (See "Activating and Registering Windows" later in this appendix.)

THE TYPICAL UPGRADE INSTALLATION

The upgrade installation is the easiest way to convert an old PC to Windows XP. Not every previous version of Windows has the same upgrade path, however. Check Table A.1 to see if and how you can upgrade from your current operating system.

TABLE A.1—UPGRADE OPTIONS FOR WINDOWS XP

If you have this version of windows	You can upgrade to this version of Windows XP
Windows 3.1	No upgrade possible; clean install required
Windows 95	No upgrade possible; clean install required
Windows 98 (first edition)	Windows XP Home Edition *or* Windows XP Professional
Windows 98 Special Edition (SE)	Windows XP Home Edition *or* Windows XP Professional
Windows Millennium Edition (Me)	Windows XP Home Edition *or* Windows XP Professional
Windows NT 3.51 Workstation	No upgrade possible; clean install required
Windows NT 4 Workstation	Windows XP Professional
Windows 2000 Professional	Windows XP Professional

In addition, you can easily upgrade from Windows XP Home Edition to Windows Professional.

Before You Upgrade

Before you upgrade, make the effort to download the latest version of all your key hardware drivers. Go to the manufacturer's Web site, or to DriverGuide.com, and grab the Windows 2000 or Windows NT version of all your drivers. (Because XP is based on Windows NT/2000, it uses those drivers—*not* the drivers used in Windows 9X/Me.) Store these drivers in a handy folder on your hard drive, in case you need to install those drivers post-installation.

(Trust me on this one. The only problems I ran into during numerous XP upgrades were with 9X/Me drivers that had to be upgraded to 2000/NT versions.) When you first start the Windows XP installation program, it runs a utility called the Windows Upgrade Advisor. This little program analyzes all the hardware and software on your system and prepares a report that lists any items that might cause problems under Windows XP.

Examine this report carefully before proceeding with the installation. If you see a critical component that Windows thinks might cause problems, cancel the installation and download any new drivers that might alleviate the problem. (Remember to get the Windows 2000 or NT drivers—unless specific Windows XP drivers are already available.) If it looks like there will be more problems than you can deal with, delay the installation until you can discuss your situation with Microsoft technical support.

It's always a good idea to close down *all* running programs before attempting any new software installation. In addition, be sure to turn off any anti-virus program that may be running in the background.

During the Installation

When you've prepared yourself as best you can for any potential problems, then you can proceed with the installation.

After running the Windows Update Advisor, the Windows XP installation program makes a backup copy of your previous operating system. This way if the installation goes bad, you can uninstall XP and reinstall your previous version of Windows.

From here on out, the installation proceeds automatically. It's slow and plodding, but rather solid. You shouldn't run into too many (if any) problems. Just be patient and wait for the entire operation to finish. Then you'll be up-and-running and ready to start using Windows XP.

THE "CLEAN" INSTALLATION

As you saw in Table A.1, some users have no choice but to do a "clean" installation of Windows XP. Other users might choose to install clean, in order to avoid any baggage (in terms of settings, and so on) associated with their previous OS.

A clean installation wipes everything off your hard disk and installs XP to what is now a completely clean disk. This is a rather drastic installation, as it also deletes any programs and personal files that are on the disk. It also means that you'll have to reinstall all your programs after you install Windows.

When is a clean installation a good idea? If your old system wasn't running right or was messed up in one way or another, a clean install makes sure that your old problems won't follow you to a new OS. A clean installation is also called for if you were running Windows 3.1, Windows 95, or Windows NT 3.51. These versions of Windows can't be easily upgraded, so you have to start from scratch if you want to run Windows XP.

There's one other reason you might want to consider a clean installation. When you do an upgrade, many of the files from the old operation are retained. When you do a clean install, you don't have these old files sticking around to clutter up your hard disk. Compare the average 2.9GB size of Windows XP installed via upgrade to the 1.7GB size after a clean installation. That's a lot of wasted disk space you can recover by doing a clean install.

Once you decide to perform a clean installation, the process is very similar to that of an upgrade install. Just follow the onscreen instructions and make sure you have a few thick magazines to read while the installation program does its thing. (Although that's another advantage of a clean installation—it should take about half the time as an upgrade install.)

ACTIVATING AND REGISTERING WINDOWS

After the installation is complete, you'll be prompted to activate your copy of Windows XP. This is something new, and totally separate from the normal registration process.

In an attempt to discourage what Microsoft calls "casual" software piracy, the company now requires that each individual copy of XP be activated before it can be used. (You do have a 30-day grace period, but after that the operating system quits working if it's not activated.) The activation process can be done online or over the phone, although doing it online is much, *much* easier.

Window Product Activation (or WPA, as the process is called) essentially marries your copy of Windows to your personal computer system. If you try to install that copy of Windows on another PC, it won't work. This limits you to one PC per copy, which is different from past versions of Windows (and most software programs), which allowed you to install on two machines (a desktop and a laptop).

If you've been following along, you've realized that you need to purchase a separate copy of Windows XP for each computer in your home. That can get expensive, but there's no easy (or legal) way around. Because you have to activate each copy before it can work, and because you can't activate a copy twice, you're stuck.

I'm not a fan of WPA. I think it's an overly complex solution to a minor problem. I also think it's too punitive. (If you break the rules, Windows won't start—which means you can't use your entire computer!)

WPA also promises to introduce a ton of user problems. Because the activation is married to your specific hardware configuration, what happens when you add to, remove, or change the components of your system? Imagine installing a new hard drive and finding that Windows no longer works! Microsoft says that WPA will figure out most common system changes, but the operative word here is *most*. If you're like me and install and uninstall a lot of peripherals—as well as perform the occasional reinstall of the complete operating system—WPA is almost guaranteed to be a real headache. Again, Microsoft says that you can call their support number and receive a case-by-case override if WPA shuts down your system, it's still an unnecessary annoyance that punishes innocent computer users more than it does any hard-core pirates.

Some critics are afraid that because WPA records information about your hardware setup and sends it along to Microsoft to create your unique product activation code, Microsoft will have private knowledge about your personal computer system. Experts tend to discount this issue, as does Microsoft, of course. It appears that product activation is totally anonymous, and completely separate from the product registration procedure.

While Microsoft has not revealed how the product activation code is generated, Fully Licensed GmbH (`www.licenturion.com/xp/`), a German consulting firm, has done some analysis of WPA and come up with the following list of components that Microsoft tracks to create the code. This list includes your Windows volume serial number, network adapter

MAC address, CD-ROM drive, graphics adapter, CPU serial number, hard drive, SCSI host adapter, IDE controller, processor model, amount of RAM, and whether your PC is dockable or not. If you've changed more than four of these items within a specified period, Windows won't start. If this happens to you, you'll need to call Microsoft and explain your particular situation—and hope they'll give you a new code to get you up and running again.

As I write this, the time frame allowed between changes has not yet been determined by Microsoft. They've kicked around 60 days, 90 days, and even six months. In any case, if you make too many changes to your system within a short period of time, you could run up against the product activation constraints. (In other words—Microsoft will think you've installed your copy of Windows XP on a second, illegal, machine.)

By the way, the version of WPA in the shipping version of XP has been softened somewhat from what Microsoft originally intended. The initial intent was to trigger the WPA protection if four items were changed *at any time* over the life of your PC. Rejigging WPA to trigger if the changes are made over a limited period of time is more palatable to users who make a lot of changes to their systems. For example, if you upgraded RAM one month, installed a new CD-ROM drive the next, and then waited six months to add a second hard disk drive and a network adapter, the changes should be far enough apart not to trigger the WPA protection. (If you made all those changes at one time, however….) Like it or not, you have to activate Windows XP in order to use it. You're prompted to activate XP at the end of the installation process, although you can delay the activation for up to thirty days if you want to. To activate XP after the installation process, click the Start button, then select All Programs, Accessories, System Tools, Activate Windows.

When you follow the onscreen instructions, you'll have a choice of activating online or by phone. If you have a modem or Internet connection, choose the online option, because this automates the entire procedure. No further action will be required on your part.

If you choose to activate by phone, you'll be given a 24/7 toll-free phone number to call. You'll have to provide Microsoft with the activation number that Windows XP has generated. In return, the operator will give you another number to enter into XP to complete the activation. As these numbers are extremely long, this process is a big pain the rear. Again, choose the online activation option, if you can.

Once you've activated Windows XP, you can then register the program. As with previous versions of Windows, registration is optional, and really doesn't gain you much—other than access to Microsoft's technical support department. Unlike activation, if you don't register your copy of XP, it doesn't quit working.

To sum up, activation is a different process from registration. Activation is required to use your copy of Windows, and totally anonymous. Registration is optional, and requires you to submit some personal information. You have to activate, but you don't have to register.

UNINSTALLING WINDOWS XP

It doesn't happen often, but once in a while a problem comes up that is so severe it requires to uninstall Windows XP. This is actually a fairly easy process in Windows XP, as a copy of your previous operating system is kept on your hard disk, just for this purpose.

To uninstall Windows XP, follow these steps:

1. From the Control Panel, click the Add or Remove Programs icon.
2. When the Add or Remove Programs utility opens, press the Change or Remove Programs button.
3. Scroll down the list of programs, select Windows XP, and click the Change/Remove button.
4. When prompted, select Uninstall Windows XP, then follow the onscreen instructions to remove the operating system.

This process removes Windows XP and reverts back to your previous version of Windows. It should work fine, except in the following conditions:

- You changed hard disk configuration from what it was at the time of installation. (For example, if you switched from FAT32 to NTFS.)
- If you upgraded from Windows NT 4.0 or Windows 2000 Professional.

Any software applications that you added or modified since the Windows XP installation may not work properly when you revert to the previous operating system. Windows XP will warn you of most potential issues before the uninstallation process begins.

APPENDIX B

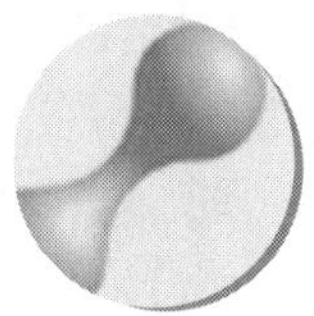

WINDOWS ACCESSORIES

- Calculator
- Character Map
- Clipboard Viewer
- Games
- HyperTerminal
- Notepad
- Paint
- Sound Recorder
- WordPad

Windows XP, like all previous versions of Windows, includes a number of built-in accessory programs that you can use for various incidental computing tasks. Most of these programs have been around for several versions, so you're probably already familiar with how they work. Just in case you've forgotten about them, I'll run down those accessories that I didn't get a chance to mention elsewhere in the book.

(To learn more about the other accessories, such as Windows Movie Maker, look them up in the index to reference their coverage elsewhere in this book.)

CALCULATOR

This is a basic onscreen calculator, with an attractive interface overhaul for Windows XP. Launch it by clicking the Start button and selecting All Programs, Accessories, Calculator. (I use this one so much I've created a shortcut to it on my Quick Launch bar!)

CHARACTER MAP

This accessory lets you add special characters to your documents. Launch it by clicking the Start button and selecting All Programs, Accessories, System Tools, Character Map.

CLIPBOARD VIEWER

This accessory lets you view the contents of the Windows Clipboard. Use Clipboard Viewer to look at material that you've recently cut or copied. Launch it by clicking the Start button and selecting All Programs, Accessories, System Tools, Clipboard Viewer.

GAMES

Windows XP provides a variety of simple games you can play on your own, or in some cases over the Internet with other users. In addition to that old standby, Solitaire, the new XP games include Spider Solitaire (I'm hooked on it!) and Internet versions of Backgammon, Checkers, Hearts, Reversi, and Spades. Access these games by clicking the Start button and selecting All Programs, Accessories, Games.

HYPERTERMINAL

This is a basic Windows-based modem dialer. You can use it to connect to any online services that aren't yet connected to the Internet. (I used HyperTerminal a lot back in the old pre-Web BBS days, but it doesn't get much use anymore.) Launch it by clicking the Start button and selecting All Programs, Accessories, Communications, HyperTerminal.

NOTEPAD

This is the original text editor, good for very small, very plain documents. Launch it by clicking the Start button and selecting All Programs, Accessories, Notepad.

PAINT

Microsoft Paint is a very, very basic graphics-editing program. It's been upgraded for Windows XP, and can now handle more file types than before. It's still very limited in functionality, and useful only for editing bitmapped images. Launch it by clicking the Start button and selecting All Programs, Accessories, Paint.

SOUND RECORDER

This is a barebones digital recording program. You can use it to record your own .WAV files, as long as you have a microphone hooked up to your system. (It can also record from any device currently playing on your system.) Launch it by clicking the Start button and selecting All Programs, Accessories, Entertainment, Sound Recorder.

WORDPAD

WordPad was meant to replace Notepad, since it can handle larger documents, provide some basic text formatting, and save documents in Rich Text Format (RTF). It's a poor man's word processor, more unwieldy than the elegant Notepad and less fully featured than a real word-processing program, such as Microsoft Word. Launch it by clicking the Start button and selecting All Programs, Accessories, WordPad.

APPENDIX C

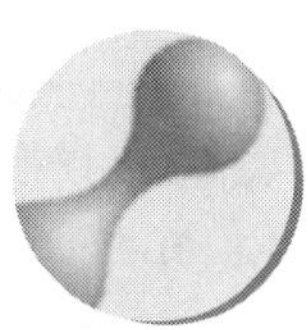

ACCESSIBILITY OPTIONS

- Control Panel Accessibility Options
- Other Accessibility Tools
- Using the Accessibility Wizard

Windows XP can be configured to enhance accessibility for vision-impaired, hearing-impaired, or mobility-impaired users. You don't need any additional hardware or software to take advantage of these accessibility options.

You can access these accessibility options from the Windows Control Panel, or by running the Accessibility Wizard.

PART 7 APPENDIXES

CONTROL PANEL ACCESSIBILITY OPTIONS

Windows XP's main accessibility options are found in the Accessibility Options utility, which is accessed from the Control Panel. Just click the Accessibility Options icon in the Control Panel to display the Accessibility Options dialog box.

This dialog box includes five tabs. Each tab serves as a gateway for specific accessibility tools.

Keyboard Options

The Keyboard tab lets you turn on or off three different tools:

- **StickyKeys**—Lets you perform multiple-key operations (such as Ctrl+key or Alt+key) by pressing one key at a time.
- **FilterKeys**—Adjusts the response of your keyboard, making it less sensitive to accidentally repeated keystrokes.
- **ToggleKeys**—Produces a sound when the Caps Lock, Num Lock, and Scroll Lock keys are activated.

This tab also provides the option of displaying extra keyboard help in programs.

Sound Options

The Sound tab lets you turn on or off two different tools:

- **SoundSentry**—Displays a visual warning when your computer makes a sound.
- **ShowSounds**—Instructs software applications to display captions for the sounds that they make.

Display Options

The Display tab lets you turn on or off the High Contrast option, which can make it easier for the vision-impaired to read the screen. It also lets you change the width and blink rate of the Windows cursor.

Mouse Options

The Mouse tab lets you turn on or off the MouseKeys tool, which lets you control the mouse from your PC's numeric keypad.

General Options

The General tab lets you configure how the accessibility options are employed on your computer.

OTHER ACCESSIBILITY TOOLS

There are other accessibility tools to be found elsewhere than the Accessibility Options dialog box. These include

- **Magnifier**—Which enlarges a selected portion of the screen. You open Magnifier by clicking the Start button, then selecting All Programs, Accessories, Accessibility, Magnifier.
- **Narrator**—Which uses text-to-speech technology to read the contents of the screen aloud. You launch Narrator by clicking the Start button, then selecting All Programs, Accessories, Accessibility, Narrator.
- **On-Screen Keyboard**—Which lets users with limited mobility type onscreen with a mouse or other pointing device. You activate the onscreen keyboard by clicking the Start button, then selecting All Programs, Accessories, Accessibility, On-Screen Keyboard.

USING THE ACCESSIBILITY WIZARD

The easy way to activate many of these accessibility options is to use the Accessibility Wizard. Like most wizards, this one guides you through a selection process and then activates the tools appropriate to your particular situation.

You start the Accessibility Wizard by clicking the Start button, then selecting All Programs, Accessories, Accessibility, Accessibility Wizard.

APPENDIX D

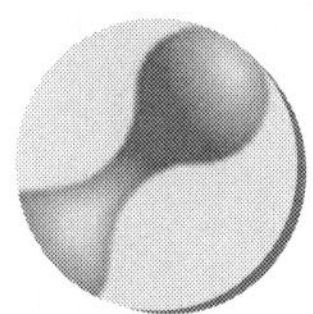

A TOUR OF TECHTV

Boasting the cable market's most interactive audience, TechTV is the only cable television channel covering technology information, news, and entertainment from a consumer, industry, and market perspective 24 hours a day. Offering everything from industry news to product reviews, updates on tech stocks to tech support, TechTV's original programming keeps the wired world informed and entertained. TechTV is one of the fastest growing cable networks, available around the country and worldwide.

Offering more than a cable television channel, TechTV delivers a fully integrated, interactive Web site. Techtv.com is a community destination that encourages viewer interaction through e-mail, live chat, and video mail.

TechTV, formerly ZDTV, is owned by Vulcan, Inc.

AUDIENCE

TechTV appeals to anyone with an active interest in following and understanding technology trends and how they impact their lives in today's world—from the tech investor and industry insider, to the Internet surfer, cell phone owner, and Palm Pilot organizer.

WEB SITE

Techtv.com allows viewers to participate in programming, provide feedback, interact with hosts, send video e-mails, and further explore the latest tech content featured on the television cable network. In addition, `techtv.com` has one of the Web's most extensive technology-specific video-on-demand features (VOD), offering users immediate access to more than 5,000 videos as well as expanded tech content of more than 2,000 in-depth articles.

INTERNATIONAL

TechTV is the world's largest producer and distributor of television programming about technology. In Asia, TechTV delivers a 24-hour international version via satellite. TechTV Canada is a "must-carry" digital channel that will launch in September 2001. A Pan-European version of TechTV is planned for 2002.

TECH LIVE QUICK FACTS

Tech Live is TechTV's unique concept in live technology news programming. Tech Live provides extensive coverage, in-depth analysis, and original features on breaking technology developments as they relate to news, market trends, entertainment, and consumer products. Tech Live is presented from market, industry, and consumer perspectives.

Mission

Tech Live is the leading on-air resource and ultimate destination for consumers and industry insiders to find the most comprehensive coverage of technology and how it affects and relates to their lives, from market, industry, and consumer perspectives.

Format

Tech Live offers nine hours of live programming a day.

Tech Live is built around hourly blocks of news programming arranged into content zones: technology news, finance, product reviews, help, and consumer advice.

Tech Live news bureaus in New York City, Washington D.C., Silicon Valley, and Seattle are currently breaking technology-related news stories on the financial markets, the political arena, and major industry players.

The TechTV "Superticker" positioned along the side of the screen gives viewers up-to-the-minute status on the leading tech stocks, as well as additional data and interactive content.

Tech Live runs Monday through Friday, 9:00 a.m.–6:00 p.m. EST.

NETWORK PROGRAM GUIDE

The following is a list of the programs that currently air on TechTV. We are constantly striving to improve our on-air offerings, so please visit `www.techtv.com` for a constantly updated list, as well as specific air times.

AudioFile

In this weekly half-hour show, Liam Mayclem and Kris Kosach host the premiere music program of its kind that dares to explore music in the digital age. From interviews with artists and producers, to insight into the online tools to help create your own music, *AudioFile* discovers how the Internet is changing the music industry.

Big Thinkers

This weekly half-hour talk show takes viewers into the future of technological innovation through insightful and down-to-earth interviews with the industry's most influential thinkers and innovators of our time.

Call for Help

This daily, hour-long, fully interactive call-in show hosted by Becky Worley and Chris Pirillo takes the stress out of computing and the Internet for both beginners and pros. Each day, *Call for Help* tackles viewers' technical difficulties, offers tips and tricks, provides product advice, and offers viewers suggestions for getting the most out of their computers.

CyberCrime

This weekly half-hour news magazine provides a fast-paced inside look at the dangers facing technology users in the digital age. Hosts Alex Wellen and Jennifer London take a hard look at fraud, hacking, viruses, and invasions of privacy to keep Web surfers aware and secure on the Web.

Extended Play

In this weekly half-hour show, video game expert hosts Kate Botello and Adam Sessler provide comprehensive reviews of the hottest new games on the market, previews of games in development, and tips on how to score the biggest thrills and avoid the worst spills in gaming. This show is a must-see for game lovers, whether they're seasoned pros or gaming novices.

Fresh Gear

A gadget-lover's utopia, host Sumi Das supplies viewers with the scoop on the best and brightest technology available on the market. In this weekly half-hour show, detailed product reviews reveal what's new, what works, what's hot, and what's not and offers advice on which products to buy—and which to bypass.

Silicon Spin

Noted technology columnist John C. Dvorak anchors this live, daily, half-hour in-depth look at the stories behind today's tech headlines. CEOs, experts, and entrepreneurs cast a critical eye at industry hype and separate the facts from the spin.

The Screen Savers

Whether you are cracking code, are struggling with Windows, or just want to stay up to speed on what's happening in the world of computers, *The Screen Savers* is here to help. Leo Laporte and Patrick Norton unleash the power of technology with wit and flair in this live, daily, hour-long interactive show geared toward the tech enthusiast.

Titans of Tech

Titans of Tech is a weekly hour-long series of biographies profiling high tech's most important movers and shakers—the CEOs, entrepreneurs, and visionaries driving today's tech economy. Through insightful interviews and in-depth profiles, these specials offer viewers a rare look at where the new economy is headed.

INDEX

Symbols

A

D

E

G–H

I

J–K–L

M

N–O

Q–R

S

T

U–V

W–X–Y–Z